The Labour Party in Wales, 1900–2000

The Labour Party in Wales
1900–2000

Edited by

Duncan Tanner, Chris Williams and Deian Hopkin

UNIVERSITY OF WALES PRESS
CARDIFF
2000

© The Contributors, 2000

JN
1159
.A8
W45
2000

British Library Cataloguing-in-Publication Data.
A catalogue record for this book is available from the British Library.

ISBN 0–7083–1586–0

Typeset at University of Wales Press
Printed in Great Britain by Dinefwr Press, Llandybïe

Contents

List of Illustrations

List of Tables

Preface

NEIL KINNOCK

I am delighted that a thorough evaluation of the history of the Labour Party in Wales has at last been made. The book is the product of many years of painstaking work in the archives of the Labour Party and it shows insights which are essential for a good, authentic history. It records a great story of the diligence, the imagination and – often – the courage and sheer slog that went into the development of the party in Wales.

Here is a saga of campaigns and struggles and of names – some known only in their locality, some recognized across the wider world. Ablett, Bevan, Griffiths, Callaghan and Foot are here, of course – and so are many of those who neither sought nor won fame but whose commitment to the cause propelled them to serve for their communities, for the labour movement and for the social and economic emancipation of people of all classes, races and creeds.

Democratic socialism is the conviction of people who believe that all commercial activity and political decisions should be made compatible with the needs of human society by means of plural democracy. And whilst Welsh people, happily, do not have a monopoly of that ideal, I have long thought that the *instinct* for it is particularly well developed in our country. That shows in this story.

Of course, it is not easy to capture both the history and the diverse character of the party across the whole of Wales in a single volume. It is, however, essential to have such a reference both as an inspiration and as an instruction. In this, the centenary year of the Labour Party and the first year of the new millennium, it is more fitting than ever to have a measure of the past and a source of the lessons that it teaches.

This reflective evaluation of the party's history in Wales rightly celebrates Labour's successes but it certainly does not overlook its past errors. Indeed, it invites us to learn from them. And any reader who is willing to consider the past, not in order to long for what is gone but to reach for what is yet to be done, will truly catch the purpose of this volume.

Notes on Contributors

NEIL EVANS is an honorary lecturer in the School of History and Welsh History, University of Wales, Bangor. He has published widely on the urban, labour, ethnic and women's history of Wales. Most recently he has published essays in Gareth Elwyn Jones and Dai Smith (eds.), *The People of Wales* (Gomer, 1999); in David Howell and Kenneth O. Morgan (eds.), *Crime, Protest and Police in Modern British History* (University of Wales Press, 1999); and edited (with Eberhard Bort) *Networking Europe: Essays in Regionalism and Social Democracy* (Liverpool University Press, 2000).

DEIAN HOPKIN is Professor and Vice-Provost of London Guildhall University and chairman of Cityside Regeneration Ltd. He taught history at the University of Wales, Aberystwyth for twenty-four years and was a founding editor of *Llafur: The Journal of Welsh Labour History*. In 1986 he was co-founder of the International Association for History and Computing.

DOT JONES recently retired from the Centre for Advanced Welsh and Celtic Studies at Aberystwyth where she was leader of the project on the Social History of the Welsh Language. Her project-related publications were *Statistical Evidence relating to the Welsh Language 1801–1911* (University of Wales Press, 1998) and *The Coming of the Railways and Language Change in North Wales 1850–1900* (Centre for Advanced Welsh and Celtic Studies, 1995). A long-time member of Llafur: The Welsh Labour History Society, her previous publications have included articles on workmen's compensation and the miner, friendly societies, and women's work in Wales.

IOAN RHYS JONES is a doctoral student at the University of Wales, Bangor, working on aspects of Welsh education, society and identity.

R. MERFYN JONES is Professor of Welsh History at University of Wales, Bangor, where he is also Pro-Vice-Chancellor. His publications include *The North Wales Quarrymen, 1874–1922* (University of Wales Press, 1988) and *Cymru 2000: Hanes Cymru yn yr Ugeinfed Ganrif* (University of Wales Press, 1999). He was co-editor of *Llafur: The Journal of Welsh Labour History* for a period of sixteen years.

RICHARD LEWIS is Deputy Director, School of Law, Arts and Humanities, at the University of Teesside. His recent publications include *Leaders and Teachers: Adult Education and the Challenge of Labour in South Wales, 1906–1940* (University of Wales Press, 1993); (with D. Ward) 'Culture, politics and assimilation: the Welsh on Teesside *c.*1850–1940', *Welsh History Review* (1995); and 'The Welsh radical tradition and the ideal of a democratic popular culture', in Eugenio F. Biagini (ed.), *Citizenship and Community: Liberals, Radicals and Collective Identity in the British Isles, 1865–1931* (Cambridge University Press, 1996).

EDDIE MAY taught British and European history at a number of universities, including Cardiff, Leicester and Glamorgan. He received his doctorate in 1995 from the University of Wales for a study of industrial and social relations in the South Wales Coalfield, 1914–21. His publications include essays on Spanish history (particularly on Anarchism) and on the themes of industrial unrest, town planning, and the First World War in Welsh history. He is currently an e-commerce consultant.

KENNETH O. MORGAN has been lecturer at Swansea; Fellow and tutor at The Queen's College, Oxford; Vice-Chancellor at the University of Wales, Aberystwyth; and Visiting Professor at Witwatersrand, South Africa. The most recent of his books are *Modern Wales: Politics, Places and People* (University of Wales Press, 1995), *Callaghan: A Life* (Oxford University Press, 1997), *The People's Peace: A History of Britain since 1945* (Oxford University Press, new edition 1999), and (jointly edited with David Howell) *Crime, Protest and Police in Modern British Society* (University of Wales Press, 1999).

DUNCAN TANNER is Professor of History at the University of Wales, Bangor. Previous publications include *Political Change and the Labour Party 1900–1918* (Cambridge University Press, 1990). He is editor (with Pat Thane and Nick Tiratsoo) of *Labour's First Century* (Cambridge University Press, 2000), a substantial history of the Labour Party in Britain.

ANDREW WALLING is a doctoral student at the University of Wales, Bangor, working on the history of the Labour Party in Britain in the 1950s and early 1960s. He worked as research assistant to the Labour Party Centenary Project, listing all archive material relating to the Labour Party in Wales.

CHRIS WILLIAMS is Senior Lecturer in the School of History and Archaeology at Cardiff University. Previous publications include *Democratic Rhondda: Politics and Society, 1885–1951* (University of Wales Press, 1996), *Capitalism, Community and Conflict: The South Wales Coalfield, 1898–1947* (University of Wales Press, 1998) and (with Bill Jones) *B. L. Coombes* (University of Wales Press, 1999).

JOHN WILLIAMS is now retired, but was formerly a university teacher at the University of Wales, Aberystwyth where he was Professor of Social and Economic History. Recent publications include the *Digest of Welsh Historical Statistics, 1974–96* (Welsh Office, 1998), *Was Wales Industrialised?* (Gomer, 1995) and 'Clark the Ironmaster', in B. L. James (ed.), *G. T. Clark: Ironmaster in the Victorian Age* (University of Wales Press, 1998).

Acknowledgements

The editors would like to thank the University of Wales Collaboration Fund and the Research Committees of both the University of Wales, Bangor, and the School of History and Archaeology, Cardiff University, for financial support. Gratitude is due to Bill Jones and Robert Smith for helping to publicize the project, to Elisabeth Bennett for assistance with photographs and to Tass Rees for help with the maps. The editors also gratefully acknowledge the expert advice and professional skills of Susan Jenkins, Ceinwen Jones, Liz Powell, Sue Charles and Richard Houdmont at the University of Wales Press. Richard Lewis would like to thank Neil Evans for providing him with advance access to his essay (co-written with Kate Sullivan) on the language of politics in Wales, 1880–1914. Eddie May would like to express his particular thanks to Chris Williams for his editorial assistance in writing his chapter. Duncan Tanner would like to thank Research Centre Wales for travel and research expenses. Neil Evans and Dot Jones would like to thank John Davies, Kate Sullivan and Ryland Wallace for help and references, and Anita Gale for kindly giving permission to examine embargoed material in the National Library of Wales.

General Election Results 1910

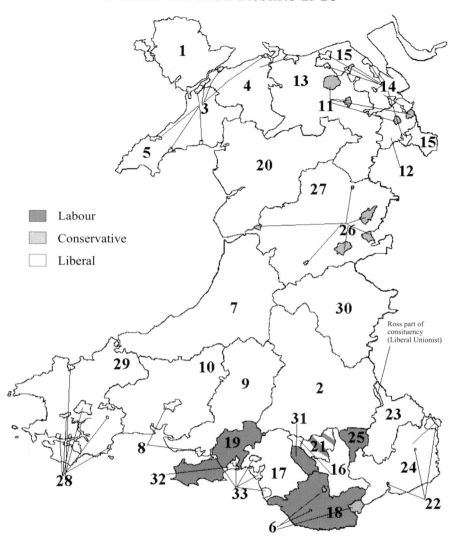

Labour

Conservative

Liberal

Ross part of
consituency
(Liberal Unionist)

1. Anglesey	12. Denbigh East	23. Monmouth North
2. Brecon	13. Denbigh West	24. Monmouth South
3. Caernarfon Boroughs	14. Flint Boroughs	25. Monmouth West
4. Caernarfon, Arfon	15. Flintshire	26. Montgomery Boroughs
5. Caernarfon, Eifion	16. Glamorgan East	27. Montgomery
6. Cardiff District	17. Glamorgan Mid	28. Pembroke Boroughs
7. Cardigan	18. Glamorgan South	29. Pembroke
8. Carmarthen Boroughs	19. Gower	30. Radnor
9. Carmarthen East	20. Merioneth	31. Rhondda
10. Carmarthen West	21. Merthyr Boroughs	32. Swansea Town
11. Denbigh Boroughs	(2 seats) 1 Lab, 1 Lib.	33. Swansea Boroughs
	22. Monmouth Boroughs	

Source: *National Atlas of Wales*

General Election Results 1922

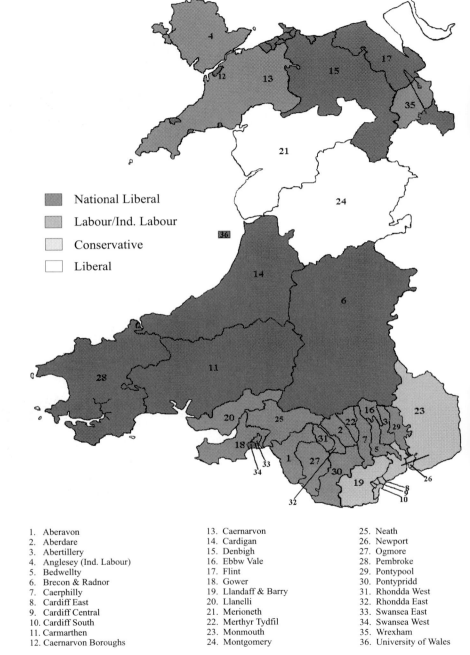

National Liberal

Labour/Ind. Labour

Conservative

Liberal

1. Aberavon	13. Caernarvon	25. Neath
2. Aberdare	14. Cardigan	26. Newport
3. Abertillery	15. Denbigh	27. Ogmore
4. Anglesey (Ind. Labour)	16. Ebbw Vale	28. Pembroke
5. Bedwellty	17. Flint	29. Pontypool
6. Brecon & Radnor	18. Gower	30. Pontypridd
7. Caerphilly	19. Llandaff & Barry	31. Rhondda West
8. Cardiff East	20. Llanelli	32. Rhondda East
9. Cardiff Central	21. Merioneth	33. Swansea East
10. Cardiff South	22. Merthyr Tydfil	34. Swansea West
11. Carmarthen	23. Monmouth	35. Wrexham
12. Caernarvon Boroughs	24. Montgomery	36. University of Wales

Source: *National Atlas of Wales* and Arnold J. James and John E. Thomas, *Wales at Westminster* (Llandysul, 1981).

General Election Results 1945

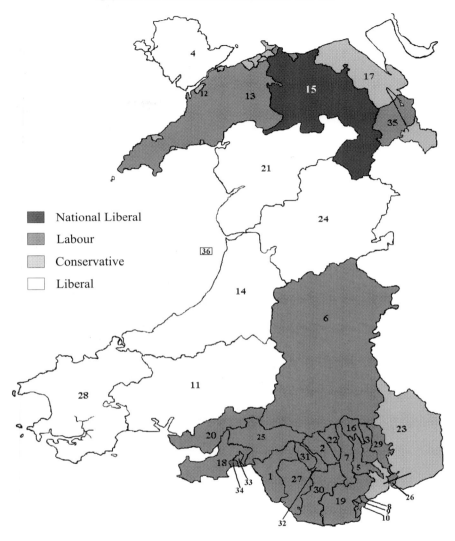

National Liberal

Labour

Conservative

Liberal

1. Aberavon	13. Caernarvon	25. Neath
2. Aberdare	14. Cardigan	26. Newport
3. Abertillery	15. Denbigh	27. Ogmore
4. Anglesey	16. Ebbw Vale	28. Pembroke
5. Bedwellty	17. Flint	29. Pontypool
6. Brecon & Radnor	18. Gower	30. Pontypridd
7. Caerphilly	19. Llandaff & Barry	31. Rhondda West
8. Cardiff East	20. Llanelli	32. Rhondda East
9. Cardiff Central	21. Merioneth	33. Swansea East
10. Cardiff South	22. Merthyr Tydfil	34. Swansea West
11. Carmarthen	23. Monmouth	35. Wrexham
12. Caernarvon Boroughs	24. Montgomery	36. University of Wales

Source: *National Atlas of Wales*

General Election Results 1966

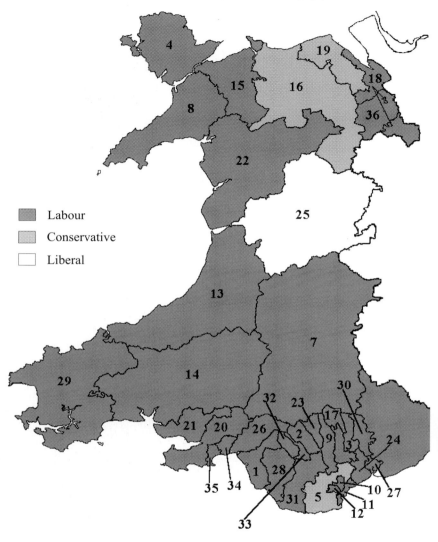

Labour
Conservative
Liberal

1.	Aberavon	13.	Cardigan	25.	Montgomery
2.	Aberdare	14.	Carmarthen	26.	Neath
3.	Abertillery	15.	Conway	27.	Newport
4.	Anglesey	16.	Denbigh	28.	Ogmore
5.	Barry	17.	Ebbw Vale	29.	Pembroke
6.	Bedwellty	18.	Flint East	30.	Pontypool
7.	Brecon & Radnor	19.	Flint West	31.	Pontypridd
8.	Caernarfon	20.	Gower	32.	Rhondda West
9.	Caerphilly	21.	Llanelli	33.	Rhondda East
10.	Cardiff North	22.	Merioneth	34.	Swansea East
11.	Cardiff South East	23.	Merthyr Tydfil	35.	Swansea West
12.	Cardiff West	24.	Monmouth	36.	Wrexham

Source: *National Atlas of Wales*

General Election Results 1979

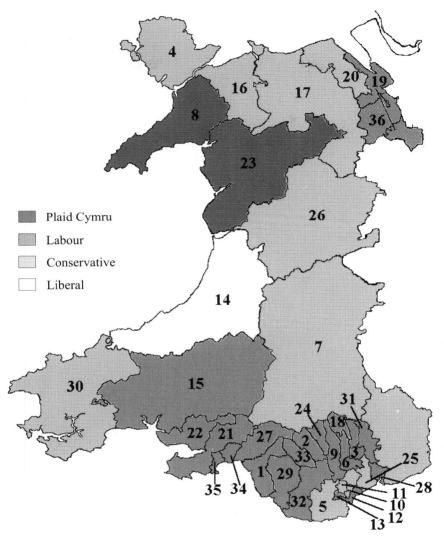

Plaid Cymru

Labour

Conservative

Liberal

1. Aberavon
2. Aberdare
3. Abertillery
4. Anglesey
5. Barry
6. Bedwellty
7. Brecon & Radnor
8. Caernarfon
9. Caerphilly
10. Cardiff North
11. Cardiff North West
12. Cardiff South East
13. Cardiff West (speaker)
14. Cardigan
15. Carmarthen
16. Conway
17. Denbigh
18. Ebbw Vale
19. Flint East
20. Flint West
21. Gower
22. Llanelli
23. Merioneth
24. Merthyr Tydfil
25. Monmouth
26. Montgomery
27. Neath
28. Newport
29. Ogmore
30. Pembroke
31. Pontypool
32. Pontypridd
33. Rhondda
34. Swansea East
35. Swansea West
36. Wrexham

Source: *National Atlas of Wales*

General Election Results 1997

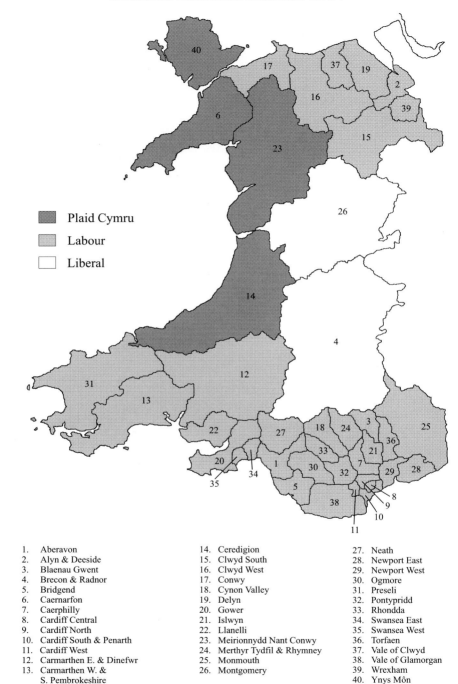

Plaid Cymru

Labour

Liberal

1. Aberavon	14. Ceredigion	27. Neath
2. Alyn & Deeside	15. Clwyd South	28. Newport East
3. Blaenau Gwent	16. Clwyd West	29. Newport West
4. Brecon & Radnor	17. Conwy	30. Ogmore
5. Bridgend	18. Cynon Valley	31. Preseli
6. Caernarfon	19. Delyn	32. Pontypridd
7. Caerphilly	20. Gower	33. Rhondda
8. Cardiff Central	21. Islwyn	34. Swansea East
9. Cardiff North	22. Llanelli	35. Swansea West
10. Cardiff South & Penarth	23. Meirionnydd Nant Conwy	36. Torfaen
11. Cardiff West	24. Merthyr Tydfil & Rhymney	37. Vale of Clwyd
12. Carmarthen E. & Dinefwr	25. Monmouth	38. Vale of Glamorgan
13. Carmarthen W. & S. Pembrokeshire	26. Montgomery	39. Wrexham
		40. Ynys Môn

Source: D. Balsom (ed.), *The Wales Yearbook 1998* (Cardiff, 1997), p.14.

Abbreviations

AL	*Aberdare Leader*	NCB	National Coal Board
AGM	annual general meeting	NEC	National Executive Committee
ASRS	Amalgamated Society of Railway Servants	NLW	National Library of Wales
CLP	Constituency Labour Party	PPS	Parliamentary Private Secretary
CND	Campaign for Nuclear Disarmament	RO	Record Office
CP	Cabinet Paper	RW	*Radical Wales*
DH	*Daily Herald*	SDF	Social Democratic Federation
EC	executive committee	SDP	Social Democratic Party
FCC	Food Control Committee	SWMF	South Wales Miners' Federation
FVC	Food Vigilance Committee	SWRCL	South Wales Regional Council of Labour
ILP	Independent Labour Party	SWV	*South Wales Voice*
LL	*Labour Leader*	TLC	trades and labour council
LRC	Labour Representation Committee	UDC	urban district council
LV	*Labour Voice*	WCG	Women's Co-operative Guild
LW	*Labour Women*	WEA	Workers' Educational Association
MFGB	Mineworkers' Federation of Great Britain	WHR	*Welsh History Review*
NAC	National Administrative Committee (of ILP)	WLL	Women's Labour League
		WM	*Western Mail*
NALSO	National Association of Labour Students Organisations	WRCL	Welsh Regional Council of Labour

Introduction

CHRIS WILLIAMS

Democratic Socialism is not a middle way between capitalism and Communism. If it were merely that, it would be doomed to failure from the start. It cannot live by borrowed vitality. Its driving power must derive from its own principles and the energy released by them. It is based on the conviction that free men can use free institutions to solve the social and economic problems of the day, if they are given a chance to do so.[1]

The Labour Party (in the form of the Labour Representation Committee) was established in 1900. By the general election of that autumn, Keir Hardie had been elected one of its two MPs, representing the Welsh constituency of Merthyr Boroughs until his death in 1915. In 1909 the largest trade union in Wales, the South Wales Miners' Federation (SWMF), affiliated to the Labour Party, along with the rest of the Mineworkers' Federation of Great Britain. By 1923 Wales was returning a majority of Labour MPs to Westminster and one of them, the MP for Aberavon Ramsay MacDonald, was about to become Labour's first prime minister. Other leaders of the Labour Party were to follow the Scots Hardie and MacDonald in representing Welsh constituencies: the English-born James Callaghan and Michael Foot and the Welshman Neil Kinnock. Aneurin Bevan and James Griffiths – two of Wales's most celebrated politicians – applied themselves at slightly less exalted levels but with barely reduced effect.

In every general election from 1922 until 1997 Labour has returned the largest number of·MPs from Wales and since 1945

Labour has had an absolute majority of all Welsh MPs. Wales contributed significantly to the Labour Party's emergence in 1918 and, dramatically, to its survival in the disastrous general election of 1931. In that year, of the fifty-two Labour MPs that were returned to the House of Commons, almost a third were from Welsh constituencies. Labour's share of the vote (which in Britain fell from 37 per cent in 1929 to 31 per cent in 1931) rose in Wales from 44 to 47 per cent, the highest share to that date but a level regularly exceeded in the 1950s and 1960s. Support reached its high-water mark in 1966 with thirty-two of the thirty-six Welsh seats and 61 per cent of the vote, a full 13 percentage points higher than the United Kingdom average. Although Labour's ascendancy has slipped since 1966, the party averaged 48 per cent of Welsh votes between 1970 and 1997 and has continued to return a majority of Welsh MPs (the low being twenty out of a total of thirty-eight in 1983 and the high being thirty-four of forty in 1997).

Much of Wales has been a Labour stronghold since the early 1920s. Yet if the Welsh contribution to the party of Hardie, MacDonald, Bevan and Kinnock is easily demonstrated, the place of the Labour Party in the history of Wales has yet to receive the attention it is due. This collection of essays marks the centenary of the Labour Party and assesses the party's contribution to Wales and the Welsh people across the twentieth century. The first task of this introduction is to capture the essence of the different currents of historical writing as they have framed the history of Welsh politics and particularly the history of the Labour Party in Wales.[2] The second objective is to evaluate the major themes that emerge from the eleven different essays gathered here and identify their collective significance. It is in the nature of historical scholarship that this volume cannot be the *definitive* study of its theme but, by illuminating the most crucial and telling relationships between the Labour Party and Welsh society, it may represent a *defining* moment in the growing comprehension of a complex century in the history of Wales.

The first monograph to deal with modern Welsh political history was Kenneth O. Morgan's *Wales in British Politics, 1868–1922* (Cardiff, 1963).[3] Morgan took as his starting-point the epoch-making general election of 1868 which placed a Nonconformist agenda at the heart of Welsh politics and which marked the start, in his words, of 'a kind of national awakening in Wales, a political and indeed cultural renaissance, a rekindling of the flame of national consciousness after centuries of isolation and neglect'.[4] Advancing into a period touched only by biographers and some of the earliest historians of trade unionism, Morgan emphasized the central significance of politics in Welsh history, arguing that '[t]he advance of democracy after 1867 made political activity the major channel for asserting the individuality of Wales'.[5] Inspired by some of the regional approaches to nineteenth-century labour history (such as Asa Briggs's edited volume, *Chartist Studies* (1959)) and with insight gained from his analogy between a 'Welsh question' and the more problematic 'Irish question', Morgan's primary concern was the development of Liberal politics in Wales.[6] Turning to the political 'periphery', rather than remaining with one's attention fixed firmly on the 'core', would, suggested Morgan, 'shed new light on the political characteristics of contemporary Britain, in which the rebirth of a sense of local, regional, or national community has been an important theme'.[7] This was not an abstract, soulless exercise: animated by a passionate pride in Welsh national identity Morgan wrote that only through a 'detached assessment' could 'the dignity and vigorous reality of Welsh nationality in the mid-twentieth century be sustained and fostered'.[8]

Morgan's detailed narrative took as its central theme the emergence of a new Welsh political identity at Westminster, centred on demands for disestablishment, land reform, education reforms and temperance, accompanied spasmodically (as in the Cymru Fydd movement) by a semi-articulate striving after 'Home Rule'. Clearly and chronologically structured, *Wales in British Politics* united the method of the scholar of 'high politics' (the scouring of personal correspondence and private archives) with an awareness of the importance of party structures and public opinion. Politics was a serious game in which individual ambitions and high-minded principles, ideological commitment and group loyalties intersected with the growing political and national consciousness of Welsh intellectuals, opinion-formers and, beyond them, the electorate, itself grappling with shifting notions of social and collective identity. As they were depicted by Morgan, political parties were not simply the expressions of class interests but were active subjects in their own right, articulating policies that changed the terms of political debate and reacting to criticism and support from external pressure groups.

Given the historical absence of any Welsh state, the fact that Kenneth O. Morgan had endeavoured to write Welsh political history at an all-Wales level was significant in itself.[9] He brought his work to a close in 1922 (the very year of Labour's emergence as *the* major force in Welsh politics). The achievement of the *cause célèbre* of Welsh Liberalism, disestablishment, effectively marked both the end of the Liberal era in the history of Wales and the disappearance from the centre-stage of British politics of a distinctively Welsh set of problems. After 1922, suggested Morgan, 'the interests of Wales were once again to become virtually indistinguishable from those of the other nations'.[10]

Nevertheless, Morgan noted that the history of the Labour Party might also 'fruitfully be investigated' if it was treated as 'a study in regional diversity'.[11] He felt that the early history of the labour movement in Wales was 'shot through with a recognition of the distinct needs of the Welsh industrial community' and in *Wales in British Politics* he devoted some attention to its rise.[12] Socialist societies had been slow to arrive in the late nineteenth century, their weakness paralleled by that of the trade union movement, at least before the growth of the 'New Unionism' and the establishment of the SWMF.[13] The miners' strike of 1898 changed the terms of the debate: it was 'the 1868 of the coalfield . . . the effective origin of the Labour movement in Welsh history'.[14] It was followed by the intermittent growth of the Independent Labour Party, the victory of Keir Hardie in Merthyr Boroughs in 1900 and the coalescence of a group of 'Lib-Lab' MPs representing mining constituencies. The success of the Welsh labour movement raised issues (both ideological and symbolic) to which 'the old Liberal platform had no solution' and although the Labour Party could not yet displace the Liberals, it was applying pressure of 'alarming proportions'.[15] Industrial relations struggles soured the old ethos of capital–labour compromise and, gradually, 'a coherent vision of a Labour Party' emerged, albeit one that remained 'largely rooted in the local issues of the villages and valleys rather than in the international cause of social revolution'.[16]

The context Kenneth O. Morgan provided for the study of the 'rise of Labour' in Wales was a robust one and although his judgements have, inevitably, been challenged in some of their particulars, or been amplified by further research, they have, on the whole, stood the test of time. No other scholar has sought to overturn his depiction of the politics of the age. Of course, his vital contribution had not been made in a vacuum. Nor was his emphasis on party politics the only approach. The work of Ieuan Gwynedd Jones, the historian of mid-nineteenth-century Wales, involved greater attention than was present in *Wales in British Politics* to the communities in which political activity took root.[17] Jones's work attempted more a *social* history of Liberal politics, the logistical demands of which in terms of research necessitated studies of smaller communities.[18] Jones's method was to be much emulated by later scholars, who found, as Morgan had predicted, that it was very difficult to replicate the all-Wales approach adopted in *Wales in British Politics* when dealing with (for instance) the inter-war years. In the sphere of industrial and trade union history John Williams's work also fringed on the early years of Labour politics and eloquently brought the economic historian's awareness of industrial relations and material circumstances into the equation.[19] Furthermore, Kenneth O. Morgan's contribution to the development of the history of the Labour Party in Wales did not begin and end with his monograph. It had been preceded by a stimulating foray into 'Democratic politics in Glamorgan, 1884–1914' and was soon complemented by an essay dealing with 'The Merthyr of Keir Hardie', in a collection edited by Glanmor Williams on the political history of Merthyr Tydfil.[20] In time Keir Hardie, one of the central figures in the story of Labour's rise in Edwardian Wales, was to be the subject of a full-length biography.[21]

By the early 1970s modern Welsh history was on the verge of a significant advance. Llafur, the Society for the Study of Welsh Labour History, was established and began publishing an annual journal (entitled *Llafur*). The Social Science Research Council funded an important project on the history of the South Wales Coalfield and the South Wales Miners' Library was opened.[22] In time these developments led to monographs, including Hywel Francis and David Smith's *The Fed*, Francis's own *Miners Against Fascism*, and Richard Lewis's *Leaders and Teachers*.[23] Equally important was the sense of communal, comradely endeavour and interest that Llafur in particular fostered, with its regular meetings, lectures and conferences. A concern for party-political history as such, however, was (and has remained) relatively marginal in the pages of *Llafur*, which rapidly broadened out into the expansive terrain of social history.[24]

Of more immediate importance for the development of the historiographical context which has informed this volume was the University of Wales Colloquium of Historians held at Swansea in 1971, from which a special issue of *Welsh History Review* emerged.[25] Of the four contributions, three dealt directly with party-political history (the fourth author, David Smith, wrote on the struggle of the south Wales miners against company unionism). Kenneth O. Morgan, in 'The new Liberalism and the challenge of Labour: the Welsh experience, 1885–1929', extended some of his views on the 'rise of Labour' debate from *Wales in British Politics*, addressing more squarely the rise of 'New Liberal' ideas and their inability either to capture the Welsh Liberal agenda or to prevent the sweeping successes of the Labour Party in the 1920s. Morgan stressed, however, the resilience of the 'old' Liberalism in Wales, at least until 1914.[26]

Cyril Parry's essay on 'Gwynedd politics, 1900–1920: the rise of a Labour Party' represented a condensed version of an earlier work.[27] As a regional study it operated within the existing interpretative framework established by Kenneth O. Morgan, stressing the 'catalytic' impact of the First World War rather than the organizational and ideological problems faced by the Liberal Party before 1914.[28] The rise of the labour movement was viewed as centred on industrial conflict, the gradual hardening of class interests and the rise of issues of social reform, although, again, this combination was insufficient to present a serious challenge to Gwynedd Liberals until after 1918.[29] Parry argued that, even when the Labour Party did begin to take control of parliamentary representation, it inherited much from its predecessors. 'The effects of the radical inheritance', he wrote, 'shaped labour's view of politics', particularly in terms of the inculcation of tolerance and optimism.[30] Labour in Gwynedd eschewed revolutionary objectives in favour of gradualism and constitutionalism and the area's experience was manifestly different from the strife-ridden politics of the South Wales Coalfield: 'the politics of conflict were alien to this area'.[31] Parry also highlighted other important trends in the evolution of the local labour movement, including the critical role played by 'the power of personalities' such as R. Silyn Roberts, David Thomas and R. T. Jones and the fact that they represented an activist élite.[32] Like Kenneth O. Morgan before him, Parry echoed the idea that after the First World War specifically Welsh political issues went into retreat, cowed by collectivism and 'the growth of scale'.[33]

Peter Stead's contribution addressed the question of 'Working-class leadership in south Wales, 1900–1920'. Stead argued that the nature of such leadership in Wales had been fixed in the 'late-Victorian and Edwardian context' and had changed little since, perceiving itself as representing a community of workers and their families that clustered together under the banner of 'labour':[34]

> The leaders of organized labour were now taking their place alongside the landowners, the industrialists, the ministers and other leaders of the groups that dominated the public life of the area. The already established consensus now had to accept this new importance of working-class leaders, but at the same time these new leaders had in turn to come to terms with the reality of the values and norms established in this self-conscious community.[35]

As 'labour' emerged as a force in Welsh life so it generated a particular form of industrial and political leadership. 'Lib-Labism' was founded both on the growth of the SWMF and the qualified welcome for the working class that came from within the 'progress-ive' coalition of Welsh Liberalism. The success of the 'Lib-Labs', argued Stead, depended on their image within the wider commun-ity as unifying and representative figures.[36] Although later scholars would emphasize different aspects of the 'Lib-Lab' experience and qualify some of Stead's judgements, his assessment of the social importance of men such as William Abraham (Mabon), William Brace, Thomas Richards and John Williams was significant.[37] Their time would, eventually, pass, as new industrial relations problems and political developments imposed their own logic but Stead reminded readers that in many ways the style of leadership developed by the Lib-Labs was carried on by their successors, of whatever political stamp and ostensible ferocity: '[t]he Labour Party that was to emerge as the dominant party in industrial south Wales after 1918 was led by men whose careers had consisted not of sectional activities but of service to the community as a whole.'[38] Exemplifying this pattern was Vernon Hartshorn, spurned by the Mid Glamorgan electorate in 1910 but returned unopposed to Parliament for the Ogmore constituency in 1918.[39] Ultimately, argued Stead, ideological purity counted for less than practicality and pragmatism, party labels for less than 'ability, industry and integrity in public affairs'.[40]

In this essay and in his subsequent contributions Peter Stead probed the relationship between the Labour Party and Welsh society. He went on to interrogate the political language of Edwardian Wales some considerable time before the study of 'discourse' became fashionable, arguing that 'culture' was the terrain on which the contested meaning of social change was fought out.[41] The victors, the proponents of an independent labour politics, were able to redefine their society as 'working-class' in a way that would continue to hold resonance for a half-century.[42] Ultimately that too was to weaken and the Labour Party would be faced with a new challenge: 'reconciling what was essentially a British party with Welsh aspirations'.[43] As Stead explained, the Labour Party 'rarely doubted that Welshness had contributed to its legitimacy and genius' but was much less clear as to whether this 'Welshness' necessitated formal constitutional recognition.[44] It is a question which has gnawed at the conscience of the Labour Party in Wales throughout its existence.[45]

Kenneth O. Morgan, Cyril Parry and Peter Stead were not the only historians to contribute to the developing history of the Labour Party in Wales in the 1970s. J. Beverley Smith's measured, informative and deeply sensitive essay on James Griffiths was as much an intellectual and social history as it was a biographical study.[46] Michael Foot completed his two-volume biography of Aneurin Bevan, both a literary *tour de force* and a perceptive celebration of a Labour hero.[47] Local and organizational studies were begun at this time that were to emerge later: Deian Hopkin's detailed reading of the politics of the Llanelli constituency represented a close fidelity to the approach of Ieuan Gwynedd Jones, and Chris Howard, though studying the national leadership of the Labour Party, also generated perceptive observations on Labour politics in south Wales.[48]

In the 1980s a greater volume of work made its presence felt: local studies of Gower and Swansea by David Cleaver, of Cardiganshire by Howard Jones and of Aberdare by Jon Parry and Anthony Mòr O'Brien and a partisan reading of the life of S. O. Davies by Robert Griffiths.[49] Although neither were directly political studies, both R. Merfyn Jones's monograph on the north Wales quarrymen and David Pretty's history of agricultural trade unionism had much to contribute to a greater understanding of the political dynamics of some of the more neglected parts of Wales.[50]

In terms of the political history of the Labour Party, John Graham Jones's work was perhaps the most significant of all appearing at this time, in that it represented an attempt to open up new areas of debate, particularly with regard to the 1920s and 1930s. Jones drew attention to the geographical and sociological diversity of Welsh constituencies, countering the impression that Wales 'as a whole was a Labour stronghold'.[51] On the contrary, the Labour Party may have secured a substantial block of Welsh seats by 1922 but moving beyond the heavy industrial constituencies proved more difficult. Jones suggested that Labour had consciously to adopt a 'new socialism', with predominantly middle-class candidates taking a moderate and constitutionalist stance in the coastal ports and north-east Wales in order to woo the electorate and eschewing industrial action as a primary political weapon. Jones may have exaggerated the commitment of working-class activists, even in the South Wales Coalfield, to a pseudo-revolutionary industrial rather than political strategy but his stress on the gradual spread of Labour Party organization across Wales and on the difficulties faced in the rural areas in particular added valuably to the burgeoning historiography.[52]

In the early 1980s Kenneth O. Morgan made another landmark contribution to the history of modern Wales in the form of his *Rebirth of a Nation* and he continued to publish incisive and ground-breaking essays on various aspects of Welsh political history.[53] The problems and challenges that had faced the Liberal Party, the reconstruction issue in Wales after both world wars and the historical context of Welsh nationalism were amongst the most prominent themes and biographical work also proceeded, including a full-length study of James Callaghan.[54] If it is possible to extract a common theme from such diverse and prodigious scholarship it is that, whatever the dramatic changes in personnel and party loyalties that Wales had undergone in the course of the modern era, Morgan nevertheless saw an essential continuity in the reformist pragmatism of the Welsh, in their readiness to accept limited gains in this world rather than wholesale transformation in the next. 'Wales', he argued, 'is not a revolutionary country', and the significance of revolutionary gestures or documents could easily be exaggerated.[55] 'For every act of civil disobedience or industrial direct action . . . there were countless, less spectacular, instances of legal, constitutional, peaceful protest that provided the essential stimulus for change.'[56] The Welsh genius was to be found in 'artistry in the uses of power' not in insurrectionary plots.[57] As with his *Wales in British Politics*, so here, in a series of interpretative essays, Ireland provided an illuminating contrast. Compared with Ireland after all, noted Morgan, 'Wales has been . . . the model of constitutionality'.[58]

Dai Smith had, at one time, dabbled in the history of Labour Party politics, but first trade union and then cultural histories claimed his attention throughout most of the 1970s and 1980s.[59] Only in the 1990s did he turn to the career of Aneurin Bevan in what may be viewed as an attempt to reconcile the south Wales that had been formed in the late nineteenth and early twentieth centuries to the society that (post-1945) it had become.[60] Rather than adopt a strictly biographical approach, *à la* Michael Foot or (more recently) John Campbell, Smith situated Bevan within the social and cultural world that gave him meaning, because, wrote Smith, '[i]magining Aneurin Bevan's culture is an essential precondition to comprehending his politics'.[61] Smith argued that this was an essentially 'offensive not defensive' modernizing culture, full of hope and ambition and that Bevan symbolized a 'Labour Socialism' uniting 'principled theory and pragmatic action', a yoking of philosophy and practice built on the Labour Party and on working-class discipline.[62] Far from Aneurin Bevan being atypical in relationship to his society, insisted Smith, he carried the socialist principles he had imbibed in south Wales into his ministerial offices under Clement Attlee: 'he had a philosophy of political action that went beyond the merely contingent'.[63]

The present author's study of the politics of the Rhondda Valleys represented a different kind of enterprise.[64] Influenced by a new wave of labour histories grounded in an appreciation of the importance of local political cultures, *Democratic Rhondda* attempted to comprehend the evolution of an area's politics across the modern chronological span.[65] As Liberalism and 'Lib-Labism' eventually gave way to independent labour politics, socialism and communism, so a picture emerged which paid attention both to change (in terms of the class basis of local politics and the priorities held by the different parties) and to continuities (in terms of the style of leadership and the pragmatic approach to power of most local politicians). Rather than emphasize the often-celebrated manifestations of syndicalism, industrial unionism and extra-parliamentary communism in the Rhondda, greater stress was placed on the strength of the Labour Party hegemony in the area (particularly from 1910 onwards) which facilitated such 'exotic' experimentations. Labour's strength involved significant risks – corruption, nepotism, complacency, ossification – but also generated a constructive rather than 'rejectionist' attitude towards local administrative responsibilities and a down-to-earth appraisal of the opportunities provided by the flexibility of the British state. This was an analysis extrapolated to the coalfield as a whole in a further publication, *Capitalism, Community and Conflict*, in 1998.[66] By the mid-1990s such work was being accompanied by other reassessments of Welsh Labour's past, drawing eclectically on urban sociology, political science and comparative studies. The result was both new information and a sizeable challenge to romantic conceptions of the nature of the Labour Party in Wales.[67]

Before the appearance of *Democratic Rhondda* plans were being laid for this volume of essays. Duncan Tanner convened a meeting at Gregynog Hall, Newtown, in April 1995 which brought together most of the contributors and at which '[i]t was unanimously felt that a multi-author history of the Labour Party in Wales could play an important part not only in helping to close a large gap in Welsh historiography but also in setting a new research agenda for the future'.[68] The editors (Duncan Tanner and Deian Hopkin, later joined by the present author) approached potential contributors and publishing contracts were signed with the University of Wales Press. A meeting of contributors took place in Cardiff in 1997 and a conference was held (jointly with Llafur) in Bangor in 1998. By spring 1999 the volume began to assume its final shape as the last of the contributions arrived, although it remains a matter of regret that two of the chapters intended for the section dealing with Wales after 1945 did not materialize. What can be stated, without much fear of contradiction, is that the 'large gap in Welsh historiography' that this volume originally and ambitiously aimed to close, remains yawningly present. Indeed, the more one examines it the larger it appears to be: testament if nothing else to the enduring interest and multi-faceted nature of the subject itself.

The second aim (of setting 'a new research agenda') is perhaps more evidently addressed. When combined with a parallel electronic publication listing Labour archival sources, this book offers new encouragement to examine various aspects of the Labour Party's history in Wales.[69] This volume highlights fresh ideas on the more researched aspects of Labour's history in Wales, identifies original areas for study (and the sources available for doing this) and reaffirms the existence of some significant gaps in our knowledge. Kenneth O. Morgan's call, forty years ago, for the story of Labour politics to be told through 'detailed, almost fragmentary, presentation against the background of local pressures and animosities in each constituency', is still valid, as is his suggestion that the local leadership of constituency parties remains a profitable area of study.[70] Many significant features of the period since 1945 are scarcely even touched on here, from the impact of urban sprawl and unemployment on Labour politics to the relationship between trade unions and the Labour Party since the 1970s. If contemporary Wales is increasingly being discussed by students of politics and social policy, the recent past remains shrouded in mystery, despite the Labour Party's willingness to open up its records to academic scrutiny.

This volume stands very much in the tradition of the four decades of scholarship that have preceded its appearance. Given that the earlier work of several contributors has already been singled out in some way or other, major or minor, as laying the ground for such an enterprise, this should hardly be surprising. Naturally, changing intellectual and historiographical fashions make their presence felt: the problematizing of 'class', the attention to political discourse, the necessary appraisal of the experience of women and the importance of gender relations being amongst the most obvious. Yet, although some earlier judgements are modified, challenged or contextualized in different ways, this work does not run against the logic of most earlier historical writing.

This is not to understate the significance of the volume. Earlier work on Welsh Labour politics was remarkably innovative, but the rather sparse recent work on British constituency politics provides no obvious alternative blueprint. It is not just that Welsh Labour parties had to face issues which were absent from politics in England (such as the challenge of nationalism and the language question), nor that Welsh economic and social trends were often an exaggerated form of trends in other parts of Britain. The Scottish experience provides possibilities for comparison and there are obvious similarities between the experience of parts of Wales and some regions within the United Kingdom.[71] It is not that Wales is unique. It is simply that the study of Labour politics in the rest of Britain has also scarcely gone forward as it might, continuing to focus in the main on national policy, internal and structural reform and individual leaders. As a result, sections of this book offer rare glimpses of life and politics away from London, which should encourage similar attention to other parts of Britain.[72]

Editorial policy has not been to enforce a 'party line' and this is not an 'official' history. Contributors have been encouraged, quite naturally, to develop views of their subjects that are, at one and the same time, balanced and independent, drawing attention both to the Labour Party's failures and its successes. But although this volume contains eleven different essays by a total of twelve contributors, five major themes emerge with regularity across the book as a whole: an appreciation of the regional diversity of the Labour Party in Wales; an exploration of the problematic links between social and economic change on the one hand and political change on the other; an engagement with the realm of political ideas and identities; a stress on what might be termed the 'social history' of Labour politics understood in terms of party culture and activism; and a reassessment of Labour's contribution to devolutionary politics in Wales in this century.

The importance of regional variation across Wales to an understanding of the Labour Party's fortunes will rapidly become apparent in reading the essays that follow. Late nineteenth- and twentieth-century Wales encompassed great variation in terms of local economies, demographic and linguistic histories and political experiences. Labour made uneven progress in spreading the socialist message, establishing party organization, winning and holding parliamentary seats and taking control of local government institutions. As Duncan Tanner puts it in Chapter 5, 'there is more to Welsh Labour politics than the politics of the coalfield' and everywhere the Labour Party had to be sensitive to the particular form of political culture with which it sought to engage, involving (as Deian Hopkin points out in Chapter 2) dockers, railwaymen and schoolteachers as well as coalminers. The 'all-Wales' level appropriate for some discussions (most obviously devolution) was irrelevant in others, where the varied nature of Welsh communities demanded a more subtle response. Wales was not and is not an 'essence'; rather, as Neil Evans has written else-where, it has its own 'coalescing and conflicting totality', reflected in all its complexity in this volume.[73]

Complexity is the most obvious characteristic of the second major theme: that of the relationship between economic and social change and politics. Boldly stated, the objective or material social and economic conditions of Wales's communities did not give rise 'naturally' to any particular set of political attitudes. However umbilical the appearance of the link between the Labour Party and the working-class communities from which its greatest and most consistent support has been derived, the relationship between one and the other was never automatic or unquestionable. Throughout much of Wales the heterogeneity of the working class, its fractur-ing along lines of gender, skill, ethnicity, language and religion, its internal differentiation through patterns of residence and con-sumption, operated, particularly in the early years of this century, to undermine expectations that Labour was the natural repository of whatever votes the working class possessed. Even in coalmining communities where social variation was relatively less marked, the generation of strong allegiances to the Labour Party was, in the Edwardian era, tentative and halting and was far from being the inevitable reflex of occupational danger and geographical concentration. As John Williams writes in Chapter 1, 'the causal connections are less direct and less immediate than is sometimes assumed' and the existence of working-class communities was 'a necessary but certainly not a sufficient condition to determine political organization'. There remained wide variations in the political experiences of ostensibly similar communities. That said, there were 'preconditions': structural features which *facilitated* the development of Labour politics, including the heavy geographical concentration of male manual workers, the development of trade unionism and the incidence of social and industrial unrest. As Duncan Tanner shows in Chapter 11, for the last thirty years, the decay of old, established industrial and social structures posed new problems for the by-then hegemonic Labour Party. The importance of social and economic factors cannot be written out of history but rarely are the links direct and unmediated: 'the logic of much recent analysis', wrote Tanner elsewhere, 'is to recognize the difficulties of making connections between "social" experience and "political" responses.'[74]

If electoral behaviour is not an unfailing barometer of social change, then historians must pay attention to political ideas, languages (sometimes systematized as 'discourse') and the construction (in the political arena) of political and social identities.[75] Social problems might, as John Williams writes, provide 'convenient and prominent pegs from which to hang fresh ideological clothes' but equally, as Richard Lewis shows in Chapter 4, not all issues were amenable to class analysis and class identity was not the only identity available. In Chapter 3 Eddie May echoes work by Peter Stead in insisting on the importance to the early labour movement of its dignity and status in Welsh public life. Even the broad lines of the political system with which we are familiar were not fixed before 1914. After 1918, as political formations hardened, so party affiliations both capitalized on class identities and also created them. Ideological inventiveness (as in the case of the Liberal Party in the late 1920s) did not automatically lead to political success as the political system polarized in the 1920s, marginalizing centrist traditions. In shaping its message to meet its constituents' needs and fears, Labour worked hard to become what was (apparently and misleadingly) the 'automatic' political expression of mining communities: perhaps, in recent years, it has been in danger of forgetting its own history and mistaking appearance for reality. Politics was and is a crucial domain in its own right, with its own dynamic: analysis of 'the rise of class politics' must not stop at 'class'.

This volume's fourth theme is the social history of Labour Party politics: not in the sense of any deterministic linkages but rather the cultural dimension to political activity and the vital role played by individual activists. The Labour Party, in its many varied forms of organization (Independent Labour Party branch, Constituency Labour Party, Women's Section, Trades and Labour Council), often spawned what Eddie May terms a 'vibrant social, cultural and educational life'. In Andrew Walling's Chapter 8 it is evident that, whether it was through dances or quizzes, whist drives or camping expeditions, mock parliaments or galas, tableaux or May Day parades, the party sustained individuals in a web of common endeavour.[76] As Neil Evans and Dot Jones document in Chapter 9, Labour Party women made an immense contribution to this 'social politics', notwithstanding the fact that their struggle within the party has oftentimes appeared to be as momentous as the struggle of the Labour Party itself. Party activists tended to be men and women enmeshed in their communities, working to generate new senses of community leadership. What emerges from virtually every chapter in this book is the often heroic nature of their efforts, their determination, commitment, evangelism and idealism. They were, as Eddie May suggests, 'the sustaining core of Labour politics'.

Finally, what unites this volume (more, it must be admitted, than it has united the Labour Party for most of its history) is a focus on Wales. Organizationally it is possible to suggest that there has only been a 'Welsh' Labour Party since the formation of the Welsh Regional Council of Labour in 1947. There has always been a sense in which the pull of external and international commonalities and interests, particularly in the South Wales Coalfield, has rendered the Welsh context secondary, even, for some, irrelevant. Kenneth O. Morgan shows in Chapter 7 how Labour was caught in a dialectical conflict over devolution ('a natural and traditionally socialist idea' according to Goronwy Roberts). To a considerable degree this has changed with the rise of the devolutionary project and there is much greater awareness now of the party as a distinctively Welsh entity than ever before. R. Merfyn Jones and Ioan Rhys Jones demonstrate in Chapter 10 how important the Labour Party has been in channelling (and, at times, frustrating) demands for a greater measure of national autonomy within the British state. Labour's struggles in this area replicate more clearly than those of any other party the ambiguous attitudes held by the Welsh people towards devolution in the twentieth century.

It has already been observed that this volume is not an official history of the Labour Party in Wales and many of the contributors have exposed Labour's failings. At times the party has suffered from limited horizons, timidity, defensiveness and particularly from male chauvinism. Yet, whatever its deficiencies, this volume's collective verdict on a century of the Labour Party in Wales is more positive than negative. From the 1920s and 1930s, as the present author shows in Chapter 6, right down to the present day, the Labour Party has delivered, at national and local levels, pragmatic policies representing tangible gains for working people. If, as Duncan Tanner suggests, the Labour Party in Wales has been 'verbally radical but vehemently practical' then perhaps it has indeed fulfilled the ambition of James Griffiths that it should be 'a faithful mirror of the life and struggles of the Welsh people'.

Notes

[1] Aneurin Bevan, *In Place of Fear* (Wakefield, 1976), 124.

[2] In thinking about this theme an essay by J. Lawrence and M. Taylor has been particularly helpful: 'Introduction: electoral sociology and the historians', in Lawrence and Taylor (eds.), *Party, State and Society: Electoral Behaviour in Britain since 1820* (Aldershot, 1997).

[3] All references are from the 3rd edn (1980).

[4] Ibid., p. v.

[5] Ibid., p. vii. For an early biography see E. W. Evans, *Mabon (William Abraham 1842–1922): A Study in Trade Union Leadership* (Cardiff, 1959).

[6] *Chartist Studies* was published in London.

[7] Morgan, *Wales in British Politics*, p. vii.

[8] Ibid., p. ix.

[9] N. Evans, 'Writing the social history of modern Wales: approaches, achievements and problems', *Social History*, 3 (1992), 479–80.

[10] Morgan, *Wales in British Politics*, p. viii.

[11] Ibid., p. ix.

[12] Ibid., 310.

[13] Ibid., 199–204.

[14] Ibid., 204.

[15] Ibid., 211, 245.

[16] Ibid., 247, 255.

[17] Evans, 'Writing social history', 481.

[18] See I. G. Jones, *Explorations and Explanations: Essays in the Social History of Victorian Wales* (Llandysul, 1981); *Communities: Essays in the Social History of Victorian Wales* (Llandysul, 1987); *Mid-Victorian Wales: The Observers and the Observed* (Cardiff, 1992). For one work with later relevance, see idem, 'Franchise reform and Glamorgan politics, 1869–1921', in P. Morgan (ed.), *Glamorgan County History, VI, Glamorgan Society 1780–1980* (Cardiff, 1988).

[19] L. J. Williams, 'The first Welsh Labour MP', *Morgannwg*, VI (1962); idem, *Was Wales Industrialised? Essays in Modern Welsh History* (Llandysul, 1995).

[20] 'Democratic politics in Glamorgan, 1884–1914', *Morgannwg*, IV (1960); G. Williams (ed.), *Merthyr Politics: The Making of a Working-Class Tradition* (Cardiff, 1966) also included two other contributions of relevance to this volume: I. G. Jones, 'The Merthyr of Henry Richard' and J. W. England, 'The Merthyr of the twentieth century: a postscript'.

[21] K. O. Morgan, *Keir Hardie: Radical and Socialist* (London, 1975). See also K. O. Fox, 'Labour and Merthyr's khaki election of 1900', *WHR* II/4 (1965).

[22] Evans, 'Writing social history', 481–2.

[23] H. Francis and D. Smith, *The Fed: A History of the South Wales Miners in the Twentieth Century* (London, 1980; Cardiff, 1998); H. Francis, *Miners Against Fascism: Wales and the Spanish Civil War* (London, 1984); R. Lewis, *Leaders and Teachers: Adult Education and the Challenge of Labour in South Wales, 1906–1940* (Cardiff, 1993).

[24] For exceptions, see, *inter alia*, W. David, 'The Labour Party and the "exclusion" of the Communists: the case of the Ogmore Divisional Labour Party in the 1920s', *Llafur*, III/4 (1983); N. Evans, 'Cardiff's Labour tradition', *Llafur*, IV/2 (1985); D. Hopkin, 'The rise of Labour in Wales, 1890–1914', *Llafur*, VI/3 (1994); C. Howard, ' "The focus of the mute hope of a whole class": Ramsay MacDonald

and Aberavon, 1922–29', *Llafur*, VII/1 (1996); I. McAllister, 'The Labour Party in Wales: the dynamics of one-partyism', *Llafur*, III/2 (1981); K. O. Morgan, 'Leaders and led in the labour movement: the Welsh experience', *Llafur*, VI/3 (1994); D. Morris, 'Sosialaeth i'r Cymry – trafodaeth yr ILP', *Llafur*, IV/2 (1985); J. Parry, 'Trade unionists and early socialism in south Wales, 1890–1908', *Llafur*, IV/3 (1986); C. Williams, ' "An able administrator of capitalism"? The Labour Party in the Rhondda, 1917–21', *Llafur*, IV/4 (1987).

[25] Evans, 'Writing social history', 486. *WHR*, VI/3 (1973).

[26] Morgan, 'The new Liberalism and the challenge of Labour: the Welsh experience, 1885–1929', reprinted in K. O. Morgan, *Modern Wales: Politics, Places and People* (Cardiff, 1995), 82.

[27] C. Parry, *The Radical Tradition in Welsh Politics: A Study of Liberal and Labour Politics in Gwynedd 1900–1920* (Hull, 1970).

[28] Parry, *Radical Tradition*, 2.

[29] Ibid., 71–3.

[30] Ibid., 73.

[31] Ibid., 73–4.

[32] Ibid., 74–5.

[33] Ibid., 76.

[34] Stead, 'Working-class leadership in south Wales, 1900–1920', 329.

[35] Ibid., 330.

[36] Ibid., 334.

[37] C. Williams, 'Democracy and nationalism in Wales: the Lib-Lab enigma', in R. Stradling, S. Newton and D. Bates (eds.), *Conflict and Coexistence: Nationalism and Democracy in Modern Europe: Essays in Honour of Harry Hearder* (Cardiff, 1997).

[38] Stead, 'Working-class leadership', 350.

[39] P. Stead, 'Vernon Hartshorn: miners' agent and cabinet minister', in S. Williams (ed.), *Glamorgan Historian*, VI (1970). See also C. Howard, 'Reactionary radicalism: the Mid-Glamorgan bye-election, March 1910', in S. Williams (ed.), *Glamorgan Historian*, IX (1973).

[40] Stead, 'Working-class leadership', 352.

[41] P. Stead, 'The language of Edwardian politics', in D. Smith (ed.), *A People and a Proletariat: Essays in the History of Wales, 1780–1980* (London, 1980).

[42] Stead, 'Language', 164. See also idem, 'Establishing a heartland: the Labour Party in Wales', in K. D. Brown (ed.), *The First Labour Party 1906–1914* (Beckenham, 1985).

[43] P. Stead, 'The Labour Party and the claims of Wales', in J. Osmond (ed.), *The National Question Again: Welsh Political Identity in the 1980s* (Llandysul, 1985).

[44] Ibid., 99.

[45] For an early attempt to square the circle, see D. Hopkin, 'Y *Werin a'i Theyrnas*: ymateb sosialaeth i genedlaetholdeb 1880–1920', in G. H. Jenkins (ed.), *Cof Cenedl: Ysgrifau ar Hanes Cymru*, VI (Llandysul, 1991).

[46] J. B. Smith, 'James Griffiths: an appreciation', in J. B. Smith (ed.), *James Griffiths and his Times* (Ferndale, 1977).

[47] M. Foot, *Aneurin Bevan* (2 vols.: London, 1962 and 1973).

[48] D. Hopkin, 'The rise of Labour: Llanelli, 1890–1922', in G. H. Jenkins and J. B. Smith (eds.), *Politics and Society in Wales, 1840–1922* (Cardiff, 1988); C. Howard, ' "Expectations born to death": the local Labour Party expansion in the 1920s', in J. M. Winter (ed.), *The Working Class in Modern British History:*

Essays in Honour of Henry Pelling (Cambridge, 1983). See also Howard, 'Reactionary radicalism', and idem, '"The focus of the mute hopes of a whole class"'.

[49] D. Cleaver, 'Labour and Liberals in the Gower constituency, 1885–1910', *WHR* XII/3 (1985); idem, 'The general election contest in the Swansea town constituency, January 1910: the socialist challenge', *Llafur*, V/3 (1990); H. C. Jones, 'The Labour Party in Cardiganshire 1918–66', *Ceredigion*, IX/2 (1982); J. Parry, 'Labour leaders and local politics, 1888–1902: the example of Aberdare', *WHR*, XIV/3 (1989); A. Mòr O'Brien, 'The Merthyr Boroughs election, November 1915', *WHR*, XII/4 (1985); idem, 'Keir Hardie, C. B. Stanton and the First World War', *Llafur*, IV/3 (1986); R. Griffiths, *S. O. Davies: A Socialist Faith* (Llandysul, 1983).

[50] R. M. Jones, *The North Wales Quarrymen, 1874–1922* (Cardiff, 1982); D. A. Pretty, *The Rural Revolt that Failed: Farm Workers' Trade Unions in Wales, 1889–1950* (Cardiff, 1989). For more on north Wales see also R. M. Jones, 'Labour implantation: is there a Welsh dimension?', *Tijdschrift voor sociale geschiedenis*, XVIII/2–3 (1992); and on rural society see D. Howell, 'Labour organisation among agricultural workers in Wales, 1872–1921', *WHR*, XVI/1 (1992).

[51] J. G. Jones, 'Wales and the "New Socialism", 1926–29', *WHR*, XI/2 (1982), 192.

[52] Ibid., 174. See also idem, 'Welsh politics between the wars: the personnel of Labour', *Transactions of the Honourable Society of Cymmrodorion* (1983); idem, 'Glamorgan politics, 1918–85', in P. Morgan (ed.), *Glamorgan County History*, VI.

[53] K. O. Morgan, *Rebirth of a Nation: Wales 1880–1980* (Oxford and Cardiff, 1981); idem, *Modern Wales*.

[54] K. O. Morgan, *Callaghan: A Life* (Oxford, 1997).

[55] K. O. Morgan, 'The Welsh in English politics, 1868–1922', in idem, *Modern Wales*, 22–3.

[56] Ibid., 23.

[57] Ibid., 24.

[58] K. O. Morgan, 'Consensus and conflict in modern Welsh history', in D. W. Howell and K. O. Morgan (eds.), *Crime, Protest and Police in Modern British Society: Essays in Memory of David J. V. Jones* (Cardiff, 1999), 30. See also K. O. Morgan, *Democracy in Wales: From Dawn to Deficit* (Cardiff, 1995).

[59] For an early essay, see his 'Leaders and led', in K. S. Hopkins (ed.), *Rhondda Past and Future* (Ferndale, 1975).

[60] D. Smith, *Aneurin Bevan and the World of South Wales* (Cardiff, 1993); idem, *Wales: A Question for History* (Bridgend, 1999). See also C. Williams, 'Searching for a new South Wales', *History Workshop Journal*, XLI (1996).

[61] Smith, *Aneurin Bevan*, 258; J. Campbell, *Nye Bevan and the Mirage of British Socialism* (London, 1987).

[62] Smith, *Aneurin Bevan*, 189, 207–10.

[63] Smith, *Wales: A Question for History*, 191.

[64] C. Williams, *Democratic Rhondda: Politics and Society, 1885–1951* (Cardiff, 1996).

[65] See, for instance, D. Howell, *British Workers and the Independent Labour Party, 1888–1906* (Manchester, 1983); M. Savage, *The Dynamics of Working-Class Politics: The Labour Movement in Preston, 1880–1940* (Cambridge, 1987); D. Tanner, *Political Change and the Labour Party 1900–1918* (Cambridge, 1990).

[66] C. Williams, *Capitalism, Community and Conflict: The South Wales Coalfield, 1898–1947* (Cardiff, 1998).

[67] For example, R. Fagge, *Power, Culture and Conflict in the Coalfields: West Virginia and South Wales, 1900–22* (Manchester, 1996); D. Gilbert, *Class, Community and Collective Action: Social Change in Two British Coalfields, 1850–1926* (Oxford, 1992); E. May, 'Charles Stanton and the limits to "patriotic labour" ', *WHR*, XVIII/3 (1996); Tanner, *Political Change*.

[68] B. Jones, 'The Labour Party in Wales: a centenary history', *Llafur*, VI/4 (1995), 147.

[69] D. M. Tanner and A. Walling, *The Labour Party in Wales: An Electronic Guide to Archival Resources* (Bangor, 2000).

[70] Morgan, 'Democratic politics in Glamorgan', 23.

[71] D. Howell, *A Lost Left: Three Studies in Socialism and Nationalism* (Manchester, 1986); I. Donnachie, C. Harvie and I. S. Wood (eds.), *Forward! Labour Politics in Scotland 1888–1988* (Edinburgh, 1989); A. Campbell, N. Fishman and D. Howell (eds.), *Miners, Unions and Politics 1910–47* (Aldershot, 1996).

[72] Noteworthy regional studies include Savage, *Dynamics*; A. McKinlay and R. J. Morris (eds.), *The ILP on Clydeside 1893–1932: From Foundation to Disintegration* (Manchester, 1991) and S. Davies, *Liverpool Labour: Social and Political Influences on the Development of the Labour Party in Liverpool, 1900–1939* (Keele, 1996).

[73] Evans, 'Writing the social history', 489. See also Smith, *Wales: A Question for History*, 25.

[74] Tanner, *Political Change*, 11.

[75] Lawrence and Taylor, *Party, State and Society*, 2.

[76] For a sense of this across Britain, see D. Weinbren, *Generating Socialism: Recollections of Life in the Labour Party* (Stroud, 1997).

I
FOUNDATIONS

1

The Economic and Social Context

JOHN WILLIAMS

Consideration of the fortunes of the Welsh economy in the four decades following 1880 requires confrontation with a prior question: was there at this time anything which could reasonably be described as a Welsh economy? In some important respects the answer must be in the negative. The economic links between the different regions of Wales – even when these regions are crudely defined as north, mid, and south – were generally tenuous and certainly of marginal significance to each of the individual regions. The rest of Wales offered insignificant markets for the industries of either the south or the north, and if the industrial south became a significant source of demand for the agricultural products of rural mid and west Wales, the south increasingly depended for its supplies on imports from Canada, New Zealand and the United States. Most consumer goods came from, or through, England – via Liverpool in the north and Bristol in the south. Perhaps the main link – and it was a significant one – was through people. Migration from rural Wales to the labour-intensive industries of coal, iron and steel had long been a feature, and it was one which substantially quickened in the decades after 1880: this, indeed, was a rare case where there was some significant connection between north and south Wales when, with the decline of the slate industry from the mid-1890s, many quarrymen were sucked into the rapid expansion of the South Wales Coalfield.

It was not only economic links which were missing: Wales also lacked the institutional structures which help to define an economy. Obviously, and probably fortunately, Wales did not have its own system of currency; there were no customs barriers between it and England; and there was no distinctive system of raising taxes and allocating public expenditure. Monetary, fiscal and trade policy were all settled elsewhere. They were also settled without any explicit reference to the situation and needs of Wales. If this could be construed as neglect it was none the less not unreasonable in the sense that these matters were considered to be issues which should be determined by reference to the perceived interest of the United Kingdom as a whole (indeed, in the grander language of the time, to be 'imperial' issues): Wales was probably not much more ignored or neglected than most other regions. The one marked exception – the export tax on coal imposed in the budget of 1900 to help meet the cost of the Boer War – perhaps merely reinforces the general point, since it was a fiscal and trading decision which seemed likely to affect an important part of the Welsh economy (or, at least, economic activity within Wales). In the event it is difficult to discern any specific impact of the tax on the upward trend of exports of anthracite and steam coal from south Wales either during the years the tax operated (1901 to 1906) or following its removal in 1906.[1]

An economy is not only defined by its economic controls: but in the Wales of 1880 there were also few distinctive social or cultural institutions. There was the National Eisteddfod, first held at Aberdare in 1861, and the (collectively more important) numerous local eisteddfodau which were 'a central development in the cultural life of nineteenth-century Wales'.[2] There were the chapels and Nonconformity, but despite the jibe (in an entry in a *New Statesman* clerihew competition) that

> Description fails
> At the chapels of Wales
> Can anything so grim
> Please Him?

these were not unique to Wales: it was only in Wales that they provided a credible basis for the specific politics of disestablishment. More significantly there was no distinctive and operative Welsh law or legal system: the Welsh Sunday Closing Act of 1881 was almost unique in being a law passed by the imperial Parliament but applying only to Wales. During the four decades which followed 1880 progress was made in closing some of these institutional gaps – the national University was established in 1893; the National Museum and the National Library received their charters in 1907 – but in 1880 the most general source of a distinct national identity sprang from the Welsh language. Paradoxically this was (proportionately) just beginning its long decline: and, ironically, this was being assisted by the encouragement given to English (as the language of 'progress') by many of the articulate and educated Welsh-speaking Welshmen who were pressing for Welsh national institutions.

Given these constraints on the general concept of a Welsh economy it is none the less the case that the nature and organization of economic activity within Wales embodied several features which, on the face of it, were favourable for the emergence of a political party based on labour. The main industries were hugely labour-intensive and the nature of the labour was overwhelmingly manual. These industries were not only manual but were also – disproportionately, compared with other economic regions of the UK – male in their employment needs. It would be difficult to establish whether this last point was of any particular political significance when, for virtually all this period, the parliamentary franchise was restricted to men. If the early establishment of the Labour Party in Wales took place in a very masculine world and made its appeal mainly to male workers, it could plausibly be argued that it was not well-prepared for widening its appeal to women voters after 1918. It is a view, however, which would need to be interpreted within the general context that, in British parliamentary elections generally, there have only been rare occasions (1945, 1997) when the Labour Party secured a majority of the female vote.

In terms of employment, coalmining was the dominant industry throughout these four decades. In the 1881 census the number of male workers in mining and quarrying (101,675) for the first time – just – exceeded those in agriculture. More than four-fifths of these were in coal and nearly 90 per cent of these were in south Wales. Both the absolute numbers and their geographical concentration carried political implications. Thus, around 1910, eleven of the south Wales constituencies contained a significant proportion of voters who were miners: even 10 per cent coming from a single occupational group (as in Breconshire) was electorally important, while in four constituencies (Rhondda, West Monmouthshire, Mid Glamorgan and East Glamorgan) miners actually constituted a majority of all the electors. In two north Wales constituencies, East Denbighshire (44 per cent) and Flintshire (13 per cent), miners carried considerable political weight.[3] This weight had been gathering momentum throughout these years: in 1881 employment in coal had only just been launched on its rocket-like path which peaked in 1920 when it exceeded 290,000 (270,000 in south Wales).[4] The descent was equally precipitous until it finally fizzled out in the 1980s. That there were political implications arising from this pattern is no doubt a truism: but it is equally obvious that the causal connections are less direct and less immediate than is sometimes assumed. In 1910, despite the number of constituencies with a strong miners' vote, there were still only four Welsh miners' MPs and the election of January 1910 was the first occasion on which they were elected as Labour Party representatives. The fact is that it was over a quarter of a century after the 1881 census before the South Wales Miners' Federation (SWMF) was formally committed to a working-class party and the conversion from Lib-Labism was less than Damascus-like for many of its leaders; the 1997 election perhaps suggests that any party-political repercussions of the virtual disappearance of a Welsh coal industry might have an equally long gestation period.

Most of the other major industrial activities were also labour-intensive, manual and male-dominated. Many of the smaller occupational categories showed similar characteristics but (outside agriculture) the four major groups (mining, metal manufacturing and engineering, transport and building) were on their own sufficient to determine the defining features of work in Wales between 1880 and 1920. In 1880 these four sectors accounted for nearly half (47.8 per cent) of the total male workforce, rising to nearly three-fifths (58.7 per cent) in 1920.

Agriculture, although declining relatively from one-fifth to one-tenth of the male occupied population during these years, was still the third largest sector. This, too, was a labour-intensive industry, although any political implications of this were still further complicated because the composition of employment in this sector embraced both landless labourers and land-owning farmers. If the politics was complicated, it was also significant: in 1901 eight of the fourteen county constituencies (Anglesey, Brecknock,

Cardigan, Carmarthen, Merioneth, Montgomery, Pembroke and Radnor) had at least 20 per cent of their voters occupied in agriculture, and five of the borough constituencies (Pembroke and Haverfordwest, together with the Districts of Carnarvon, Denbigh, Flint and Montgomery) embraced such small towns as Winston, Nefin, Ruthin and Mold which were dependent on agriculture.[5] If it is generally hazardous to read off political affiliations by correlating them with the relation to the ownership of the means of production, the predominance of small-scale tenant farmers makes this doubly hazardous in Wales: but, equally, it could be argued that the radical traditions in Welsh agriculture should induce caution about any notion that rural equals apathetic. If the Labour Party was to become the party of the whole of Wales it was necessary to break into these areas: the strong radical Liberalism displayed in those localities before 1914 suggested that this need not be a forlorn enterprise.

Equally difficult to interpret is the significance, if any, of the other aspect of work and employment which has been up to now neglected in this brief account: the paid occupation of women in Wales. It may be that the overriding consideration lies in the simple fact that women were, for parliamentary elections, totally unenfranchised until 1918, but there were women engaged in Welsh politics before this, whilst some women (householders) were able to take part in local elections.[6] Indeed, women were not uncommon as candidates in elections to Poor Law boards of guardians and, while they lasted, school boards: and these bodies – touching on aspects crucial to their local communities and often embedded in the passions of religious denominational differences – could be significant areas for any new party wishing to break into the established political game. These are speculations. The main facts, or at least tendencies, are that the level of female paid employment, especially for married women, was much lower in Wales than the average for the UK (this, of course, is well known, but it is less widely appreciated that the relative gap was increasing throughout these years); and that this arose overwhelmingly from the very low employment possibilities in coalmining areas, for in rural Wales female activity rates were rising during these years. Thus between 1851 and 1911 the female activity rate in Glamorgan fell by a quarter, from 27 to 20 per cent, whereas in Cardigan it rose by a quarter, from 28 to 36 per cent. The heavy dependence in industrial areas on male wage packets carried with it an additional social cost in times of high unemployment in heavy industries.

This last feature emphasizes another major characteristic of the economic and social development of Wales in the late nineteenth and early twentieth centuries: the extent of variation between the different regions of Wales. What is important here is not that there were differences, but that in most major respects these differences were increasing sharply. The trend can be illustrated from three pervasive and strategic aspects: the distribution of the population, the variation of the broad economic structure, and the proportion of Welsh speakers.

The industrialization which had already taken place by the mid-nineteenth century – mostly in the form of iron production along the northern ridge of the South Wales Coalfield and in Denbigh-shire – had necessarily influenced the distribution of the population, but not too sharply. The most affected county, Glamorgan, with just over 10 per cent of the acreage, had just under 20 per cent of the population in 1851. By 1880 the pace had quickened and Glamorgan accounted for nearly one-third of the population. None the less it was between 1880 and 1920 that the real shift took place, with the weight of population sinking very firmly to the bottom of Wales: in 1920 nearly two-thirds (64 per cent) of the population was in Glamorgan and Monmouthshire, and nearly half (47 per cent) in Glamorgan alone. The dominance of the South Wales Coalfield is even greater if attention is focused on the location of the overall increase in the population of Wales. Nine-tenths of the population increase of nearly 1.1 million were in the two counties of Monmouthshire and Glamorgan. It is equally remarkable that half of the counties of Wales saw little or no increase during these four decades: three (Cardigan, Merioneth and Montgomery) actually saw an absolute decline in their population, and three others (Anglesey, Pembroke and Radnor) were in this respect stagnant. Interpretation, particularly the political interpretation, of these population shifts is even more complicated when particular subregions are considered. For example, the major coal-exporting ports of the south – Cardiff, Newport, Swansea and Barry – all experienced a mushroom growth. This was almost literally true of Barry, with less than 500 inhabitants in 1881 and over 33,000 by 1911, but in the same period the population of Cardiff increased by 100,000, Newport by 46,000 and Swansea by 67,000. It was not just the numbers: these towns, especially the latter three, had a social composition which was more complicated than their coalfield hinterlands, in particular having what was for Wales a large middle class.

It is, as we are generally finding, not easy – and perhaps danger-ous – to see direct causal connections between population distribu-tion and political activities or flavours. It may seem, and may indeed be so, that the extra fact that Glamorgan and, to a much lesser degree, Monmouth were the only counties to experience significant net in-migration (especially from outside Wales) made them more exposed to the newer, leftish political trends: caution and scepticism are injected by the equal fact that when these counties really experienced the establishment of Labour Party dominance, in the inter-war years, they were subject to massive net out-migration. Perhaps the only reasonably certain political effect of the heavy concentration of the population of Wales into the counties of the southern coalfield was that the representation of those counties in Parliament would be increased. The occasional redistribution of seats tended to reflect population shifts. In 1880 just six of the thirty-three Welsh seats were in Glamorgan, this became ten out of thirty-four between 1885 and 1914, and then from 1918 sixteen of the thirty-six Welsh seats were from this one county. It follows therefore that a political party which could capture all or most of this geographical area would already be a significant force in Wales.

The geographical disaggregation of the occupied population reveals equally wide variations. Naturally these variations in effect simply reflect the shift in population distribution. Naturally, because it was the areas which experienced growing industrial activity which attracted in-migration: population shifts were largely determined by the location of those economic activities which were, relatively, growing or stagnating. What was perhaps distinctive was the scale of this differentiation within Wales, largely because of the high labour intensity of its most rapidly expanding industry. Thus the number of males employed in mining in Glamorgan in 1921 was greater than the total population had been in every other county (apart from Monmouth) in 1880. Two out of every five occupied males in Glamorgan were in coalmining, but only one in fifty was in agriculture: Cardigan, in contrast, still had over 40 per cent of its occupied male population engaged in agriculture.

Also interconnected was the trend in the proportion of Welsh-speakers in the different counties of Wales. Any presumption of an inverse relationship between the language and the spread of industrialization needs, however, to be treated with considerable care. There are other, and complicated, influences at work. This is suggested, for example, by the contrast in the first official language census in 1891 between the new growing commercial centre of Cardiff, with its 14 per cent Welsh-speakers, and the old industrial centre of Merthyr Tydfil where more than two-thirds of the population over three years old spoke Welsh. One obvious influence was proximity to the English border so that in 1891 Radnor had only 6 per cent and Monmouth 15 per cent of Welsh-speakers. None the less, trends over time suggest some inverse connection with economic activity: there was a general decline from 54 per cent in 1891 to 37 per cent in 1921 in the proportion of the residents in Wales able to speak Welsh (which includes both monoglot Welsh-speakers and those able to speak both Welsh and English). The sharpest declines were in the industrial counties of Glamorgan (49 to 32 per cent), Denbigh (64 to 48 per cent) and Flint (68 to 42 per cent), whilst, proportionately, the fall in Monmouth (15 to 6 per cent) was even more dramatic. In contrast, in the counties with little industrial growth – Anglesey, Cardigan, Merioneth – four out of five of the population in 1921 were still Welsh-speaking. The complications are perhaps indicated by the ambiguities of Carmarthen – partly on the coalfield, very agricultural – which also maintained this high proportion of Welsh speakers.

If there is any political pertinence to be read from the emerging pattern of language mix, it is not easy to understand. It is sometimes suggested that the early twentieth-century surge of migrants from England into the South Wales Coalfield might have loosened the hold of the Welsh language and also brought with it more progressive ideas and attitudes. It is difficult to reconcile the latter view with the relative political inertia of the agricultural counties of south-west England from which most of these migrants were escaping; nor is it obvious that there was necessarily less intellectual liveliness brought by the concurrent stream of movement to the same areas from the rural Welsh-speaking counties of Wales which, whether or not it gave the Welsh language a second chance, certainly slowed down its decline in the industrial south.

What seems to emerge from the survey of the trends in some of the very broad characteristics – population, occupations, language – is that it is misleading to infer any strong, direct, mechanistic causal connections between these trends and the emergence of a Labour Party in Wales. Such caution can be overdone – acute scepticism is a disease to which historians are particularly prone – and it would certainly be folly to allow more indirect links to be overlooked. In particular the trends which have been briefly examined did influence and shape the emergence of a significant trade unionism in Wales as well as being the source of some aspects of social and industrial unrest; and both these developments were more organically connected to the nascent Labour Party.

A few specific unions had all their members within Wales, and in a very few cases the number is known with reasonable accuracy. Given the dominance of mining it is fortunate that the major example was the SWMF which still retained essential autonomy in this respect even as a constituent of the Mineworkers' Federation of Great Britain (MFGB). Yet tracking the total number of trade unionists in Wales during these years – and, indeed, at any period until very recent times – is a forlorn enterprise. Apart from the general absence of records, many of the minority which did join a union were enrolled in a national (British or, more usually, England and Wales) organization which did not keep separate its Welsh membership. If there were regional figures, those in south Wales were likely to be bundled in with Bristol and the south-west, and those in north Wales with Liverpool and the north-west. A judgement that trade unionism became an active force and a perceived presence during these years must, therefore, partly rest on more impressionistic bases. None the less, it is a judgement which is made and offered with some confidence.

To begin with, it is more or less a truism that, during this period, it was easier to recruit and maintain members in heavily populated areas with concentrations of male manual workers. It has already been indicated that south Wales exhibited these features to a strong degree. This can be seen in the persistence from the early 1870s of a separate, if relatively ineffective, union amongst the tinplate workers around Llanelli and Swansea, until it was undermined by personal dissensions and the sharp setback to the industry in the 1890s imposed by the US McKinley tariff. John Hodge's British Steel Smelters' Union was also active in the same area and absorbed many of the tinplate millmen from the 1890s on.[7] Railwaymen, because of their geographical dispersion and occupational diversity, would not (with obvious exceptions such as railway towns like Swindon and Crewe) be seen as a concentrated workforce. However, the exceptional density of the rail network serving the South Wales Coalfield and its ports modified these disadvantages in this region. At all events, this was one of the pioneering centres of railway unionism, symbolized by the attendance of delegates from Merthyr, Cardiff, Pontypool, Aberdare and Newport at the 1872 London meeting at which the Amalgamated Society of Railway Servants was founded. Railwaymen were also involved in several of the most crucial industrial conflicts such as the 1890 stoppage and the strike leading up to the notorious Taff Vale judgment of 1901.[8] In a different region, it could be claimed that the continued existence of the North Wales Quarrymen's Union from the early 1870s represented a similar instance, but it was an organization which only commanded the 'lukewarm allegiance' of the workforce.[9] Despite these various exceptions it was still the case that the favourable conjunction of population density and concentrations of male manual workers had, up to the 1880s, most obviously manifested itself amongst the skilled craft workers in the major towns. A significant part of the opening ceremony for the Roath Dock in Cardiff in 1887 was a great parade of friendly societies and trade unions. The banners of the union marchers proclaimed them as members of local branches of the national societies for carpenters and joiners, plumbers, boiler-makers, shipwrights, masons, tailors, engineers, steam-engine makers, plasterers, iron moulders and printers. In the same year the Trades Union Congress held its annual meeting at Swansea (although this may have been more a missionary move than a recognition of local strength: some contemporary comment suggests that trade unionism in Swansea was not only, as was general, limited to élite groups, but was also on a very small scale).[10]

From these modest footholds there was a great leap forward in union activity in Wales in the 1890s. In Britain as a whole, the years from 1889 to 1891 saw a vigorous push towards extending union membership to the much wider range of unskilled manual workers, and in few centres was this wave of New Unionism more marked than in south Wales. In a ferment of enthusiasm saddlers, tramway workers, riggers, blacksmiths, bakers and even laundry women were sucked into the movement, and national trade union leaders Ben Tillett and Tom Mann were frequent visitors. It is true that, as is the habit of waves, this one receded fairly rapidly with the general economic downturn of the early 1890s. But it left its mark partly because of the continuing, if attenuated, presence of general unions such as Tillett's Dockers' Union (the Dock, Wharf and Riverside and General Labourers' Union of Great Britain and Ireland, affectionately known in south Wales as the 'union with the long name'). It was equally important that the outburst of sometimes bizarre activity (attempts at strikes by schoolboys and housewives) around 1890 had been reported in enormous detail in the local press and with more sympathy than antagonism.[11] Perhaps the shift in both the level and the spread of activity can be illustrated most forcibly from its brief appearance amongst one of the most downtrodden, dispersed and difficult-to-organize groups. For a time in the 1890s the agricultural workers of Anglesey were brought together by the remarkable John Owen Jones ('ap Ffarmwr') to form a union.[12] Thus, in addition to favourable objective conditions in the form of a concentrated and aggrieved workforce, there was, from the 1890s, an air of opportunity and possibility for union organization which went beyond dependence on such factors.

Looming behind all this were the developments in coalmining. The general outline is familiar enough: a long and chequered history of unionism had by the 1890s ended in a series of structurally and geographically separate bodies loosely linked together for the occasional negotiations with the more coherent Coalowners' Association over the terms for the Sliding Scale. The humiliating defeat in the long 1898 stoppage precipitated a move to a much firmer federal structure, a stronger financial base and an application to join the MFGB, the 'English' union whose incursions into Wales had been so vehemently resisted for the previous decade. The mere scale of the SWMF was of enormous significance, not only for itself but as a beacon of unionism. From the first year of its effective operation in 1899 until the First World War the SWMF always mustered over 100,000 members. None the less, to read into these absolute numbers a relatively unproblematic establishment of trade unionism (with whatever political implications that entailed) would be mistaken. The 'Fed' consistently struggled (and with limited success) to maintain its membership. In 1899 the 104,212 members constituted 79 per cent of those employed in the industry, but by 1912 the 114,207 members represented only 51 per cent of those so employed.[13]

Even after the formation of the SWMF it took another decade before this was translated into a formal political commitment to affiliate to the Labour Party in 1908. South Wales had in fact voted for such affiliation in an earlier ballot in 1906 but it was not until 1908 that a majority across the MFGB was achieved.[14] This will be taken up and subjected to critical analysis in chapter 3: the immediate purpose is to make a simpler point. The experience of the miners can be taken as an illustration of a more general observation: the mere existence of predominantly working-class communities, like the mere existence of trade unions, might have been a necessary but was certainly not a sufficient condition to determine political organization. Right up until 1914 there were still only four constituencies which returned miners as their MPs. Moreover these were the same four as in 1906 though, of course, Mabon as the first Welsh miners' MP had served in this capacity since 1885. They were also the same four candidates who, in 1906, had stood as Lib-Labs and all four would have happily continued to do so had they not been 'precipitated in [sic] the Labour Party' by the MFGB's decision on affiliation.[15] Attention is clearly needed to the overall social context within which these features were evolving.

One such aspect was the emergence and growth of trades councils which brought together local trade union organizations, often specifically as electoral organizations.[16] In this respect and at this period they were the labour institutions most directly focused on party politics: it is thus significant that, whereas in 1894 there were just six trades councils in Wales representing 16,000 trade unionists, these figures had grown to thirty-six representing 126,000 in 1913, and seventy-one representing 261,000 in 1920 (their peak). Another feature of the general social context within which political allegiances and class consciousness were being forged during these years was the scale and extent of industrial conflict. In particular the symbolic reverberations of the six-month lock-out of the miners in the south in 1898, and of the three-year lock-out of the Penrhyn quarrymen between 1900 and 1903 in the north. Welsh involvement in the so-called 'Great Unrest' of 1911–14 ensured that this momentum was maintained right up to the First World War (and beyond, as the 1915 coal strike demonstrated).

Along the way, the previous Liberal consensus was significantly undermined, although not overthrown. There was increasing recognition, on both sides of the class divide, that the pressures of growing competition in the worldwide markets for coal, tinplate and steel were making earlier notions of identity of interest less tenable. These rifts were especially difficult to disguise in industries, like those which dominated Wales, in which labour accounted for a high proportion of costs: capital reacted not merely by attempting to cut wages, but by worsening working conditions and eroding customs (for example, by refusing to close a pit for the rest of the day if there was a fatal accident); labour reacted both by resisting and attempting to formalize previous conventions. On the labour side this could be epitomized by the shift from the widespread acceptance by south Wales miners in the 1890s of the Sliding Scale to regulate wage rates, to the production and publication of *The Miners' Next Step* in 1912 (without implying that most, or even large numbers, accepted the ideology of the latter). On the side of capital the shift could be summarized through the personal trajectory of D. A. Thomas (Lord Rhondda): in 1898 he did not join the coalowners' lock-out but frequently and publicly criticized the owners' obduracy; by 1910 he had fashioned the vast Cambrian Combine and presided over the long and bitter struggle which is still evoked by the word 'Tonypandy'.

The wide and varied social context within which policies were evolving in Wales during these decades is here given peremptory treatment. One justification is that the causal links between the social and the political are even more tenuous than those between the economic and the political. Another is that some aspects are given fuller, and more informed, treatment in other chapters. Even so, some brief comments can be ventured. Religion, for example, is an inescapable influence. But the extent and nature of its pertinence for the specific political developments of this period are less obvious. In relation to the emergence of a Labour Party there are some obvious negatives: the long-established alliance of Nonconformity and Liberalism, firmly held together – in Wales – by the cement of disestablishment; the generally unfriendly and often hostile attitudes of most clergymen; the well-perceived failure of Nonconformity to address the problems of industrialism; and the related effect of a theology rooted in individual salvation:[17] 'Nonconformists concerned themselves exclusively with the individual.

No adequate social philosophy or theology was developed apart
from the claim that social improvement was an implicit factor in
individual regeneration. Welsh Nonconformists had never had
specifically social *theology*.'[18] Against this were several positive
links, pervasive if intangible, between religion and the rise of
working-class politics in Wales at this time. A common theme
pressing the case for some, usually loosely defined, form of
socialism was to present it as a way of ushering in God's Kingdom
on earth. Keir Hardie particularly stressed that the primary
concern of Christians should be with social rather than individual
morality. A few Nonconformist ministers relayed a similar
message, one or two of these – like T. E. Nicholas ('Niclas y Glais')
– particularly addressing Welsh-speakers.[19] Most working-class
leaders at this time had themselves grown up within a tradition of
Sunday school teaching and biblical discussion. The political
language was soaked in allusions such as those to the Israelites in
captivity: they were the common coinage even of internal union
disputes, as when one dissatisfied miner during the long 1898
stoppage asserted that 'had Mabon been at the head of the children
of Israel in Egypt they would still be making bricks'.[20] Numbers
are not everything, especially in so elusive an area. But at a time
when the 1906 Royal Commission found that total church
membership amounted to an extraordinarily high level of one-
third of the total population (when a further third was below the
age of fifteen) it would be folly to discount a religious influence on
almost all aspects of life.

None the less, Labour activists found more favourable opportunities for rousing political awareness in more mundane and tangible
social issues. In this they were assisted by the general absence of a
social theology amongst Welsh Nonconformist clergy which left
most ministers acquiescent on such pressing contemporary issues
as housing. They could proclaim to sinners the Christian message
that in the hereafter 'in my Father's house are many mansions', but
social reformers forcibly pointed out that such luxuries were not
much in evidence in Merthyr or Ferndale, and were certainly not
available for general consumption. Moreover the housing problem
was – as it was generally in Britain before 1914 – seen largely as a
health problem. Thus the degree of overcrowding in the Rhondda,
where the number of persons per inhabited house was consistently
much higher than in such northern towns as Bradford and

Huddersfield, was the reality behind the Labour Party's campaigns in local elections in many coalfield areas in the early twentieth century. If these conditions were partly the result of the very rapid rise of population, they were also reflected in the much greater infant mortality figures: in Aberdare in 1910 infant mortality at 213 per 1,000 live births was almost twice the average of 122 for England and Wales, and Rhondda and Merthyr registered rates of 183 and 173 respectively.[21] At the very least these social problems provided convenient and prominent pegs from which to hang fresh ideological clothes. That they were not sufficient in themselves to precipitate political change is evidenced by the fact that deprivation – whether of housing, health or bleak poverty – was most acute in rural areas such as Cardiganshire, where Labour's electoral support was always limited.[22]

The messages of neglect and class subordination were also conveyed through the framework and operation of the legal system. A dramatic example such as the Taff Vale judgment, which made unions liable for losses to employers caused by industrial action, was of some significance, as was the far from accidental fact that it arose from the peculiar obduracy of employers in south Wales led by, in this case, Amon Beasley (general manager of the Taff Vale Railway company) and Sir W. T. Lewis (later Lord Merthyr). More pertinent, however, was the general atmosphere, the persistent drip, drip, drip of employers using the courts to enforce industrial action. In the whole of Britain by the beginning of the twentieth century only one major group of employers, the south Wales coalowners, continued to make direct, deliberate and persistent use of the courts to bring actions against their workmen for breach of contract.[23] These employers also frequently challenged in the courts claims for injuries made by workmen under the Workmens' Compensation Acts, and used legal means to curtail many traditional working practices. Besides the class antagonisms which these actions nourished, they also directly encouraged union membership since it became increasingly clear that individual workers needed the support of union representation in the courts.

There were other structural features such as the odd imbalance in the broad demographic structure of Wales around the turn of the century: young and lively in industrial Wales, ageing in the rural heartland; a remarkable excess of males in Glamorgan and Monmouthshire but with most counties having a more normal excess of females, especially marked in Cardiganshire. Multiplying the examples, however, does not in itself answer the more interesting issue of the influence of religion, social policy, the law, population or whatever on the emergence of the Labour Party in Wales.

Even in a chapter where the main object is to provide background it is impossible to avoid all engagement with the question of whether – and how, and how far – the structural conditions outlined above (economic and industrial as well as social) contributed to the rise of the Labour Party. If the overall outcome seems to suggest that the influence of structural factors was powerful but not compelling, necessary but not fully sufficient, it is still of some significance that the varying intensity with which these structural forces operated in Wales is clearly linked to the scale and pace of the emergence of the Labour Party. Structural conditions were least favourable in mid Wales since Welsh agriculture was small-scale and with a composition of employment dominated by tenant farmers rather than agricultural labourers – but even here some union activity emerged and, just before 1920, this was being more directly linked to the Labour Party.[24] In north Wales coalminers and quarrymen gave a greater structural stiffening but the former were neither numerous enough nor sufficiently spread and the latter were by 1900 a fast-fading force. It was in the context of south Wales that the presumed favourable structural influences were most marked and it was here that a political party based on manual workers, fostered in industrial conflict and appealing to a class consciousness, found its strongest earliest expression in Wales.

None the less, it is necessary to remind ourselves about how elusive explanations are in social sciences and to note that concentrating on the background structural factors has necessarily ignored other possible influences. As Harold Macmillan observed when asked what most bothered him in politics: 'Events, dear boy. Events.' On that basis what shaped the political flavour of Wales around the beginning of the twentieth century were such 'happenings' as: the 1885 election of Mabon; the 1898 stoppage; the 1901 Taff Vale judgment; Tonypandy 1910; Llanelli 1911; the 1915 coal stoppage. Even in hindsight it is not obvious that each of these sprang naturally from the structural context. These difficult issues of causation and explanation will be explored in later chapters, but it is always prudent to keep in mind a dictum of John Maynard

Keynes that 'In social events, the inevitable never happens. It is the unexpected always.'

Notes

[1] R. Church, *The History of the British Coal Industry, III, 1830–1913 – Victorian Pre-eminence* (Oxford, 1986), 66.

[2] J. Davies, *A History of Wales* (London, 1993), 363.

[3] R. Gregory, *The Miners and British Politics, 1906–1914* (Oxford, 1968), 138.

[4] J. Williams, *Digest of Welsh Historical Statistics*, I (Cardiff, 1985), 103–32. Unless otherwise stated the statistics used are taken or calculated from the *Digest*.

[5] H. Pelling, *Social Geography of British Elections, 1885–1910* (London, 1967), ch. 15.

[6] A. V. John, ' "Run like blazes": the Suffragettes and Welshness', *Llafur*, VI, 3 (1994), and K. Cook and N. Evans, ' "The petty antics of the bell-ringing boisterous band"? The Women's Suffragette movement in Wales, 1890–1918', in A. V. John (ed.), *Our Mothers' Land: Chapters in Welsh Women's History, 1830–1939* (Cardiff, 1991).

[7] W. Minchinton, *The British Tinplate Industry* (Oxford, 1957), 112–38; A. Pugh (One of Them), *Men of Steel* (London, 1951).

[8] L. J. Williams, 'The New Unionism in south Wales, 1889–92', *Welsh History Review* (*WHR*), I/4 (1963), 418–19; P. S. Bagwell, *The Railwaymen* (London, 1963).

[9] R. M. Jones, *The North Wales Quarrymen, 1874–1922* (Cardiff, 1981), ch. 5.

[10] *South Wales Daily News*, 25 Aug., 2 Sept. 1887.

[11] L. J. Williams, 'New Unionism', 413–29.

[12] D. A. Pretty, *The Rural Revolt that Failed: Farm Workers' Trade Unions in Wales, 1889–1950* (Cardiff, 1989), ch. 2.

[13] HMSO, *Abstracts of Labour Statistics* (London, 1899–1912); and R. Page Arnot, *The Miners*, I (London, 1949), 334–5. Some of those employed (such as craftsmen) might have been members of other unions.

[14] Gregory, *Miners*, 28–33.

[15] Ibid., 138–43; and Pelling, *Social Geography*, 362.

[16] C. Williams, *Democratic Rhondda: Politics and Society, 1885–1951* (Cardiff, 1996), 77–8.

[17] R. Pope, *Building Jerusalem: Nonconformity, Labour and the Social Question in Wales, 1906–1939* (Cardiff, 1998), 58–70, 226–7 and ch. 4 generally.

[18] Ibid., 240.

[19] Ibid., ch. 2.

[20] J. Harvey, 'Work and worship: mining and religion in the paintings of Nicholas Evans', *Llafur*, VI/1 (1992), 62–4.

[21] E. D. Lewis, *The Rhondda Valleys* (London, 1959), 202, 214.

[22] Pretty, *Rural Revolt*, ch. 1.

[23] J. Williams, 'Miners and the law of contract, 1875–1914', *Llafur*, IV/2 (1985).

[24] D. Howell, 'Labour organisation among agricultural workers in Wales, 1872–1921', *WHR*, XVI/1 (1992).

2

Labour's Roots in Wales, 1880–1900

DEIAN HOPKIN

When the twentieth century arrived, the nineteenth century was still very much alive. Symbolically, Queen Victoria was still on the throne and the Prime Minister, Lord Salisbury, would not have been out of place in an earlier era. The political leaders of the day were shaped in the political worlds of Gladstone and Disraeli. In 1900 William Abraham (Mabon), the first MP in Wales to stand explicitly in the Labour interest, albeit taking the Liberal whip, was fifty-eight years old, born at a time when Chartism was in full swing and indeed before either Gladstone or Disraeli had reached prominence. William Brace, who would become another prominent Lib-Lab MP in 1906, and Keir Hardie, the first official Labour MP, were both forty-four. On the other hand, Noah Ablett, often seen as the most radical spokesman for the labour movement immediately before the First World War, was just seventeen, while Aneurin Bevan was a three-year-old child. The men and women who made the crucial breakthrough for Labour in the elections of 1918 and the subsequent decade were either very young in 1900, or had not yet been born. Yet their political roots and the terms of the political debates in which they were themselves to be engaged, lay in the decades before 1900.

Finding a starting-point for the rise of Labour in Wales, as in Britain as a whole, however, is a somewhat arbitrary business. Do we begin with the striking puddlers of Cyfarthfa in 1812 who ran mortal risk by swearing the Luddite oath, or the spontaneous protesters of 1816? Are the Scotch Cattle the first manifestations of working-class consciousness, or were they the culmination of an even longer process extending back to the grievances of iron-workers in the late eighteenth century? If public expressions of radical dissent and concrete proposals for change are the key indicators then we should perhaps start with John Frost, Hugh Williams and the Chartists. On the other hand, if we are looking for a moment when the electoral prospects for representatives of the working class began to be realized, then is not 1868 the most feasible starting-point?

In truth, there are many starting-points in history, but there are also as many false dawns. Many of these earlier moments of awareness, however, do not form part of a continuum of develop-ment which leads, seamlessly, to the foundation of the modern Labour Party; they are historical cul-de-sacs. Then there is the question of geography. If Labour began to develop in Wales, it was by no means everywhere. Indeed, in purely geographic terms, Labour was confined for many years to a limited part of Wales, largely the industrial belt of south Wales and to a lesser degree the smaller industrial areas of the north-east and north-west. At all political levels, parliamentary and local, Labour advanced only in certain communities.

The idea of independent labour representation was, none the less, current long before the formal reality. In the 1880s, Gladstone had referred to the 'Labour Party' not in reference to the newly arrived socialist groups, the Social Democratic Federation or the Socialist League, but as a generic concept which acknowledged the distinct contribution of the Lib-Lab wing of his own party. 'Labour' in this sense was a slogan rather than a political philosophy. This idea of labour took root more widely in the 1890s, even though it was not always clear what this new 'party' consisted of. The *South Wales Daily News*, for example, heralded the arrival of what it called 'the new . . . Labour Party' in 1892: 'It is already formed . . . and it is a party which cannot be overpowered or ignored . . . The Labour Party is with us, not yet organised, but the great work of organisation yet to be achieved.'[1] This was the description of a mood and aspiration, rather than of any formal political party. In this sense, the spirit of the Labour Party preceded its formal creation.

In the late nineteenth century, Wales was a rapidly changing society, its urban and industrial population growing at an unpre-cedented rate and with new towns and cities emerging as powerful agents of political change. As the population grew, so the quality of life was changing. Literacy was improving, educational standards rising, incomes generally growing, and patterns of leisure and consumer consumption undergoing secular change. The modern newspaper was emerging at this time, electricity and gas were widely distributed in urban areas, and networks of road and rail were extending. All of these had an influence on the dissemination of political ideas. Wales was becoming ever more accessible from London, for example, so that political meetings addressed by London socialists and radicals became commonplace. Their newspapers could be read in the remotest parts of Wales. Batches of the Independent Labour Party (ILP)'s *Labour Leader* were received in Aberystwyth in the 1890s while the *Fabian News* was read in Llandysul and the *Clarion* in Caernarfon. Socialists visited coastal north Wales with greater ease than their radical predecessors, John Ruskin or William Morris and, easier still, they could now organize regular missions to most parts of south Wales.[2]

And yet politics was changing at a slow pace, largely because the electorate did not always grow quite as rapidly as did the population as a whole. After the reform of the franchise in 1885 extended the vote to male lodgers and as legal and registration processes altered, there was significant relative growth in the electorates of industrial Wales. Between 1885 and 1910 the electorate of Rhondda, for example, grew at ten times the rate for Anglesey, while the electorate of East Glamorgan, the fastest growing of all, was growing at almost 6 per cent per annum and Cardiganshire's electorate was, to all intents and purposes, static. Yet not every industrial constituency was growing at the same rate and, indeed, a notable feature of this period is the displacement of Merthyr Boroughs as the largest south Wales constituency by Cardiff and Rhondda. Merthyr was, it is true, the exception to the rule, having declined in size by almost 15 per cent between 1885 and 1900. Between 1900 and 1910, the rate of growth tended to increase everywhere, with even some rural communities such as Radnorshire or Caernarfon seeing a noticeable rise. Yet, even the most rapidly expanding electorates still left voters in the clear minority of the population. The population of Merthyr Tydfil and Aberdare in 1900 was 110,000, the electorate just 15,000. Such growth as there was, moreover, did not produce a visible change in

Table 2.1. Growth in the Welsh electorate, 1885–1910: selected constituencies

	1885	1900	1885–1900		1910	1900–10	
			% change	annual rate		% change	annual rate
Anglesey	9,777	10,000	2.2	0.15	10,300	3.0	0.30
Caernarfon	22,590	23,500	4.0	0.26	25,200	7.2	0.70
Cardiganshire	12,308	13,299	8.0	0.50	13,405	0.8	0.08
Radnorshire	4,539	5,219	15.0	1.00	5,971	14.0	1.40
Pembrokeshire	10,883	11,100	1.9	0.10	11,750	5.8	0.50
Carmarthen East	8,669	9,967	15.0	1.00	12,268	23.0	2.30
Rhondda	8,210	12,549	53.0	3.50	17,640	40.0	4.00
Merthyr Boroughs	20,000	17,024	−15.0	−1.00	23,219	36.0	3.60
Swansea Town	7,597	9,097	19.7	1.30	12,935	42.0	4.20
Cardiff	12,605	22,361	77.0	5.10	28,273	26.4	2.60
Glamorgan East	8,544	15,315	79.0	5.30	23,979	56.6	5.60
Gower	10,500	12,267	17.0	1.10	14,712	19.0	1.90

Source: J. Williams, *Digest of Welsh Historical Statistics*, II (Cardiff, 1985), 130–2.

the political landscape of Wales. The electoral boundaries of Wales did not change to reflect a shifting population.[3] As a result, few constituencies were dominated by the emergent industrial working class.

It is not surprising, therefore, that from the late 1860s to the end of the First World War, the supremacy of the Liberal Party in Wales was largely unchallenged. The electoral system may have disadvantaged radical parties but it did not inhibit Liberal success. Even in the worst election year, 1886, the party still took twenty-five out of thirty-four Welsh parliamentary seats and in 1906 the party won all but one of the Welsh constituencies, a result which no political party has since rivalled. Over that half-century, the Liberals did evolve in Wales, the place of Liberal Wales within the imperial system was widely discussed, and a new emphasis on regional and national self-determination began to surface, most notably in the Cymru Fydd movement. Even a 'New Liberalism' was beginning to emerge, with a greater emphasis on collective responsibility and greater public enterprise. This evolution was reflected, in a very real sense, through the development of the Lib-Lab section within the party. While not a discrete political movement, the Lib-Labs none the less challenged some of the older political arrangements.

Much of the Liberal Party's strength derived from its association with the Nonconformist chapels and its role as their defender against Anglicanism. Most Nonconformist congregations were dominated by men who were natural allies of the Liberal Party, a party which served the purposes of the whole community. As Merfyn Jones has pointed out, many communities in north Wales grew around the chapel which became more than a place of worship: 'it was also an organizer and an identity, the focus and the expression of the organizers of the community's values.'[4] These values, which traditionally had included the demand for the franchise, the defence of the tenant, and the disestablishment of the Anglican Church, were embodied in the Liberal Party's political programmes. As a result Nonconformist ministers were generally little interested in the idea of independent labour representation.

On the other hand there appears to have been little outright hostility to the labour movement. Trade unionists, in south Wales as much as in north Wales, used chapel premises for their meetings; John Hodge once contrasted the drunken and violent behaviour of Glasgow workers with the several hundred well-behaved and respectable men who came to hear him in a chapel schoolroom in south Wales 'with not a drunk among them'. That particular meeting began and closed symbolically with a hymn.[5] Churches often supported strikes; for example, the Llechwedd strike of 1893 was sustained by chapel collections, while the strikes in Nantlle in 1906 were organized by the chapels rather than the union lodge.[7] Yet this was not a comfortable situation for Nonconformists in general. The election of Mabon in 1885 created some discord among the Rhondda's Baptists and in some cases a ban was placed on the use of chapels for political purposes. By 1889 a lively debate had broken out in the pages of *Seren Cymru*, the Baptist newspaper, over the appropriateness of ministers playing any part in politics. On the other hand, a number of prominent Baptists began to criticize the absence of working men on local and county councils.[7] Yet, on the whole, the loyalty of the Nonconformist establishment to the Liberal Party remained solid until well after 1900.

To a large extent, the alignment of Liberalism and Nonconformity within working-class communities depended on industrial harmony and economic prosperity. With the advent of depression in the tinplate industry and the beginnings of significant industrial unrest from 1889 onwards, new strains began to show. An interest in labour representation began to grow within a number of congregations and communities which the Liberals were slow to recognize. The party remained preoccupied with the traditional issues of land reform and disestablishment, and took for granted the loyalty of organized labour. Always a federation of radical interests, the Liberals were not inclined to focus on a range of issues which were beginning to preoccupy many urban workers. Indeed, the mainstream of Welsh Liberalism was resistant to the idea of labour representation and reluctant to adopt working-class men as Liberal candidates, as indeed were their English counterparts.[8] Even 'New Liberalism' seems to have been ineffective in staunching the loss to the Liberal Party of a new generation of well-educated, politically sophisticated young men and women.

On the other hand, it would be quite wrong to regard the Liberal Party in Wales as enduring a slow death. It is true that the party experienced internal problems and challenges. As yet, there was no external challenge. In 1900, the Liberals were still, for the vast majority of Welsh electors, the party which best defended their interest against aristocratic, Anglican landowners and English coalowners and industrialists. The party, after all, had the most exciting and compelling political spokesman for Wales in David Lloyd George, who was supported by able colleagues such as Tom Ellis.

The labour movement, then, was not a serious challenger to the Liberal Party in Wales before 1900. In this respect, Wales was typical of most of the United Kingdom. Bradford, hailed as the birthplace of independent labour, was a significant exception. Generally, the Liberals were not only unchallenged, but held to be the main advocate of working-class interests. Trade union leaders, by and large, stood by the party. This is as true of the north-east of England as it is of the industrial midlands or, indeed, of Wales. Studies of areas as diverse as South Shields or Wolverhampton, Liverpool or Nottingham have shown that the Liberal ascendancy held firm in most parts of the country long after 1900, while in most parts of West Yorkshire the Liberals held onto slim but convincing electoral leads until the First World War.[9]

And yet the conditions for change were forming very rapidly and did not always remain beneath the surface. There were some important landmarks in the late 1880s and 1890s in the history of the labour movement. In the past trade unionism had enjoyed mixed fortunes in Wales. The best organized industries were the coal and railway industries, while the engineers were reasonably well-organized in the coastal towns of south Wales.[10] Such areas produced committed labour leaders. Some of the best-known national leaders of the Amalgamated Society of Railway Servants (ASRS), formed in 1872, came from Wales, among them Richard Bell, Edward Harford and, later, J. H. Thomas. These were politically stable unions, at this time linked closely to the Liberal Party and Lib-Labs.

In the late 1880s, moreover, there were a few straws in the wind. At the Trades Union Congress held at Swansea in 1887, Keir Hardie made his first major foray into national politics with a vigorous denunciation of the veteran leader of the Northumberland miners, Henry Broadhurst MP, for his support for the chemical manufacturer, Sir John Brunner, in the Northwich by-election. By implication, this was seen as an attack on the whole strategy of accommodation practised by the Parliamentary Committee of the TUC. On this occasion, the highly experienced and respected Lib-Lab leaders of the Congress comfortably defended themselves against such attack.[11]

Shortly after, the skilled unions were more seriously challenged by the arrival of 'New Unionism', and this heralded the beginning of a period of more difficult industrial relations culminating in the 'Great Unrest' of 1911–14. These 'New Unions' which made such a huge impact in England after the Great Dock Strike of 1889 had actually made their appearance in Newport and Swansea six months earlier.[12] At the time the significance of this wider unionism was not fully understood, partly because the best organized trade unions, such as the coalminers, were relatively unaffected at the outset; their Lib-Lab leaders did not face any significant challenge to their own authority for another twenty years or so. On the other hand, even the miners were beginning to evolve organizationally; during the 1890s, different local miners' unions began to seek greater co-operation with their counterparts elsewhere and by 1900 they were in the throes of creating a new and effective federation. Elsewhere in Welsh trade unions, there were moves to create new associations and federations, as in the tinplate industry. Yet the horizons of Welsh trade unions, like their English counterparts, were strictly limited. Their immediate concerns of wages and conditions were far more pressing than longer-term political change. Many if not most of their members were in any case outside the parliamentary franchise and, frankly, saw little prospects of being included. Recognizing this hiatus, Lib-Lab MPs claimed to speak for the widest community, voting or not, and this was accepted by the leaders of the most powerful trade unions in Wales. At the same time, there was sufficient radical energy in the Welsh Liberal MPs to head off any major diversion down the road to independent labour representation.

But there is something else. Many of the Welsh industrial communities were relatively new, their populations swelled by the arrival of young, single men looking for work in the mine or the metalworks. By contrast, the textile communities of Lancashire and West Yorkshire, where the early labour movement grew up, were longer established, with a more robust framework of workingmen's clubs and mechanics' institutes. This may explain, in part, the relative tardiness of organized socialism in Wales before 1900.

John Williams has noted the development of the trades councils which, in time, became key elements in the matrix of power which sustained the Labour Party through industrial Wales. Yet the direct link between the trades councils and the *formation* of the Labour Party is not easy to establish. For one thing, the trades councils did not really come into their own until well into the first decade of the twentieth century. Even so, those that were established continued to maintain far stronger relationships with the mainstream Lib-Lab MPs and local government officials than with the Labour Representation Committee (LRC).

The first trades council in Wales was established in Swansea in 1873, with 4,000 members and twenty-six affiliated societies. Its most influential member was the General Union of Carpenters and Joiners and from the outset it was reluctant to become involved in politics, and only then with the Liberals.[13] Newport tried to follow seven years later, though this first attempt failed and it was not until 1889 that Newport Trades Council really came into being. By this time, however, the Cardiff Trades Council had been formed (in 1884) and was soon substantially larger than any other trades council in Wales. In the early 1890s, smaller trades councils were formed in Barry, Pontypridd, Neath and Briton Ferry, and smaller still in Merthyr, but it is significant that even at the end of the century there were no separate trades councils for the mining valleys of Glamorgan and Monmouth, and none at all in north Wales.[14]

By 1897 there were still only six registered trades councils in Wales with 16,705 members, less than 3 per cent of the total for the UK (169 with over 700,000 members).[15] And those trades councils which had been formed were kept at arm's length from the new Labour Party. By 1906, only two (Cardiff and Merthyr) had affiliated to the LRC; by 1909 this had risen to seven, perhaps symbolizing the changing mood within the trades councils.[16] At the turn of the century, however, this was some distance away.

Historians are nowadays more inclined than hitherto to take seriously the role and significance of the Lib-Labs and the radical wing of the Liberal Party in preparing the ground for the eventual emergence of a distinct Labour Party. It is still true that on the debit side the failure of Liberals generally to widen the basis of their representation created a degree of disillusionment in some sectors; the Lib-Labs themselves were a product of that disillusionment, with Lib-Lab MPs more often than not elected in the teeth of traditional Liberal Party opposition. In 1885, for example, a bitter conflict broke out between the emerging Rhondda Steam Coal Miners' Association and the local Liberal caucus, the Rhondda Three Hundred, over the selection of the Liberal candidate for the Rhondda.[17] The Liberal establishment first rejected the preferred candidate of the miners, William Abraham, in favour of the coalowner Lewis Davis and then compounded the suspicion that this was a class-based decision by accepting Lewis Davis's twenty-two-year-old barrister son, Frederick Lewis Davis, as an alternative candidate when the coalowner himself decided not to stand. The outcome was the first major breach between trade unionism and the Liberal establishment, resulting in the decisive victory of William Abraham, standing as a 'Labour' candidate. Ironically, this also led to the collapse of the Liberals' own local organization and its absorption into a new Rhondda Labour and Liberal Association. It is difficult to tell, however, how many potentially valuable candidates may well have been lost to the Liberal Party because of similar, but less publicized, behaviour of some local caucuses.

Yet this does not lead inexorably to the conclusion that the Liberal Party's demise was obvious in the 1890s. The very existence of the Lib-Labs and their capacity to gain control of coalfield seats, demonstrates the continued importance of the Liberal Party as the main point of reference for working-class politics in late Victorian Britain.

Paradoxically that very dominance was a stimulus to the evolution of independent labour representation. Some sections of the Liberal Party outside the Lib-Lab group were highly sympathetic to the claims of labour but beyond the coalfields were unable to force local associations to select labour leaders as Liberal candidates. The co-operation between some Liberals, even MPs, and the burgeoning labour movement went far beyond anything in which Mabon or his colleagues might have engaged. David Randell, the Liberal MP for the Gower constituency, for example, was prepared to try his hand at anything. In 1887 he helped the young Richard Bell to organize a branch of the ASRS in Swansea in 1887 and a little later he helped others to form the Tinplate Workers' Union in the area.[18] Generally, when the crunch came, he did his duty; during the 1892 election, he joined Mabon and others in fully supporting Dillwyn, the veteran MP for Swansea Town. Perhaps Randell was a confused young Liberal, a harbinger of things to come. He continued to flirt with the labour movement and increasingly with its more exotic wings. Not long after the 1892 election, he was found chairing a number of meetings organized by the Marxist Social Democratic Federation (SDF) during one of which he is reported to have declared himself 'tending more and more in the direction of socialism'. He joined Keir Hardie in protest meetings during the tinplate lock-out in Llanelli in 1894. Years later, long after he left Parliament, he presided over a major Labour rally in Swansea.[19] Other Liberals moved more slowly but, over time, there was a gradual shift of sentiment, even in north Wales with the disaffiliation of W. J. Parry, Brigadier Sir Owen Thomas and, of course, E. T. John.[20] In general, however, main-stream Liberals and Lib-Labs were disinclined to take any of these new developments seriously.

It was into this unpromising landscape that the socialist mission-aries began to make forays in the last quarter of the nineteenth century. The ground had been prepared to some extent by radical thinkers in Wales such as R. J. Derfel, whose eclectic mixture of co-operation, romantic nationalism and ecumenical socialism harked back, in no small way, to Baptist dissenters such as William Richards and Morgan John Rhys.[21] From the 1860s onwards, there were interesting discussions in the literary and religious press over the need for change. The debates over Darwinism and secularism formed a context for more wide-ranging explorations of individualism, collectivism and communitarianism. In the 1880s the tempo began to accelerate. Henry George's famous book, *Progress and Poverty*, often regarded as a seminal intellectual influence on the radical movement, was published in England in 1879. The arrival of Eastern European immigrants at around the same time produced a flurry of socialist activity in London. The Democratic Federation, the first recognizable socialist party in Britain, was formed in 1881, and evolved into the Social Democratic Federation (SDF), Britain's first Marxist party, by 1884. In that same year, the Fabian Society, the ethical fellowship committed to a gradualist and evolutionary path to socialism, was formed.

However, the problem was that there were several competing versions on offer, of varying degrees of comprehensibility. Socialist journals often had to run whole series of articles seeking to explain what all this socialism meant, and the remarkable success of Robert Blatchford's *Merrie England* can be compared to the equivalent success of books in the late twentieth century on computing or strategic management, explaining the mysterious language of those disciplines to a hungry lay readership.

Almost as soon as the SDF was formed in 1881 its London-based members began to see Wales as an important challenge. It may appear to some contemporary observers that south Wales, despite its rapid industrial development, remained 'terra incognita' to most Englishmen in the 1880s, but it was none the less enticing. Individual socialists had often visited north or mid Wales in the past, usually on vacation, but from the mid-1880s they began to turn their attention more systematically to the south. They were a strange, rather privileged lot. William Morris, one of the most prominent advocates of socialism at this time, did not exactly earn the average industrial wage, more like the wage of a nineteenth-century equivalent of a modern City futures trader. Indeed the founder of the SDF, H. M. Hyndman, often drew critical attention because of his early income from West Indies plantations. Others too came from the upper echelons of the middle class, a long distance away from the working class they sought to influence: J. L. Joynes, H. H. Champion, Eleanor Marx, to name but a few.

It is not surprising, then, to find that the early audiences in Wales for the socialist message were university students, professors of economics, teachers, doctors, even some clergymen.[22] Many of these names have long disappeared, largely because there were no parliamentary victories to immortalize them. It was such people who introduced the Fabian Society to Wales, making its first appearance in Wales in the mid-1880s, ahead of any other socialist group. In 1886 a branch was formed at the University College of Wales at Aberystwyth, through which Thomas Jones, among others, passed.[23] Soon, other branches were formed, notably in Cardiff, where the Fabians became quite visible in local politics. It is difficult to judge the impact of the Fabians in terms of numbers. There was a significant ebb and flow in the membership of the society, reflecting its strength in the university colleges of Wales and among professional, mobile occupations. While membership lists are not a reliable indication of the real strength of political parties or groups, still the Welsh Fabians remained numerically a tiny group. Twenty years after its first appearance in Wales, the total registered Welsh membership was just twenty-three, including several whose addresses were outside the Principality.[24] They may have made little impact on the electorate but their influence, in the longer term, far outweighed their numbers, largely because of their social position and their determination. They played a key part in preparing the intellectual ground and proved to be an incomparable training ground for a future generation of civil servants, politicians, academics and others who occupied positions where they could influence affairs. In the early 1890s, for example, the Cardiff Fabians ran full programmes of lectures each winter, addressed by distinguished men and women such as Sidney Webb, Herbert Bland, W. S. de Mattos, Hugh Holmes Gore and Katherine Conway, and these were regularly reported in the local press. It was through his activities in the Fabian Society in London, moreover, that Ramsay MacDonald began to visit and speak in Wales, his earliest recorded meeting there being organized by the Cardiff Fabians at the May Day Rally of 1892.[25]

Another vital task for the Fabians was to penetrate parts of Wales which other socialist groups or even trade unions conspicuously failed to reach, including rural Llandysul (or Orllwyn Vale as the Fabians called it) which at one time in 1892 claimed an astonishing twenty-six members.[26] The Llandudno group, which met in a cellar, were said to have been chiefly responsible for keeping the socialist spark alive in the area for two decades.[27] In any case, the kind of people attracted by the Fabians over the years were unconcerned by their minority status; in 1911, writing to David Thomas, the socialist organizer and theorist, a local journalist in Colwyn Bay, Edward Downs, described himself as one of just three socialists in the area, a fact which clearly did not deter him from continuing to organize meetings and seek to influence his editor to publishing stories favourable to socialism.[28]

Wales was important to the Fabians for other reasons. From 1908 onwards the Fabians held their national summer school in Llanbedr, near Harlech, and brought there some of the most eminent radical thinkers of the day, including R. H. Tawney, R. C. K. Ensor, Sydney Herbert, Mary MacArthur, Graham Wallas, Sidney and Beatrice Webb, Granville Barker and the theorist of imperialism, J. A. Hobson.[29]

The Fabians were an important bridgehead rather than a conventional political party. The emphasis, moreover, on discussion and debate encouraged into the society's ranks a number of individuals, including a number of ministers and academics, whose names do not appear anywhere else in the socialist movement: Professor H. J. Fleure, the eminent Aberystwyth geographer, the Revd Richard Parry of Llangollen, or, indeed, Clement Edwards, who was a member in 1896 and later became a Liberal MP for Denbigh and a vigorous opponent of Labour.

The Fabians, of course, were not seeking to win elections or to organize a political party. The SDF, by contrast, did wish to do so, and found Wales to be exasperating territory. The SDF was rather late making its first appearance in Wales. It was five years after its formation, in 1886, that the party's leader, H. M. Hyndman, finally visited Wales, and only then to the Dinorwic district of Caernarfonshire, where he expressed the view that: 'We shall be able to organise social-democracy throughout the District. The ideas are already spreading.'[30] Hyndman's expectations were illfounded. No branch of the SDF was ever recorded in Dinorwic, Caernarfonshire, or for that part anywhere else in north Wales, and there is no solid evidence of any individual members ever being recruited in the area.

Indeed, in the mid-1880s, it was the Socialist League, the splinter group which William Morris had stripped away from the SDF, which appeared to be in the vanguard. In the summer of 1887, a member of the League on holiday in Barmouth sought out the local

Welsh-speaking quarrymen. Neither could speak the other's language, but this did not dampen Haydn Saunders's enthusiasm for the prospects for advanced socialism in the area.[31] At about the same time, a hundred miles to the south, a London-based engineer was conducting the first recorded socialist tour of industrial south Wales. Sam Mainwaring, born forty-five years earlier in Neath, was already a veteran of the struggles for free speech in London and would presently become one of the actors in the political campaigns leading to the matchgirls' strike. Accompanied by Frank Kitz, a young dyer at William Morris's Merton Abbey Works, Mainwaring sought to spread the Socialist League's message among the miners, ironworkers and brickmakers of Pontypridd, Dowlais, Tylorstown and Aberdare. Promises were given to establish branches and the two returned to London satisfied that they had made a great breakthrough.[32] It was not to be, of course, and the Socialist League soon melted away.

Despite a hesitant start, the SDF eventually returned to Wales. In 1892 a speaking tour was organized for H. W. Hobart, a London party officer, to the anthracite districts of west Wales where he addressed meetings in towns such as Llanelli, Pontarddulais, Kidwelly, Ammanford and Gorseinon. It was a bizarre affair. The local contact turned out to be David Randell, the maverick Lib-Lab MP, while the metropolitan missionaries found local practices difficult to cope with: the vigorous observance of the Welsh Sunday in Llanelli, for example, did not quite accommodate the normal weekend activities of London socialists.[33] None the less, in the following year, a further tour took in the Swansea and Neath districts.[34] On each occasion there were encouraging numbers of recruits and by 1896 active branches were being claimed in Cardiff, Pontypridd, Treharris and Aberdare. Above all, in Barry a highly active membership maintained substantial premises and owned and ran a successful and long-established newspaper and publishing business, the *Barry Herald*.[35]

Yet, as elsewhere in Britain, the SDF failed to make the expected long-term breakthrough. At no time did the party manage to maintain more than half-a-dozen branches and its members were never elected to any council or board. The branches that were formed were relatively short-lived, collapsing more often than not through internal wrangling and argument, the stock-in-trade of so many left-wing groups.

As the industrial climate began to change, the conditions improved for an increase in working-class representation. It was the Independent Labour Party (ILP), not the SDF, which gradually made the greater headway in Wales. Yet the history of the ILP in Wales began inauspiciously enough with the often-quoted episode of the only Welsh representative proposing to attend the inaugural conference in Bradford in 1892 sadly missing his train at Cardiff station. It is doubtful, of course, if Sam Hobson's presence at that conference in itself would have accelerated the progress of the ILP in Wales. Unlike Yorkshire, the North-West or even London, there were no Labour Unions or Labour Churches to form an initial infrastructure and the Labour Electoral Association had made no recorded appearance in Wales after its inauguration at the Swansea TUC in 1888. In its early years, as David Howell has suggested, the ILP occupied mere islands in Wales.[36]

The ILP could not count on a large audience in Wales when it came into existence in February 1893. When Joseph Burgess, editor of the widely read Yorkshire paper, the *Workman's Times*, invited his readers to submit their names and addresses so that he might build up a national network of contacts for a new party, barely three responded from Wales and even some months later, when many hundreds had declared their support for Burgess's initiative, there were just twelve Welsh names, all of them in Cardiff or Newport.[37] This may not tell the whole story, of course, since it is hardly likely that the *Workman's Times* reached many parts of rural Wales. Even so, support from Wales was thin; in comparison with eleven from a rapidly growing city such as Cardiff, there were over fifty from Hull, a smaller town, and even fourteen in Carlisle. The Welsh signatories, moreover, included familiar names from the ranks of the Fabian Society. This was typical of the Labour movement's early period. The average activist might well subscribe to a variety of socialist projects. A fine example in this period is Edward Robinson, one of the few who did sign Burgess's petition. A customs officer by profession, Robinson was the backbone of several socialist and radical groups over two decades of activity. He was an early member of Cardiff Fabians, and was elected secretary of Cardiff ILP when it was formed. In 1896, he became the first secretary of the South Wales and West of England ILP Federation. His job, however, required him to move around the country. Some time in the early 1900s he was transferred to west Wales, and in

1906 he reappeared as the founding secretary of the Pembrokeshire ILP.[38]

Despite the obstacles it faced, in early 1894 the ILP was enthusiastic about the prospects for Wales. In March Keir Hardie visited south Wales and proclaimed the arrival of the ILP. A conference was subsequently held, and a constitution drawn up. Hardie asserted that 'The people are very advanced not only politically but socially'.[39] A Welsh National Administrative Committee (NAC) was formed with the colourful Sam Hobson as chairman, and with representatives from Swansea, Neath, Cwmavon, Morriston and Cardiff. By the early summer it was reported that branches were being formed in a dozen south Wales towns and in July 1894 the London officers of the ILP submitted some glowing reports:

> South Wales has made progress. Hitherto they have not been part of the national organisation. But as a result of careful deliberations consequent upon a special series of meetings, they have decided to become part of the main body, and be subject to the common discipline. There is enormous scope for development in Wales, and a rich reward in the form of successful contests ought soon to be theirs.[40]

In common with practice elsewhere in the country, an ILP Federation was soon established for south Wales, and several thousand copies of the new ILP constitution were printed.[41] Keir Hardie himself was very active in the area, speaking at meetings and writing about Wales in the *Labour Leader*. Then, over the autumn and winter, the enthusiasm gradually waned. In 1895, in the first general election fought by ILP candidates, there were no financial contributions from Welsh branches and, with the exception of two highly unsuccessful independent labour candidates in Merthyr Boroughs and Swansea District, no official ILP candidates either.[42]

For the remainder of the decade, Wales became less of an ILP island than a socialist desert, continually visited by 'missions' to try to recapture this lost land, especially south-east Wales; in 1897, it was even admitted that the only progress being made was by 'forcing new branches in some villages', given that 'the elements [were] dead against them'.[43] A titanic struggle was taking place within the ILP over its future, with a number of experienced campaigners arguing for a merger with the SDF and a reinauguration of the party as a more explicit 'Socialist Party'. There is no doubt that this struggle sapped the energies of local activists and all over the country membership began to dwindle. In order to combat this, the NAC began to focus on particular areas which might be reinvigorated. One of these was Wales. In 1898, an experienced campaigner from the north of England, Willie Wright, was appointed to visit south Wales for six weeks to try to revitalize the local organization. His task was made unexpectedly easier by the sudden outbreak of industrial trouble.[44] In April 1898, 100,000 Welsh miners were locked out after a dispute with the coalowners. Within a week of his arrival in Wales, Wright was reporting enormous interest; thirteen meetings, three new branches, almost 120 members; by July eight more branches had been added. During the course of the summer thirty-two further branches were created and an estimated thousand members enrolled.[45]

This seems to reinforce the idea that the fortunes of the socialist movement and, conversely, the difficulties of the Liberal Party, were intimately linked with industrial politics. It was in times of strike and unrest that the ILP, the SDF and others could gain the oxygen of publicity. In 1898, Keir Hardie took full advantage of the situation to write some highly emotional newspaper articles, address a host of public meetings, and launch a popular relief fund, all of which assisted his own election in Merthyr Boroughs two years later.[46] At the same time, the ILP were well-organized thanks to the efforts of Willie Wright. And as long as he remained, all was well. Unfortunately, despite the entreaties of the local ILPers and an offer of an extended contract at an increased salary, he was forced to resign, probably for health reasons.[47] The effect on the ILP was dramatic. As one local organizer put it, 'once Wright went, [the branches] collapsed because no-one knew what to do next'.[48]

By early 1900 with just seven active branches, the ILP was back where it had been five years earlier. And so it continued for a few years to come. There was the pretence of vigour; in 1904 the recently revived South Wales ILP Federation claimed to have thirty-five branches but could only give the addresses of four branch secretaries. Even in 1904, and despite the election and energy of Keir Hardie himself, the ILP in Merthyr was facing serious problems.[49]

Yet in 1900 Wales played its part in the founding conference of the Labour Party. Delegates from many parts of Britain gathered at Farringdon Hall, and they included a small group of Welsh delegates – R. Dommett from the Swansea branch of the Dock, Wharf and Riverside Union, C. M. Stenner of Cardiff from the National Amalgamated Labourers' Union, J. Jenkins from the Associated Shipwrights. They played no part in the debates and made little impact back home. But then the entire conference was largely ignored outside the labour movement itself; indeed, even the *Labour Leader*, the official newspaper of the ILP, gave relatively little space to this first meeting and only gradually began to provide space for the LRC's activities.

This is not entirely surprising. The dominant political issue of the moment was the South African War, which not only split the Liberal and radical movement, but created considerable discomfort among those who had never questioned Britain's imperial domination and military prowess. The surprising Boer victories, and the profoundly embarrassing failures of British generalship, cast a huge shadow over the political landscape itself.

The election of October 1900 revolved around questions of loyalty to leadership. And yet, in that election, the first Labour MP was actually elected in Wales. Keir Hardie's victory was, to a large extent, a psephological accident and certainly could not be regarded, seriously, as the sign of a socialist breakthrough. None the less, the victory was an enormously powerful symbol, marking the beginning of a continuous process. Once Labour secured this toe-hold on the parliamentary constituency, it never lost it.

And so, in 1900, the Liberals may well have remained the senior party in the two-member seat of Merthyr Boroughs and, despite the public mood, the dominant party of Wales. They may not have even noticed the birth of the Labour Party and have felt that an industrial conflict such as the protracted and debilitating Penrhyn strike which started in the same year was irrelevant to their own destiny. Yet, little by little, the roots of change were spreading. Eventually, within a generation, the rhizomes of Labour and socialism would break through the surface, inexorably strangling the Liberal Party which towered above. In this sense, at least, Labour in Wales begins in 1900.

Notes

[1] *South Wales Daily News*, 3 May 1892.

[2] For Ruskin's 1876 visit to north Wales see B. Atkinson, *Ruskin's Social Experiment at Barmouth* (London, 1900).

[3] I. G. Jones, 'Franchise reform and Glamorgan politics, 1869–1921', in P. Morgan (ed.), *Glamorgan County History*, VI, *Glamorgan Society 1780–1980* (Cardiff 1988).

[4] R. M. Jones, *The North Wales Quarrymen, 1874–1922* (Cardiff, 1981), 55 ff.

[5] J. Hodge, *From Workman's Cottage to Windsor Castle* (London, 1931), 127.

[6] For example, a multi-denominational group of clergy, including the local Anglican rector, formed a committee to give aid and assistance during the ironworks lock-out at Dowlais in 1875; NLW, pamphlets, box XHD 5306, *Y Cload Allan*; see also R. M. Jones, *Quarrymen*, 62–3.

[7] For the attitude of Baptists to the Liberal Party and the labour movement, see T. M. Bassett, *Bedyddwyr Cymru* (Swansea, 1977), 285 ff.

[8] All four Welsh Lib-Lab MPs faced considerable opposition from Liberal Party organizations before winning their seats and Mabon was twice rejected by the Rhondda Liberal Three Hundred; C. Williams, 'Democracy and nationalism in Wales: the Lib-Lab enigma', in R. Stradling, S. Newton and D. Bates (eds.), *Conflict and Coexistence: Nationalism and Democracy in Modern Europe: Essays in Honour of Harry Hearder* (Cardiff, 1997).

[9] For Wolverhampton see J. Lawrence, 'Popular politics and the limitations of party: Wolverhampton, 1867–1900', in E. F. Biagini and A. J. Reid (eds.), *Currents of Radicalism: Popular Radicalism, Organised Labour and Party Politics in Britain, 1850–1914* (Cambridge, 1991); for other regions of England see, for example, A. W. Purdue, 'The ILP in the North-East of England' and B. Lancaster 'Breaking the moulds: the Leicester ILP and popular politics' in D. James, K. Laybown and T. Jowitt (eds.), *The Centennial History of the Independent Labour Party* (Halifax, 1992); D. Clark 'The South Shields Labour Party', in M. Challcott and R. Challinor (eds.), *Working Class Politics in North East England* (Newcastle, 1983); M. Crick, 'The Independent Labour Party in the heavy woollen areas of West Yorkshire 1893–1902', in K. Laybourn and D. James (eds.), *The Rising Sun of Socialism* (Bradford, 1991); P. Wyncoll, *The Nottingham Labour Movement, 1880–1939* (London, 1985); S. Davies, *Liverpool Labour: Social and Political Influences on the Development of the Labour Party in Liverpool, 1900–1939* (Keele, 1996).

[10] Webb Trade Union Collection (Webb TU), British Library of Political and Economic Science (BLPES), section A, vol. xvi, f. 191. The Amalgamated Society of Railway Engineers had some 1800 members in four south Wales towns in 1892.

[11] F. Reid, *Keir Hardie: The Making of a Socialist* (London, 1978), 104 ff.

[12] L. J. Williams, 'The New Unionism in south Wales, 1889–92', *WHR, I/4* (1963), 413–19; D. Hopkin and J. Williams, 'New light on the New Unionism in Wales, 1889–1912', *Llafur*, IV/3 (1986).

[13] T. J. McCarry, 'Labour and society in Swansea, 1887–1918' (Univ. of Wales Ph.D. thesis, 1986), 50. By 1887, the Swansea Trades Council had shrunk to some 500 members and was severely criticized for inactivity in the Webbs' survey of that year.

[14] Webb TU, A iv, fos. 1–7.

[15] 16th Abstracts of Labour Statistics, British Parliamentary Papers (PP) 1914, vol. lxxx, Cmd 7131.

[16] Annual Conference Reports, Labour Party, 1906 and 1909.

[17] C. Williams, *Democratic Rhondda: Politics and Society 1885–1951* (Cardiff, 1996), 31–8.

[18] *Cambria Daily Leader*, 9 July 1888; McCarry, 'Labour and society', 71.

[19] *South Wales Press*, 8 Dec. 1892; *LL*, 23 June 1894, 23 Oct. 1898.

[20] D. A. Pretty, *The Rural Revolt that Failed: Farm Workers' Trade Unions in Wales, 1889–1950* (Cardiff, 1989).

[21] D. G. Jones (ed.), *Detholiad o Rhyddiaeth Gymraeg R. J. Derfel* (Aberystwyth, 1945); F. P. Jones, *Radicaliaeth a'r Werin Gymreig yn y Bedwaredd Ganrif ar Bymtheg* (Cardiff, 1975).

[22] R. Lewis, 'The Welsh radical tradition and the ideal of a democratic popular culture', in E. F. Biagini (ed.), *Citizenship and Community: Liberals, Radicals and Collective Identities in the British Isles, 1865–1931* (Cambridge, 1996).

[23] For Thomas Jones, see E. L. Ellis, *T.J.: A Life of Thomas Jones, CH* (Cardiff, 1992).

[24] Fabian Society Archives, 136 ff. (Nuffield College, Oxford).

[25] *SWDN*, 3, 5 May 1892.

[26] BLPES Coll Misc 375 (local Fabian Societies).

[27] *North Wales Weekly News*, 20 March 1924.

[28] David Thomas Collection, NLW, folio (a) 1, 3.3.11.

[29] *Fabian News*, June 1908.

[30] *Justice*, 23 Jan. 1886.

[31] *Commonweal*, 22 Oct. 1887.

[32] For Mainwaring's life and views, and his account of the tour, see K. John, 'Sam Mainwaring and the autonomist tradition', *Llafur*, IV/3 (1986).

[33] *Justice* (3, 17 Dec. 1892). Colne branch member, John Patterson, had urged that English branches might organize a fund to help start a mission in Wales; *Justice*, 12 Nov. 1892.

[34] *Justice*, 23 Sept. 1893.

[35] See issue no. 1, 21 Feb. 1886.

[36] D. Howell, *British Workers and the Independent Labour Party, 1888–1906* (Manchester, 1983), 241–53.

[37] The lists appeared in the *Workman's Times* from 14 May 1892 onwards.

[38] Fabian Society Archives, fo. 139; *LL*, 14 Nov. 1896; *Pembrokeshire County Guardian*, 18 Oct. 1907.

[39] *LL*, 26 May 1894.

[40] Independent Labour Party National Administrative Committee Mins, Secretary's monthly report, July 1894.

[41] *LL*, 5 May 1894.

[42] *LL*, 6, 13 Oct. 1894.

[43] *LL*, 18 Sept. 1897.

[44] An attempt was made to form a South Wales ILP Federation early in 1898 and approaches were made to Wright, among others, to assist with organizing new branches; see *LL*, 19 March and 30 April 1898. The coal dispute began in early May. Wright arrived at the same time, his salary of 30s. already guaranteed by local organizers; Keir Hardie to John Penny, 5 May 1898; Francis Johnson Papers, 1898/22 (BLPES).

[45] See NAC Mins, 23 May, 17 July 1898. For Wright's activities in the Swansea Valley see *Llais Llafur*, 3 Sept. 1898.

[46] *LL*, 2, 9 July 1898.

[47] *LL*, 8 Oct. 1898. Watts to NAC; NAC Mins, Oct. 1898; see also letter from T. Harrington, Chairman and J. Watt, Secretary respectively of the South Wales ILP Federation, *LL*, 3 Dec. 1898.

[48] E. Vaughan, Maerdy, to NAC, NAC Mins, Oct. 1898.

[49] In April 1904, the branch was said to have been languishing for some time: *LL*, 30 April 1904. In Sept. it was said to be in a state of 'suspended animation'; *LL*, 16 Sept. 1904.

3

The Mosaic of Labour Politics, 1900–1918

EDDIE MAY

As should be evident from previous chapters, 'Wales' was not a single entity and the development of the Labour Party in Wales was not a singular, linear process. Instead, a mosaic of individuals, groups, organizations and events were pieced together, against a background of rapid and sometimes traumatic social change, to create a party which slowly replaced the Liberal Party as the political choice of most of Wales. This chapter examines the main constituents of that mosaic: the individual activists, many of whom belonged to the Independent Labour Party, the trades councils and the trade unions that comprised them, all of whom were essential to the development of the Labour Party. It concludes by assessing the extent to which, by 1918, Labour was sustainable as an alternative political tradition and the degree to which it challenged the hegemony of Liberalism in parts of Wales.

The emergence of the Labour Party in Wales and the pattern of Labour politics were in large part reflections of the changing social and economic structure of Wales. Yet this process of political transformation was not an automatic reflex but the outcome of a conscious, complex and sometimes contradictory attempt on the part of political activists to understand their society and their place within it. The cornerstone of this project was the 'politics of dignity'. The demand for independent working-class representation arose, in part, from the frustrated attempt to have labour's contribution to the commonweal appropriately recognized by sharing in the administration of public life. It affronted the dignity of the working class and their representatives that their claims for inclusion, based upon the individual achievements of respectable leaders such as William Abraham and the collective endeavour of their class, were ignored by their social superiors in the selection and election of public representatives.

Yet the politics of dignity encompassed more than asserting the 'rights of labour' in the political arena. This could have been accommodated by a more enlightened and less socially exclusive Liberal political machine. What Liberalism could not accommodate so easily was the perceived threat posed to working-class dignity, especially working-class masculinity, by developments in the economy and the responses of their employers and political masters. The dignity and self-respect of many working-class men were challenged by the apparently increasingly limited opportunities for advancement at work and by the erosion of occupational differentials and real incomes by a combination of structural changes in the economy and inflation. The chronic housing shortage further curtailed aspirations to respectability. With individual social mobility thereby constrained, after 1901 collectivist methods also appeared circumscribed by the courts. Rather than independent manhood, many saw a future of emasculated serfdom. These gendered concerns added to and made personal the conflict between capital and labour.

Labour activists were able to articulate and organize around these concerns by arguing the need for political action in order to reassert their 'lost prestige as Trades' Unionists and men'.[1] At the parliamentary level it was argued that Labour MPs could help safeguard and advance the claims of organized labour, particularly by reversing the Taff Vale judgment, and could introduce bills dealing with unemployment, the eight-hour working day, and the minimum wage, as well as reform of the Poor Law. In this manner the working man and his family would be protected from the vituperative employer and the vagaries of the labour market. Locally, party activists campaigned for the extension and municipalization of services, particularly housing, in order to improve the comfort and respectability of the working-class home. Independent working-class political representation would, then, raise the status and dignity of that class, 'giving the working class a new feeling of hope and confidence in themselves' as they realized their own importance as 'the foundation upon which the whole superstructure of Society rests'. It was claimed that the rise of labour meant that the slum dweller and the miner 'are feeling the stirrings of a New Manhood within them'.[2]

The individuals who articulated this discourse were also responsible for the tireless, and what must have sometimes seemed fruitless, activism which provided the sustaining core of Labour politics. Without their activism the party would not have developed and the quality of their intervention could be crucial to the party's early success or failure. At the national or regional level, activists usually shared a prominent position in the world of organized labour. These included Vernon Hartshorn, James Winstone and other miners' agents such as Charles Stanton, all of whom worked for the affiliation of the South Wales Miners' Federation (SWMF) to the Labour Representation Committee (LRC).[3] At the local level individual miners' leaders and lodges could play an important part, but other groups of workers were often responsible for the first initiatives.

One important occupational group was that of the railway workers. Faced by employers noted for their hostility to trade unionism, and confronted with the problems of sectionalism and organizing on a national basis, railway workers were more alive to the need for political representation than other trade unionists. This was of course emphasized by the historic setback that the Amalgamated Society of Railway Servants (ASRS), the most important of the railway unions, suffered in the Taff Vale case. That it occurred in Wales added particular significance to the local situation. Thus, in 1903, it was the Barry branch of the ASRS which took the initiative in adopting William Brace to contest the South Glamorgan constituency.[4] In Newport the National Union of Railwaymen played a leading role in local Labour politics, and in Bangor the ASRS was behind many of the initiatives to secure independent labour representation.[5]

School teachers, who occupied a socially ambiguous position between the working and middle classes, were another occupational group well represented in early Labour politics.[6] In Aberdare, W. W. Price, schoolmaster, was a founding member of several local socialist groups and secretary of the Aberdare Valley ILP, and other local teachers active in the party included Ted and Rose Davies, and Matt Lewis, a member of the urban district council. Morgan Jones, one of the leading members of the ILP in Wales, was also a teacher in Bargoed.[7] In Swansea, Richard Littlejohns, an art teacher, was a leading light in the Swansea Socialist Society and was adopted as a prospective parliamentary candidate for the LRC before becoming disillusioned and severing his connection with Labour politics altogether. William Jenkins, of the Assistant Teachers' Union, was, as secretary of the Swansea Trades and Labour Council (TLC), instrumental in forwarding the cause of the LRC locally.[8] In north Wales, another school teacher, David Thomas, was a crucial figure in the development of the Labour Party in that area.

In the ports it was the seafront workers, particularly the dockers, who predominated. In Newport, for example, John Twomey, district secretary of the National Amalgamated Labourers' Union, was a shareholder in the *Labour Leader* and a leading figure in the Newport TLC. In his capacity as union leader he attended the LRC's 1904 annual conference and may have been instrumental in persuading the constituent members of the Newport TLC to affiliate to the LRC.[9] In Swansea local dockers' union leaders such as Harry Lewis, R. Dommett and Tom Merrells were largely responsible for the revival and transformation of the local labour movement.[10]

Features common to all these activists were their sense of belief, their dedication and their unrelenting efforts on behalf of what for many of these people might prove an unrequited endeavour, particularly in the first decade of the twentieth century. The impression left by some of these people is that adherence to the cause of independent labour politics set them apart from most of their contemporaries.[11] They drew on a range of social, cultural and ideological influences: Fabianism and an ethical socialism, heavily influenced by new Christian teachings, were common reference points. Indeed, there was more than a hint of religion in Labour politics for many of these pioneers, as with leading Labour figures like Keir Hardie and Philip Snowden.[12]

The vast majority of Labour activists were men, and this reflects not just the importance of the trade unions to the party, but also contemporary attitudes towards women's primary responsibilities in the domestic, private sphere. As Chris Williams has written, the labour movement, from which the Labour Party emerged, in many senses mirrored the patriarchal attitudes of the wider society.[13] Women activists also faced further, and sometimes insuperable, barriers to their involvement. Even for those women who sought involvement, their domestic responsibilities could prove a burden too great to allow for any engagement in political activities. Dorothy Lenn, for example, the Women's Labour League organizer, explained poor attendances at meetings in the coalfield by writing that 'the women are tied to their homes dreadfully'.[14]

Some women did surmount these obstacles to play an important part in early Labour politics. A number of women were involved as branch secretaries and delegates in the ILP.[15] One notable example was Rose Davies, a school teacher in Abernant until her marriage in 1908 to Ted Davies, a fellow teacher and ILP member, with whom she was to have five children. A close personal friend and political colleague of Keir Hardie, Rose Davies was secretary of her local ILP and was co-opted onto the Education Committee of Aberdare Urban District Council to become the first female chairman of such a committee in Wales in 1915. She was also a member of the South Wales District Committee of the Women's Co-operative Guild, and the first woman to preside over the Aberdare TLC in 1917. She then became one of the first women magistrates in Wales in 1920 and was the first woman elected to the Aberdare UDC.[16] Rose Davies's political career was notable but not exceptional. Elizabeth Andrews, a miner's wife, played an active part in Labour politics in the Rhondda. Like Rose Davies, she was a member of the South Wales District Committee of the Women's Co-operative Guild, she served on the Rhondda War Pensions Committee and the Executive Committee of the Rhondda Borough Labour Party. She was active in campaigns for improved housing and pithead baths, and gave evidence before the Sankey Commission on housing conditions. In 1919 she was appointed Women's Organizer for the Labour Party in Wales.[17]

Yet the majority of women in the labour movement played less prominent but none the less important background roles. Through the Women's Labour League and the Women's Co-operative Guilds, they were largely responsible for the running of the 'social' side of party life, organizing fundraising, teas, socials, dances, as well as making rosettes and staffing the campaign rooms. If many of these activities could be characterized as 'domestic', they were also vital for the companionship and sociability that helped bind the party together, as well as aiding the recruitment and socialization of new members. They helped to give life to the party beyond election campaigns and meant that distinctions between the social and political were blurred whilst each was mutually supportive.[18]

These activities give us some idea of what helped sustain the commitment of Labour activists. A well-organized ILP branch provided its members with a vibrant social, cultural and educational life, as well as a political one. Deian Hopkin has recently shown the extent to which the ILP in Aberdare could be said to be creating an alternative society. With its own institute, the party offered weekly meetings, regular concerts, an ILP Band of Hope, its own football team, annual teas, a children's Christmas party, education classes, numerous committee meetings and the chance to see famous figures such as Victor Grayson, the 'victor of Colne Valley', at the Market Hall. The ILP in Merthyr even had its own tobacconist and newsagent, whilst the Swansea Socialist Society ran a shop and boot club.[19] These individuals could do much to affect the tenor of politics in their own communities but for the Labour cause to move centre stage its activists needed to convince the trade unions and their members of the need for a distinctive party to represent their interests.

Given the popularity of Liberalism in the mining communities at the turn of the century, those Welsh workers that were involved in the formation of the LRC tended to be in the 'New Unions', or those unions whose industrial position was felt to be more precarious than the SWMF.[20] Although not all Welsh unions affiliated to the LRC were 'New' or national ones (for example, the Cardiff, Penarth and Barry Coal Trimmers' Union, which occupied a privileged position in the labour market of the docks, was akin to a 'craft' union), most of the Welsh affiliates were part of national unions.[21]

The attraction of the LRC for the unions lay in a mixture of concerns over the unions' legal position after Taff Vale which, by allowing employers to sue unions for damages caused by strike action, added to a general sense of unease within the labour movement. For example, the involvement of the Trimmers' Union in independent labour politics stemmed from a sense of organizational insecurity. By the eve of the First World War the upsurge of militancy and unrest on the waterfront and the successes of the dockers' union had persuaded Trimmers' officials of the need to consider united action and it reluctantly joined the National Transport Workers' Federation in June 1914.[22]

The key union in the development of the Labour Party in Wales was, of course, the SWMF. With over 150,000 members concentrated in the most densely populated counties of Wales, with an unrivalled organization and sense of occupational solidarity, capturing this union was essential for the party. Yet for the first half of the new decade the union's leadership, and the majority of the rank and file, remained faithful to the Liberal cause. However, intensive propaganda by the ILP and the permeation of the local union structure by its activists, along with the application of the Taff Vale decision to the coal trade, when the SWMF was success-fully sued for £57,562 damages for a 'stop day', led delegates at the annual conference in 1904 to call for affiliation to the LRC. Although Lib-Lab leaders such as William Brace were able to delay the ballot, they were now struggling against an increasingly powerful current in favour of affiliation to the LRC. When the ballot was taken in 1906, a majority of 10,316 was returned for affiliation (although nationally the vote of the Mineworkers' Federation of Great Britain (MFGB) was against). After this ballot both Brace and Thomas Richards declared openly for affiliation and in 1908 a second ballot produced a clear majority across the MFGB in favour of joining the Labour Party.[23]

The speed of the transition of the South Wales Coalfield from a Lib-Lab stronghold to a putative Labour battalion is startling. Although one should be careful not to exaggerate the degree to which popular political loyalties and the nature of political rep-resentation were transformed, a quickening in the pace of political change after 1906 is noticeable.[24] One sign is the growing number of requests for information and advice about forming local Labour parties that Ramsay MacDonald received at this juncture. From Abertillery to Llanelli, TLCs began the process of forming Labour parties and the effects for the Labour Party of the miners' affiliation were seen in the party's improving organizational and financial situation in the coalfield. Meth Jones, T. I. Mardy Jones and William Harris were appointed as political organizers for Gower, Glamorgan and Monmouthshire respectively, with Zachariah Andrews, chairman of the Varteg miners' lodge, agent for the North Monmouthshire Labour Party. Miners' lodges were also pulled more closely into the plans of Labour activists to contest constituencies, as in Mid Glamorgan, although largely without the degree of success for which activists might have hoped.[25] After 1909, the SWMF quickly became the key to the party's success in south Wales. In part this was a testimony to the

profound nature of the social changes occurring within the
coalfield and the effect this had on the political loyalties of the
mining communities. The affiliation of the SWMF to the Labour
Party was also in large part due to the efforts of the ILP.

Before 1909, the key organizations in the development of Labour
politics were the ILP and the TLCs. Prior to 1918, membership of
the Labour Party was only possible through membership of an
affiliated socialist society or trade union. This meant that, for
those who did not belong to a union, or whose union was not
affiliated to the local TLC, the ILP was often the only way in which
to participate in formal Labour Party politics. After a number of
false starts, by the middle of the 1900s the ILP had slowly rebuilt its
strength. The twenty-three branches active in south Wales in 1903
had grown to forty-nine branches by 1906 and two years later the
ILP claimed 130 branches, some 4,000 members, and five full-time
organizers. The ILP also had ninety-nine councillors or Poor Law
guardians in Wales. In a town such as Aberdare, the party was a
powerful force in local politics, with seven elected representatives
on the twenty-member UDC, and a network of active branches
with good links to the local TLC.[26] Similarly impressive branches
were active in Merthyr Tydfil, Briton Ferry and Neath. Although
there was a temporary collapse in 1909, by 1910 the ILP could
claim over 100 branches, and a paid-up membership of around
2,000.[27] It began a number of ambitious national campaigns, such
as its 'War Against Poverty', which also revealed the party's ability
to draw non-socialist groups into its orbit.[28]

The ILP could also claim that it was now a party that almost
covered the whole of Wales. The efforts of Tom Platt and David
Thomas in north and west Wales had established a network of
some sixteen branches by 1910. The party's success in these areas
was, in part, due to its ability to spread the word through the Welsh
language and also helped by its ability to attract a number of
Nonconformist ministers to the cause. Such developments coun-
tered opponents' claims that socialism was both ungodly and alien
to Wales. The economic difficulties of the slate industry also aided
the party's efforts. Thus the Caernarvonshire Labour Council,
established in 1911, was joined by the North Wales Quarrymen's
Union in 1913 and could claim 6,063 affiliates and sixty-five
Labour councillors on various elected councils in the county by
1915. David Thomas followed up this success by organizing a

North Wales Labour Council shortly afterwards.[29] During this time activists of the Undeb Gweithwyr Môn (Anglesey Workers' Union) also had some success in laying the organizational foundations of the party.[30] Yet these achievements represented a step forward rather than a huge stride towards redefining the nature of political representation in north and west Wales.

Although local ILP branches and activists could prove to be extremely influential in the timing and tenor of Labour politics, the ILP was generally too small and financially weak to sustain unaided a prolonged political challenge. Thus another crucial element in the development of independent Labour politics was the creation of TLCs. The TLCs brought together the various trade unions of a district to discuss common labour problems. They provided an arena where the voice of the smaller unions could find a hearing and where (in some cases) socialists could make contact with organized labour. The agenda of these trade unions varied according to local circumstances, but common features were a commitment to defending trade union rights, and to protecting the terms and conditions of members employed by local authorities. This was not least because local authorities were important employers and contractors in their own right and council employee terms and conditions could act as an important benchmark in the local labour market. These factors inevitably involved the TLCs in considering local politics in relation to these aims, especially as councillors and guardians were constantly awake to the concerns of the ratepayers for the good husbandry of local revenues and this could provide an opportunity for socialists to make their case.

The origins of independent labour politics thus can often be located in the seemingly less heroic questions of street lighting, public nuisances, the terms and conditions of council employees, as well as the expansion of local services, such as cottage hospitals, or particularly the provision of better housing. Housing was an important campaigning issue and labour activists expended considerable energy in compiling housing surveys which exposed the overcrowded and often insanitary housing conditions found in most Welsh towns.[31] Many of these demands, of course, required public finances, and this was usually the nub of the political conflicts that facilitated the development of independent labour representation. Existing parties and independent councillors sought to defend the ratepayers' interest while labour activists stressed the requirement for an active municipal policy to meet the needs of working-class residents. In this manner the Labour Party created for itself a distinctive political programme, in the mean time being identified with extravagance and financial irresponsibility by its opponents.

What the history of the TLCs also indicates is the gradual extension of labour organization in and beyond the coalfield. At the turn of the century in Wales there were only eleven TLCs, representing just over 41,000 trade unionists. By 1910 these figures had increased to twenty-seven and 86,000 respectively, and had grown again to forty and 133,000 on the eve of war. The First World War witnessed a significant extension of labour organization, so that in 1919 there were sixty-eight TLCs representing 237,000 trade unionists in Wales. Initially the TLCs had been predominantly but not exclusively located in south Wales. By the end of the war, however, TLCs were also established in Aberystwyth, Blaenau Ffestiniog, Colwyn Bay and Wrexham, and a North Wales Federation had been organized by David Thomas. The extension of the TLCs across Wales indicates how the First World War had been an integrating experience for the labour movement.[32]

Although the establishment of a TLC did not necessarily indicate a commitment to independent labour politics, none the less they often proved crucial in the development of the Labour Party in many parts of industrial Wales. In practice, the establishment of a TLC was usually a necessary precursor to the development of labour politics since it presented other parties, most notably the local Liberal Party, with the prospect of organized working-class opposition. The Pontypridd TLC, established in 1897, was almost immediately pushed into fielding 'Labour' candidates by the refusal of the middle-class Liberal Association to countenance working-class candidates. This move to direct labour representation was as yet far removed from *independent* labour representation, as these early Pontypridd TLC-sponsored candidates were solidly Lib-Lab in their politics. This was reinforced by the decision in April 1901 to reject an attempt by the local branch of the ILP to affiliate to the TLC. Yet, just over a year later, the council's members distanced themselves from the Liberal Party too, resolving that 'this council must maintain a clear independent existence from political parties, whether Liberal or Tory'.[33] The long journey to independent labour politics in Pontypridd had been commenced and the example of Pontypridd suggests that it was, in part, the product of the prejudice and short-sightedness of local Liberals.

Elsewhere the establishment of a TLC was part of a clear commitment to the development of independent labour representation, as was the case in Merthyr Tydfil. The TLCs also became an important focus for the ILP, which adopted an early form of 'entryism' to transform local TLCs into vehicles for independent labour representation. A notable example occurred in Swansea, where members of the Swansea Socialist Society, affiliated to the ILP, were successful in getting the TLC to affiliate to the LRC. This led in turn to the Swansea TLC and the local Socialist Society forming the Swansea Labour Association. This development was of key importance for the history of labour in the town.[34] Swansea's example was replicated elsewhere. In 1906 the newly formed Treherbert TLC ran Griffiths Evans, a railway guard, as a Labour Party candidate for the Rhondda UDC. By 1914 there were five TLCs in the Rhondda performing a similar electoral function for Labour.[35]

Yet it was not all onwards and upwards, as is made clear in the case of Tredegar. Here the first TLC, established in 1907, collapsed shortly afterwards as a result of a combination of confusion over the definition of 'Labour', apathy and the defeat of their candidate for the local district council. A second effort was made in 1908, with Alfred Onions of the SWMF as president, and Sam Filer as secretary. History repeated itself almost immediately, the farce being that one of its nominees was defeated by an 'independent Labour' candidate in 1910, who condemned the TLC as a 'very effete concern'. Soon afterwards an ILP branch was established in Tredegar and affiliated to the TLC in 1911. Ted Gill, of the newly formed West Monmouthshire Labour Association, visited the town about the same time to proselytize for the Labour Party but neither he nor the ILP had much immediate effect: the TLC decided against affiliation to the West Monmouthshire Labour Association. By 1914, the TLC in Tredegar was languishing.[36]

Thus, on the eve of the First World War, the organizational foundations of local Labour parties, some more rudimentary than others, existed in most of the major centres in Wales. Some Labour parties already existed. The Rhondda Labour Party, which does not appear to have been untypical, was formed in October 1911 but struggled to define a clear role for itself, remaining a 'floating and rather powerless' body in Rhondda politics before the war. Labour parties, in all but name in some areas, also existed for Mid Glamorgan, Newport, North and South Monmouth, Abertillery, the Merthyr Boroughs and Swansea.[37]

In organizational terms, therefore, much progress had been made before 1914. If one takes a broad conception of the party's structure – including those institutions, TLC, ILP, LRC and Labour Party, that formed the nucleus of the party – then it does appear that in parts of industrial Wales many of the foundations for the Labour Party's post-war success had already been laid. However, the party's coverage of Wales was sketchy and often reliant upon the ILP. Local parties were often inactive from one election to another, and were rarely in a robust state of health.

Such a condition was not unusual in the Edwardian period. The Liberal Party's structure was often moribund outside elections, while the Conservatives were more noticeable by their absence. However, this might indeed suggest the weakness, rather than the strength, of the movement for independent labour representation in Wales. For, if a weak Liberal organization could still outperform the Labour cause, in which so much organizational effort had been invested, then it is suggestive of the continued strength of popular Liberalism rather than the clamour for political change. An examination of the Labour Party's electoral performance is therefore necessary to test the relative position of the parties before 1918.

One of the key debates on the origins and development of the Labour Party hinges on the timing of the party's breakthrough to replace the Liberals as the main opposition to the Conservative Party in British politics. Some, arguing that the rise of 'class politics' accounts for the growth of the Labour Party and the decline of the Liberal Party, point to Labour's success in the 1906 general election and the party's growing municipal presence thereafter to suggest that the breakthrough predated the post-war collapse of the Liberal Party. Others, who suggest that with the development of 'New Liberalism' the Liberal Party was able to withstand the challenge of Labour, point out that parliamentary successes by the Labour Party were usually the result of Liberal goodwill and further suggest that the party's 1910 performances point to its weaknesses, concluding that it was the war-induced collapse of the Liberals that allowed Labour to break through after the war.[38]

More recent contributions have attempted to move the debate forward. Accepting that social change is an important contributory factor in explaining the rise of Labour but also stressing the need to focus attention on how competing political ideas and strategies affected Labour's development, these historians have directed attention to the need to examine the differing social and political contexts within which the Labour Party operated and to explore the complexities inherent in political mobilizations. They have, therefore, emphasized the contingent connectedness between the social and the political, between space and place, between the national and the local and between time and historical location.[39]

This debate has obvious relevance to the situation in Wales but the hegemony of the Liberal Party there suggests that a different perspective needs to be adopted in terms of measuring and dating the Labour Party's breakthrough to second-party status in Wales. Given the Liberal Party's dominance in Wales and the Conservative Party's problem in securing parliamentary representation, it could be suggested that the Labour Party was already the second party in Wales before the outbreak of the First World War. From 1906 onwards Labour consistently won more Welsh seats than the Conservatives at general elections.

With regard to the Liberal Party, however, Labour remained very much its junior. Labour's first success, Keir Hardie's election for the dual-member Merthyr Boroughs constituency in 1900, was as the junior member to the Liberal coal magnate D. A. Thomas. So closely did they run together that Hardie's election posters were prominently displayed in Thomas's campaigning rooms. Thereafter Hardie's relationship with the Liberals in his constituency was never quite so close.

Other Lib-Lab miners' leaders had more troubled relationships with local Liberals. Mabon in the Rhondda, William Brace in South Glamorgan, Thomas Richards in West Monmouthshire and John Williams in Gower all faced considerable opposition from local Liberal associations when adopted as prospective candidates by Labour groups. In the case of Brace and Richards, intervention by the Liberal Chief Whip was required to stymie opposition and John Williams had to defeat an independent Liberal opponent in

1906. Their experiences reveal a paradox in the political history of south Wales at this time. All these men were essentially Liberal in their politics, and their success during the 1906 general election can be read as testimony to the continued strength of Liberalism. Yet the reluctance of local Liberal associations to choose or to endorse working-class candidates, even in a constituency like West Monmouthshire, an archetypal mining seat with a mining electorate of 67 per cent of the total franchise, points to a crucial weakness: Liberalism's inability to accommodate itself to the changing political aspirations of organized labour in industrial south Wales. The Liberals liked leading but not being led by the workers.

However, Labour's electoral performance before the war does illustrate the continued appeal of Liberalism to the electorate and the limits this placed on the party's ambitions. Labour performed best when opposed by a Conservative but when a Labour candidate stood against a Liberal he usually lost. There were exceptions – John Williams for Gower in January 1906 and December 1910, and Keir Hardie against unofficial Liberal candidates at Merthyr Boroughs after 1900. The Labour candidates defeated by Liberals include John Hodge for Gower in 1900, James Winstone for Monmouth District in 1906, Vernon Hartshorn twice in Mid Glamorgan in 1910, Ben Tillett for Swansea Town in 1910, Charles Stanton in East Glamorgan the same year and Dr J. H. Williams for East Carmarthen in 1912.

These defeats also tell us something else about the nature of Labour's parliamentary representation prior to the war. Everywhere except Merthyr, socialism was rejected and nowhere more decisively than in Swansea. Despite the successes of the Swansea Labour Association in municipal politics, Tillett's aggressively socialist campaign was counter-productive and he came bottom of the poll.[40] Those Labour candidates who were successful, again with the exception of Hardie, were Liberal in their politics. This is illustrated best in the difficulties that Thomas Richards's selection for West Monmouthshire caused the LRC. Richards, secretary of the SWMF, was very much a man of the Welsh radical tradition and many on the executive of the LRC shared J. R. Clynes's concern that Richards was really a Liberal candidate. There was considerable dissension within the executive, before Ramsay MacDonald and Arthur Henderson, who supported Richards, eventually won out. Will Crooks and Henderson were then permitted to campaign on Richards's behalf, as did David Lloyd George. Richards subsequently took the Liberal whip on being elected.[41]

Yet there were signs that within these limits Labour was consolidating. Hardie increased his vote between 1900 and January 1910, as did Richards in West Monmouthshire, being returned unopposed in December 1910. Even Hartshorn could take some consolation from improving slightly his performance in the second general election of 1910. These successes also came in the face of the financial difficulties faced by the party in the light of the Osborne judgment, which temporarily restricted union funding of the Labour Party. Furthermore, if the party's performance in December 1910 was far from spectacular, it should be placed in the context of a lower turnout in December 1910. Still, on the eve of war, Labour remained very much the Liberal Party's junior. Indeed, some Liberal associations were preparing for a possible counter-attack. Liberal restlessness forced William Brace, for example, to seek a safer seat than that of South Glamorgan.

The underlying causes of the apparent weakness of Labour's parliamentary challenge before the war is the subject of considerable debate. Of key importance are the differences in interpretations of the inequities of the Edwardian franchise for the Labour Party.[42] Some doubt has been cast on the extent to which the limited franchise was, in practice, biased against the working class. The borough franchise of 1867 has been described as 'capricious both in its inclusions and exclusions', owing to the sheer complexities of the registration procedures, so that while it remained exclusive, 'it was not in any conscious way selective'.[43] In south Wales, however, it has been suggested that the working class, who represented the overwhelming majority of its population, was proportionately under-represented in the electorate. This was for a number of related reasons. The first is that the number of parliamentary seats did not keep pace with the explosive growth of population. Between 1885 and 1910, the population of Cardiff Boroughs grew by 248 per cent (unparalleled elsewhere in Britain), in South Glamorgan by 197 per cent and in Rhondda by 147 per cent. The result was that south Wales was grossly under-represented in Parliament. The second reason is that proportionately the number of electors may have declined significantly between 1885 and 1910, so that the franchise was becoming increasingly restricted.[44]

A third reason is that the franchise also discriminated against young men, who were usually excluded from the franchise due to the rateable and residential qualifications. The particular significance of this to the South Wales Coalfield at least, is the youthfulness of the age structure of the region. One can suggest that the significance of this generational factor for the Labour Party is itself threefold. The first is that this cohort, reaching maturity in the first decade of the new century, was less likely to be either Welsh-speaking or chapel-attending than earlier generations. Therefore, it is probable that it was more detached from the cultural and religious bedrock of Welsh Liberalism than older cohorts. Secondly, this age group was also well-represented in the in-migration to the coalfield at this time and this cohort would surely have been less influenced by the milieu of Welsh Liberalism. The third effect of the generational factor is that it was this cohort that contemporaries identified as being in the vanguard of the political radicalism for which south Wales was gaining renown before the First World War. As such, they were the generation to which the ILP and more radical groups addressed themselves with some success. Their absence from the electorate probably shortened the Labour Party's chances at the polls.[45] However, one should be cautious about assuming that this cohort would have voted as one for the Labour Party.[46]

There is also another explanation for Labour's relatively poor electoral performance and this lies in the weakness of its electoral machinery in many constituencies. When Hardie was elected in 1900, a key theme in his victory speech was the need for a strong organization in the constituency. Fourteen years later this had yet to be accomplished. Despite much activity elsewhere, Labour's electoral organization was similarly wanting.[47]

Whatever the weaknesses of Labour's parliamentary position on the eve of war, one thing had become clearer: the 'Progressive Alliance' was decaying. In key areas of Wales, Labour and Liberal candidates prepared to stand against each other in straight contests for the leadership of their community. The task now is to discover whether a similar situation prevailed at the local level and to determine if Labour's challenge there was stronger than in contests for parliamentary seats.

At one level, by the eve of the First World War, Labour was indeed poised to take over the mantle of leadership of the community from the Liberals in parts of the South Wales Coalfield. Within the coalfield, senior Labour figures were making the transition from representatives of a sectional interest to elder statesmen of their local community. ILP veterans such as Vernon Hartshorn, for example, rejected twice by the electors of Mid Glamorgan in 1910, had nevertheless sat on Maesteg UDC from 1906 and had been its chairman in 1908, before being elected to Glamorgan County Council. James Winstone, also defeated when he stood as the LRC candidate for Monmouth District in 1906, was chairman of both Risca and then, in 1911, of Abersychan UDCs. His local standing was such that he was often returned unopposed for the Pontnewynydd North ward, and later he was elected chairman of Monmouthshire County Council.[48] Other lesser Labour figures were also carving out a significant role for themselves in local government. The first two mayors of Merthyr Tydfil Borough Council were members of the ILP. Early ILP successes in Neath led to both Jonah Jones and Daniel Harry being elected chairman of the town council, and David Davies became its first Labour mayor in 1909.[49]

With regard to securing power locally, Labour's position in 1914 is more difficult to assess, owing to an absence of consistent records and the problems of nomenclature in identifying the political loyalties of local representatives. However, it is possible to give an impression of Labour's performance in local government elections between 1900 and 1913. The picture that emerges suggests that Labour slowly established its presence in authorities across the South Wales Coalfield, to the point that it was poised to assume control in some by 1914, but that elsewhere it was only effective spasmodically within and beyond industrial south Wales.

Labour's performance in UDC elections was uneven but the trend appears to have been upwards almost universally across the South Wales Coalfield. In Monmouthshire, Labour gained some of its first major successes. As early as 1904 Abertillery had a Labour mayor and the party took control of the UDC in 1912. As such Abertillery has some claim to being the first Labour town in Wales. Tredegar could make no such claims, however, with only three Labour members on the Liberal-dominated council by 1913.[50] In Glamorgan, the Labour Party made considerable progress. Labour's five members on Rhondda UDC in 1901, for example, were swamped by the sixty-one other, mostly Liberal, councillors.

Yet Labour's position on the council improved incrementally, and by 1913 it was the second largest party, with twenty-three councillors compared with the Liberals' twenty-five.[51] In the neighbouring and more socially heterogeneous Pontypridd, the Labour Party found it harder to establish itself. The party made some ground but not sufficient to ensure the return of an important figure in the development of the Labour Party, T. I. Mardy Jones, who was defeated by a Liberal as late as 1912.[52]

Labour had more success in Aberdare. Attempts to return Labour candidates early in the new century were easily rebuffed and the resulting loss of confidence led to the TLC failing to run any candidates in 1903. Yet three ILP candidates were returned in 1904 and by 1909 Labour was the largest party on the council, with seven councillors, and was an established presence in local government in the town, a position it retained at the outbreak of war in 1914.[53]

At the level of town and borough council representation, Labour's most notable strongholds were Merthyr Tydfil and Swansea. At Merthyr the party increased its representation from three to fourteen councillors in 1905, making it the largest party on the thirty-two-member council, subsequently going on to consolidate its position. Labour also enjoyed considerable success in Swansea: by 1914 it had twelve councillors on the forty-member town council.[54] In the other boroughs, Labour had some success in Newport but this tended to be concentrated in a few dockland wards.[55] In Cardiff, where the break with Liberalism had not been completed fully before the outbreak of war, Labour made little headway. In 1910, for example, J. H. Thomas, standing as a 'Labour and Socialist' candidate, came within 104 votes of defeating John Chappell, a 'Lib-Lab' candidate and a prominent figure in Cardiff's Labour movement. The result was seen as 'promising' because Chappell, described as being 'one of the ancient type of "Labour" men who still cling to the skirts of Liberalism', was likely to become the next mayor of Cardiff. This 'promising' result illustrates how far independent labour representation still had to go in the city.[56]

In Carmarthenshire progress was similarly uneven but less impressive overall. In Llanelli, the Labour Association secured the return of five of its nine candidates in the first elections to the borough council in 1913, although the party was still far from securing a commanding position on the council.[57] The situation in Llanelli illustrates the difficulty in reading the level of support for the Labour Party from local election results. Unable to capture the town council until long into the inter-war period, Llanelli nevertheless became a safe Labour seat from 1922 onwards. Labour's pre-war success in local elections in Merthyr Tydfil, however, did not immediately translate into parliamentary domination, particularly after the death of Hardie. Again, it was not until after 1922 that Merthyr Tydfil became a safe Labour seat. Yet within the South Wales Coalfield, the successes of SWMF political organizers had resulted in a spate of local party-building and the closer linking of miners' lodges to local parties. The party's electoral performance was also improving. On the eve of war, the political map of the coalfield was more of a patchwork quilt, with islands of putative Labour dominance, than a red blanket covering the entire region.[58]

Beyond the industrial south, the evidence suggests that Labour's performance was very much weaker. For most of this period the party appears to have failed to field any candidates for town or borough elections in most of rural Wales. No Labour candidates are recorded as having stood for election in Kidwelly, Tenby, Llandovery, Abergavenny, Monmouth, Lampeter or Cowbridge, for example. Only once, in 1908, did a 'Socialist', P. Handley, stand for the Conservative-dominated borough of Brecon, coming bottom of the poll.[59] Labour had greater success at Carmarthen, securing its first councillor in 1913. The same year Griffith Williams topped the poll in Aberystwyth, giving Labour its first success there too. Although three Labour candidates were unsuccessful at Pembroke, a TLC candidate headed the poll at Pembroke Dock in the same year.[60] In Bangor, Labour's first and only town councillor before the war was elected in 1906.[61] If these latter successes are indicative of Labour beginning to broaden its appeal and ambitions beyond industrial south Wales, they also serve to remind us that it was far from being the party of local government in most of Wales before 1914.

The First World War did much to accelerate and consolidate the social, cultural and political changes already evident before its outbreak. Yet the war did more than this. As Kenneth O. Morgan has written with regard to Wales, 'the war marked an immense break with the past, in social and ultimately in political terms. In no part of the British Isles was the contrast between pre- and post-war conditions more pronounced.'[62] At the conclusion of the First World War the Labour Party was well placed to stake out its own claim to be the first party of choice in industrial Wales. Generally speaking, Labour had a good war and this was in large measure due to the labour movement's ability to reflect and represent the popular mood. Thus, as Wales responded to the war with an outpouring of popular patriotism, the majority of union and Labour leaders committed themselves wholeheartedly to the national cause. In consequence, a number found themselves co-opted into the domestic management of the war effort. William Brace was seconded to the Home Office, Thomas Richards joined his opposite number, Finlay Gibson, the secretary of the Monmouthshire and South Wales Coal Owners' Association, on various committees dealing with the coal industry. Vernon Hartshorn, rejected earlier by the electors of Mid Glamorgan for his socialist extremism, was now acceptable enough to the government to sit on the Coal Organization Committee and later the Coal Controller's Advisory Board. Such official recognition of the competence and importance of such Labour leaders did much to raise their status within the wider community and to reflect back on the working class their own importance.

At the local level Labour activists made themselves indispensable to their community. They pressed local authorities to take action to ameliorate the effects of unemployment or the distress of the dependants of servicemen and women. Labour councillors often took the initiative and used their position to galvanize municipal bodies into action. As a growing number of local committees evolved to deal with the exigencies of war, Labour expected to be represented on them and pressed to secure representation when overlooked. As a consequence, Labour leaders and activists were soon found on pensions, rent and distress committees, and after 1916 military tribunals. Yet Labour activists often had to rally their forces to overcome the resistance of the local authorities in order to gain representation on important committees. A case in point was Labour's effective exclusion from the local Food Control Committees (FCCs), established by the Ministry of Food to police the local food supply, in many areas of Wales. In response, trade unions and TLCs were galvanized into action, and local Food Vigilance Committees (FVCs) were formed to police commercial interests and to pressurize the FCCs into according greater working-class representation. As shortages became increasingly common, activists such as Noah Ablett accused the local authorities of protecting the 'profiteers in our midst', and sought to challenge the legitimacy of the authorities' mandate to deal with the problem. Frank Hodges was accused in turn of 'setting class against class' when he attacked the Bridgend FCC for favouring the interests of shopkeepers and retailers above those of working-class consumers. Demands from FVCs for rationing and greater working-class control over the local food supply were sometimes conceded, especially after localized disorder in the South Wales Coalfield in January 1918. Shortly afterwards the Ministry of Food went to considerable lengths to consult with the labour movement. Labour's food campaign did much to raise the movement's profile and to heighten and articulate a sense of working-class grievance against the perceived class bias in the administration of the domestic war effort. It also had the effect of placing local authorities on the defensive, sensitive as they were to the criticism that the wartime political truce compromised their claim to be representative of public opinion.[63]

The food campaign, with its attacks on local élites and its calls for greater working-class control, was part of a heightened sense of working-class consciousness and militancy evident from 1917 onwards. However, the results of such shifts in the popular mood for the Labour Party were somewhat mixed in the short term. Wartime collectivism and Labour's participation in the management of the war effort did much to raise the party's profile, as did its role in defending working-class interests. The challenges made to the party by the war effort resulted in a spate of party-building and reorganization, which Henderson's reforms to the national party pushed forward. By 1916, federations of Labour parties existed in north and south Wales, joined shortly afterwards by the South Wales Federation of Labour Members (of local authorities). Reports from the party's national agents spoke of the enthusiasm for the party and Henderson's reforms as being greater in the Principality than elsewhere in Britain.[64] Yet the militancy evident in the South Wales Coalfield threatened the party's relevance there, as some saw the industrial struggle as taking precedence or rejected the party for its moderation.[65]

The consequences of the war for the ILP were far more deleterious. Although the party regained its strength and flourished in parts of the increasingly militant cauldron of the South Wales Coalfield, the ILP never recovered from the distance its attitude towards the war placed between it and the wider labour movement. Its isolation was compounded by Henderson's reforms which removed much of its previous *raison d'être*. The party was also challenged by the emergence of the Communist Party which became the natural home for many critics of the Labour Party's moderation. The First World War thus helped to shift the ILP from the centre stage of Welsh Labour politics.

Whatever the immediate effects of the First World War, its consequences were to consolidate the Labour Party as the voice of organized labour in industrial Wales. With the electorate increased by 50 per cent under the Representation of the People Act, Labour gained ten seats and almost 31 per cent of the vote in December 1918. This was a 'notable advance' in itself, but the fracturing of the Liberal ascendancy caused by the rift in the Liberal Party pointed to the Liberals' long-term decline in industrial Wales.[66] In the South Wales Coalfield in particular, the Labour Party was poised to assume control of local government in many areas. Domination of the parliamentary representation of large swathes of industrial Wales was soon to follow. From its base in the coalfield, the Labour Party would gradually extend its influence.

By 1918, the rather loose alliances of activists in the ILP and the unions, whose efforts had done much to create an alternative working-class political culture, had been replaced by a more structured movement that was poised to replace the hegemony of the Liberal Party with their own in much of industrial Wales. In the rest of Wales Labour's challenge was still largely in its infancy. Yet, in the most vital centres of Welsh political life, it was the Labour Party that now prepared to speak for its own conception of Wales and its peoples.

Notes

[1] Labour Representation Committee, 9/353.

[2] K. Hardie election address, Dec. 1910, Aberdare Library (AL), PY3/4/3; 'Labour Representation on Different Bodies. An Address by Keir Hardie, MP, 4 March 1901', AL, PY3/1.

[3] V. Hartshorn to R. MacDonald, LRC 14/164, 25 April 1904, LRC 14/233, 24

April 1904; J. Winstone to R. MacDonald, LRC 7/414, 21 March 1903, LRC 9/294, 18 May 1903, LRC 24/509, 8 July 1905, LRC 24/275, 25 July 1905.

    [4] LRC 9/353; K. O. Fox, 'The emergence of the political labour movement in the eastern section of the South Wales Coalfield, 1894–1910' (Univ. of Wales MA thesis, 1965), 98–9.

    [5] Newport Labour Party Mins, 2 July 1913, 7 May 1914; P. E. Jones, *Bangor 1883–1983: A Study in Municipal Government* (Cardiff, 1986), 126–7.

    [6] Aberdare Valley Teachers' Association, General Meeting Mins, 22 May 1903; Glamorgan RO, D/D NUT 1/2.

    [7] J. Bellamy and J. Saville (eds.), *Dictionary of Labour Biography*, IX (London, 1993), 145–50.

    [8] D. Hopkin, 'The membership of the Independent Labour Party, 1904–10: a spatial and occupational analysis', *International Review of Social History*, XX (1975); idem, 'The rise of Labour in Wales, 1890–1914', *Llafur*, VI/3 (1994); LRC 2/28, 31/360.

    [9] LRC, 2/22, 11 April 1901.

    [10] T. J. McCarry, 'Labour and society in Swansea, 1887–1918' (Univ. of Wales Ph.D. thesis, 1986), 582–603.

    [11] Emrys Hughes papers, GRO, D/DX868/2; W. J. Edwards, *From the Valley I Came* (London, 1956); A. Mòr O'Brien (ed.), *The Autobiography of Edmund Stonelake* (Bridgend, 1981); B. Thomas, *History of the Llynfi Valley* (Cowbridge, 1982), 202.

    [12] D. Morris, 'Sosialaeth i'r Cymry – trafodaeth yr ILP', *Llafur*, IV/2 (1985).

    [13] C. Williams, *Democratic Rhondda: Politics and Society, 1885–1951* (Cardiff, 1996), 16–17.

    [14] C. Collette, *For Labour and for Women: The Women's Labour League, 1906–1918* (Manchester, 1989), 83.

    [15] ILP Annual Conference Reports, British Library of Political and Economic Science (BLPES), ILP6, Box 54.

    [16] Rose Davies papers, GRO, D/DXik 1–47.

    [17] Report and Minutes of the Royal Commission on the Coal Industry (Cmd. 359, 360), 1919, 1019–20; C. White and S. R. Williams (eds.), *Struggle or Starve: Women's Lives in the South Wales Valleys between the Two World Wars* (Dinas Powys, 1998), 271; C. Williams, *Democratic Rhondda*, 16–17.

    [18] Letters from Keir Hardie to Rose Davies (n.d.), GRO, D/Dxik 31/2, 30/22; D. Weinbren, *Generating Socialism: Recollections of Life in the Labour Party* (Thrupp, 1997), 1–6; P. Graves, *Labour Women: Women in British Working-Class Politics 1918–1939* (Cambridge, 1994), 156–62.

    [19] Hopkin, 'Rise of Labour in Wales', 132; *Souvenir of the Twentieth Annual Conference of the Independent Labour Party*, BLPES, ILP5, 1912/42; Swansea Socialist Society Report and Balance Sheet, 1911, BLPES, ILP5, 1912/32.

    [20] Letters from D. Davies, secretary of Merthyr, Dowlais and District Trades and Labour Council, to R. MacDonald, 28 June 1900, 6 Aug. 1902, LRC 2/208, 5/254.

    [21] *The Labour Party Foundation Conference and Annual Conference Reports 1900–1905* (London, 1967).

    [22] P. Leng, *The Welsh Dockers* (Ormskirk, 1981), 14–15, 19, 25, 39, 65–8.

    [23] Fox, 'Emergence', 92–136.

    [24] Ibid., 136; P. Stead, 'Establishing a heartland: the Labour Party in Wales', in K. D. Brown (ed.), *The First Labour Party 1906–1914* (London, 1985), 65; Hopkin, 'Rise of Labour in Wales', 129.

[25] Labour Party General Correspondence (LPGC) 5/10, 5/329, 16/213, 224; *Labour Year Book, 1916* (Brighton, 1971), 316–17; *Colliery Guardian*, 3, 24 Aug. 1917; Fox, 'Emergence', 128–33; C. Howard, 'Reactionary radicalism: the Mid-Glamorgan bye-election, March 1910', in S. Williams (ed.), *Glamorgan Historian*, IX (Barry, 1973); D. Tanner, *Political Change and the Labour Party 1900–1918* (Cambridge, 1990), 215, 218.

[26] Stead, 'Heartland', 73–4; *Souvenir of the Twentieth Annual Conference of the Independent Labour Party*; Aberdare Valley ILP Mins, GRO, D/DXhj2; Aberdare Socialist Party Mins, 1901–6, AL, PY4/5, Aberdare Socialist Party, Aberaman Branch ILP, Treasurer's Book, 1901–3, AL, PY4/4.

[27] Stead, 'Heartland', 76–7.

[28] Swansea Socialist Society Report and Balance Sheet, 1911, BLPES, ILP5, 1912/32; Cardiff 'War Against Poverty' Conference, Nov. 1912, BLPES, ILP5 1912/47; Annual Conference of the ILP, South Wales Division, Feb. 1911, BLPES, ILP5, 1911/5; Summaries of New and Lapsed Branches, 1914–1918, BLPES, NAC Papers, ILP3, Item 59.

[29] *ILP Annual Conference Reports, 1905–10*, BLPES; C. Parry, *The Radical Tradition in Welsh Politics: A Study of Liberal and Labour Politics in Gwynedd 1900–1920* (Hull, 1970), 41–4, 51–3; Hopkin, 'Rise of Labour in Wales', 130–1, 134.

[30] D. Pretty, 'Undeb Gweithwyr Môn: Anglesey Workers' Union', *Transactions of the Anglesey Antiquarian Society and Field Club* (1998), 115–48.

[31] J. Parry, 'Labour leaders and local politics, 1888–1902: the example of Aberdare', *WHR*, XIV/3 (1989).

[32] *Labour Year Book, 1916, 1919* (Brighton, 1974), 165–74, 386–9; J. Williams (ed.), *Digest of Welsh Historical Statistics*, I (Cardiff, 1988), 163.

[33] Pontypridd Trades Council and Labour Party Mins, 10 April 1901, 10 Sept. 1902.

[34] Letter to MacDonald from M. Giles, secretary of the Swansea Socialist Society, 25 Nov. 1901, LRC 3/362; McCarry, 'Labour and society', 592–8.

[35] C. Williams, *Democratic Rhondda*, 74–6.

[36] S. E. Demont, 'Tredegar and Aneurin Bevan: a society and its political articulation 1890–1929' (Univ. of Wales Ph.D. thesis, 1990), 83–90, 108–26.

[37] C. Williams, *Democratic Rhondda,* 101–3; Tanner, *Political Change, passim*.

[38] K. Laybourn, 'The rise of Labour and the decline of Liberalism: the state of the debate', *History*, LXXX (June 1995).

[39] Tanner, *Political Change*, 1–16; idem, 'Class voting and radical politics: the Liberal and Labour Parties, 1910–31', in J. Lawrence and M. Taylor (eds.), *Party, State and Society: Electoral Behaviour in Britain since 1820* (Aldershot, 1997); D. Howell, *British Workers and the Independent Labour Party, 1888–1906* (Manchester, 1983); C. Williams, *Democratic Rhondda*, 1–11; J. Lawrence, *Speaking for the People: Party, Language and Popular Politics in England, 1867–1914* (Cambridge, 1998).

[40] D. Cleaver, 'The general election contest in the Swansea town constituency, January 1910 – the Socialist Challenge', *Llafur*, V/3 (1990).

[41] LRC17/331–2, 402–24, 563–7; Fox, 'Emergence', 101–2; R. Gregory, *The Miners and British Politics, 1906–1914* (Oxford, 1968), 122–3; Demont, 'Tredegar', 66, notes that Richards was careful to appeal to middle-class electors.

[42] D. Tanner, 'Elections, statistics and the rise of the Labour Party, 1906–1931', *Historical Journal*, XXXIV/4 (1991).

[43] J. Davis and D. Tanner, 'The borough franchise after 1867', *Historical Research*, LXIX (Oct. 1996), 327.

[44] I. G. Jones, 'Franchise reform and Glamorgan politics 1869–1921', in P. Morgan (ed.), *Glamorgan County History*, VI, *Glamorgan Society 1780–1980* (Cardiff, 1988), 54–60; J. G. Jones, 'Glamorgan politics, 1918–85', ibid., 72.

[45] M. Childs, 'Labour grows up: the electoral system, political generations and British politics 1890–1929', *Twentieth Century British History*, VI/2 (1995); D. Tanner, 'The Labour Party and electoral politics in the coalfields', in A. Campbell, N. Fishman and D. Howell (eds.), *Miners, Unions and Politics 1910–47* (Aldershot, 1996), 77; idem., 'Class voting and radical politics', 115.

[46] Tanner, *Political Change*, 239, 246.

[47] *Western Mail* (*WM*), 4 Oct. 1900; Tanner, *Political Change*, 214.

[48] J. Bellamy and J. Saville (eds.), *Dictionary of Labour Biography*, I (London, 1972), 150–2, 350–1; *WM*, 6 April 1910.

[49] Fox, 'Emergence', 64; G. Eaton, *A History of Neath from Earliest Times* (Swansea, 1987), 143–7.

[50] *WM*, 2 April 1912, 9 April 1913; Demont, 'Tredegar', 90–126.

[51] C. Williams, *Democratic Rhondda*, 91, 215.

[52] *WM*, 12 April 1912; A. Adams, 'Working class organisation, industrial relations and the labour unrest 1914–1921' (Univ. of Leicester Ph.D. thesis, 1988), 50.

[53] *WM*, 8 April 1902, 5 April 1910; Fox, 'Emergence', 82–91; A. Mòr O'Brien, 'A community in wartime: Aberdare and the First World War' (Univ. of Wales Ph.D. thesis, 1986), 70–3.

[54] *WM*, 2 Nov. 1905; J. Gross, *A Brief History of Merthyr Tydfil* (Risca, 1988), 72; McCarry, 'Labour and society', 595–8.

[55] Tanner, *Political Change*, 241.

[56] *Llais Llafur*, 6 Nov. 1910; N. Evans, 'Cardiff's Labour tradition', *Llafur*, IV/2 (1985).

[57] *WM*, 3 Nov. 1913; D. Hopkin, 'The rise of Labour: Llanelli, 1890–1922', in G. H. Jenkins and J. B. Smith (eds.), *Politics and Society in Wales, 1840–1922: Essays in Honour of Ieuan Gwynedd Jones* (Cardiff, 1988), 171; Tanner, *Political Change*, 243.

[58] Tanner, *Political Change*, 218–19.

[59] *WM*, 3 Nov. 1908.

[60] *WM*, 3 Nov. 1913.

[61] P. E. Jones, *Bangor 1883–1983: A Study in Municipal Government* (Cardiff, 1986), 126–7.

[62] K. O. Morgan, *Rebirth of a Nation: Wales 1880–1980* (Cardiff and Oxford, 1981), 177.

[63] War Emergency Workers' National Committee, WNC, 10/1/68, 12/377, 10/1/128, 11, 29 Dec. 1917, 10 March 1918; E. May, 'A question of control: social and industrial relations in the South Wales Coalfield and the crisis of post-war reconstruction, 1914–1921' (Univ. of Wales Ph.D. thesis, 1995), 108–44.

[64] Labour Party National Executive Minutes, 28 Nov. 1917.

[65] *SWDN*, 28 Oct. 1919; M. Woodhouse, 'Rank and file movements amongst the miners of South Wales, 1910–1926' (Univ. of Oxford D.Phil. thesis, 1969); D. K. Davies, 'The influence of syndicalism and industrial unionism on the South Wales coalfield, 1898–1921: a study in ideology and practice' (Univ. of Wales Ph.D. thesis, 1991).

[66] Morgan, *Rebirth*, 181.

4

Political Culture and Ideology, 1900–1918

RICHARD LEWIS

Wales in the early twentieth century was still to experience full integration into a 'national' political culture, mediated through a London-based popular press. It was still to undergo the changes to political life brought about by the advent of the electrical forms of mass communication, the cinema and radio. Before 1918, contact with the 'high' politics of Westminster and Whitehall, and with international and imperial affairs, was through the local and regional press, which itself was intensely political, aimed at the politically enfranchised, its values often shaped by politically partisan owners and editors. Many, if not most, newspapers, local and regional, were overtly biased in their opinions, though they would carry, often in a depth and detail unimaginable today, the speeches and statements of politicians with views hostile to their own editorial stance. The Tory *Western Mail* was challenged by the Liberal *South Wales Daily News* but even smaller weekly papers could assert a firm political stance. In Barry, for example, the battle for the minds of the electorate was conducted through the columns of the radical *Barry Herald* and the conservative *Barry Dock News*. A journalism which could attract the young and the female readerships was developed, and found its most successful outlet in the 'new' journalism of Northcliffe and the *Daily Mail*, but the London dailies were not to break the hold of the local press in Wales until after the First World War.[1]

The political press was not confined to the local and regional dailies and weeklies, as the late nineteenth and early twentieth centuries saw innumerable attempts to publish periodicals which dealt in political debate. The Welsh labour movement was targeted by various groups, and English radical socialist journals were circulating in Wales from the days of the Chartists. By the end of the century copies of socialist papers such as Blatchford's *Clarion* and the Marxist *Justice* could be found in some Welsh homes and reading rooms. Attempts to create a Welsh labour press resulted in the Edwardian era in several publications, mostly rather short-lived, the most successful being *Llais Llafur* and later the *Merthyr Pioneer* and *Y Dinesydd Cymreig*. Important as a means of disseminating ideas and argument amongst activists, they probably had little impact on the wider population.[2] However, in the age of the limited electorate, and before the saturation of society's view of the world by modern mass communications, the mechanisms of opinion formation were more intimate and personally focused. Opinion formation in Edwardian society relied rather more, as one would expect, on the older agencies of the chapel and the school, than on the newspaper. But for those in employment, there was also the workplace, and here the activist, if he or she held a position of trust and responsibility, could be crucial. Those who constituted what might be termed the 'secondary' leadership, below the national officials and the 'sponsored' members of Parliament, at the level of the elected local branch or lodge official, the local councillor or Poor Law guardian, were in day-to-day contact with the rank-and-file union member or their immediate family. The pivotal role of the union activist in shaping the world-view of the wider membership was recognized by all who knew anything about the labour movement.[3] It is no accident that in this era, just as the political aspirations of organized labour began to become a significant factor in national party politics, many sought to influence the thinking of this critical element in the political culture of urban and industrial Britain, and of south Wales in particular. Following the major industrial conflicts of the 1890s, industrial Wales was seen as something of a crucial battleground in the conflicts between capital and labour. Evidence of the emergence of a politics which was based on class conflict, dreaded by some if eagerly anticipated by others, became a key stimulus to attempts to gain access to the minds of the working-class activist. In addition to the political press and the pamphlet, this was still the era of the 'soapbox' and the open-air meeting. A common sight in Edwardian south Wales would have been socialist missionaries of various kinds delivering their message on street corners to the sometimes receptive, but often indifferent and even hostile, audiences in the mining and coastal towns. The most sustained and successful challenge was to come from the Independent Labour Party, with its demand for a break with a form of Labour politics which was locked into the older working-class radical traditions associated with popular Liberalism. The impact of the ILP was not dramatic, only slowly did it make conversions, and even more gradually did these converts insinuate their way into key positions within the 'secondary' leadership of organized labour in Wales.[4]

The task that confronted advocates of independent labour politics in Wales after 1906 was a daunting one. Far from being a time when popular Liberalism appeared to be giving way to new perceptions of politics amongst the working-class electors in Wales, it was a high point for the Liberal Party. The 1906 general election saw the total elimination of Conservative parliamentary representation from Wales. There were 'Labour' MPs from Wales but they mostly took the Liberal whip and stood as Lib-Lab candidates, such as Mabon the veteran member for the Rhondda, or, as with Keir Hardie's election as the 'independent' Labour MP for Merthyr in 1900, actually returned with the tacit acquiescence of the dominant forces in local Liberalism. The truth is that labour politics in Wales was still locked into the well-established patterns of working-class radical politics which had evolved since the late 1860s, and which were only slowly being eroded by a complex interaction of social, economic and attitudinal change. It was a process that was not to result in dramatic shifts in terms of parliamentary representation in Wales until after the First World War.

The 'labourism' of Welsh Lib-Lab MPs such as Mabon or William Brace rested on a belief that organized labour should be acknowledged as a powerful, legitimate and beneficial element in public affairs which should be represented in Parliament and that the Liberal Party was the best vehicle for securing such recognition.[5] Aside from specifically 'labour' issues, such as restrictions on hours and ages of employment, or industrial injuries and safety matters, these MPs did not consider that the term 'labour' meant their interests were separate from the other concerns of popular Liberalism. They were as attached to the main shibboleths of Welsh radicalism as any other Welsh Liberal MP and, in this regard, they probably reflected the attitudes of most electors. For in another key respect the popular politics of the early twentieth century was significantly different from today: a very different set of issues engaged the attentions of voters, parties and politicians. These issues seem to be unrelated to the political concerns that were to dominate the new century, which tended to focus on the economy and social policy. The prime example is the long-running campaign to control, or even prohibit, the production, distribution and sale of alcoholic beverages, commonly known as the temperance movement. This cause no longer registers at all as a factor in the electoral politics of Wales, let alone the rest of Britain, yet at the turn of the century the temperance lobby was one of the most pervasive forces within Welsh radicalism.[6] For many Welsh working-class voters at the beginning of the twentieth century the brewers, distillers and publicans were seen as a far bigger menace to the well-being of Welsh workers than the activities of exploitative employers or greedy financiers. Sobriety, not social security, was the remedy for poverty and joblessness. It certainly would be a profound misunderstanding of the scale of popular support for the various forms of temperance activity in Wales to see it simply as an issue of middle-class hostility to working-class recreations. Though often linked to the more puritanical, not to say pharisaical, elements within Welsh Nonconformity, there were many leading lights within the trade union movement who were deeply committed to the temperance cause. Nor did they all belong to the older Lib-Lab traditions: Keir Hardie was not alone amongst ILP men in proclaiming hostility to the drink interest. This made the task of creating a Labour Party separate from the Liberal Party much more difficult, because in trying to shift attitudes with regard to the place of organized labour within the existing political process, the advocates of independent labour politics had to contend with a widespread perception of issues and policies which naturally assumed that the existing agencies of popular Liberalism were likely to be the most effective in obtaining change and reform. In so far as it was possible to secure social improvement through political action rather than individual endeavour, the party built by Gladstone was seen as embodying the key virtues of moral fervour and detachment from selfish and corrupt, as opposed to legitimate and beneficent, influences. Combined with pervasive beliefs in progress and the perfectibility of society through the enlightenment of individuals and the abolition of privilege, it was a frame of mind which was deeply embedded in the limited electorates of Wales. It was a perfectly rational outlook; it was not immediately obvious how a political party which stressed its exclusive linkage to one, albeit broadly based, interest would be more successful in pursuing the wider radical agenda than the Liberal Party. In addition to which, it was often difficult to persuade the Edwardian Welsh working-class voter to think of himself as a working-class voter, or even a trade unionist voter, rather than say a Nonconformist voter or as a ratepayer or simply a resident. The issues that would excite the interest of voters, especially the older, settled, married householders that made up the bulk of late Victorian and Edwardian electorates, were ones which simply do not resonate in the modern age. The drink question may have peaked as a popular political issue in the 1890s but disestablishment of the Anglican Church, and its associated controversial areas such as ratepayer subsidies to denominational education, emanating from the same Welsh Nonconformist source as the temperance movement, still had a saliency in political debate in Wales, which exposes the limited extent to which the advent of a 'Labour' challenge altered the fabric of popular politics before 1918.[7]

The key element in this political culture was, of course, the chapel. In Wales the Nonconformist chapels were always more than purely religious institutions. Throughout the nineteenth century they were the focal points of communal and social life, whether in the rural areas or in the rapidly expanding coalfield communities. The ministers, deacons and elders provided a leadership élite which enjoyed a status and authority within their localities derived not from social deference, or the privileges of an established religion, but from the fact that they genuinely embodied the dominant attitudes and mentalities of the communities from which they came. Sometimes the chapels enjoyed the patronage of employers or landlords, but it would be wrong to see them exclusively as agencies of social control. The chapel was usually a 'popular' institution in the truest sense of the word, an agency of independence not just for the tenant farmers and rural labourers but also for the urban proletariat in Wales. It was an institution which bridged that divide, it brought into the urban and industrial environment the habits of thought and action which had evolved in the Welsh countryside. It was essentially a communitarian institution, it sought to give a coherence and a focus to the lives of those thrust into the initially very raw societies of industrial Wales. They fostered habits of sobriety, diligence and self-improvement. They opposed the power of the established church, the privileges of the landed élites and the influence of drink. But above all they gave the communities in which they functioned a sense of identity which nothing else did, at least before the end of the nineteenth century. The services, the Sunday schools, the festivals, the Bible classes and the opportunities for self-improvement all combined to give the chapels a centrality which was made concrete by the fact that they were by the end of the century easily the largest and most imposing buildings in most small Welsh towns and villages.

Many writers have noted that the monopoly status the chapels enjoyed within most Welsh communities was being challenged by a range of forces by 1900.[8] Some of these were social, such as the intrusion of non-Welsh in-migrants usually not as imbued with the culture of the chapel as the Welsh in-migrant, or the spread of other sources of entertainment and diversion, such as the early cinema, spectator sport and the public house. The development of miners' institutes outside the direct control of the Nonconformist churches created alternative venues for community events and informal education. But it is the emergence of the agencies of organized labour, especially the rapid growth in the pervasive influence of the South Wales Miners' Federation, its districts, lodges and officials, which is often cited as one of the key factors behind the relative loss in authority and status of the chapels within significant areas of Welsh society. In rural north and west Wales, where the chapel retained its social potency, the Labour Party found the Liberals much harder to displace in the realm of popular politics.

It is certainly true that by the Edwardian era the Federation lodge in most coalmining towns provided a communal leadership which matched that of the local chapels. The full-time officials, especially the miners' agents and lower down the checkweighmen, soon acquired a status to match that of the local preacher and deacon. However, the lodge did not displace the chapel; rather there was a relative loss of power, as an alternative focus of leadership emerged. It was a subtle process: as indicated above, many of the leading lights of the SWMF were active and staunch Nonconformists, their bedrock trade unionism matched by their religious fervour. A Lib-Lab MP such as Mabon was almost as well-known for his pulpit as for his platform oratory. Many union officers learned their organizational, secretarial and administrative skills in the chapels and the Bible classes offered opportunities for developing competence in study and debate. Thus there was no sharp cleavage between the leadership élites of the chapel and the union branch. There was rather a seamless shift to a more secular leadership. The ILP offered an alternative source of enlightenment and also of encouragement to engage in the work of the union. But even here it is possible to detect echoes of the methods and language of the chapel culture. The ILP activists preached their message. Their vocabulary was often riddled with biblical references and analogies. There were innumerable allusions to the 'gospel' of socialism. The Edwardian era saw many examples of young men brought up in the chapel, some of them setting out on a path which would have led them in due course to ordination as ministers of various denominations, undergoing some process which resulted in rejection of their faith. (Auto)biographical studies of some leading figures in the history of the SWMF, such as Frank Hodges, A. J. Cook and Arthur Horner, lay great emphasis on the abandonment of their Christian faith and their adoption of a world-view based on a materialist conception of history and a belief in an earthly salvation for the human race in general and for the south Wales miners in particular.[9] This trend had become more pronounced by the first decade of the twentieth century. At the same time, the chapel remained the single most important influence on the outlook and mentality of many active trade unionists in Wales well into this century. It inculcated a belief in some kind of objective truth, some view of the world and the processes which make it function that could be revealed by a book. It is neither trite nor fanciful to see the links between the close textual analysis employed in chapel Bible classes and the attempts to decipher and interpret the thoughts of Marx and Engels in the classes of the Plebs' League.

Absolute abandonment of the chapel culture and total displacement of religious ideas was probably unusual. The process involved a shift of emphasis and priority for most activists. Religion was central to the lives of Mabon and Brace but it was increasingly peripheral for many of their successors. Many Labour MPs from Wales retained links with chapels and were lay preachers or deacons but over the years their numbers declined, and religion lost its saliency as a factor in the personal and intellectual development of labour leaders, whether locally or nationally. More typical than Noah Ablett was James Griffiths, who never rejected his religious upbringing but, influenced by the spread of a 'social' gospel, decided that his energies were better directed towards activity in the labour movement than the chapel. Perhaps even more representative was David Bevan, the father of that other Welsh giant of the 1945 Labour government, Aneurin Bevan. Once a pillar of the Carmel Baptist chapel in Tredegar, David drifted away from his religious commitment as more and more of his time was taken up with work for his miners' union lodge where he was treasurer. This process of drift rather than outright rejection is also reflected in the fact that chapel attendance in Wales only declined markedly after the First World War, and church membership only in the later 1920s. In the Edwardian era the chapel still shaped the political mentality of many electors in Wales.[10]

Whilst the strength of the Nonconformist churches is a key feature of Welsh political culture in the early years of the twentieth century, it was not entirely unique within the United Kingdom. Methodism in the north-east of England, and the strength of the 'free' churches in the Scottish coalfields, produced similar patterns of political support for the labour movement. What distinguished Wales, however, was the continued strength of the Welsh language, which gave to popular Liberalism another mechanism for marginalizing hostile political philosophies and portraying them as alien and inimical to the interests of the Welsh people. For most of the late nineteenth century the Tories were the chief target of this linguistic stigmatization.[11] However, it was a device that was soon deployed against the various forms of socialist propaganda brought into Wales in the 1890s and 1900s. Very little socialist literature was published in Welsh and few socialist speakers were fluent in the language which was still the vernacular in large tracts of industrial as well as rural Wales. The inability of many advocates of socialism and, by extension, of independent labour politics, to engage in debate in the tongue of the people made them easy targets for the defenders of popular Liberalism. The language was not just a medium of communication; it was an emblem of

Welsh national sentiment and the vehicle for the transmission of chapel culture. Therefore ideas which could not be expressed readily in the Welsh tongue could be dismissed as alien and irreligious. It is significant that some of the earliest socialist literature in Welsh tried to confront the question of the extent to which socialism, an outlook which made great play of its internationalism, could be reconciled with Welsh nationalism and Christianity. Socialism was, in the minds of many chapelgoers, a very materialist world-view, often associated with outlandish lifestyles and disreputable behaviour, thus efforts to reconcile socialism with the Christian gospel also figure prominently amongst the pamphlets published in Welsh in this period. The pioneers of socialist propaganda produced in the Welsh language such as the veteran anti-capitalist R. J. Derfel, and the indefatigable ILP organizer David Thomas, ploughed lonely furrows in the Liberal strongholds of rural west and north Wales.[12]

For advocates of independent labour politics it was, however, an uphill struggle everywhere in Wales. The agencies of popular Liberalism did not simply roll over in the face of the rising political aspirations of organized labour. Within the SWMF the Lib-Lab leadership fought against affiliation to the Labour Party until the membership of the wider Mineworkers' Federation of Great Britain supported the move in 1908. Subsequently they took the Labour whip, and swelled the ranks of the new party in Parliament, but the habits of mind and activity did not change overnight. In any event, the independence of the Labour Party in Parliament as in the country was compromised by political reality. It is important to remember that before 1918 the Labour Party was not, by any stretch of the imagination, a party of government. After 1910, despite attempts by more militant elements within its ranks to deepen the divide with Liberalism, the Labour Party had no choice but to collaborate with the Liberal government to secure some of its still limited and sectional objectives. The Labour Party was still a fairly loose coalition of trade unions and socialist societies, of which the ILP was far and away the most significant. Individual membership and organizations in many constituencies were not established until after the First World War. In this respect again the Edwardian Labour Party belonged to an older political culture, as by today's standards the constituencies still had enormous autonomy. Party labels, and especially the term 'Labour', did not belong exclusively to one political organization. One of the chief objectives of the early Labour Party leadership was to try to assert some authority over who could be described 'officially' as a 'Labour' candidate. Throughout Britain up to 1914, it was not unusual to see wealthy Liberal candidates, barristers and iron-masters, tacking the term 'Labour' on to their candidature descriptions. Each constituency had to create its own Labour representative body, each had its own mix of trade union and socialist groupings, each had to decide whether to mount a challenge and then to seek endorsement from the national Labour Party, whose judgement would be affected by the clandestine understandings agreed with the Liberal leadership.[13] In these circumstances, with the limited size of the electorates, the choice of candidate was vital. The personality and character of the candidate could often determine success or failure far more than policies and programme. Local service to the community was a powerful advantage, but not necessarily enough. The case of Vernon Hartshorn illustrates the problem for the early Labour Party in Wales. The miners' agent for the Maesteg district of the SWMF, a man highly regarded as a skilled negotiator, with a prodigious grasp of the details of the industry and a very competent administrator, he also possessed the necessary social skills to make a successful politician. He was a local councillor and, despite his rising profile in the coalfield, no one could doubt his dedication to the interests of the people of the Mid Glamorgan constituency. As a long-standing member of the ILP he was keen to challenge the local Liberal caucus in Mid Glamorgan. His chance came in 1910, at a by-election in March and again in the general election in December. In both cases, standing as the Labour candidate, he failed to break the hold of the Liberal élite. They brought in orthodox Welsh Liberal candidates, first a businessman in the March by-election and then a journalist in December, but both embodied the older radical traditions. The local Liberal establishment campaigned against Hartshorn's suitability to represent the area. They cast aspersions on his Welshness (he was born in Risca in the most anglicized part of the coalfield); they questioned his religious commitment for, like so many of the younger labour leaders, he had drifted away from, though not wholly rejected, his early chapel-based upbringing. It was sufficient, in a straight fight, to win over enough working men to ally with those in the electorate hostile to the political aspirations of organized labour, to prevent him winning the seat. The local Liberal élite portrayed Hartshorn as an extremist and by their lights he might have been seen as such. Despite his defeat he polled a strong and solid vote, which in a three-way contest might have been enough to win the seat. Lib-Labism, resting as it did on a notion of political representation which saw organized labour as just one pillar of a broad 'Progressive' consensus in Wales, embodying the aspirations of religious dissent and Welsh national sentiment, was decaying – but it was not dead.[14]

Outside the coalfield, in rural areas where the Welsh language and the chapel showed few signs of incipient decline, or in the coastal towns where the labour movement did not dominate the communities as in the coalfield, the Labour Party was still seeking to establish a presence and was even further from displacing the older political order. Even in the slate-quarrying district of north Wales where memories of the bitter struggles with the local Tory magnate Lord Penrhyn were still fresh, a break with Liberalism was not seen as practical politics. Socialist ideas gained a foothold, the ILP was established, but the North Wales Quarrymen's Union leaders and members knew that they were an island of organized labour in a sea of Welsh rural radicalism, where landlordism and the Anglican Church remained the chief enemies. The influence of ILP activists such as the Revd R. Silyn Roberts and David Thomas began to result in subtle changes in the vocabulary and rhetoric used in union meetings and conferences and it became more socialistic and anti-capitalist in tone. ILP members became branch officials, and local councillors and one of their number, R. T. Jones, became general secretary of the quarrymen's union. But it was not until 1920 that the quarrymen affiliated to the Labour Party and not until 1922 that R. T. Jones felt secure in standing as a purely 'Labour' parliamentary candidate.[15]

Scale apart, the north Wales experience was not so different from the more industrialized and urban parts of Wales. The Labour Party was making slow progress through the branches of unions and in the local councils and boards of guardians. It was winning over the activists and the 'secondary' leadership of unions. It is also important to realize that the divisions and distinctions between the various varieties of radical activity and that of socialist groups such as the ILP was not quite as clear-cut as most historians would like. The socialist ideology of the ILP was always rather nebulous, and its strong ethical basis meant that it could accommodate most working-class radicals without trespassing too heavily on their ideological inheritance. The key shift was the refocusing of the world-view in an anti-capitalist direction. It was a process made easier by changes in the nature of Welsh capitalism. The growth of joint-stock companies, where the functions of ownership and management were separated, made it easier to see the exploitative or victimizing manager as a lackey of capitalism rather than just a bad and unchristian man.

The labour movement in Edwardian Wales existed, for political purposes, in a radical continuum which stretched from the Liberal caucuses to small Marxian groupings. It is difficult to draw hard and fast ideological, or even organizational boundaries, within this complex network. Individuals complicate the story. At both extremes there were those that wished to disrupt this zone of contact and debate, to lay down the limits of legitimate discussion. The liberal élite produced those, such as J. Hugh Edwards, Hartshorn's opponent in December 1910, who tried to initiate a virulent anti-socialist crusade. He combined hostility to the idea of independent labour representation with well-established arguments about the extent to which socialist ideas ran counter to religious precepts, national sentiment and orthodox Liberal economic thinking.[16] Rising anti-socialist sentiment coincided with, or possibly was related to, the emergence of advanced socialist ideas, often defined, not entirely accurately, as syndicalism, in south Wales. These 'syndicalist' ideas tended to reject the wisdom and question the efficacy of political action by the labour movement. In fact, for the vast majority of those active within the labour movement in south Wales, this was a period of intense debate about the best strategies to be pursued.

Just as with the north Wales quarrymen, most trade unionists were entirely pragmatic, seeking gains in the political world as in the industrial, weighing up the costs and the benefits of particular policies and actions. Few were wedded in principle to either Lib-Labism or independent representation: they wanted direct political representation to pursue union objectives. Typical of this attitude was the Shropshire-born treasurer of the SWMF, Alfred Onions. By 1906 Onions was the miners' agent for the Tredegar district, a local and county councillor and a magistrate. He was what the Liberal

South Wales Daily News described approvingly as a 'Methodist and progressive of the trade union type'.[17] A pillar of old-style labourism, he would have been perfectly at home with Brace or Mabon. Yet he made the transition to Labour with little apparent difficulty, and became the Labour MP for Caerphilly in 1918. It is a process that has been described as one of translation not displacement and there were often only subtle differences in the career patterns which might tip one man towards Labour, whilst another stuck with Liberalism.[18] It is particularly well illustrated by the careers of two leading figures within the Cardiff Coaltrimmers' Union. This was a key waterfront union, which occupied a strategically important position at the height of the coal-exporting boom. The president of the union was John Chappell. He made his name in Cardiff, building up his union in a hostile environment where organization was difficult and victimization easy. In 1898 Chappell was returned as a 'Labour' councillor for the Splott ward but, despite the fact that he enjoyed a good press from the local socialist journal regarding his campaigns against 'sweated' labour, he soon threw in his lot with the local Liberal Association. He became a pillar of the local Liberal establishment, becoming Lord Mayor of Cardiff in 1909. He served as an army officer in the war and subsequently was a senior civil servant. The general secretary of the coaltrimmers was the devout Baptist and teetotal Rechabite, Samuel Fisher. Unambiguously Liberal in his politics in the early 1900s he soon fell foul of the rising influence of the ILP on Cardiff Trades Council. When his union affiliated to the Labour Party, as a loyal servant, Fisher accepted the shift; but as late as 1920 he was still describing his politics as 'Liberal now Labour'.[19]

Thus the shift from Lib-Labism (or Liberal 'labourism') to socialist labourism in Wales was far from complete or certain by the outbreak of the First World War. If there were Liberals who wished to crusade against socialism, there were also those who wished to preserve the old 'progressive' alliance with Labour by adapting and reinventing Liberal radicalism in a way which could accommodate the political aspirations of organized labour. Historians have tended to give attention to those who were seeking to break the old alliance, and the enemies of Lib-Labism were many; however, there were also operating in the Welsh radical continuum those who could not see the logic of a decisive break. They felt a split between working-class and middle-class radicalism could only benefit the enemies of 'progress' and in particular the Conservatives. In Edwardian south Wales there emerged a small but influential group of academics and professionals who tried to redefine the radical agenda, to give it a stronger social dimension. This coterie of 'social' radicals targeted the labour activist, and through adult education and social work, they established contacts with trade unionists and sought to shape their view of the world – and how it should be changed. There was no ambiguity about their agenda. In 1907 P. Wilson Raffan, the radical Liberal owner of the *South Wales Gazette* and first chairman of the Welsh district of the Workers' Educational Association, stated the position most starkly:

> The WEA also realizes that the democracy of this country will, in the near future, be called upon to play an important part in the affairs of the Empire; hence it is of the highest importance that those upon whom the greatest responsibility devolves have such knowledge as is necessary, to use the powers wisely and discharge their duties in a manner as will bring the greatest good.[20]

The theme of the rule of the many 'under the guidance of the wise' was repeated many times by this network of 'social' radicals. They were acutely aware that this required a decisive shift in thought and policy by existing 'progressive' politicians. Many of them, such as Thomas Jones, later to earn some fame as deputy secretary to the Cabinet of four inter-war prime ministers and as a supreme fixer and networker, were heavily influenced by neo-idealist philosophy, which laid a great stress on the role of the state in moral and social improvement. This was often combined, as with Daniel Lleufer Thomas, the stipendary magistrate for the Rhondda, with a genuine sympathy for the broad aspirations of organized labour, and a desire to see Welsh Nonconformity shift its emphasis from individual salvation to broader social concerns. They were anxious to preserve the ideals of community within existing radical thought, often articulated on the basis of an idealized notion of harmonious relations within Welsh rural society, which they wished to see re-established in urban and industrial Wales. What distinguished this loose coterie was their willingness to contemplate assaults on the main shibboleths of Liberal economic thinking, to appease the emerging anti-capitalist ethos within the ranks of organized labour.[21] It usually took the form of ideas of co-operative control or co-ownership of enterprises, or even evolved into 'corporatist' notions of institutionalizing relations between capital and labour, but they were major departures from the free-market ideology of classic Liberal economic thought. In their own way this grouping helped to reinforce and legitimize the spread of an anti-capitalist sentiment and to assist in the growth of state socialist ideology within the Welsh labour movement.

Before 1914 these ideas made little impact on the main body of Welsh Liberal politicians who did not feel the need to appease organized labour but simply to contain its political ambitions and, on occasion, to confront working-class militancy. However, in the inter-war years this social radical coterie was to be profoundly influential within the labour movement and in the various voluntary and state responses to the economic crises which afflicted Wales. Nevertheless, the years just before the outbreak of war saw unprecedented industrial unrest in Wales. This is not the place to detail this discontent, which was seen at the time in the popular press as indicating a decisive shift in the temper of an industrial area which, the Chartist era aside, up to the late nineteenth century was not automatically seen as one of the great storm centres in the relations between capital and labour. The search for explanations for this break with the Lib-Lab assumptions of mutuality, sliding scales and conciliation inevitably focused on the spread of ideas. They did not have to look too far to find the 'men of intellect and the men of action' who were 'behind' the unrest.[22] By 1910 there existed a cadre of activists within the miners' union imbued with a deep sense of class consciousness, absorbing a developed Marxist critique of capitalism (what they always called 'scientific' socialism) and a belief in the mission of the organized working class to overthrow capitalism. Through the influence of charismatic and inspirational figures, such as Noah Ablett and A. J. Cook, they established a tradition of militancy and direct action within the south Wales miners which was to remain with them almost until the recent effective demise of the industry. These men, combining the arts of leaders and teachers, challenged not just the old 'progressive' consensus, but the logic of old-style trade unionism and its leadership. Their mission was not to improve the workers' lot under the capitalist system but to attack and change the system itself. It was a view which saw the common ownership of the mines in terms of workers' control rather than the state ownership advocated by some of the other 'socialist' leaders within the Federation.[23] In fact, whilst the presence of the semi-syndicalistic activists gave a slightly revolutionary tinge to the events in the coalfield in the years just prior to the First World War and they enjoyed being identified by the capitalist press as the authors of the discontent, they were a symptom and not a cause of the unrest. Changes within the structure of the coal industry made conflict with the owners almost inevitable, and the older union leaders were losing the initiative, their 'progressive' rhetoric and solutions finding less and less support amongst the activists. However, the debate was not 'won' by the direct action men: rather there was an ongoing debate. Charismatic leaders such as Ablett converted many later leaders to a Marxist critique of capitalism but few became simon-pure syndicalists and state socialism, especially nationalization, became the objective of most of the rising generation of socialist labour leaders in Wales. Noah Ablett was a key figure in the foundation of the Marxist alternative to the WEA, the Labour College movement, and its journal *Plebs*. His closest ally in building support for the new movement in south Wales was Ted Gill. Although Gill accepted the Marxian critique of capitalism he eschewed notions of workers' control, and in a well-known debate with Ablett at Trealaw in 1912, Gill attacked what he saw as the impracticality and ideological illusions of its advocates.[24]

Ablett and Gill had attended Ruskin College in Oxford together, and upon their return to south Wales in 1908 both became active in the local labour movement. Both devoted much of their time to raising the political consciousness of their fellow workers. Through his writings and his classes Ablett entrenched Marxism within key elements of the miners' leadership in south Wales. Gill, however, sought to provide a platform for debate, to tap into the ferment of ideas which swirled around Wales in the years before the outbreak of war. In 1909, Gill helped establish the New Era Union in Abertillery. This organization was, in many ways, very representative of the state of popular political debate in south Wales in the late Edwardian era. The 'superintendent' of this body was a local Baptist preacher dismissed for promoting a 'social' rather than an individual salvationist gospel. It sought in the words of its press publicity written by Gill and the local miners' agent and future Labour MP for the area, George Barker, to help 'through true thought, and Scientific methods' to create a more just society. It rejected 'dogmatic creeds' and aimed instead at making 'intelligence victorious over unreason, universal love over individual selfishness, true civilization over brutality and savagery'. Classes in Marxist economics and sociology were combined with visits from 'social' gospel preachers; even those bringing the messages of Marxist 'scientific' socialism couched their language in the rhetoric of the chapel. Frank Hodges, a leading militant and protégé of Ablett at the time, delivered an address on 'The religion of social democracy' which would give the workers a 'Kingdom' of social democracy on earth, its 'Redeemer' being the 'conscious social organization of labour'. One week in 1913 saw a talk by a vicar from Bristol suggesting that the Established Church, rescued from 'Mammon', could be a vehicle for socialism and a few days later Guy Bowman stated that political action of any kind by the workers' movement was a waste of time and argued instead for a war of 'sabotage' against the agencies of capitalism. It was a rigorously and relentlessly anti-capitalist diet. That was not uncommon in the urban and industrial centres of Wales. The rhetoric was changing but it was a subtle change, long on critique but diverse and disparate when it came to solutions.[25]

Wales entered the war with the Liberal Party still very much in the ascendancy in both national and local government, with islands of independent labour representation and limited and diverse socialist penetration of its political consciousness. It ended with the Liberal Party deeply, possibly fatally, divided and with independent labour representation making significant advances in both local and national government. Nothing perhaps illustrates the scale of the change better than the career of Vernon Hartshorn, the miners' agent for the Maesteg district who failed to break down popular prejudice against Labour men and socialists in the pre-war political culture of Wales. In the general election of 1918 he was returned unopposed for what was effectively the same seat which had rejected him in the bitter election battles of 1910. It was a personal triumph for Hartshorn but it reflected deep shifts in the political culture, especially of industrial Wales, in the war years.[26] It is always difficult to assess the impact of a major war. Because, after hostilities have ended, circumstances appear to have changed from pre-war years, it is too tempting to assume that the war was exclusively, or even in large part, responsible for those changes.

Nowhere is this problem better highlighted than in the Welsh political landscape of 1914 compared with that of 1918.

The war experience was not one which automatically benefited the Labour Party. Its outbreak exposed profound differences over the war within the leadership of the party. As is well known, the outbreak of the European war shattered Keir Hardie and his death in 1915 made those problems even more pronounced with the return of the former left-wing miners' agent for Aberdare, C. B. Stanton, as a rampant anti-pacifist, and pro-war candidate for Hardie's former seat in Merthyr. His defeat of James Winstone, the moderate ILP socialist, the acting SWMF president and miners' agent for the Pontypool area, seemed to indicate that the ILP activists had lost much ground because of their hostility to, or lukewarm support for, the war effort. Certainly there is no evidence that opposition to the war, as such, was very strong amongst the Welsh working class.[27] Army recruitment from the ranks of the south Wales miners, already seen as amongst the most militant and politically conscious workers in Britain, was, if anything, above the average. However, the war was to have a dramatic impact on relations between capital and labour in Wales, as it did in most countries caught up in the conflict. Successful prosecution of the war required a compliant workforce, especially in those industries such as coal, steel and rail transport on which a modern 'total' conflict depended. When patriotic fervour gradually gave way to a more critical pattern of genuine support for the men at the 'Front', questions were asked about who was making the sacrifices and who was benefiting from the conflict.[28]

The slow but very perceptible rise of an anti-capitalist ethos amongst working-class political and union activists in industrial Wales before the war, was given a significant boost by the war and immediate post-war experience.[29] Yet here again the process was neither simple nor straightforward. Even amongst those within the labour movement hostile to the war there were differences about why the conflict was wrong. Some, such as John Thomas, an ILP member and the first full-time organizer for the WEA in Wales, argued that the war transgressed his ethical and religious principles. He did not have an easy time and was exiled from his home area to undertake farm work, but he avoided prison. A similar fate befell David Thomas, the leading light of the ILP and the WEA in Gwynedd. Those, such as Mark Starr (a product of the Labour

College movement), who argued that the war was a capitalist and imperialist endeavour, hostile to the interests of the workers, received even less consideration. Telling his court martial that he wanted to fill the workers' heads with ideas rather than 'blow them off' earned Starr a period of reflection in Wormwood Scrubs prison.[30] These differences of perspective on the war mirrored other ideological conflicts on the left that became even more pronounced as the effects of the war on the lives and aspirations of the working class in Wales became more and more profound. If the bulk of the Welsh working class never abandoned their initial support for the war effort, they became increasingly sceptical about issues of equality of sacrifice. War profiteering reinforced an underlying gut hostility to the employing classes and anti-capitalist rhetoric could now be flavoured with the suggestion that in many ways the capitalists were unpatriotic. The need for the state to step in to end abuses, that taxation policy should be used to deprive the profiteers of their tainted gains and that the workers' interests should come before those of the financiers and rentiers, were ideas which resonated amongst the mass of Welsh workers in a way which they did not before 1914. Yet, the left was neither consistent nor coherent in its response to this new atmosphere. From about 1916 the exigencies of war had changed the relative bargaining power of capital and labour and the state was obliged to come to terms with a more assertive and demanding trade union movement. Often only patriotic restraints prevented direct challenges to the existing order. Rationing, rent controls and the direct state control of key industries rode over the shibboleths of free-market capitalism. The state could be seen as an agency for social improvement and the process lent more and more credibility to arguments of the state socialists. Nationalization of the commanding heights of the economy, and the use of the apparatus of the state to secure a more equitable distribution of the wealth of the nation, became a realistic concept and a realizable policy objective in a way that it was not before 1914. Yet by the late war period the advocates of state socialism were already being outflanked by those arguing for a much more radical assault on the existing social and political order. 'Scientific' socialism which had fingernailed its way into the arena of activist debate in Wales before the war, was now being more actively and broadly canvassed. By 1916 the Labour College movement was able to tap into a widespread feeling that the capitalist system was in a state of crisis, that the war exposed the nature of the system and that the state, forced to intervene in the economy more and more to sustain the war effort, was either about to expose its coercive class oppression role, or could be seized by the workers to bring in a new social and economic order. George Barker, the miners' agent for the Western Valleys of Monmouthshire, who, along with Ted Gill, had denounced the concept of workers' control of the mines as 'lunatic' in 1912, by 1917 was arguing that 'The industrial worker of the coming generation will be intellectually equipped, not for "Collective Bargaining" with his employer, but for taking over and controlling his own industry.'[31] By November 1917 over 1,200 workers in industrial south Wales were attending Labour College classes and being imbued with a Marxist view of the world. The Bolshevik revolution was to stimulate excitement and interest in revolutionary doctrines and was to reshape the world-view of many within the organized working class in Wales.[32]

Yet dramatic as the later war years were, it is unwise to overstate the revolutionary climate of the time. Hostility to anti-war campaigners among rank-and-file workers remained strong. The credibility and acceptability of 'Labour' men as candidates for public office came from their inclusion within the political system, not from their rejection of it. This was pointed out at the time by left-wing critics of 'scientific' socialism, who were especially scathing about the 'pedantic, narrow, doctrinaire young men' who peddled 'formulae' rather than policies.[33] The irony is that, despite the spread of 'scientific' socialism, the late war period saw the triumph of the ILP strategy pursued in Wales since the turn of the century. The claim by the young apostles of Marx that they were responsible for a fundamental shift in the political outlook of the industrial workers of Wales brought derision from more orthodox advocates of independent labour politics. Keir Hardie's son-in-law, Emrys Hughes, pointed out that such advances as had been made by organized labour owed far more to the ground-breaking labours of ILP activists over previous decades than to the revolutionary posturing of the Labour College classes.[34] This shift was also due to the war experience. The term 'profiteer' came into regular usage at this time and linked patriotic feelings with anti-capitalist sentiment. State socialist or even 'corporatist' solutions to the problems of society gained credibility, as did many personalities

associated with organized labour. When the government appointed
a commission of inquiry into the industrial unrest which afflicted
industrial Wales in the late war period, its chairman was D. Lleufer
Thomas and its secretary was Edgar Chappell, both members of
the social radical coterie which had sought to foster Welsh
progressivism in the pre-war era.[35] The leading labour member of
the commission was Vernon Hartshorn, already the acceptable face
of socialist labourism amongst the populace and the political
élites. The commission detected a steady deterioration in relations
between capital and labour, and sought solutions which would
humanize and harmonize such relationships, through more state
intervention and the institutionalization of employer/employee
negotiations.[36] Even in semi-official publications the shift to an
anti-capitalist ethos could be detected. Not a new socialist order
but not free-market capitalism either; these ideas were ultimately
rejected by both sides in the bitter battles of strike, lock-out and
chronic joblessness which were to make industrial Wales a
'problem' area in the inter-war years.

By 1918 the initiative in Welsh politics was to be with men such
as Hartshorn: they understood the language of the new era, they
had the credibility within their communities, they had the
organizations of labour behind them; just as the old agencies of
popular Liberalism rotted at the roots from leadership splits at the
top. The older, fragmented patterns of political behaviour amongst
the Welsh working class did not disappear, especially in the febrile
political atmosphere at the end of the war. The Bolshevik revolution frightened many more Welsh voters into a reactionary cast of
mind than it inspired those who wished to emulate their Russian
counterparts. Rather the war reinforced a process which allowed
Labour to inherit the traditions of Welsh working-class radicalism
as easily as former Lib-Lab miners' MPs such as Mabon, William
Brace and Thomas Richards were returned unopposed as Labour
men in 1918. The legacy of progressivism was also carried into the
new political culture by the social radical élites that had emerged in
the Edwardian Wales and that were personified by Thomas Jones.
He rejected the rhetoric of class conflict but endorsed the idealism
of the Labour Party. The Liberal Party, divided at the top and
struggling to reposition itself in relation to the emergence of
Labour as a possible party of government, often opted for an anti-
Labour and anti-socialist stance. Increasingly it was seen as a party

of the right, of the defensively minded middle classes. In industrial south Wales, when the miners' aspirations were broken on the wheel of decontrol and an employers' assault on their wages and conditions, then Labour, with its state-socialist policies and its army of activists with their anti-capitalist rhetoric and their class-conscious vocabulary, offered the only viable alternative in the changed political culture of the inter-war years. In rural Wales the process was more protracted and Liberalism remained a force in popular politics. Personalities still counted for much but, with the greatly expanded electorates, organization counted for far more. The face-to-face, street-based electoral politics of the pre-1914 era were to give way to the politics of the national programme and the negative stereotyping of the press-based 'scare' stories. The political influence of the chapels was eroded further by the war experience when able and articulate ministry-bound young men abandoned the pulpit. In 1915 the future communist and miners' leader Arthur Horner found the ability of so many preachers to abandon 'the Prince of Peace' for the god of 'patriotism' too much and Noah Ablett was to complete his conversion to a different world-view.[37] Biblical language withered in political debate and the rhetoric of class conflict and revolutionary change became more common. Of course such usages alienated as well as converted, reinforcing fear as well as hope. But the agencies of organized labour in Wales were firmly in the hands of those that used the new vocabulary of progress with ease and, just as often, with conviction.

Notes

[1] A. G. Jones, *Press, Politics and Society: A History of Journalism in Wales* (Cardiff, 1993).

[2] Ibid., 138–41; D. Hopkin, 'The rise of Labour in Wales, 1890–1914', *Llafur*, VI/3 (1994).

[3] The leading light of Marxist workers' education in south Wales, Noah Ablett, had no doubt about the pivotal role of the activist 'for in the present loose democracy of the trade unions, individuals count for much', *Plebs* (Feb. 1909).

[4] Hopkin, 'Rise of Labour', 125–34; P. Stead, 'Working-class leadership in south Wales, 1900–1920', *WHR*, VI/3 (1973); D. Howell, *British Workers and the Independent Labour Party, 1888–1906* (Manchester, 1983), 241–53; C. Williams, *Democratic Rhondda: Politics and Society, 1885–1951* (Cardiff, 1996), 56–82; C.

Parry, *The Radical Tradition in Welsh Politics: A Study of Liberal and Labour Politics in Gwynedd, 1900–1920* (Hull, 1970), 22–44.

[5] Stead, 'Working-class leadership', 331–3; Williams, *Democratic Rhondda*, 31.

[6] W. R. Lambert, *Drink and Sobriety in Victorian Wales, c.1820–c.1895* (Cardiff, 1983), 247–54.

[7] K. O. Morgan, *Rebirth of a Nation: Wales 1880–1980* (Oxford and Cardiff, 1981), 134–55; D. Tanner, *Political Change and the Labour Party, 1900–1918* (Cambridge, 1990), 207–8.

[8] D. Gilbert, *Class, Community and Collective Action: Social Change in Two British Coalfields* (Oxford, 1992), 64–70; R. Pope, *Building Jerusalem: Nonconformity and the Social Question in Wales, 1906–1939* (Cardiff, 1998), 93.

[9] F. Hodges, *My Adventures as a Labour Leader* (London, 1925), 19–20; P. Davies, *A. J. Cook* (Manchester, 1987); A. Horner, *Incorrigible Rebel* (London, 1960), 14.

[10] J. Griffiths, *Pages from Memory* (London, 1969), 14; M. Foot, *Aneurin Bevan* (London, 1997), 19–20.

[11] N. Evans and K. Sullivan, ' "Yn llawn o dân Cymreig": the language of politics in Wales, 1880–1914', in G. H. Jenkins (ed.), *The Welsh Language and its Social Domains, 1801–1911* (Cardiff, 2000).

[12] Ibid.; Parry, *Radical Tradition*, 23–44; Pope, *Building Jerusalem*, 31–70. Financial constraints also played a part in preventing the production of much socialist propaganda in Welsh, see the correspondence between D. Thomas and the National Labour Press, Manchester, 17 Jan. 1913 (David Thomas MS, University of Wales, Bangor, 19182).

[13] Tanner, *Political Change*.

[14] P. Stead, 'Vernon Hartshorn: miners' agent and cabinet minister', in S. Williams (ed.), *Glamorgan Historian*, VI (1970), 89–91.

[15] R. M. Jones, *The North Wales Quarrymen, 1874–1922* (Cardiff, 1981), 295–321; Parry, *Radical Tradition*, 45–70.

[16] K. O. Morgan, 'The New Liberalism and the challenge of Labour: the Welsh experience', *WHR*, VI/3 (1973), 303. See also C. B. Turner, 'Conflicts of faith? Religion and Labour in Wales, 1890–1914', in D. R. Hopkin and G. S. Kealey (eds.), *Class, Community and the Labour Movement: Wales and Canada, 1850–1930* (Aberystwyth, 1989), 67–85; Pope, *Building Jerusalem*, 58–70.

[17] *SWDN*, 6 Dec. 1906.

[18] G. A. Williams, *The Welsh in their History* (London, 1982), 186.

[19] *Labour Pioneer, Organ of the Cardiff Socialist Society* (Oct. 1900); K. O. Morgan, *Wales in British Politics, 1868–1922* (Cardiff, 1963), 204; *Who's Who in Wales* (Cardiff, 1920).

[20] *SWDN*, 1 Dec. 1907.

[21] R. Lewis, 'The Welsh radical tradition and the ideal of a democratic popular culture', in E. F. Biagini (ed.), *Citizenship and Community: Liberals, Radicals and Collective Identities in the British Isles, 1865–1931* (Cambridge, 1996).

[22] A. J. Jenkinson, 'Reflections on a pamphlet entitled *The Miners' Next Step*', *Economic Review* (July 1912).

[23] D. Egan, ' "A cult of their own": syndicalism and *The Miners' Next Step*', in A. Campbell, N. Fishman and D. Howell (eds.), *Miners, Unions and Politics, 1910–47* (Aldershot, 1996).

[24] K. O. Morgan, 'Socialism versus syndicalism: the Welsh miners' debate, 1912', *Bulletin of the Society for the Study of Labour History*, XXX (1975).

[25] R. Lewis, *Leaders and Teachers: Adult Education and the Challenge of Labour in South Wales, 1906–1940* (Cardiff, 1993), 94–6.

[26] Stead, 'Vernon Hartshorn', 92.

[27] A. Mòr O'Brien, 'Patriotism on trial: the strike of the south Wales miners, July 1915', *WHR*, XII/1 (1984).

[28] B. Waites, *A Class Society at War: England 1914–18* (Leamington Spa, 1987), 55–75, 221–31.

[29] E. May, 'Charles Stanton and the limits to "Patriotic Labour"', *WHR*, XVIII/3 (1996).

[30] Lewis, *Leaders and Teachers*, 105, 121. Details of Thomas's conflicts with the military authorities can be found in the David Thomas MS (see n. 12) 19190.

[31] G. Barker, 'Foreword', in M. Starr, *A Worker Looks at History* (Oxford, 1917).

[32] Lewis, *Leaders and Teachers*, 113.

[33] *Merthyr Pioneer*, 29 June 1918.

[34] *Merthyr Pioneer*, 11 May 1918.

[35] Chappell had been editor of the monthly *Welsh Outlook* which mirrored the views of the social radical group which included Thomas Jones himself, an earlier editor. Chappell's radicalism often proved to be too advanced for the journal's financial backer, the Liberal MP and coalowner, David Davies. See T. L. Williams, 'Thomas Jones and the *Welsh Outlook*', *Anglo-Welsh Review*, 64 (1979), 38–46, also G. Jenkins, 'The *Welsh Outlook*, 1914–33', *National Library of Wales Journal*, XXXIV/4 (1986).

[36] *Commission of Enquiry Into Industrial Unrest, Division 7 (Wales and Monmouthshire)*, Cd. 8668 (1917).

[37] *Merthyr Pioneer*, 24 July 1915.

II
ESTABLISHING CONTROL

5

The Pattern of Labour Politics, 1918–1939

DUNCAN TANNER

There are two popular images of the Labour Party in Wales after 1918: Labour Wales, in which MPs were returned inevitably and with huge majorities; and radical Wales, where left-wing Labour parties challenged both Labour's own leaders and Tory governments. Neither image is entirely mythical. There were areas in or around the South Wales Coalfield where Labour expanded dramatically in the aftermath of war.[1] The South Wales Coalfield also spawned a series of crusading anti-establishment heroes, including Noah Ablett, Aneurin Bevan and S. O. Davies, and a rank and file with the socialist passion to protest against unemployment, fascism and war.[2] Yet there is another Wales, in both the geographical and political sense, which is too often neglected but which is equally important. In this Wales Labour was much less radical, its progress much less rapid. The lion had two heads; and only one of them roared.

Earlier chapters have noted Labour's limited and varied pre-war progress and its mixed ideological inheritance. This chapter builds on these and on works that have shown there is more to Welsh Labour than the politics of the coalfield.[3] It highlights the rather different political situation which existed in the little studied towns of the south *and* north Wales coasts and in the rural areas. At the same time, it is suggested that in both these areas and in the coalfield Labour was often less voluble, less triumphant and more concerned with delivering practical policies than the popular image might suggest. In the north and south, in coalfields and in tourist areas, Labour was organized by a small band of activists. There was much that these activists shared with each other and with the national leadership. In particular, they developed a 'practical socialism', a commitment to making real changes in the material world through direct intervention by the state. They also developed policy orientations which demonstrated how these material changes might be achieved, furthering and augmenting the ideological inheritance outlined by Richard Lewis in Chapter 4. This is not to deny the radical alternatives advocated by powerful currents within the Welsh labour and trade union world, nor the tensions which developed between 'moderates' and 'radicals' and between the Welsh left and London in the 1930s (which are also discussed below). It is not to suggest that Labour had answers for all the problems which Wales faced, or that its 'practical socialism' was uniquely effective or innovative. Within Labour politics there were divisions, deficiencies and failures. However, what Labour did well was more striking that what it did badly, the areas of agreement within the party were more significant than the examples of discord, at least until the later 1930s, and what Labour advocated was on the basis of reflective concern for the people. No other party in Wales could make the same claims, nor boast the same record.

The economic and social circumstances which faced Labour after the First World War provided both political opportunities and challenges.[4] Wales paid a heavy price for its dependence on coal, steel and agriculture. These sectors were subject to pronounced and escalating economic problems in the 1920s and 1930s. Over-capacity resulting from expansion during the First World War was followed by increased international competition, long-term decline and finally world slump. However, Wales's economic problems also created potential campaigning opportunities; in particular they seemed to demonstrate that Labour's critique of capitalism was valid. At the core of Labour's understanding of the world was the implicit assumption that capitalism produced cut-throat competition, unemployment and low wages. Labour politicians of all kinds routinely attacked the economic madness of unplanned capitalism during the war and in the 1920s. By the 1930s they had an answer: the planned restructuring of the Welsh economy.

High rates of unemployment – one of Labour's most pronounced concerns since before the war – had evident potential as an electoral issue. Agricultural prices and employment never really recovered after the war and crashed in 1922. Post-war unemployment rates in coalmining varied from more than 20 per cent in Glamorgan to half that in Wrexham, but they were high everywhere. Unemployment rates also ranged between 10 and 25 per cent in the south Wales coastal towns. In the 1930s, the position became famously worse. In industrial south Wales unemployment rates reached 32 per cent by 1930; they were to rise still higher, especially in the coalmining areas. In 1935 70 per cent of coalminers in Merthyr and Dowlais were unemployed. Nor was this a temporary problem. In Brynmawr, just one year earlier, investigations determined that nearly 60 per cent of miners had been unemployed for two years or more.

Social problems also provided potentially fertile ground for Labour propaganda. Surveys and reports undertaken in the 1930s – when the well-meaning descended on Welsh social problems in vast numbers – revealed a mixture of ill-health, poverty and social dislocation. Housing was a particular difficulty. By 1920 two-thirds of agricultural labourers' cottages in Wales were unfit for habitation. Moreover, pre-war overcrowding along the south coast had been intensified by wartime neglect and now reached crisis proportions.[5]

Notwithstanding these economic and social problems, Labour's electoral success was no more inevitable after 1918 than it had been before the war. The party faced considerable political competition. Even given Labour's political and social base in some mining areas before 1914 and the wartime events which reinforced its potential appeal, old political allegiances were still strong. This was not just a consequence of tradition, but of traditionalism. Labour challenged so many old ways of behaving and thinking, whether in fact or in the propaganda of its opponents, that recruitment was no easy matter in many parts of Wales. In north Wales, for example, Labour was portrayed as anti-religious, anti-Welsh, anti-national, anti-rural, opposed to the upward mobility of the small man. It was the sharp voice of a vulgar proletarianism, rising above its cultural and intellectual station and masquerading as the workers' party.[6] There were alternative images and allegiances which Labour could emphasize, and in mining areas at least it had some roots in people's experiences and loyalties. But the social bases of solidarity were much weaker outside the coalfield and were not wholly dominant within it. Nor did the diversity of Wales help. Labour

Table 5.1. Welsh constituencies held by the Labour Party, general elections
1918–1945

1918	1922	1923	1924	1929	1931	1935	1945
10	18	20	16	25	16	18	25

Note: There were 36 constituencies.
Source: F. W. S. Craig, *British Parliamentary Election Results 1918–49* (London, 1983).

had to create an appeal which was as relevant in Llandudno or Newtown as it was in Merthyr or Newport, despite both this diversity and localized fluctuations from the prevailing economic misfortunes of Wales as a whole. Even in the 1930s, there were areas where employment conditions were improving, or where new industry was altering economic and social prospects.

As Labour gained ground after 1918 it also faced the problem of its own success. Once it achieved office, in local and national government, it had to administer the system it had previously attacked. It was required to address the housing problems, provide the educational opportunities and services, tackle the consequences of mass unemployment. Party members were not content to let voters suffer; voters themselves expected Labour to be a practical and not simply a rejectionist party. Labour had to show it could make a difference whilst operating a system which it attacked and could not alter.

In part as a result of these problems, Labour's electoral domination of Wales developed gradually and by 1939 was still far from complete. As Table 5.1 indicates, it was only in 1929 and 1945 that Labour won an overwhelming majority of Welsh seats; generally it captured around half. Labour's organizational and electoral expansion also took place more slowly than one might think.

The period began inauspiciously, with the 'khaki' election. Fortunately for Labour it faced a divided Liberal opposition in 1918, for it had no established organizational and electoral presence even in some mining constituencies and internal differences over the war were often still unresolved.[7] In northern and rural Wales the position was even worse. Despite the enthusiasm of some activists and the evident progress made towards independence during the war, some unions proved hesitant. R. T. Jones of the Quarrymen's Union, for example, declined to stand as official Labour candidate in Caernarfonshire, thereby tactically avoiding identification with the 'pacifist' Independent Labour Party (ILP). Despite initial reservations the Anglesey Workers' Union supported the 'Independent Labour' candidate, Brigadier-General Sir O. Thomas (a former Liberal candidate for Oswestry who had been knighted for his work in recruiting soldiers and who lost two sons to the war).[8] In many rural seats Labour was unable to find candidates in 1918 and the older parties were unopposed.

After the election there was a frantic rush to establish ward committees, to select candidates for local government elections and especially to found local Labour newspapers.[9] Labour aimed to root itself in the concerns and lives of working-class communities. As Jim Griffiths wrote in the first issue of the *Llanelli Labour News*, the party wanted to be 'a faithful mirror of the life and struggles of the people'.[10] This meant campaigning for real improvements in services, from maternity clinics to better unemployment benefit and especially for better municipal housing provision. In Llanelli Labour believed provision of public housing was part of the state's 'social responsibility', a sentiment echoed across Wales.[11] In the industrial areas union branches and trades councils provided many of the leaders, much of the impetus and most of the money for new constituency organizations.

Individuals from within these organizations subsequently took the party forward, often acting independently of their union branch. In the post-war years, crusading pioneers became community leaders. Historians have rightly stressed the ethical drive which drove these pioneers to make considerable personal sacrifices in the interests of the 'cause'. Yet an idealistic commitment to Labour's creed was not confined to the south, nor to industrial workers. Educated individuals, often pacifists and declared socialists, played a vital part in expanding Labour's credibility and its organization after 1918. In the affluent and rural areas, the establishment of Labour organizations in 1918–19 was heavily dependent upon a handful of dedicated and often middle-class activists or trade union organizers. Examples include Caradog Jones, the ILP school teacher who organized Labour branches and the Lleyn agricultural labourers' union by travelling around the area on a bicycle, or E. P. Harries and Evan Anthony, who established and developed the Pembrokeshire Labour Party.[12]

Perhaps the best example, however, is the pacifist school teacher, Workers' Educational Association official and trade union organizer, David Thomas. Thomas had been active in Bangor ILP politics before the First World War. His pre-war attempt to root Labour in the values of Welsh-speaking Wales has attracted some attention; his post-war activities tell another important story.[13]

Like others who sat within a Welsh radical tradition which enthusiastically embraced chapel, literature and education, Thomas had been a conscientious objector during the war. Immediately after the war he threw himself into building a Labour infrastructure. He sought to organize Labour branches, to establish trade unions, village clubs, the North Wales Labour Federation and the network of contacts necessary to support Labour's aims. Even before 1914 he had recognized the need to 'keep in touch with local socialists and ensure that they are continually made to feel part of "Y frawdoliaeth" ' (the Brotherhood). Although he knew that waking up the agricultural districts was also a 'gorchwyl mawr iawn' (a huge undertaking), his commitment to that task was striking.[14]

Less practical, but also significant, was the support which Labour attracted from the preachers and poets of Welsh-speaking Wales. Labour's apparent hostility to a xenophobic British nationalism gave it an almost spiritual respectability in the eyes of some Welsh Nonconformists and allowed it to incorporate many of those rooted in the progressive reformist tradition. George Maitland Lloyd Davies, a good example of this type, described socialism in 1917 as a moral revolution which would prevent the hideous events of the recent past from ever being repeated:

> The only untried principles, the only parties in Europe whose objects have not been discredited by the war is that of Socialism. It is without doubt the political power of the future . . . I believe we may well see a spiritual revolution, a renaissance beyond our dreams, a veritable coming of the kingdom of love on earth.[15]

The Labour Party's London head office could afford little organizational assistance to Wales in 1918–19, so parties sought to support one another. Federations of constituency Labour parties were formed in both the north and south. The south Wales organizer, B. P. Watts, raised the question of merging these two

Table 5.2. *Seats contested by Labour, 1918–1945: mining and semi-mining constituencies, south Wales (% votes won)*

	1918	1922	1923	1924	1929	1931	1935	1945
Caerphilly	54.8	57.2	58.7	59.0	57.9	67.6	76.3	80.2
Gower	54.8	54.2	59.1	57.2	54.0	53.4	66.8	68.5
Neath	35.2	59.5	62.3	unop	60.2	64.0	unop	79.2
Ogmore	unop	55.8	unop	unop	56.7	61.0	unop	76.4
Pontypridd	42.8	47.2	54.9	55.9	53.1	58.3	unop	68.6
Aberdare	21.4	57.2	58.2	61.6	64.6	unop	unop	84.3
Merthyr Tydfil	47.3	53.0	60.1	59.8	59.6	69.4	68.0	81.4
Rhondda East	unop	55.0	71.9	unop	50.2	68.1	67.8	48.4
Rhondda West	unop	62.1	65.4	unop	65.1	84.3	unop	unop
Abertillery	unop	unop	unop	unop	64.5	unop	unop	86.6
Bedwellty	53.6	63.0	67.6	unop	79.0	unop	unop	82.1
Ebbw Vale	unop	65.4	65.6	unop	60.3	unop	77.8	80.1
Pontypool	39.0	40.6	50.6	52.6	51.5	56.3	67.9	77.3

Note: Bold type represents Labour victories. 'Unop' represents 'unopposed'.

sections into 'some sort of national council', arguing that 'the national sentiment for such a proposal exists'. He was supported by William Harris, secretary of the South Wales Labour Federation, a miners' organizer in Monmouthshire and member of the National Executive Committee (NEC). Harris insisted (successfully) on the appointment of an all-Wales organizer, and pushed (unsuccessfully) for the establishment of an all-Wales Advisory Council, similar to that granted to Scotland.[16] In these discussions about the devolution of institutional power within the Labour Party, the question of 'Home Rule all Round' was more than a subtext; it was a key concern. If the enthusiasm of Labour recruits like E. T. John for this policy is well-known, the enthusiasm of many in south Wales for addressing the 'national question' merits more attention.[17]

Labour organizers also recognized that in the new political world they needed to attract support from women. A women's organizer, Elizabeth Andrews, was appointed to encourage this. She established a series of women's advisory committees and regional federations to give women a clearer voice. By 1921 federations had met in six different locations in south and west Wales.[18]

The subsequent pattern of Labour expansion between 1918 and 1929 demonstrates both the enduring quality of the difficulties and the partial success of Labour's response. By 1929 Labour had made substantial progress in some areas at least. Table 5.2 shows that Labour MPs were returned for every seat with a substantial mining vote after 1918, although not with the huge majorities common since 1945. In the coalfield Labour built on deep social and industrial loyalties, blurring the distinctions between the union, Labour, the council, the working class, the community, even the chapel. Its impassioned support for communities during the 1926 dispute reinforced its moral authority. During the 1920s, miners' institutes and labour clubs became the bedrock of community life. Labour miners led and organized most activities. However, in the Rhondda and Tredegar at least, the party also tried to create its own political culture, featuring annual May Day celebrations (a declaration of labour's universal importance) and a welter of choirs, orchestras, education classes, children's outings and party dances and suppers. In Tredegar membership was opened out, with women and professionals (notably teachers) playing a role in the party. As frequently, individual membership was paid little attention or was even actively discouraged.[19] Sometimes a number of union branches did not even bother to affiliate; it was unnecessary.[20] Labour parties were often as élitist as the Liberals had been, and as dependent on a small circle of respected leaders rooted in community organizations. Labour assumed control of a great many local councils and became responsible for the delivery of services. In some mining areas during the 1920s it combined this with loud campaigns against unemployment and in favour of action on a variety of issues, notably against the exclusion of Russia from international trade. Labour was becoming the establishment and its support a political reflex. It did not have many members or much organization because it did not need them. The position was impregnable. Labour leaders became barons in one-party states.

Outside the South Wales Coalfield, however, Labour failed to replicate this position, even in the strongly industrial seats on the south Wales coast or in urban north Wales. As Table 5.3 indicates, only Swansea East and Llanelli consistently returned Labour MPs in

Table 5.3. Seats contested by Labour, 1918–1945: non-mining constituencies, south Wales (% votes won)

Constituency	No. of contests	1918	1922	1923	1924	1929	1931	1935	1945	by-election
Swansea East	10	36.4	**50.9**	**57.4**	**54.6**	**56.5**	**56.5**	**unop**	**75.8**	46.9 (1919); **unop (1940)**
Llanelli	9	46.9	**59.5**	**55.1**	**52.9**	**55.4**	**65.3**	**unop**	**81.1**	66.8 (1936)
Cardiff Central	8	22.4	29.4	32.0	33.8	**39.1**	30.8	36.7	49.1	
Cardiff East	8	28.5	31.4	32.7	32.8	**39.0**	31.8	37.8	**50.7**	
Cardiff South	8	26.3	31.4	37.9	40.3	**45.3**	40.2	49.1	**60.2**	
Newport	10	41.0	45.7	38.6	47.2	**39.5**	40.9	48.3	**54.2**	33.8 (1922); ILP 45.5 (1945)
Llandaff & Barry	9	30.8	30.4	27.0	43.3	**40.8**	39.3	48.7	**47.5**	I.Lab 40.3 (1942)
Carmarthen	11	–	–	24.8	31.5	**38.2**	36.4	**47.4**	48.3	28.8 (1924); 35.4 (1928); unop (1941)
Swansea West	8	25.6	32.1	**34.8**	33.4	**40.6**	41.5	47.1	**58.0**	

There was no Labour candidate in Carmarthen in 1918 or 1922. Bold type represents Labour victories.

Table 5.4. Seats contested by Labour, 1918–1945: urban constituencies, north Wales (% vote won)

Constituency	No. of contests	1918	1922	1923	1924	1929	1931	1935	1945	by-election
Wrexham	8	23.7	**35.8**	**39.0**	44.4	**46.4**	47.9	**56.3**	**56.0**	
Caernarfon Boroughs	9	–	–	–	17.5	15.8	–	–	30.6	– (1945)
Caernarfonshire	8	–	**53.0**	47.3	49.2	38.5	37.2	44.5	55.3	

Notes: Occupational information drawn from the 1921 and 1931 census. Caernarfonshire, a mixed seat, is included here because (quarry) mining villages were an important element in the constituency even in 1931. Bold type represents Labour victories.

the 1920s; in urban north Wales (Table 5.4) not even the mining constituency of Wrexham could boast the same record. Only in 1929 did Labour fare much better, winning most industrial seats and capturing a series of socially mixed urban seats for the first time.

Labour politics in the coastal seats of south and north Wales were in some ways very different from Labour politics in the coalfields. As in the coalfields, trade unions made important contributions at general elections. Union branches also pressurized councillors and selected and funded municipal candidates. But mass support was not 'delivered' by the unions, nor does it seem that union branches were as noticeable in other aspects of party life as were the miners' lodges. Much of the work was done by a small group of committed activists. These could be drawn from the National Union of Railwaymen, miners' unions or Transport and General Workers' Union, but frequently they were drawn from the ward committees. In Wrexham, for example, a solicitor and a teacher – Cyril O. Jones and Chris Davies – played a major role. In Caernarfonshire, there was the familiar alliance between professionals and individual union officials. Trade unions often paid affiliation fees sporadically, especially during trade depressions and local parties needed an individual membership and often ingenious fundraising to stay afloat. As the Swansea Executive Committee reported in 1927, 'our time is taken up trying to explore every channel to raise sufficient funds to meet our liabilities'.[21] Attempts to turn links with union officials into links with union members were frequently unsuccessful. It was difficult to replicate the 'Labour culture', based on union/Labour identification, which had been created in the coalfield. The labour halls set up in urban centres like Pontypridd and Cardiff did not play the same part as the miners' institutes, although they tried (and incurred huge debts as a result).[22] Where labour clubs and halls were strong (as in Newport) they could be a source of revenue and members. Yet the party was not usually at the centre of community life in quite the same way as it was in the coalfields, nor as respected and as authoritative in the eyes of union members. If May Day demonstrations could be successful spectacles, brass band and choral concerts and related cultural and social activities were often poorly supported by the trade union rank and file. The Llanelli sports day organized in 1932 'could not be termed successful in view of the poor attendance'. In Swansea children attended galas and Christmas treats every year, 'but the parents kept away' and took 'very little interest' in membership campaigns.[23] Even the May Day demonstration held at Newport in 1926 was a failure 'owing to the trade union branches taking no action'. Following a similar failure in 1928 the secretary criticized 'the apathy on the part of the trade union movement in relation to the political party'.[24]

Savage's seminal study of Labour's inter-war development in the constituencies contends that labour clubs enabled the party to become established as a 'neighbourhood' organization, with strengths outside the union/party relationship.[25] The unusually full records for Newport show that in some wards such clubs drew a large section of the population into the party's ambit through their dances and social activities. Alongside this (and unlike the position in Savage's case-study of Preston) Newport's Labour Party organized successful daytime meetings for women. By 1924 the women's section was 'one of the chief driving forces of the party'. As a result of these twin activities Newport had the largest individual membership in Wales, was amongst the largest parties in the UK and was fêted by national leaders and other constituency Labour parties as an organizational model.[26]

Although the Llandaff and Barry Labour Party made similar strides, few other Labour parties in Wales had a substantial individual membership, or clubs and women's sections which were quite so successful. One alternative method of securing support (used with dramatic success across London between 1928 and 1935) was the establishment and mass delivery of free Labour newspapers. Welsh Labour saw the value of this but its Labour newspapers lurched from one crisis to another, surviving on the credit of printers and the hard work of a tiny editorial team. The Swansea, Merthyr, Caernarfon and Llanelli publications collapsed in the 1920s. Papers started in north-east Wales and the Rhondda in the 1930s suffered a similar fate.[27] Having a national paper – the *Daily Herald* – was no compensation. Its circulation in Wales was low and party members were sometimes reluctant to promote further sales.[28] Neither the approach identified by Savage nor that practised in London were simply replicated in Wales. Other explanations for Labour's successful expansion need to be advanced.

Labour's national programme was inevitably part of Welsh Labour's 'constructive' image. Head office expected local parties to disseminate this message but often MPs, candidates or the election agent were expected to fill this role (and many others) by the local branches. Conflicts ensued when they failed to do so.[29] Outdoor meetings and propaganda campaigns on national issues were generally unpopular with party members. The Llanelli propaganda committee noted not untypically in 1921 that 'prominent Labour councillors and Labour workers were fighting shy of the open air meetings'.[30] There were often too few party workers for canvassing or literature distribution to be carried out thoroughly. Mass meetings involving major outside speakers were a different matter. The grand theatre of the public meeting remained popular. Weaker parties complained when not supplied with a 'star turn' by head office (or when the star turn failed to materialize).[31] Mass meetings demonstrated that Labour had arrived but they were not especially effective as a means of communicating Labour's message.

Labour parties in urban north and south Wales developed their roots during the 1920s by addressing real problems faced by ordinary people. The focus of much local party activity were the annual municipal elections and the unglamorous process of raising funds, finding candidates, developing a municipal programme and ensuring its implementation. The process was often haphazard. Policy was far from uniform (nor was it always implemented as activists thought it should be). None the less, the intentions and the message were broadly consistent.

Labour policies and propaganda did not of themselves create mass support. They helped reinforce or create an image in the voters' minds; they made its claims to be the workers' party seem credible. The huge majorities of some Labour councillors and MPs in the later 1920s were a clear indication of the party's now socially rooted electoral support. Labour did not entirely create class loyalty but it certainly used it as an electoral tool.

Although Labour had expanded its support in the industrial and semi-mining constituencies in both north and south Wales by 1929, it was unable to achieve the same level of electoral success which it managed in the coalfield. As Table 5.5 indicates, Labour's majorities were surprisingly small in many industrial and semi-mining constituencies between 1918 and 1924. Moreover, Labour failed to achieve control of town councils in industrial boroughs like Swansea and Caerphilly until the late 1920s, whilst other councils in these areas did not fall to Labour until the 1930s or later. Labour performed so much better in 1929 because, in addition to roots in working-class urban areas, it had absorbed enough of a progressive radical appeal to be a credible party of the 'intellectual' middle classes.[32]

None the less the appeal developed between 1918 and 1929 had not so broadened Labour's image that it had become the party of all Wales. In rural and semi-rural Welsh seats, Labour was much less successful, even though it did better in 1929 than in previous

Table 5.5. Labour election performance, 1922–1924: selected seats

Constituency	Election	Size of Labour majority
Pontypool	1922	2544
Swansea East	1922	407
Swansea West	1923	115
Gower	1922	2086
Llanelli	1924	2259
Wrexham	1922	1098
	1923	1881

Table 5.6. Seats contested by Labour, 1918–1945: rural and semi-rural Wales
(% vote won)

Constituency	No. of contests	1918	1922	1923	1924	1929	1931	1935	1945	by-election
Pembrokeshire	8	28.0	31.0	27.7	23.4	26.9	–	27.6	49.8	
Monmouth	10	–	–	–	28.2	24.9	29.2	36.6	48.1	25.0 (1934); 39.9 (1939)
Brecon and Radnor	9	–	32.6	–	30.5	**33.7**	40.2	47.4	**46.8**	53.4 (1939)
Cardiganshire	9	–	–	–	–	–	24.0	38.9	36.2	19.2 (1932)
Montgomery	8	–	–	–	22.7	14.8	–	–	–	
Merioneth	8	–	41.7	39.5	33.1	32.5	32.6	35.2	35.4	
Anglesey	9	(ILab)	(ILab)	–	36.1	28.4	–	27.6	47.8	30.5 (1923)
Denbigh	8	16.7	–	–	–	–	–	14.3	28.7	
Flintshire	8	–	16.2	–	19.1	22.0	28.6	27.2	37.4	

Note: Pembrokeshire, Denbigh and Flintshire are included here although they contained a large but not entirely dominant rural population.

elections (Table 5.6). It had not developed the institutional structures or the ideas which could help it tackle this weakness and broaden its image.

In areas like Caernarfonshire, where quarrymen and railwaymen were well-represented, commentators had hoped Labour might 'sweep the county' in 1918. However, by the end of 1919 there was still 'little mutual understanding, still less co-operation' between the unions. The explanation was clear: 'the rank and file are prepared neither to pay for their politics nor to give unquestioned allegiance to their own selected candidates'. There were similar problems in Pembrokeshire, where the existence of a disparate union base was again seen as a source of potential strength. Once again, formal union support was not enough. Other supporters had to carry the load. 'It is really surprising to find the people who join our movement', wrote the local secretary; 'schoolmasters, tradesmen etc form a part of every District Committee.' A school teacher himself, he went on to reveal the extent of Labour's problem and the central role of the dedicated activist in sprawling rural constituencies: 'Addressing four meetings after school last week I had to cover over 60 miles in a side-car.'[33] After the agricultural wages board was abolished and rural confidence diminished, the role of urban missionaries became even more pronounced. Unsurprisingly many rural seats went uncontested by Labour candidates until 1923 or 1924.

The problems facing Labour in rural seats is well illustrated by the position in Brecon and Radnor, in social composition the most favourable of these constituencies. Typically Labour responded to the problem of its limited roots by selecting a wealthy, moderate, parliamentary candidate with rural interests. The ex-Liberal MP, E. T. John, lavished money on paid subagents, a full-time organizer and expert agricultural speakers. On the advice of one, the Revd Gordon Lang, he sought support from prominent community leaders in the smaller rural villages. Lang reported on the gratifying success of the campaign in attracting ministers and influential people to public meetings.[34] None the less, E. T. John's approach failed to create a powerful organization rooted in popular support. As John's successor as candidate, the businessman Peter Freeman, learnt, it was difficult to break down rural tradition, especially given Labour's own organizational weakness. With small local parties strewn across a diverse constituency there was little commitment to the divisional organization and the candidate was expected to cover the gaps. Having industrial elements in the constituency helped but maintaining their enthusiasm when rural interests had to be stressed in the parliamentary campaign was not easy. In 1939 the South Wales Miners' Federation had to remind its members in Brecon and Radnor: 'it is just as important to the miners and their families to secure the election of Labour members for agricultural and other constituencies as it is to elect federation MPs for mining divisions.'[35] Freeman and his election agent, the future Lord Watkins, made huge personal contributions, including funding and writing a local election sheet. Following NEC policy, Freeman asked for some local financial contribution towards his mounting costs. The Divisional Labour Party (truthfully) pleaded poverty, having once again failed to extract money from the branches. It suspended its activities and attacked Freeman, stating: 'the present position is largely due to the amount received from you not being up to expectations.'[36] Labour branch parties had not cracked the problem of traditionalism nor established Labour's practical worth. Nor could a lone if enthusiastic and wealthy candidate compensate for Labour's limited roots within rural communities. Here, as in similar seats across Britain, the 'solution' augmented internal problems.

In similar manner, Labour made only partial progress with the progressive middle classes and Welsh-speaking intelligentsia during the 1920s. The *Welsh Outlook* and the existence of middle-class Labour activists demonstrated that such groups were not essentially anti-socialist.[37] The 'progressive' radicalism outlined by Richard Lewis did not disappear. Yet problems remained. If E. T. John, George Maitland Lloyd Davies and other Welsh-speaking nationalists retained their faith in Labour as the party of international fellowship, reason, moral progress and Welsh nationalism, their doubts on particular matters were felt more keenly by others.[38] Even more than in England, pressure groups, 'good causes' and Liberalism provided a counter-attraction, whilst a 'non-political' enthusiasm for preserving Welsh culture was an additional vehicle for demonstrating social concern.

Labour faced serious obstacles in attempting to broaden its appeal to this constituency. There was still no single policy forum for the whole of Wales which could engage highly educated activists who wanted to use their talents within the party. Policy committees were mooted but little seems to have materialized. Regional federations never really played this role; indeed, the NEC was so concerned about creating power bases for constituency radicals that it consciously restricted the federations' activities.[39] The South Wales Labour Federation formed after the war was soon moribund. The North Wales Labour Federation became a channel for specific grievances (the need for material in Welsh, an all-Wales advisory committee, rural campaigns, a Welsh edition of the *Daily Herald* and a north Wales organizer). Its annual meetings were important to weaker branches but unlike the county Labour federations in south Wales, it could not even divert workers from 'strong' to 'weak' areas.[40] There were too few members even in the stronger seats within north Wales and little enthusiasm for the task.[41] Middle-class members in weaker areas became isolated.

Expanding the party's base was not easy. Labour's small team of Welsh organizers could not fill the gaps noted above. Nor could they make male-dominated local parties take women (or the young) as seriously as they wished. This was not for want of trying, nor of tactical acumen. Labour's chief woman organizer, Elizabeth Andrews, portrayed herself as a 'Labour woman' rather than a feminist. Like Rose Davies, the first ever woman county councillor in Glamorgan and a powerful figure in the coalfield, she encouraged female involvement in all areas of policy but thought issues such as the provision of nursery schools and of advice on birth control should be paid considerable attention by the whole party.[42] It would be wrong to dismiss Labour's efforts in this direction. There were seats where women were strongly represented at executive level in the 1920s. Labour councils were not necessarily unsympathetic on many matters which concerned women (especially maternity and child welfare). Nor was Labour policy necessarily unattractive to women voters, even when it did not have a 'feminist' tinge. However, Andrews and Davies were brave campaigners in a very masculine world, not powerful and respected elements in a national Welsh leadership which included and considered women. In the constituencies similarly strong-minded characters often fought hard against the limits imposed by the party and its local leaders. Labour's appeal and organization had been broadened by 1929, but the party was still firmly rooted in a male working-class culture.

In the 1930s Labour faced a new challenge. Mass unemployment indicated, to Labour activists, the inadequacy of capitalism as a means of delivering a decent and respectable lifestyle. However, the consequences of unemployment and the threat of fascism in Europe underlined the need for a constructive alternative to be placed before the voters. Labour had conspicuously failed to provide this when in government between 1929 and 1931. It would need to find new ideas or new resolve if it was to meet the challenge.

The response of the Labour left in Wales to the crisis of the 1930s has been well-documented.[43] Coalfield Labour parties refused to accept what they saw as moderate and vacillating NEC policies. The SWMF led demonstrations against the Means Test in 1935 and called for mass opposition to the policy of non-intervention in Spain. Many were willing to accept the Communist Party as allies and form a Popular Front against fascism. Militancy and extra-parliamentary action were a significant part of a dramatic chapter in Labour's history.

Outside the coalfield, Labour was hardly classically 'moderate', at least in south Wales. There had been support for the ILP's 'living wage' policies in the 1920s, despite the collapse of ILP membership in Wales.[44] Some parties had refused to expel Communists when ordered to do so by the NEC.[45] Only Bedwellty emulated the Poplar councillors in their revolt against government restrictions on unemployment benefit payments, but strong and radical views were regularly expressed on this and other issues by parties outside the coalfields. By the 1930s, calls for extensive nationalization and for the socialization of credit were common across Wales. In north Wales the Wrexham party shifted substantially to the left and a north Wales strategy document called for 'a bold and comprehensive socialist policy', instead of 'flirting with Financial autocrats and a policy of subordination to the Money Kings and Banks'.[46]

For a time the NEC lost the initiative. It was not that London was opposed to fighting on issues like the Means Test and Spain (on the contrary, it was increasingly developing its own campaigns); but organizers were concerned that any initiative on these matters in south Wales would inevitably include the Communists. Whilst London prevaricated, the SWMF backed Stafford Cripps's call for a United Front and later a Popular Front against fascism.[47] Support for this was not confined to the coalfields. In Pontypool, Cardiff and Swansea, for example, the Communist Party and the Socialist League had permeated the constituency parties.[48] In Swansea rank-and-file activists thought the NEC's Victory for Socialism campaign in 1934 too moderate; by contrast a door-to-door collection for Spanish Aid Relief raised nearly £300 and there was massive support for a demonstration addressed by Stafford Cripps. Swansea delegates deemed a conference on election strategy in 1939 a failure, 'The National Party being apparently unaware of the feeling in South Wales regarding the Means Test, Munitions and Rearmament, Distressed Areas and Spain'.[49] There was even more conflict in Pontypridd. Many members caught up in the fight against fascism, militarism and war sought to co-operate with the Communist Party through Council of Action committees and mass rallies.

But should coalfield 'militancy' mould our image of Labour across Wales in the 1930s? And should we see those parties which took a different line as pale reflections of their dramatic coalfield neighbours? There was another and less well-known side to Labour politics in Wales during the 1930s, which gradually developed into an alternative approach. Initially Labour's support for a practical and constructive socialism coexisted with the 'militant' approach advocated by the SWMF. Labour's attempt to develop practical municipal programmes in the 1920s has already been noted. By 1931, 'practical' measures meant making hard and distinctly non-socialist choices. Labour councillors were forced to discuss economies, sometimes opting to cut teachers' salaries or discourage women from working to ensure there was 'one wage per family'.[50] Generally, however, Labour councillors tried to protect employment, notably through direct labour schemes. Trade unions valued and supported these endeavours. In Newport, for example, the Labour Group, party leaders and unions were brought closer together, as the party attacked attempts by the dock, tram and railway companies to shed jobs.[51] This did not necessarily mean abandoning those welfare issues which had helped Labour to expand in the 1920s, contrary to Savage's suggestion. His second point – that 'neighbourhood' welfare issues were more prominent where women were especially active within the Labour Party – merits more attention. The Newport example seemingly supports his hypothesis, since strong female representation on the Executive Committee coincided with lengthy discussions of matters which were not traditional male concerns.[52] However, the union-dominated Swansea Labour Party also developed a municipal strategy which involved a large housing initiative, slum clearance, ward clinics to improve maternity and child welfare and provision of a central municipal hospital 'as a priority over other central services'. Membership amongst women and on the council estates had grown but neither group was as powerful as other sections of the party. Electoral realities, civic pride, changing circumstances and control of the council had also helped to generate Labour's concern with such issues.[53] Its rounded programme embraced concern for both employment and for social welfare.

A further component of Labour's practical and constructive emphasis was the need to attract new industries to Wales. The Depressed Areas Bill in 1934 focused discussion. Pontypridd established a subcommittee to develop a response, since they were 'in favour of new industries being set up in the area'.[54] Not that they or others were sanguine about the prospects. Oliver Harris for the SWMF accepted that pits would close and that new industries must be bought in but regarded the government's effort to do so as half-hearted. He advocated industrial planning and job-sharing – a reduction of the working week, retirement at sixty, a school-leaving age of sixteen, with proper support for those who stayed on in school – in short, the national Labour programme.[55]

Practical discussions of this kind drew in many progressive intellectuals. Academics carried out an industrial survey of south Wales. The report concluded: 'a deliberate effort to secure the introduction of new industries into the region is not only desirable on sentimental or compassionate grounds, but is justifiable as a sound measure of public economy.' The newly formed South Wales Regional Council of Labour (SWRCL) and many of its affiliated unions agreed with this emphasis. It wanted south Wales to be 'considered as an economic unit, and its future systematically planned'. This would mean central government support and direct intervention.[56] To achieve this Wales needed a powerful advocate within the Cabinet. Growing Labour support for appointing a Secretary of State for Wales culminated in 1944, with the SWRCL presenting its case to government 'not (as) an application for Home Rule or a separate Parliament but (as) a sincere and desirable effort towards the rehabilitation of Wales'. This did not fully appease the devolutionists, but it accorded with wishes expressed by party organizers and executives in north Wales since the second Labour government (when Peter Freeman had suggested this to Mac-Donald). Attlee turned down the request.[57]

Despite this disagreement between Welsh Labour representatives and Labour's national leaders, the 'practical socialism' being generated within Wales accorded well with the national emphasis on planning and state welfare developed by Dalton, Morrison and Attlee himself in the 1930s. The national party's opposition to the Means Test also lent it moral authority, reinforcing its position as the 'natural' party of the coalfield. The NEC had wanted to rekindle popular enthusiasm for socialism through a series of nation-wide campaigns. The 'million members' campaign in 1932 was followed by a rural campaign in 1933 (reflecting growing and specialist Labour attention to these areas) and the Victory for Socialism campaign in 1934. Such efforts involved the distribution of party literature and the promotion of party newspapers, the *Daily Herald* and the new TUC-backed publication, the *New Clarion*. A new idealism, combined with a practical approach, would win over the young and the professionals. There was some support for this in Wales. As the Wrexham MP and Bangor economics lecturer Robert Richards put it:

> This is a task for which many of the younger intellectual members of the party are admirably equipped. This is not a task that we can expect the middle-aged trade union official to perform. It is for the visionaries and the dreamers to do this. But the vision must be tested in the everyday actualities of the world of politics and economics.[58]

As unemployment and its consequences escalated, the pressure to be 'practical' grew. By the late 1930s tensions between 'moderates' and 'radicals' in constituency parties were mounting. Labour's desire to protect working-class communities meant rejecting some 'militant' proposals for confronting capitalism. When the Labour-controlled Abertillery Urban District Council took a generous (and possibly illegal) line on the feeding of school children in 1934, Labour parties across south Wales declined to follow suit. In Pontypridd, for example, one delegate 'pointed out that there was an impression . . . that if the scheme was put into operation the increase in rates would prevent new industries coming into the town'. The motion to implement the Abertillery scheme was lost. Similarly, the left's call for Labour members to resign from public assistance committees, rather than administer capitalism's problem and dispense the pittance allowed by the state, was rejected. Labour used tact and humanity to minimize the degradation and the impact of poverty. Not untypically, in Newport Labour representatives were told to stay on committees and 'obtain the best possible rates they can secure'.[59]

The radical alternative of a Popular Front was rejected by most parties. The NEC's implacable opposition to working with Communists was reported and (narrowly) accepted, even in Pontypridd, during a series of conflicts throughout 1936 and 1937. In Newport,

NEC expulsions of those breaking conference policy were accepted by larger majorities.[60]

The NEC's views were shared by Welsh Labour Party officials. The organizer George Morris reported that 'the Communists . . . have made a definite attempt to capture our party machine . . . they are pursuing their efforts in this direction and it has taken all our time to combat their activities . . . [the SWMF] is being used to further their cause'. Regional federations were successfully encouraged by Welsh organizers to back the national party, as were branch meetings.[61] The Rhondda Party was disaffiliated for ignoring conference policy and several other parties were warned. The South Wales Regional Council of Labour investigated 'irregularities' in Cardiff, reforming the party in July 1939.[62] Many union leaders felt the Communist-backed National Unemployed Workers' Movement was attempting to recruit 'their' members, and had objected to being portrayed as 'social fascists' in Communist propaganda. The same people opposed Cripps, turning the SWRCL into a powerful ally of the NEC. The left was marginalized by two elements – the new Welsh party machine and non-mining unions – both of which continued to play a major part in Welsh Labour politics after the war.

However, the left's failure was not simply a by-product of machine politics. The main reason for rejecting the Popular Front strategy was a desire to address the practical problems facing Wales. George Ridley MP spoke for many when he attacked the six years of discussion which had taken place since 1931: 'Party leadership had been derided, loyalty had been impaired and differences very much over-emphasized . . . Dialectical discussion and ideological arguments are not helpful.' Through its own constructive programme, including official campaigns and rallies on unemployment, the Means Test and Spain, the NEC was closing down the space for an alternative approach. 'Practical socialism' and 'militancy' had often been complementary; now people had to choose.[63]

It is also possible that Cripps and his allies assisted in the defeat of the Welsh left. As the crisis in Europe intensified, so Cripps's line on fascism, militarism and war became less credible. In 1935 the NEC had called on local parties to consider air-raid precautions which would 'mitigate the possible effects of disastrous air raids upon the defenceless civilian population'. Like Cripps, many Welsh Labour parties had objected that this was both talking up the threat of a war and a poor defence against mass bombing. A similar TUC resolution raised difficulties in Pontypridd during 1937, and was passed by the chair's casting vote.[64] However, by 1938 fascism clearly had to be fought; Britain had to be armed, democracy protected. Cripps's contention that a proto-fascist National government could not be trusted with armaments was never really understood in Wales.[65] When Cripps was expelled in 1939, many parties were sympathetic but even so a majority backed the NEC. 'Disruption' of Labour's need to face the crisis at home and abroad had gone too far.[66]

By 1939 Labour had regained much of the support obtained at its high point in 1929. In the coalfield there were certainly larger majorities in the 1935 general election than ever before. Outside the coalfield, in the early 1930s, Labour lost some of the socially mixed seats on the south Wales coast first won in 1929 but regained some momentum thereafter. Several councils were captured or recaptured. There was municipal expansion in Newport, Barry and Swansea (although not in Cardiff). In urban north Wales Labour performed better in 1935 and in subsequent county council elections than it had done previously, although its roots in local government remained weak.[67] The rural campaigns organized by the NEC and county federations may have had some impact: Brecon and Radnor once again fell to Labour at a by-election in 1939. Support for a Secretary of State, opposition to fascism and militarism and a more tangible approach to economic problems were all attractive to some progressive intellectuals, even if the nationalist party was a new rival for this constituency in parts of Wales. There was still no policy, or structure for determining policy, for the whole of Wales. However, the formation of an active regional organization for the whole of south Wales and support for appointing a Secretary of State for Wales were steps towards a broader policy focus.

By 1939 Labour had proven its worth. It was no longer strong because others were weak. In urban Wales it had become the workers' party but it had also developed contacts with a broader section of the Welsh population. The party's ethical idealism was significant in this respect; it also inspired the activists who kept the party alive. The explanation of Welsh Labour's expansion and evolution advanced here also has implications for our understanding of British Labour politics, especially in the 1930s. There was more to Welsh Labour politics than the defence of working-class interests and a passionate commitment to a crusading socialism. The party was more than a collection of colourfully abrasive radicals, always ready to attack the establishment, although the party's internal culture (and its subsequent history) has valued their contribution and stressed their significance. Equally significant was Welsh Labour's commitment to a practical socialism, an approach which paralleled that of the party across Britain. If the revisionist right and socialist left have received all the historical attention, it was the 'direct intervention' advanced by many parties in Wales and simultaneously developed by party leaders at the British level into a clear programme which invariably delivered the political goods. Of course, parties across Britain advanced different versions of the national leadership's approach; Welsh Labour similarly developed its own character. Verbally radical but vehemently practical in its policies; containing many who were 'loyal' but many more who were wary of 'loyalism'; concerned with issues which affected all Wales but without the institutional mechanisms for devising more complete policies or for influencing government, it was overly dependent on a small group of dedicated and powerful activists. These were strengths and weaknesses which were to become even more significant in the post-war years.

Notes

[1] C. Williams, *Democratic Rhondda: Politics and Society, 1885–1951* (Cardiff, 1996), 84–99; D. Hopkin, 'The rise of Labour: Llanelli, 1890–1922', in G. H. Jenkins and J. B. Smith (eds.), *Politics and Society in Wales, 1840–1922* (Cardiff, 1988), 172–82.

[2] H. Francis and D. Smith (eds.), *The Fed: A History of the South Wales Miners in the Twentieth Century* (London, 1980); D. Smith, *Aneurin Bevan and the World of South Wales* (Cardiff, 1993); H. Francis, *Miners Against Fascism: Wales and the Spanish Civil War* (London, 1984).

[3] For detail, C. Parry, *The Radical Tradition in Welsh Politics* (Hull, 1970); D. A. Pretty, *The Rural Revolt that Failed: Farm Workers' Trade Unions in Wales 1889–1950* (Cardiff, 1989); J. G. Jones, 'Wales and the "New Socialism", 1926–29', *WHR*, XI/2 (1982); K. O. Morgan, 'The challenges of democracy', in R. A. Griffiths (ed.), *The City of Swansea: Challenges and Change* (Stroud, 1990), 60–3; P. Stead, 'The town that had come of age: Barry 1918–1939', in D. Moore (ed.), *Barry: The Centenary Book* (2nd edn, Barry, 1985), 394, 398.

[4] For much of the following see R. M. Jones, *Cymru 2000: Hanes Cymru yn yr Ugeinfed Ganrif* (Cardiff, 1999); and K. O. Morgan, *Rebirth of a Nation: Wales 1880–1980* (Oxford, 1981), ch. 8.

[5] Morgan, *Rebirth*, 219, 223–5, 235. Swansea Labour Association passed a resolution 'to prevent public expenditure being incurred for other purposes until the Housing problem has been taken seriously in hand' (Swansea Labour Association (SLA), General Committee (GC) Mins, 30 Oct. 1919, West Glamorgan RO).

[6] *Caernarfon and Denbigh Herald*, 10, 17 Nov. 1922. I owe this reference to Andrew Edwards, who also helped with Welsh-language material from the David Thomas papers.

[7] D. Tanner, *Political Change and the Labour Party, 1900–18* (Cambridge, 1990), 393, 400; K. O. Morgan, *Wales in British Politics, 1868–1922* (3rd edn., Cardiff, 1980), 285.

[8] C. Parry, 'Gwynedd and the Great War', *WHR*, XIV/1(1988), 114–15; Pretty, *Rural Revolt*, 113. For dissatisfaction with this, J. Williams to D. Thomas, 30 Jan. 1919, David Thomas MS 1919 (Univ. of Wales Bangor (UWB)); D. Thomas to R. T. Jones, 26 Jan. 1918, David Thomas MS file 67 (National Library of Wales (NLW)).

[9] For example, Pontypridd Trades and Labour Council (TLC) 15 Jan. 1919 (microfilm NLW); SLA Executive Committee (EC) Mins, 21 Aug. 1918.

[10] *Llanelli Labour Party News*, 4 Oct. 1924.

[11] *Llanelli Labour Party News*, 1 Oct. 1925. For other examples, *Newport Labour Searchlight*, 10 Oct. 1923; *Swansea Labour News*, 2 Sept., 30 Dec. 1922; Stead, 'Town come of age', 387.

[12] Pretty, *Rural Revolt*, 80, 94–101; P. Harries, 'Edgar Phillip Harries: some aspects of his life', *Journal of the Pembrokeshire Historical Society*, IV (1990–1), 74–8.

[13] See D. Hopkin, 'Y *Werin a'i Theyrnas*: ymateb sosialeth i genedlaetholdeb 1880–1920', in G. H. Jenkins (ed.) *Cof Cenedl: Ysgrifau ar Hanes Cymru*, VI (Llandysul, 1991); D. Morris, 'Sosialaeth i'r Cymry – trafodaeth yr ILP', *Llafur*, IV/2 (1985).

[14] See, for example, D. Thomas to R. T. Jones, 26 Jan. 1919, J. Williams to D.T., 30 Jan. 1919, David Thomas MS (UWB) 1919 and E. Jones to D.T., 31 March 1920, David Thomas MS (UWB) 19197. For the pre-war quotations, 'Notes on the organisation of meetings', MS 19159. Other local and educated supporters included Percy Ogwen Jones, who edited the Labour newspaper, Y *Dinesydd Cymreig* (Parry, 'Gwynedd and the Great War', 93–4).

[15] G. M. Ll. Davies to T. Jones, 30 May 1917, Thomas Jones MS W3 fo. 133 (NLW).

[16] B. P. Watts to D.T., 19 Feb. 1919, David Thomas MS 19196 (UWB); W. Harris to D.T., 23 March 1920, DT MS 19197; W. Harris to T. Jones, 3 May 1920, Thomas Jones MS H21 fo. 3; W. Harris to E. T. John, 16 July 1920, E. T. John MS 2622 (NLW).

[17] J. G. Jones, 'E. T. John, devolution and democracy 1917–24', *WHR*, XIV/3 (1989).

[18] Labour Party, *Annual Report* (1920), 32. See also E. Andrews, *A Woman's Work is Never Done* (Ystrad Rhondda, 1948).

[19] Williams, *Democratic Rhondda*, 112–13; S. E. Demont, 'Tredegar and Aneurin Bevan: a society and its political articulation 1890–1929' (Univ. of Wales Ph.D. thesis, 1990), 350–6. However, by the 1930s it was noted that 'for some years past', the Tredegar party 'have not encouraged nor promoted individual membership' (G. A. Wilcox to W. Citrine, 16 June 1934, TUC archive, Modern Records Centre, Univ. of Warwick, TUC MS 292/79T/20). Only Caerphilly had a substantial individual membership.

[20] For non-participation, D. Gilbert, *Class, Community and Collective Action: Social Change in Two British Coalfields, 1850–1926* (Oxford, 1992), 89–93, 122–38. In Caerphilly six South Wales Miners' Federation lodges and at least twelve other branches were not affiliated in 1929, whilst in 1927 there were seven unaffiliated union branches in Aberdare (TUC MSS 292 79R/13, MSS 292 79C/56).

[21] SLA Annual Meeting, 21 April 1927. See also Newport Labour Party (LP), *Annual Report* (1925), South Wales Coalfield Archive (SWCA). For north-east Wales, D. Hopkin, 'Labour in north-east Wales', unpublished paper.

[22] Pontypridd TLC Mins, 24 April 1928. Cardiff's 'delinquent' branches and the party's unchecked expenditure created organizational chaos (Cardiff TLC circulars, 21 Sept. 1926, 16 May 1927, TUC MSS 292/79C/9).

[23] Llanelli LP Mins, 4 April 1932 (Carmarthenshire RO); SLA, *AR* (1932 and 1933).

[24] Newport LP, GC Mins, 12 Feb. 1926, 18 May 1928.

[25] M. Savage, *The Dynamics of Working-Class Politics: The Labour Movement in Preston, 1880–1940* (Cambridge, 1987), 173–80, 194–200.

[26] Newport LP, *AR* (1924); *Labour Organiser* (Aug. 1934, Feb. 1937); Gloucester LP Mins, 13 May 1937 (Microfilm, British Library of Political and Economic Science).

[27] SLA Mins, 3 May 1928, noting debt of £1,028 on the *Labour News*, whose income had peaked in 1920 and 1921; Llanelli LP Mins, 19 Jan. 1926. See also the warning that Y *Dinesydd Cymreig* (Caernarfon) 'may go under' without a wealthy patron (G. M. Ll. Davies to T. Jones, 3 June 1920, Tom Jones MS W3 fo. 147).

[28] See criticism of the paper's 'reactionary' policy from Aberdare miners, D. E. Thomas to O. Harris, 14 June 1937, SWMF MS NUM/3/3/58 (SWCA). For critical comments at Cardiff in 1936, J. Wood, 'The Labour left and the constituency parties 1931–1951' (Univ. of Warwick Ph.D. thesis, 1982), 74.

[29] For the forced resignation of the notoriously inactive Evan Davies MP, J. G. Jones, 'Evan Davies and Ebbw Vale: a note', *Llafur*, III/3 (1982). In Llanelli Councillor W. D. Hughes supported a resolution asking the MP 'to resign at the conclusion of the life of the present Parliament' (Llanelli LP Mins, 11 April 1931). Labour asked a great deal of its representatives. As agent to the next MP, Jim Griffiths, Hughes was expected to run the division. He organized over 100 meetings and dealt with 700 advice cases in 1937–8 alone. (Llanelli Divisional LP, *AR* (1938), Llanelli LP papers, box 3.)

[30] Llanelli LP Mins, 21 May 1921.

[31] Chepstow LP Mins, Sept.–Oct. 1938, Jan. 1939 (Gwent RO) and letters between Rhys Davies and David Thomas in 1923, David Thomas MS (UWB) 19203. George Lansbury was especially popular, but was rather unreliable. As Davies commented 'Y mae dipyn yn "wit-watog" ' (He is a bit scatter-brained).

[32] This image was increasingly projected by educated and respectable parliamentary candidates in the socially mixed Cardiff and nearby Llandaff and Barry seats. This included the ex-Tories D. Graham Pole and J. A. Lovat-Fraser, and the ex-Liberals Hugh Dalton and E. N. Bennett.

[33] For Caernarfonshire, B. Evans to E. T. John, 6 Nov. 1919, E. T. John MS 2401 and for Pembrokeshire, D. T. Lewis to E. T. John, 23 July 1920, MS 2628.

[34] G. Lang to I. Morgan, 5 Sept., 13 Sept. 1922, E. T. John MS 3611, 3646.

[35] SWMF circular, Brecon and Radnor LP misc papers, box 41 (NLW). Brynmawr had delivered less support than anticipated in 1922 (E. T. John to I. Davies, 21 Nov. 1922, E. T. John MS 3703).

[36] Brecon and Radnor LP Mins, 3 June 1932.

[37] G. Jenkins, 'The *Welsh Outlook*, 1914–33', *The National Library of Wales Journal*, XXXIV/4 (1986).

[38] G. M. Ll. D. to D.T., 3 Oct. 1920, David Thomas MS 86 (NLW); G. M. Ll. D. to E. T. John, 20 Mar. 1923, E. T. John MS 3818 and E. T. John's support for pacifism, nationalism, and 'institutionalised Christianity', John to G. M. Ll. D., 4 Oct. 1923, E. T. John MS 3996. For John's continuing faith in MacDonald (who was 'more completely in accord with Welsh Nationalism than you appear to anticipate'), E. T. John. to G. Lang, 1 Jan. 1923, E. T. John MS 3756.

[39] This was especially evident in the National Executive Committee's observations on the Constituency Parties Movement in the later 1930s (B. Pimlott, *Labour and the Left in the 1930s* (Cambridge, 1977), ch. 12). For projected Welsh policy committees, papers re conference at Llandrindod Wells, E. T. John MS 5521.

[40] 'Review of the political situation in north Wales', n.d. or author but probably Huw T. Edwards in 1931, Thomas Jones MS H21; resolutions for North Wales Labour Federation meetings, Wrexham LP Mins, 28 March, 11 April 1933. For the 'considerable enthusiasm' generated by the 1930 conference, Colwyn Bay LP Mins, 2 April 1930 (Clwyd RO).

[41] According to its own leaders, Wrexham, the only strongly Labour seat, treated membership campaigns with 'a tremendous apathy and indifference' and could hardly sustain local parties, let alone send help elsewhere (Wrexham LP Mins, 16 Aug. 1932, Brymbo branch LP Mins, 21 Oct. 1932, noting 'stagnant' and low membership, Clwyd RO). When trying to develop a north Wales body in 1919, David Thomas had complained that 'not a single person in the Wrexham division seems to care a brass button whether the NWT&LC lives or dies' (D.T. to J. W. Williams, 9 April 1919, David Thomas MS 67, NLW).

[42] For example, East Glamorgan Labour Women's Advisory Council, 6 March 1926, 24 Sept. 1927 (NLW). See also chapter by Evans and Jones below.

[43] Francis and Smith, *The Fed*, 268, 273; Smith, *Bevan*, 238–9.

[44] There was even support in the 'moderate' Newport party (Newport LP Mins, 13 Sept. 1926, 19 Sept. 1928, 13 Dec. 1929). For falling ILP membership and branch closures, Welsh Divisional Council of the ILP, mins and circulars 1923–29 *passim*, BLPES Coll, Misc 371.

[45] Williams, *Democratic Rhondda*, 154; W. David, 'The Labour Party and the "exclusion" of the Communists: the case of the Ogmore Divisional Labour Party in the 1920s', *Llafur*, III/4 (1983). See also Llanelli LP Mins, 17 Oct. 1925; Pontypridd TLC Mins, 19 July 1926, 24 Jan. 1927.

[46] Wrexham LP Mins, 10 May 1932, opposing the formation of any further minority governments and 'Review of the political situation in north Wales', Thomas Jones MS H21.

[47] Labour's General Secretary turned down SWMF calls for demonstrations against Italy's invasion of Abyssinia, arguing it would 'not be the most helpful course to pursue' at this time (J. S. Middleton to O. Harris, 25 April 1936, NUM 3/3/58).

[48] W. James (Pontypool) to E. P. Harries, 29 Jan. 1934 (TUC MSS 292 79T/14); NEC Mins, 27 July 1938, 'Report of an enquiry held at Cardiff; report from Mary Sutherland on Socialist League activities in Swansea, 5 March 1936' (Labour Party archives, Museum of Labour History, Manchester), LP/SL/35/21.

[49] Swansea LP, *AR* (1935, 1938, 1939). For other adverse comments on Victory for Socialism, e.g. Rhondda Borough LP Mins, 6 July 1934 (NLW).

[50] For example, Llanelli LP Mins, 10 Oct. 1931.

[51] Newport LP EC Mins, 3 May 1937. Some union branches remained too poor or disinterested to become involved. In Neath local figures complained 'many branches pay what they think' whilst ten out of twenty-eight local branches did not even affiliate (Neath Trades Council and Labour Party, *AR* (1938–9), TUC MSS 292 79N/2).

[52] A series of meetings on the Maesglas and Somerton estates culminated in a 'lengthy statement on linoleum' (Newport LP GC Mins, 14 Nov. 1930).

[53] Swansea LP, *AR* (1936, 1937). The Swansea women's section always had to stress its right to be considered (EC Mins, 26 Jan. 1926, 6 Dec. 1933, 6 May 1936). Newport's women's section had similar problems with its views on birth control, although the issue was discussed at EC level.

[54] Pontypridd TLC Mins, 19 Sept., 10 Oct. 1932, 15 April 1934.

[55] *Miners' Monthly* (Dec. 1934).

[56] Board of Trade, *An Industrial Survey of South Wales* (1932); H. A. Marquand, *South Wales Needs a Plan* (1936); SWRCL Mins, 4 May 1938 (NLW).

[57] 'Memo by J.G. Davies, Post war reconstruction: status of Wales' n.d. but probably 1944, D. R. Grenfell MS D/207/1 box 9 (Glamorgan RO). For Freeman's proposal, 'Review of the political situation in north Wales'.

[58] *North Wales Labour Searchlight* (Dec. 1931).

[59] Swansea EC Mins, 4 June 1934; Pontypridd TLC Mins, 19 Sept. 1931, 10 Sept. 1934; Newport LP Mins, 2 Sept. 1934.

[60] A resolution protesting against the Socialist League's expulsion was lost 28–13 (Newport LP Mins, esp. 31 July 1936, 23 April 1937).

[61] For example, comments of Elizabeth Andrews, Caerphilly Federation of Women's Sections Mins, 7 May 1935 (NLW); East Glamorgan Women's Council Mins, 20 April 1937, 25 March 1939. See also SWRCL Mins, 4 May 1938, 8 March 1939. For Morris's views, Wood, 'The Labour left', 91.

[62] Williams, *Democratic Rhondda*, 153–5, and on Cardiff, lengthy correspondence and memos in TUC MSS 292/79C/9. For warnings to local parties, for example, G. Morris to W. J. Bevan (Tredegar), 22 Feb. 1938: 'If a Local Party is unable or unwilling to take such steps as may be necessary to ensure party discipline they cannot be permitted to remain affiliated.' TUC MSS 292/79T/20.

[63] SWRCL Mins, 23 Feb. 1937.

[64] Rhondda Borough LP Mins, 21 Sept. 1935; Pontypridd TLC Mins, 8 Nov. 1937.

[65] A Socialist League meeting in Swansea had backed Cripps's representative J. T. Murphy on this issue in 1935, but Murphy reported that the members 'were not quite convinced that we were right' (Wood, 'The Labour left', 61).

[66] For sympathy, see *Miners' Monthly* (March 1939). Significantly, however, the paper also noted that whilst socialism was the ultimate objective, 'the rank and file of the party are anxious to enjoy some of the fruit while working their way to the promised land'. The SWRCL and eight of the fifteen divisional and borough parties who submitted resolutions supported the NEC (SWRCL 8 March 1939, Wood, 'The Labour left', 191).

[67] There were comparatively few Labour councillors even in Wrexham, and elsewhere Labour activists often stood and acted as independents (see T. Baxter, Holyhead TLC, to E. P. Harries, 26 Oct. 1938, TUC MSS 292 79H/45 and Colwyn Bay LP Mins, 16 May 1931).

6

Labour and the Challenge of Local Government, 1919–1939

CHRIS WILLIAMS

Mae yna deip sylfaenol o gynghorydd Llafur, on'd oes. Maen nhw i gyd 'run peth. Maen nhw'n fyr, maen nhw'n dew ac yn seimlyd . . . Maen nhw'n sylfaenol llwgr . . .[1]

(There's a basic type of Labour councillor, isn't there? They are all the same. They are short, they are fat and slimy . . . They are fundamentally corrupt . . .)

I found them [members of local authorities in south Wales and Monmouthshire] very intelligent, with a thorough grasp of all duties and functions falling on their Councils. Both on the County Councils and the Urban District Councils, I was much impressed with the fact that they spoke on their subjects without any reference to the permanent officials, which is quite unlike my experience in the Southern Counties of England. They have been trained in a political atmosphere unlike my experience in any part of England. They knew a great deal about national politics and what is going on in other parts of the country.[2]

The Labour Party's rise to power in Welsh politics took place in the arena of local government as well in Parliament. During the inter-war years, the structure of local government, with its pattern of annual and triennial elections, offered the party, in some parts of Wales, a more sustained opportunity for the exercise of political power than did the two minority governments of 1924 and 1929–31. To party activists, even in those parts of Wales where Labour was weak, local elections provided a regular challenge that served as a marker of progress, whether measured in seats won in victory or votes polled in defeat. Where it was possible to gain control of local authorities Labour endeavoured to confound its critics by administering in a responsible and constructive manner. It sought to implement policies designed to improve the lot of its constituents and to secure their long-term loyalty. For some on the left of the party, the control of the local state was considered an important weapon that could reinforce the wider industrial and political struggles of the working class.

In the 1920s and 1930s, local authorities had powers and scope for autonomous action considerably greater than those they were to retain in the second half of the twentieth century. Centralization did intensify during the inter-war decades, principally with regard to the relief of poverty and the financial independence of local bodies. Yet, any local authority, by the management of permissive legislation in matters of housing, the feeding of necessitous children, or the municipalization of public services, or by the liberal interpretation of regulations concerning the administration of outdoor relief, could make a significant difference to the standard of living and the quality of life enjoyed by its constituents. In 1908, Rhondda activist Tom Morris, later to be the Labour Party's organizer in Wales, argued that '[i]f the measures of social reform now vested within the administrative powers of District and County Councils were put in force, they would to a very great extent mitigate the evils of unhealthy environment which surrounds [sic] us to day'. To Morris, local government was 'the most democratic institution at our very doors which can be made a powerful lever for social reform through its administrative powers'.[3]

Local government, whatever its opportunities, did not normally head the list of labour movement priorities and was rarely considered the primary arena for the class struggle. As one Labour supporter put it in 1935, 'the masses will not be emancipated by the process of administration on local bodies, however humane and sympathetic our representatives may be'.[4] Yet, whether it is assessed by reforms achieved, or by power gained, the increasing influence that the Labour Party possessed in Welsh local government between the wars contributed significantly to the shift from a public 'Liberal Wales' to one that was markedly 'Labour'. Furthermore, the election of working-class men and women as Labour councillors and Poor Law guardians and the control they often exercised over the local state in industrial districts, facilitated a

Table 6.1: Labour-controlled local authorities, 1919–1939

AUTHORITY	DATES OF LABOUR CONTROL
County Councils	
Glamorganshire	1919–22, 1925–39
Monmouthshire	1919–22, 1925–39
County Borough Councils	
Merthyr Tydfil	1920–39
Swansea	1927–30, 1933–39
Municipal Borough Councils	
Kidwelly	1934–39
Neath	1932–39
Port Talbot	1923–39
Urban District Councils	
Abercarn	1921–39
Aberdare	1921–22, 1926–29, 1930–39
Abertillery	1919–39
Ammanford	1921–39
Bedwas and Machen	1919–39
Bedwellty	1919–22, 1924–39
Blaenavon	1922–39
Brynmawr	1919–39
Caerphilly	1928–39
Cwmamman	1919–39
Cwmbran	1935–39
Ebbw Vale	1919–22, 1925–39
Gelligaer	1927–39
Glyncorrwg	1922–39
Llwchwr	1931–32, 1933–39
Maesteg	1919–39
Mountain Ash	1919–39
Mynyddislwyn	1919–22, 1925–39
Nantyglo and Blaina	1919–39
Ogmore and Garw	1919–39
Pontypool	1935–39
Pontypridd	1920–39
Rhondda	1919–39
Rhymney	1921–22, 1926–27, 1938–39
Risca	1921–39
Tredegar	1919–22, 1928–39
Rural District Councils	
Llanelly	1931–39
Neath	1934–35, 1937–39
Pontardawe	1919–39
Ystradgynlais	1931–39

Note: Elections for county councils were held in March, for borough councils in November, for urban/rural district councils in March or April. County councils and boards of guardians elected their members every three years. Other bodies elected a third of their members annually.

redefinition of community identities that was, essentially, both democratic and egalitarian.[5]

An assessment of the Labour Party's impact on Welsh local government must begin by establishing a clear picture of its successes and failures across the country. Table 6.1 lists those county, borough, urban district and rural district councils which were controlled by Labour at some point during the 1920s and 1930s.[6]

This indicates that, although the structure of Welsh local government was multi-tiered, the pattern of the Labour Party's success was set by geography rather than by type of authority. Map 6.1 of the local government areas of south Wales encompasses all the Welsh local authorities listed in Table 6.1. The limits to Labour control of local government during this period were set, more or less, by the geographical boundaries of the South Wales Coalfield, with its associated industries of iron, steel, and tinplate. Labour's total domination of a block of sixteen parliamentary constituencies in this area (fifteen in the coalfield plus Swansea East) from 1922 onwards was imitated, if imperfectly, at local level.

Chronologically, Labour's attainment of local power was much more contingent, uneven and often considerably later than the blanket nature of its parliamentary success. Labour had had a significant presence (even occasional control) on some urban district councils (UDCs) at Aberdare, Abertillery, Cwmamman and Rhondda, and on Merthyr Tydfil and Swansea Borough Councils before the First World War, but it was the first peacetime election in spring 1919 that catapulted it into power in a dramatic fashion.[7] For instance, on the Glamorgan County Council, Labour leapt from having only eleven pre-war representatives to enjoying a substantial majority of fifty-one of a total of seventy-eight councillors and aldermen.[8] In some coalfield UDCs, 1919 was the beginning of an – as yet – unbroken sway over the local state. In other cases, Glamorgan and Monmouthshire County Councils amongst them, defending such gains three years later was an impossible task and Labour was forced to retreat into temporary 'opposition'.[9] During the mid to late 1920s control was often regained and Labour also battled successfully to take hold of additional authorities including Swansea, Port Talbot and Caerphilly. Although Swansea slipped away again in 1930, Labour could take heart from its return to power there in 1933, which followed a long-planned struggle to win

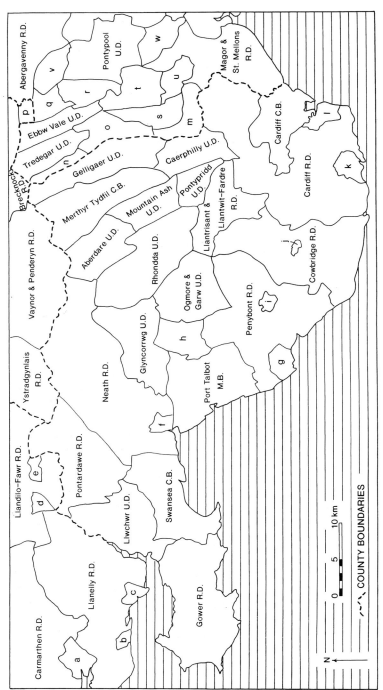

Map 6.1: Local Government Areas of South Wales, 1937

Neath in 1932. By the mid to late 1930s Labour could be highly satisfied that traditionally less radical authorities were now succumbing to their efforts, including Kidwelly, Cwmbran and Pontypool.

However, on the eve of the Second World War, Labour had still failed to win control of local authorities across vast areas of Wales. In some, including the north-west, south-west, and rural mid Wales, it had gained virtually nothing at all. In much of Pembrokeshire, Cardiganshire and Radnorshire, for instance, it was often commented that 'political issues were not predominant', or that the elections were 'devoid of political significance'.[10] Colwyn Bay Labour Party felt in 1931 that it suffered from 'The very parochial nature of the issues determining the civic attitude of the electors . . . selfish policies aimed at the parish and the parish alone.'[11] In 1937 one Labour county councillor confronted sixty-nine non-Labour colleagues in Pembrokeshire, and in Anglesey five faced fifty-five.[12] In the borough councils Labour was barely stronger, with only three out of eighteen councillors in Aberystwyth and two out of twenty-four in Bangor.[13] In mid Wales Labour enjoyed occasional successes in the towns of Brecon, Newtown and Llanidloes but, especially in the countryside, the old alignment of 'Church-Tory versus Nonconformist-Radical' persisted.[14] In north-east Wales the Labour Party and trade unions were much more powerful but even here the party struggled to gather momentum. According to the *North Wales Labour Searchlight* of January 1932:

> Labour in North Wales does not take Local Government seriously enough. Of all the Local Government bodies in the six counties, I doubt whether Labour could muster sufficient representatives to form a decent parish council! As far as West Denbighshire goes, its two boroughs, Denbigh and Ruthin, have not a single representative; in fact I should be surprised to hear that the workers of those towns had shed the inferiority complex sufficiently to have dared to challenge the powers that be.

By 1937 this was no longer an accurate picture of the state of politics in the north-east, as Labour had twenty-two out of a total of eighty-one representatives on Denbighshire County Council, but the party remained a long way from power in the boroughs of Colwyn Bay (four out of twenty-eight representatives), Flint (five out of twenty-four) and Wrexham (seven out of thirty-six).

Labour enjoyed greater, if still only partial, success, on the periphery of the South Wales Coalfield. Most of the Labour representatives on Breconshire County Council (twenty out of a total of seventy in 1934) were returned by wards in the Ystrad-gynlais and Brynmawr areas and a similar pattern was evident from the eastern districts of Carmarthenshire (where Labour had twenty out of seventy-six on the county council in 1937).[15] On Carmarthen Borough Council Labour had fought its way to a quarter of the seats by 1937 but, surprisingly, remained unable to win more than a minority representation on Llanelly Borough Council throughout the inter-war decades, its best performance being a third of the seats in 1936.

In south-east Wales, Labour struggled to get anything more than one or two seats on the borough councils of Cowbridge, Monmouth and Abergavenny but was able to develop and sustain serious bids for power in the ports of Cardiff, Newport and Barry. In the latter, Labour came close to power in 1936, with ten out of the total of twenty-one seats, and in Newport in 1934 Labour managed to take half of the thirty council seats, only to be denied control by the ten anti-Labour aldermen. One more seat for Labour would have allowed the party to put its own people on the aldermanic bench but this success proved elusive.[16] In Cardiff Labour gained ground steadily in the 1920s, with regular victories in working-class wards such as Splott and Adamsdown and occasional advances in Cathays, Grangetown and Ely.[17] The challenge was not sustained in the 1930s, although by 1937 Labour could manage seventeen out of the fifty-six councillors and aldermen.

The degree of influence Labour representatives wielded on bodies where they lacked an overall majority varied greatly from authority to authority, according to the party's own local political traditions, culture and the nature of the opposition it faced. On Breconshire County Council in 1919 Labour joined with the Liberals in a 'progressive alliance' to end Conservative control.[18] In Barry, Peter Stead writes that the Labour minority 'kept up a fight for more and cheaper municipal housing and especially for a far more dynamic response to local unemployment' and brought 'far more urgency into local government elections'. Labour chairmen, even those seen as 'socialist', won the respect of their opponents for their energy and efficiency.[19] On some councils Labour's minority status did not prevent the party from exercising a degree of control, assisted by superior cohesion, organization and leadership. Thus, in Merthyr in 1919, although Labour remained two seats short of an absolute majority on the borough council, it enjoyed an effective working majority, dominating committee appointments and chairmanships. In 1920 unequivocal control followed.[20] Equally, the *South Wales Daily Post* of 2 November 1926 commented that, although in Swansea the Independents had a majority of six over Labour, the latter's 'usually superior cohesion and [the] more regular attendance of that party's members upon the council have in the past discounted their numerical inferiority'. On the Rhondda UDC, although the size of the official Labour group fell below 50 per cent in 1924, the indistinguishable nature of the work and behaviour of three or four 'Independent Labour' councillors ensured that there was no break in the continuity of council administration and an official absolute majority was regained in 1926.[22] Even in positions of greater weakness, Labour could still make its presence felt. In his retiring speech as chairman of Denbighshire County Council in 1938 Alderman Richard Edwards commented that when he had joined the council 'there were only two Labour representatives and they were of a very mild type. But although they were mild they got a good deal out of us because of their mildness.'[22]

Explaining the mosaic of Labour's progress in local government is an even more difficult task than documenting the frustratingly elusive petty chronologies of advance and retreat. To a degree, only detailed local studies rooted in an understanding of the economy, society and political culture of individual areas can provide satisfactory answers and relatively few of these have been completed.[23]

That said, one can identify a number of factors common to many of the authorities which Labour came to control in the course of the 1920s and 1930s. Most obviously, they covered areas of heavy industry, particularly coal but also iron, steel and tinplate. Manual workers in these industries dominated local electorates and, in south Wales as in many other areas of Britain, gradually they came to identify more with each other, fellow members of a British working class, than with older, ideological continuities of race, religion or with the rhetorical promise of Edwardian Liberalism. In its local electoral campaigns and literature Labour stressed that it was the party 'of the workers', with the interests of working men and women at heart.[24] In Ystrad Rhondda in 1925, James James defended his council seat against a challenge from an 'Independent' candidate by pointing out in his election address that:

> James is a collier – one of yourselves. Workingmen be true to your own class. Vote like Men for Your Own Man. Do not be misled by your enemies. What they say of him they think of you. Vote for James James – The Workers' Champion and retain the Only Labour Seat in the Ward.[25]

This is not to suggest that Labour's message was simply sectional, or that it paid no heed to the needs of other social groups in the authorities it contested. To be successful Labour had to convert appeals to class interest and class loyalty into a more general sentiment that its return would be in the interests of the community as a whole.[26]

Successful bids for local power by Labour often relied on effective organization and leadership, combined with a judicious selection of candidates designed to appeal to what might remain a sceptical electorate, together with a vigorous and lively set of policies. The great contrast between Labour's success on Port Talbot Borough Council, where the party had held sway since 1923, and its comparative weakness on that of Neath, was ascribed in part to the organizational and inspirational qualities of Port Talbot's Labour councillor Joe Brown. The critical victories on the Neath authority that finally brought Labour control in 1932 were credited to the 'magnificent organization of the [Briton] Ferry Socialist movement', along with the 'apathetic behaviour of the other section of the electorate'.[27] The advances made by the Merthyr Labour Party in 1919 were generated in part by a major organizational push, with a total canvass of electors and many public meetings, led by local miners' leaders Noah Ablett and S. O. Davies.[28] Labour's progress in Swansea in the mid-1920s was held to be due to the party's adroitness in selecting as candidates people who had given 'useful services' as Poor Law guardians, building up a reputation for themselves as sympathetic but efficient administrators and Labour was also believed to be far more effective in getting its supporters out to vote. In contrast, an Independent candidate bemoaned that 'our organisation is of a scratch or temporary character, which is just resuscitated before each November election'.[29] It was a common complaint of anti-Labour newspapers that their preferred candidates were poorly organized, whether they fought as Independents, Liberals, Conservatives, Ratepayers, or (as sometimes happened) 'Anti-Labour'.[30]

Labour candidates also tended to possess the political initiative in bringing to the local government arena a distinct set of policies and, at least in the early 1920s, a determination to implement change for the better. This could be quite vague, as in the case of the Revd Howard Ingli James in Barry, Labour candidate for Glamorgan County Council in 1919, who wished to 'uplift and better the condition of all the people who are unfairly and unjustly treated, and to make life a brighter and gladder thing for everybody'.[31] Or it might be very specific, as with the Labour slate at Tredegar in the same year. As early as November 1918 the Labour Party locally had compiled a 'definite comprehensive programme' to which all candidates were required to subscribe. It consisted of nine points, ranging from housing reform to the improvement of local transport facilities and from the municipalization of the milk supply to the creation of a stipendiary magistracy. According to the *Merthyr Express*:

> Possibly the programme will be considered Utopian by many, and others, while approving of it, will consider the programme too ambitious, even if it is practicable. But whatever may be said about it, it will focus the attention of the electorate and give a definiteness which is absent from most municipal elections.[32]

Labour's ability to 'focus the attention of the electorate' was critical to its progress, in a period when its opponents all too often became defined as much by the fact of their opposition as by any original policies of their own. As the *South Wales Daily Post* admitted on 1 November 1927, 'it is inevitable that the party whose policy is static is at a disadvantage when opposed to a party whose policy is dynamic'.

It may have been the individual popularity of Labour's candidates, which often stemmed from a much wider range of activities than simply the political, that did most to win the party support. All studies of local politics and local communities, however restricted in scope, stress the importance of individual men and women in driving forward political change and social reform.[33] In Ynysybwl, Richard Woosnam was Labour councillor (sitting on Mountain Ash UDC) from 1919. Woosnam was prominent in the local chapel, in all village activities, was checkweigher and compensation secretary at the local pit and chairman of the local welfare institute.[34] Henry Harvey Williams, elected Labour county councillor for Palleg Eastern ward, Breconshire, was lodge secretary at Yniscedwyn and Ystradfawr and was well-known as 'one of Wales's champion euphonium players', conductor of the local male voice party and former leader of the Ystradgynlais Prize Band.[35] Ioan Matthews notes that 'nearly all those elected to the UDC in Ammanford under the Labour banner were long-serving lodge officials and respected community leaders', giving as examples Tom Davies, chairman of the Tirydail lodge for nineteen years and a founder member of Elim chapel, and Cathan Davies, an active trade unionist for twenty years who was treasurer of the Pantyffynnon lodge and deacon and secretary of Capel Newydd, Betws.[36] Labour's most prominent figures in Wrexham were Chris Davies, who was president of the Denbigh National Union of Teachers and a popular local headmaster, and Cyril O. Jones, son of Garmonydd the poet and a successful solicitor. Both rose to be Labour mayors of Wrexham and aldermen, as did Joseph Parton, originally from Wolverhampton, a railway guard and activist in the National Union of Railwaymen whose prowess as a bowler for the local cricket team endeared him even to those of a different political persuasion.[37] Increasingly, in the inter-war decades, the Labour Party and the working class in which it was rooted, generated their own public representatives. These were men and women who, in most respects, were cut from the same cloth as the majority of their constituents. Philip Massey, in his study of Nant-y-glo and Blaina, cited one elector who judged Labour candidates to be 'men who have lived our lives, known poverty and should be able to represent our interests best'.[38] The trend of inter-war election results, at least in south Wales, show such a judgement to have become increasingly common.

Evaluating the record of the Labour Party in local government office in Wales between the wars is a complex task. First, there is the problem that one is assessing not a single record but many: if one includes the boards of guardians then there were at least forty local authorities in Wales that, at some time, were controlled by

Labour, each of which has its own copious (and often near-impenetrable) records. It is only through detailed local studies that a truly satisfactory impression is likely to be gained. Second, one always has to consider the extent to which the achievements and the disasters, claimed by or blamed upon local authorities, were the result of their own actions, or whether they were the consequences, more or less unavoidable, of exogenous events and decisions. One is forced, therefore, to calibrate the performance of the local states: clear-cut pronouncements of either success or failure are unlikely to be unattainable.

These cautionary remarks notwithstanding, one may, in three stages, measure to what extent Labour fulfilled its local government objectives. First, one must explore the policies and priorities, the blueprints and dreams, that Labour activists carried with them when they stepped into the council chambers. Second, one needs to assess how these initial plans (and others that were developed subsequently) fared in office: to what extent Labour back-pedalled, whether by accident or design, and how changes in the implementation of policy generated their own tensions within local Labour movements. Finally, one may turn to the political balance-sheet as it stood at the end of the 1930s: for even if Labour had not conjured up the social revolution that some of its grander pronouncements of the immediate post-war years may have promised, the verdict on its administration, in the light of the many difficulties of the inter-war decades, may still be a positive one.

There was no single agreed approach towards local government amongst Labour local authorities and nor was there any clear and detailed direction of Labour's efforts in the localities from the Labour Party nationally. Labour head office was rarely anything more than indifferent to local government issues and produced very little in the way of policy directives.[39] At the all-Wales level the situation was no better. Thomas Isaac Mardy Jones, one-time registration agent for the Labour Party and the South Wales Miners' Federation, MP for Pontypridd 1922–31 and one of the more obviously intellectual Labour figures of his day, did produce an argument for the creation of large unitary authorities in the central coalfield, which had the support of progressive thinkers and policy-makers, including Daniel Lleufer Thomas and Edgar Chappell, but nothing came of this.[40] Some prominent Labourites, including Vernon Hartshorn, James Winstone and William

Jenkins, were on the fringes of the housing reform and garden city movements which also enjoyed a brief popularity in the immediate post-war period, but the movement's grand schemes for 'dormitory villages' outside the coalfield which would enshrine new ideals of community and citizenship fell victim to the economic depression that afflicted south Wales from the early 1920s onwards.[41] Only occasionally, as in 1922 when local authorities in West Monmouthshire met to discuss how to support the local boards of guardians, battling against high levels of unemployment and poverty, was there much co-operation between individual bodies, even if they were controlled by members of the same political party.[42] As late as 1938 the South Wales Regional Council of Labour proposed holding a conference on local government policy because, as so many councils were by this time under Labour control, 'it would seem to be an appropriate time for consultation so that a greater measure of uniformity could be achieved'.[43] Probably more frequent than such attempts at co-ordination were instances of diametrically different policies being followed by two adjoining Labour-controlled authorities, as was the case in the setting of rates between Abertillery UDC and Nantyglo and Blaina UDC in the late 1930s.[44]

Rather than Labour having a general approach to the problems and opportunities of local power, therefore, it was up to individual groups of councillors, as Sue Demont puts it, 'to chart their own courses through the bureaucratic, legal and financial structures of local government'.[45] Although this led to considerable diversity, a lack of unity in the face of central government pressure or sometimes even conflict between different Labour-controlled bodies, it is also the case that many Labour councils began their terms, in 1919 or shortly after, with similar lists of priorities.

Labour's 'nine point manifesto' for Tredegar UDC has already been mentioned and similar documents were developed by Labour activists in Rhondda (concentrating on the provision of mothers' pensions for widows with children and on the need for free education, house-building, rates reform and direct labour to combat unemployment) and in Pontypridd (where Labour advocated the provision of public parks, better sanitation, prevention of river pollution, improved housing standards and the municipalization of the milk supply).[46] In Merthyr Labourites proclaimed the need for the municipalization of gas, trams and electricity services and to build a town hall, a public library, public baths, a public abattoir and a 'refuse destructor'.[47] However, when they took office, Labour groups often found that converting policy into reality was extremely difficult. Britain in the 1920s was a society and an economy in flux. Wartime inflation had rendered the prices of building materials, for instance, punitively high. The absorption of demobilized servicemen back into the local economy brought with it serious problems of adjustment. The coal industry, on whose prosperity the society had largely been built, was in a turbulent state. The coalition government's promises on reconstruction, involving help to local authorities, were either slowly delivered or forgotten. The net result was that Labour struggled to implement any of the policies it had championed whilst in opposition, as well as having to impose wage restraint upon its employees, facts that contributed to its ejection from office in some areas in 1922.[48]

Labour's tardiness frustrated many of its supporters and led to an increase in tension in the relations between party and trade union rank and file on the one hand and public representatives on the other. To some extent the former believed that councillors should take their orders from the local party, acting very much as delegates in the council chamber. Many councillors, however much they might have supported such a policy before taking office, rapidly distanced themselves from it once elected and fell back on claims that they represented all their constituents and not just those who attended party meetings. 'I represent the Labour Party, but I recognize that I am not there to represent one class but to look after the interests of all', proclaimed Joseph Parton on becoming mayor of Wrexham in 1934.[49] These difficulties are never far from the surface in any democratic system but they clearly appeared in the early 1920s in areas of the coalfield where expectations had been high. A partial resolution of the problem was achieved in some authorities through the creation of 'Labour groups' of councillors, which met before council meetings to clarify policy, strategy and tactics and which thus placed a protective foil between councillor and activist, as well as reinforcing collective discipline within the council chambers.[50]

The catalyst both for the most dramatic expressions of internal dissent (resembling internecine warfare at times) within the labour movement over local government issues, and for highly strained relations between the agents of central and local power, was the

General Strike and miners' lock-out of 1926. The events of this year and of 1927 represented a culmination of trends that had been developing since 1919. They centred, most obviously, upon the Poor Law boards of guardians, which had the responsibility to relieve poverty in their areas. Some of these bodies had fallen under Labour control in 1919 and had experienced a change in the principles under which they were conducted. Labour guardians tended to be more generous in the scales of relief they offered and more liberal in applying the regulations under which relief might be granted. It was believed, in the Ministry of Health, that such a policy was, in effect, the granting of a minimum wage to the unemployed, underemployed and even to those in full-time employment who were on low wages. Whereas, before the First World War, acceptance of Poor Law relief had been seen as something shameful, civil servants were alarmed that it was becoming much more socially acceptable 'to claim a share in a fund that is coming to be regarded not, as hitherto, a modest legal provision for the relief of real "destitution", but as a source to which men can conveniently and . . . rightfully look for the augmentation of their reduced earnings'.[51] Under such circumstances, and with the increasing levels of unemployment in the coalfield in the early 1920s, the costs of Poor Law relief multiplied considerably. As boards of guardians were, ostensibly, financially supported from the rates levied in their localities, which were increasingly ill-equipped to supply the revenue necessary, it was not long before many boards had to apply to the Ministry of Health to sanction loans or overdrafts. This gave the Ministry opportunities to demand reductions in scales of out-relief and a tightening of procedures under which relief was granted.[52]

It was at this point that many Labour-dominated boards of guardians had to clarify their strategy. It is possible broadly to identify two approaches in the policy statements and actions of Labour guardians (and councillors in similar cases) in the 1920s. On the one hand, there were those on the left of the party (some of whom were also members of the Communist Party of Great Britain) who advocated what might be termed a 'rejectionist' line. They counselled defiance of central government threats and spoke, albeit often vaguely, of 'forcing' central government to take over the administration of the unemployed and of poor relief. They justified such a policy by referring to the admittedly often-parlous condition of the local poor and unemployed and took great heart from the struggles of the Poplar Board of Guardians in London. Beatrice Webb may have been thinking of 'rejectionists' when she wrote that in south Wales Labour's policy was 'to get as much as possible for the workers irrespective of any consequence'.[53]

Most Labour guardians and other public representatives adopted what might be seen as a more 'pragmatic' approach. That is, they attempted to get as much from the system as possible but remained aware both of the coercive mechanisms open to a hostile central government and of the responsibilities that they had to their constituents. Recognizing, perhaps, that the revolution would not be won in a council chamber, they were prepared to argue and petition central government but, eventually, to accede to the demands made upon them. Keeping their hands on the reins of power, if only to administer relatively harsh regulations as sympathetically as possible, was considered preferable to any abdication of control.[54]

Virtually all Labour-dominated local authorities ultimately adopted a 'pragmatic' line in their dealings with the Ministry of Health. In 1926 this consisted of obeying Circular 703, which set out the maximum scales of outdoor relief and also demanded strict adherence to the terms of the Merthyr Tydfil judgment, outlawing any relief of striking miners. The exception was the Bedwellty Board of Guardians, which remained defiant and which by the beginning of October 1926 was the second most highly indebted board in Britain. By November the Ministry had decided that it would have to be superseded and in February 1927 the democratically elected board was dissolved. Within a fortnight it had been replaced by a three-man team, all of whom had political connections to anti-Labour groups. A fortnight later, both the number of people being relieved and the costs of that relief had been halved, although there was no appreciable change in the levels of unemployment and poverty in the district. Other local authorities that were putting up some resistance to dictates of the Ministry were given explicit warnings that they would be treated in the same way as Bedwellty if they did not comply with centralized directives. The Merthyr Board of Guardians, recognizing that the levels of relief in the Bedwellty area were inadequate, decided that 'it would be in the interests of the poor' for them to cut their scales, rather than risk being superseded themselves.[55] Within eighteen months senior civil servants were quietly wondering whether 'the screw may not have been turned too tight in some of the bad South Wales areas' and finding serious cases of hardship in the Bedwellty district.[56]

The vast majority of Labour-dominated local authorities evaded rather than sought direct clashes with central government. Even before the Bedwellty denouement they could look upon the ways in which non-Labour bodies were operating to see the dire consequences of having power removed from their grasp. The Pontypool Board, on which Labour had only six of the twenty-three guardians, was too draconian even for the Ministry of Health. Having implemented a scale of relief well below that recommended in Circular 703 for the duration of the dispute, on 1 December 1926 the Pontypool guardians attempted to stop giving out any relief at all, before they were reminded by the Ministry that this was incompatible with their legal obligations. During 1926 the board had given relief to less than a quarter of those registered as unemployed, compared with ratios of three-fifths in Merthyr and four-fifths in Bedwellty. In Carmarthenshire, the Carmarthen and Llandilo-Fawr guardians pursued similarly parsimonious policies.[57]

One strategy that provided greater relief than that permitted by the spirit, if not the letter of the law, was for local education authorities to supply school children with meals. As the actual cost (and value) of these meals was higher than the sums deducted as a consequence from the scales of out-relief, it was a minor way in which strikers' families could be subsidized. This policy was implemented in Merthyr and the Rhondda Valleys, although when, at the end of 1926, the proximity of financial collapse forced the latter authority to bring this to a close, a major split between left and right within the local Labour Party was the consequence.[58] But 'rejectionist' policies were hardly ever again pursued in south Wales: when serious worries arose over the administration of the Means Test in 1932, representatives of Labour-controlled councils met with the Labour Party's National Executive Committee Means Test subcommittee to agree that continued sympathetic administration would be in the best interests of the unemployed, whatever the failings of the regulations. The evidence suggests that it was the correct decision: between January and September 1932, 35 per cent of applicants for transitional benefit in non-Labour-controlled Birmingham had their applications refused, whereas the similar figure for Labour-controlled Merthyr was under 1 per cent.[59] Neil Evans points out that such a policy represented the effective *non*-administration of the Means Test. Across Britain, 65 per cent of applicants received the maximum amount of relief: in Glamorgan the figure was 94 per cent and similar conditions obtained in Monmouthshire.[60]

All local authorities in the South Wales Coalfield took a long time to recover from the effects of the 1926 stoppage. The abolition of the boards of guardians, in 1930 closed a sorry chapter in the history of the relief of the poor, but their indebtedness was passed on to the remaining authorities, which then had to struggle with what were often high rates that few, either private individuals or companies, could afford to pay. With unemployment climbing higher still in the early 1930s, 57 per cent of Merthyr's rates, and 60 per cent of those levied by Monmouthshire County Council, were being spent on public assistance.[61] In these circumstances Labour-controlled authorities could only battle against the tide of economic and social disaster that threatened to engulf the area. All expenditure programmes had to be slashed and efforts had to be focused on maintaining vital services.[62] Where Labour faced opposition on its left, as it did in the form of the Communists in the Rhondda Valleys and elsewhere, economy programmes offered easy targets for often vitriolic criticism. It was relatively simple for Labour groups to be accused of, variously, 'starving the children', 'betrayal' of the unemployed and a 'no hope philosophy'. But as, occasionally, Communists discovered when they gained elected office, there were no easy answers to many of the problems being faced. As Labour Alderman Jack Evans of Nantyffyllon pointed out:

> every member of the [Glamorgan County Council Labour] Group retains his belief in Socialism and is prepared to play his or her part in propagating the idea of social ownership and control, but not one pretends that he can establish and practise Socialism in County administration when the whole country is so obviously unripe for such a change. All the Labour County Councils can do is to introduce as much humaneness into its administration as is possible, and thereby make the lives of the people a little bit easier during these terrible hard and difficult times.[63]

Elizabeth Andrews, the Labour Party's woman's organizer in Wales, observed more succinctly, 'it is the PLODDERS that do the work

of the WORLD, not the SHOUTERS'.[64] There is no denying that
Communist members of local authorities did their fair share of
'plodding' but it is also the case that the degree of co-operation
between Labour and Communists was probably greater than either
liked to admit. As Mavis Llewellyn, a Communist councillor in
Ogmore Vale, explained:

> I don't know that there was all that great deal of difference between the
> Communists and those who were – of course even then there were lefts
> in the Labour Party, and there were the old die hards, who were
> certainly not socialists, and there was always a very close working
> relationship with some of the Labour Party councillors, in fact, it got so
> obvious that if Communists wanted to move a motion on the council
> we had to find allies before the meeting . . . otherwise there would be a
> solid block once the Labour group had met. . . . But we worked very
> well together.[65]

However, Communists were responsible, in the course of the 1930s,
for making the most explicit allegations of corruption and nepotism against Labour-dominated local authorities, criticisms that
have, with or without foundation, passed into political folklore.
Teasing out the intricate strands of truth and legend is another
task that demands detailed case-studies. Work undertaken to date,
on Rhondda, Swansea and Wrexham, suggests that there was at
least some foundation to such allegations, particularly in the early
to mid-1930s. Some councillors did find jobs for their relatives and
others may have been part of a more or less organized system of
bribe-taking in the fixing of teaching jobs. But there is no evidence
that anything more than a minority of councillors were involved.
Most public representatives cannot be accused of such practices
and some made it their business to expose wayward comrades, even
if this led to the political and electoral embarrassment of the
Labour Party. Wrexham Labour Party was so concerned about the
issue that it developed a 'code of honour' for Labour members of
public bodies, outlawing 'canvassing', the receipt of 'favours or
hospitality' and the appointment of 'near relatives' to the local
councils.[66] Then again, some councillors with supposedly tarnished reputations continued to be elected many times and to serve
their constituents in other important ways. This suggests that, as in
many things, the people who witnessed these events at first hand
had a better sense of proportion than many who have commented

subsequently. One Labour politician who did suffer for his involvement in a scandal, Aberdare's Edmund Stonelake, was not only innocent of corruption but also a serious loss to the calibre of leadership on the local UDC.[67] There was the odd crook, in the Labour Party as in other political parties, but it is important to place the occasional malfeasance in its wider context of community service and common struggle. What sometimes ended up as corruption or nepotism may have begun in a common and understandable desire on the part of a parent, relative or friend to secure some advantage for a loved one in what otherwise were times of great disadvantage. Philip Massey considered that many Labour leaders in Nant-y-glo and Blaina owed much of their support to creating a personal sense of obligation by their willingness to assist people in the completion of forms or the resolution of 'little matters of difficulty which arise'. For some, this was the context in which a gift might be offered or received and there was often little more to it than that.[68]

What, by 1939, had the Labour Party achieved in those areas where it had held local power, in some cases for two decades? Most Labour authorities administered the Poor Law and its successor system in ways that, given the unfavourable context of the times, probably could not have been bettered. Of course, it still had to contend with public criticism and sometimes intense pressure, as was the case during the Means Test demonstrations of 1935. Nevertheless the 'pragmatic' strategy of remaining in power and working the system as effectively as possible was sensible, realistic and endorsed by democratic majorities time and again. But although Labour's record here was overwhelmingly defensive, in matters of public health it managed, in the 1930s, many more progressive achievements. Labour-controlled authorities were at the forefront of the development of maternity and child welfare clinics in the South Wales Coalfield. They established schemes whereby expectant and nursing mothers and young children were supplied with free milk. Bursts of school meals for necessitous children and the supply of boots occasionally staved off some of the worst effects of the Depression.[69] According to one Ministry of Health report in 1931, the incidence of malnutrition amongst school children was directly related to:

> the completeness and efficiency in the arrangements made by the Local Education Authorities for the Medical supervision and treatment of

malnutrition by the administration of milk or the provision of meals. In those areas where the arrangements are systematic, as example, Rhondda, Pontypridd, Aberdare, Merthyr Tydfil, there is no increase.[70]

Significantly, all four councils named were controlled by the Labour Party. Labour-dominated authorities were also to the fore in the anti-tuberculosis campaign. When the Clement Davies committee reported in 1939 it paid them fulsome tributes for their positive contributions, particularly in the context of the economic problems and demographic outflows experienced since the 1920s.[71]

Notwithstanding such necessarily impressionistic evidence, there remains some doubt over the overall impact upon health and disease of the Labour administration of local government services. J. M. Winter, as part of a wider consideration of the impact of economic distress on public health, argues that, across England and Wales, the record of Labour-controlled municipalities in the reduction of infant mortality rates (used as the most sensitive indicator of changes in public health) was no better than that of non-Labour-controlled authorities. Winter bases his argument on a sample of three groups of seven boroughs 'of similar geographic distibution', the first of which includes boroughs consistently controlled by the Labour Party, the second group boroughs intermittently controlled by Labour and the third group boroughs which were never Labour-controlled. Using an index of infant mortality rates between 1926–9 and 1938, Winter's results show the rates for the first ('Labour') group of boroughs falling to 78 per cent of the 1926–9 rate by 1938, in comparison with greater falls to 75 per cent and 72 per cent for the second and third groups. On this basis Winter claims that there is no support for the hypothesis that Labour's control of local government made a significant difference to the public health of its constituents.[72]

Winter's methodology, however, is open to question. It assumes that the relative differences between the groups of boroughs in terms of economic and social conditions (including, most obviously, the rates of unemployment) remained constant throughout the period under consideration. If, however, the differentials worsened, then such changes may in themselves help to explain the greater difficulties experienced in reducing infant mortality in 'Labour boroughs'. If one compares the Welsh boroughs included in Winter's sample (Merthyr Tydfil in the first group, Swansea in the second and Cardiff in the third) then it is evident that the gap in experiences between these urban areas widened throughout the late 1920s and 1930s, with Merthyr Tydfil averaging between 50 and 60 per cent unemployment amongst its insured population after 1931, more than double the rates of either port.[73] Winter's own data indicate that the South Wales Coalfield was even more badly hit by the social effects of unemployment than 'Special Areas' elsewhere in Britain and he concedes that its traditionally high levels of fertility, infant and maternal mortality 'set this area apart from the general demographic development of Britain'.[74]

Furthermore, there are other problems with Winter's argument. His categorization of his chosen boroughs in one of three distinct groups may obscure essential similarities between them: Swansea, which was Labour-controlled for ten of the thirteen years under scrutiny, may not be the most suitable candidate for the category of 'intermittent' Labour administration; nor is it obvious that, when Labour lost control in the town, policies were dramatically put into reverse. To deny the Labour Party credit for whatever advances were made in the field of public health in the town on the grounds that Labour control was not constant throughout the period appears to distort the historical record and fly in the face of qualitative and contemporary evidence. Finally, Winter himself acknowledges that local-authority-led campaigns to improve antenatal, child welfare and maternal health levels, all of which were heavily emphasized by Labour-controlled authorities in south Wales, had a significant impact for the better, suggesting that the reasons for the differences in the decline in mortality rates between 'Labour boroughs' and 'non-Labour boroughs' lie outside the realm of local government policy-making.[75] Winter's argument serves as a valuable reminder both of the need for analytical rigour in evaluating the impact of political action on social conditions and of the heuristic problems such evaluation involves.

James Griffiths believed that 'the services rendered to our people by our councils' during the Depression had been impressive. It was his judgement that 'their salvage work saved our community life from complete dissolution'.[76] Such a view, like that of Jay Winter, involves too many imponderables to be endorsed without reservation but it has a ring of truth. Labour-controlled authorities may sometimes have acted, in the words of John Rowett, as 'working-class benefit societies', but they did so in a world which offered the working class precious few other benefits.[77] In arriving at any judgement on Labour's record in local government it needs to be remembered that Labour councils were, by popular mandate, the self-image of the communities they represented. A complete understanding of the society that so obviously committed itself to Labour control should not neglect the world of local government.

Notes

[1] Rod Richards, in 'Gêm Galed', *Barn* 383/384 (Rhagfyr 1994/Ionawr 1995), 13.

[2] *Report on the Derelict Areas*, III, *South Wales and Monmouthshire*, by Lt.-Col. Sir Wyndham Portal, 2 July 1934, 127.

[3] *Glamorgan Free Press*, 10 Jan. 1908.

[4] J. Thomas, in *Rhondda Clarion*, 3 (Dec. 1935).

[5] D. Smith, 'Tonypandy 1910: definitions of community', *Past and Present*, 87 (1980); D. Gilbert, *Class, Community and Collective Action: Social Change in Two British Coalfields, 1850–1926* (Oxford, 1992); M. Savage, 'Urban history and social class: two paradigms', *Urban History*, XXI/1 (1993).

[6] This table is based upon many sources, including a wide variety of newspapers, and D. S. Wilson Rumsey, *Labour Rule in the Welsh Valleys, 1919–21* (London, 1922). J. Rowett, 'The Labour Party and local government: theory and practice in the inter-war years', Univ. of Oxford D.Phil. thesis, 1979, contains valuable appendices, although they are not completely accurate as far as Wales is concerned. The lack of any consistent, comprehensive source for the party-political complexion of local authorities represents a major difficulty in establishing the accuracy of this table, and it should be regarded only as the author's best current estimate. Boards of guardians have not been included owing to the absence of exact data, although Labour did win those of Bedwellty, Merthyr, Neath, Pontardawe and Swansea in 1919.

[7] T. J. McCarry, 'Labour and society in Swansea, 1887–1918', Univ. of Wales Ph.D. thesis, 1986.

[8] *WM*, 10 March 1922.

[9] *WM*, 8 March 1922, 7 March 1925

[10] *WM*, 10 March 1919, 11 March 1922; *South Wales Daily Post*, 3 Nov. 1930.

[11] Colwyn Bay Labour Party General Committee Mins., 18 April 1931 (Clwyd RO).

[12] Rowett, 'Labour and local government', 381.

[13] *Daily Herald*, 8 Nov. 1937.

[14] A. D. Rees, *Life in a Welsh Countryside: A Social Study of Llanfihangel yng Ngwynfa* (Cardiff, 1996), 157–8.

[15] *DH*, 14 Feb. 1934.

[16] P. Stead, 'The town that had come of age: Barry 1918–1939', in D. Moore (ed.), *Barry: The Centenary Book* (Barry, 1985), 413–14; *DH*, 15, 18 Oct., 3 Nov. 1934.

[17] N. Evans, 'Cardiff's Labour tradition', *Llafur*, IV/2 (1985).

[18] *Labour Voice*, 15 March, 10 May 1919.

[19] Stead, 'The town come of age', 396, 411–13. Similar achievements have been identified in Cardiff, by Evans, 'Cardiff's Labour tradition', 82–3.

[20] *Merthyr Pioneer*, 15 Nov. 1919, 6 Nov. 1920.

[21] C. Williams, *Democratic Rhondda: Politics and Society, 1885–1951* (Cardiff, 1996), 91–2.

[22] D. Hopkin, 'Labour and politics in north-east Wales', unpublished paper, 1986, 29.

[23] Apart from *Democratic Rhondda*, see S. E. Demont, 'Tredegar and Aneurin Bevan: a society and its political articulation, 1890–1929', Univ. of Wales Ph.D. thesis, 1990. A. J. Adams, 'Working class organisation, industrial relations and the labour unrest 1914–1921', Univ. of Leicester Ph.D. thesis, 1988, contains material on Pontypridd, and I. A. Matthews, 'The world of the anthracite miner', Univ. of Wales Ph.D. thesis, 1995, has much to offer on the politics of the anthracite coalfield.

[24] *Merthyr Pioneer*, 9 Nov. 1918.

[25] Williams, *Democratic Rhondda*, 97.

[26] K. O. Morgan, 'The challenges of democracy', in R. A. Griffiths (ed.), *The City of Swansea: Challenges and Change* (Stroud, 1990), 60.

[27] *Neath Guardian*, 7 Oct., 4 Nov. 1932.

[28] *Merthyr Pioneer*, 1 Nov. 1919.

[29] *SWDP*, 2 Nov. 1926.

[30] *SWDP*, 1, 2 Nov. 1927, 3 Nov. 1928, 2 Nov. 1929; *South Wales Evening Post*, 2 Nov. 1934; Williams, *Democratic Rhondda*, 167; Demont, 'Tredegar', 378–80.

[31] Stead, 'Town come of age', 394.

[32] 23 Nov. 1918, cited in Demont, 'Tredegar', 227–8.

[33] Williams, *Democratic Rhondda*, 205–8.

[34] Gilbert, *Class*, 127.

[35] *LV*, 1, 8 March 1919.

[36] Matthews, 'Anthracite miner', 338.

[37] Hopkin, 'Labour and politics', 24–6.

[38] Philip Massey, *Portrait of a Mining Town* (Fact 8, London, 1937), 44.

[39] Rowett, 'Labour and local government', 34, 53–5.

[40] *The Good Government of Glamorgan* (Pontypridd, 1920).

[41] E. May, 'Coal, community, town planning and the management of Labour', *Planning Perspectives*, XI (1996).

[42] Demont, 'Tredegar', 341.

[43] South Wales Regional Council of Labour Mins, 11 June 1938, National Library of Wales.

[44] Mass Observation, 'Mining Town – 1942' File Report 1498 (Mass Observation Archive, University of Sussex), 9–10.

[45] Demont, 'Tredegar', 332–3.

[46] Williams, *Democratic Rhondda*, 96; Adams, 'Working class organisation', 55–6.

[47] *Merthyr Pioneer*, 1 Nov. 1919.

[48] Williams, *Democratic Rhondda*, 127–30; Adams, 'Working class organisation', 56–8; Demont, 'Tredegar', 332, 340.

[49] Hopkin, 'Labour and politics', 29.

[50] C. Williams, ' "An able administrator of capitalism?" The Rhondda Labour Party, 1917–1921', *Llafur*, IV/4 (1987); Adams, 'Working class organisation', 58–62; Demont, 'Tredegar', 335; Matthews, 'Anthracite miner', 340.

[51] Ministry of Health (MH) file 57/107, memo by J. Evans, 9 Dec. 1921 (Public Record Office).

[52] MH 57/106, 57/125, 57/126, 68/265, 79/297; Williams, *Democratic Rhondda*, 133–5.

[53] M. Cole (ed.), *Diaries 1924–32* (London, 1956), 187, cited in Rowett, 'Labour and local government', 22.

[54] Williams, *Democratic Rhondda*, 119–20; Demont, 'Tredegar', 298–302.

[55] S. R. Williams, 'The Bedwellty Board of Guardians and the Default Act of 1927', *Llafur*, II/4 (1979); P. Jeremy, 'Life on Circular 703: the crisis of destitution in the South Wales Coalfield during the lockout of 1926', *Llafur*, II/2 (1977); Williams, *Democratic Rhondda*, 135–50; MH55/691, 57/94, 57/110A, 57/117, 57/118, 57/119, 57/122, 68/266, 68/370, 68/371; *Merthyr Express*, 18 June, 2 July 1927.

[56] MH 57/109, Memorandum from Sir W. A. Robinson to the Minister of Health, 1 Nov. 1928; MH 79/304, Memorandum from Sir A. Lowry to the Minister of Health, 15 Jan. 1929.

[57] MH 57/117; D. M. Lloyd, 'Some aspects of the Poor Law in south Wales, 1870–1930', Univ. of Wales M.Sc.Econ. thesis, 1978, 208–10; D. J. Davies, 'Guardians of the needy found wanting: a study in social division during the industrial crisis of 1926', *Carmarthenshire Historian*, XIX (1982).

[58] Williams, *Democratic Rhondda*, 146–9; C. Webster, 'Health, welfare and unemployment during the Depression', *Past and Present*, 109 (1985); H. Williams, 'Merthyr Tydfil and the General Strike of 1926', *Merthyr Historian*, II (1978).

[59] Rowett, 'Labour and local government', 308–11.

[60] N. Evans, ' "South Wales has been roused as never before": marching against the Means Test, 1934–1936', in D. W. Howell and K. O. Morgan (eds.), *Crime, Protest and Police in Modern British Society: Essays in Memory of David J. V. Jones* (Cardiff, 1999), 181–2.

[61] Portal Report, 166–7; *DH*, 6 Feb. 1934.

[62] Williams, *Democratic Rhondda*, 171–3; Demont, 'Tredegar', 342–4.

[63] *Rhondda Clarion*, 1 (Sept. 1935).

[64] *Rhondda Clarion*, 2 (Oct. 1935).

[65] Interviewed by H. Francis, 20 May 1974 (South Wales Miners' Library); Williams, *Democratic Rhondda*, 186.

[66] Wrexham Trades Council and Divisional Labour Party, Joint Group of Labour Councillors, 'Code of Honour', 13 April 1935, Clwyd RO.

[67] Anthony Mòr O'Brien, 'The Aberdare housing scandal, 1919–1922', *Morgannwg*, XXVI (1982).

[68] Williams, *Democratic Rhondda*, 173–81, 193–5; Massey, *Portrait of a Mining Town*, 41–2.

[69] MH 55/629, 55/691, 79/312; Williams, *Democratic Rhondda*, 192–3; Webster, 'Health', 222–5; *The Lancet*, 6 July 1935.

[70] MH 57/3: Dr J. E. Underwood, 'Enquiry into physique, and general health and state of clothing and boots of school children in the South Wales mining districts', Jan. 1931.

[71] Ministry of Health, *Report of the Committee of Inquiry into the Anti-Tuberculosis Service in Wales and Monmouthshire* (London, 1939), 169, 175.

[72] J. M. Winter, 'Infant mortality, maternal mortality, and public health in Britain in the 1930s', *Journal of European Economic History*, VIII (1979), 451–3.

[73] J. W. England, 'The Merthyr of the twentieth century: a postscript', in G. Williams (ed.), *Merthyr Politics: The Making of a Working-Class Tradition* (Cardiff, 1966), 88.

[74] Winter, 'Infant mortality', 454–5.
[75] Ibid., 458–9.
[76] *Pages from Memory* (London, 1969), 174.
[77] Rowett, 'Labour and local government', 22–3.

7

Power and Glory: War and Reconstruction, 1939–1951

KENNETH O. MORGAN

On 2 September 1939 Arthur Greenwood rose in the House of Commons to give Labour's backing for the government's ultimatum to Hitler. As he did so, he was urged, in a famous intervention by Leo Amery on the Tory benches (heard by everybody but not recorded in *Hansard*), to 'speak for England'. Greenwood, a social patriot to his core, could equally well have been told, 'Speak for Wales'. For his and his party's uncompromising commitment to going to war was exactly the view of all parts of the labour movement in Wales as it was in Britain as a whole. In the First World War, the party and the unions had been bitterly divided: significant dissenters opposed declaring war on Germany, the imposition of conscription and the policy of fight to a finish. This time, there was virtually no dissent. The Welsh party at all levels and all the major unions were loyalist throughout. They accepted warmly the formation of Churchill's coalition (memories of the troops at Tonypandy set aside) and the policy of unconditional surrender. Indeed, the main line of criticism took the form of urging that the war be fought with greater zeal, notably opening up a second front in 1943 to assist our Russian allies. Whereas in 1917–18 there had been major movements of protest, many inspired notably by the Russian Revolution, in favour of a negotiated peace, this time there were none. Even many of the Welsh Communists were part of the wartime consensus: Arthur Horner was but one who refused to compromise his resistance to Nazi totalitarianism because of the Molotov–Ribbentrop Pact on the eve of Britain's entry into war. There were some cases of individual

Labour conscientious objectors, such as the little-known Cardiff school teacher, George Thomas. Some left-wing protesters were mistreated, such as the highly individual minister-bard and un-licensed dentist, the Revd T. E. Nicholas, harassed by the Aberystwyth police and imprisoned without trial in Swansea gaol. There were attacks on civil liberties such as the dismissal of the socialist nationalist, Iorwerth Peate, from his post in the folk studies department of the National Museum of Wales, which produced a memorable clash between Lord Plymouth and Aneurin Bevan at the meeting of its governors.[1] But in general the attitude of the Welsh labour movement throughout these six years was one of solidarity, loyalty and social patriotism.

This was in part because the labour movement itself was now part of the governing process. The Labour Party was fully represented in Churchill's government from May 1940 until after VE Day. Labour local authorities were involved in maintaining wartime services, notably in Cardiff, Barry and especially Swansea which suffered severely from wartime bombing. In ferocious fire-bomb attacks on 19–21 February 1941, the entire town centre was destroyed, with the death of 387 people and 412 others seriously injured.[2] The unions were fully involved in the corporatist industrial policy laid down by Ernest Bevin as Minister of Labour. In return for their role in control of the labour market, they accepted even such disagreeable proposals as Order 1305 which suspended the right to strike. The outcome of the war years in Wales was dramatic. After a decade of industrial stagnation and mass unemployment in the valleys, the economy was transformed. New life was breathed into coal, steel, tinplate and the docks. Full employment returned. The government itself stimulated new growth through a distribution of industries policy operated by the Board of Trade, following the lines of the Barlow Report for the relocation of industry. War contracts led to the opening up of Royal Ordnance factories at Bridgend, Hirwaun, Glascoed and Pembrey in the south, and Marchwiel near Wrexham in the north, a huge new aircraft factory at Broughton in Flintshire, and the massive expansion of the pre-war trading estate at Treforest near Pontypridd. Wales lost its depressed area atmosphere as the economy hummed with new life not known since before 1914. The long march for a somewhat ill-defined New Jerusalem led by pacifists like Keir Hardie over the decades seemed to have reached its appointed end in a time of total war.

Even so, it is obvious that the strains of loyalty and dissent occasioned by wartime circumstances led to inevitable tensions within the Welsh labour movement after 1939, despite the relative quiescence of the South Wales Regional Council of Labour and the unions. Historians like Stephen Brooke who have questioned the wartime consensus certainly find some evidence in Wales.[3] There were dissenting Welsh Labour MPs, especially after Russia's entry into the war in June 1941. Aneurin Bevan was a constant and powerful critic of government war strategy, as well as of Ernest Bevin's suppression of union protest, as will be seen. Bevan's onslaught on Bevin's Regulation 1AA (supported, it is often forgotten, by Dai Grenfell, a former Mines Minister) led to his temporary suspension from the party in 1944 and cast an ironic light on his advice to Jennie, his Independent Labour Party wife, to leave her nunnery and the impotence of isolation in the wilderness. S. O. Davies, the sombre-clad Marxist member for Merthyr, was a frequent critic, too, condemning the government for its failure to pursue a second front and its intervention in the civil war in Greece. W. G. Cove, member for Aberavon and the Commons representative of the National Union of Teachers, was another frequent gadfly, especially over the 1944 Education Act, to the annoyance of Labour's Chuter Ede who worked with Butler in pushing through that Act.[4] Perhaps the most dramatic opposition of all, however, came from a solid loyalist, James Griffiths of Llanelli. His powerful motion in February 1943 attacking the government for its failure to endorse the social insurance proposals of the Beveridge Report, attracted over 100 supporters in the House, among them nine Welsh Labour members, and also the veteran David Lloyd George, pioneer of the welfare state before 1914, now casting his last vote in the House of Commons. In time, Griffiths's motion became politically valuable for Labour. They could have it both ways, appearing as the voice of conscience and protest at the same time as being a loyal partner in the Churchill coalition.

In the Welsh constituencies, mostly quiescent and ill-organized during the wartime years, there were motions of protest too, as membership of the wartime coalition produced its strains. The SWRCL protested in 1942 when Labour MPs were asked to speak on behalf of Sir James Grigg, a Tory, in the Cardiff East by-election, in addition to his having a free run under the terms of the wartime election truce.[5] Some Welsh constituency parties also protested at the National Executive Committee's decision to suspend the King's Norton constituency party for running a Labour candidate, Elizabeth Pakenham, in a Tory-held constituency in 1941. A more frequent source of protest, however, was not that the government was too consensual, but that it was paying insufficient attention to Wales. The SWRCL, along with individual MPs such as Dai Grenfell, Jim Griffiths and S. O. Davies, led protests for a fuller recognition of Wales as a distinctive region within the framework of wartime economic planning. They received some apparent encouragement from Harold Laski, a NEC member, when he met them in October 1941.[6] They pressed on with an interim report on post-war planning in April 1942 which took a strongly national line and went on to propose a Secretary of State for Wales. But Transport House was sternly resistant to Welsh separatism in any form, as it was to Scottish. This was very much the view of Morgan Phillips, the Welsh-speaking son of an Aberdare miner, who was strongly opposed to any concessions to nationalism. When he became general secretary of the party in 1944 Transport House's stern centralism and unionism were reinforced.

The main evidence of strain within the Welsh labour movement during the war years, however, lies rather in the domain of industrial and indeed of cultural history. Some historians have spoken of the possibility of a 'radical moment' in wartime Britain, an opportunity for genuine socialist revolution, hinted at by Laski in a famous book of 1943. Marxists like E. P. Thompson linked it with a lack of imagination or plain betrayal by the Attlee government after 1945. There is some evidence that the unions and the workers in Wales shared in a mood of wartime revolt, comparable to the miners of Betteshanger in Kent who caused Ernest Bevin such anguish. The miner-writer, B. L. Coombes, wrote powerfully in these terms. The miners in 1943–4 in south Wales engaged in a variety of strike or 'go-slow' activities or in unexplained absenteeism. In February–March 1944, 100,000 Welsh miners were at one time on strike following dissatisfaction with the Porter pay awards. It took all the diplomacy of Arthur Horner and other South Wales Miners' Federation (SWMF) officials (many of them Communists) to persuade them to resolve local pay disputes through the usual collective bargaining procedures.[7] The strikes of apprentice boys in

1942–3, initially in the Rhondda and then in the anthracite pits of the western coalfield, testified to a wider mood of industrial protest over wages and working conditions.[8] They served as a reminder that industrial radicalism in the valleys could not be confined in a wartime cocoon of consensus and industrial harmony. It was a constant worry for loyalist Labour leaders in the SWMF that Communists were making the pace, taking up local grievances as agents (or as shop stewards in factories) and winning converts in such areas as the Rhondda Valleys. Throughout the war years, this current of rebellion seethed below the surface, and Mass Observation evidence of public opinion frequently detected its presence.

But in the main these strikes were limited. Compared with 1914–18 industrial revolts in Wales were relatively sporadic. In general, even in so traditionally radical a community, wartime patriotism prevailed. Far more characteristic were socialist protests conducted within traditional channels. The key figure here is not S. O. Davies, throughout his career too maverick a figure to have much influence outside his constituency, but Aneurin Bevan. His constant crusade for seeing the war as a launchpad for socialist change found its main outlet in his widely reported speeches in the Commons. But his impact can also been seen in *Why Not Trust the Tories?*, a fierce short tract of social criticism published by Victor Gollancz in 1944 under the pseudonym 'Celticus'. In this Bevan angrily recapitulated the betrayals of the people's hopes after the previous war and the evils of resultant Tory role at home and abroad. 'Lying is a necessary part of a Tory's political equipment', Bevan told his readers.[9] He poured scorn on the inadequacies of the 1944 white paper on employment, based on taxing the workers through higher social contributions and giving private enterprise another chance. He denounced the refusal of a Tory-led government to commit itself to the Beveridge Report. He condemned the reluctance to build the houses needed post-war: instead the government offered the people 'half a million steel boxes' in return for their wartime sacrifices. A capitalist government was cynically preparing the way to entrench the old order instead of engaging in the total reconstruction for which the people cried out. In a favourite historical parallel, he recalled Colonel Rainboro of the Levellers in the Putney debates in 1647 calling for the poor to mobilize democracy to destroy the power of property. It was a theme Bevan picked up again years later in his memorable *In Place of Fear* (1952). His pamphlet showed that constitutional democratic socialism was a powerful force behind the façade of wartime consensus and that social power was swinging over to the workers after the inequalities of the locust years. It is a sign of the mood of impatient anger in Wales and elsewhere that Bevan's tract sold over 80,000 copies despite its plain appearance and poor wartime paper. It is indicative too that, later that year, he was elected to Labour's NEC for the first time and that the stormy petrel of the war years now became seriously mooted as a possible Cabinet minister.

In the later stages of the war, the broad tendencies of social and economic policy tended in a socialist or Labour direction. All the debate and dialogue was in favour of central government planning. This was the thrust of the Welsh Advisory Council, chaired by the distinctly Fabian Professor J. F. Rees, principal of the University College at Cardiff, and whose dominant figure was the Labour MP, James Griffiths. Appointed in 1942, it reported in 1944 in terms which might well have provided the Labour Party with its post-war programme *en bloc*. It emphasized once again the need to avoid the disasters of the inter-war years when there was a net loss of 430,000 people migrating from Wales.[10] There was a emphasis on 'pulling through together', on the general will and on common sacrifice. Collectivism and indicative planning were everywhere the agents of change. The Board of Trade, under the Welsh-born Hugh Dalton and his able assistant, the economist Douglas Jay, used the powers of the state purposively to transform the Welsh economy. New light industries were steered to the valleys, such as the watch factory established in Ystradgynlais, an old anthracite mining town at the head of the long-depressed Swansea Valley. Douglas Jay, in later life, would recite a litany of the various south Wales mining villages through which he had conducted a kind of progress during the war years.[11] The Factories and Warehouses department of the Board of Trade, under Sir Cecil Weir and Welsh civil servants like Emrys Pride, allocated new industrial space in the older mining areas and set up new regional planning centres for civil servants and businessmen, from Cardiff to Ruthin.[12] The Distribution of Industry Act of 1945 embodied the 'development areas' policy of the Board of Trade during the wartime years, with vigorous powers given to government to direct firms to the former depressed areas. The kinds of policies advocated by labour economists in the 1930s like Professor Hilary Marquand of Cardiff now became the conventional wisdom. Industries were taken under state-wide control, such as through the National Coal Board (NCB), though this implied operational direction rather than full nationalization.

But in general it was a Labour agenda and understood as such. It chimed in with the strong pro-Labour swing shown in the Gallup Polls from the fall of Tobruk in 1942 onwards, even if hardly anyone paid them attention at the time. The mood, too, was one of solidarity and a united movement of workers by hand and by brain. The most dramatic evidence of this came in the mining industry. Early in 1945, the SWMF, the old 'Fed' which had fought the miners' cause from the days of Taff Vale and Tonypandy, agreed by an immense majority of ten to one to become part of a Britain-wide National Union of Mineworkers, with South Wales as one district within it.[13] It was an inevitable consequence of nation-wide rather than district wage agreements. But it was also further evidence of the integration and unionization of Britain, at least at the organizational level. All the Welsh miners' leaders, from Arthur Horner downwards, gave it their blessing.

These forces revealed their full significance in July 1945. Shortly after VE Day, the Labour leaders left Churchill's coalition and a general election soon followed, scheduled for 5 July, with time allowed for organizing a forces' vote which would mean the result would be known on 25 July. How well-prepared for the fray Labour was organizationally is open to debate. The SWRCL, with Cliff Prothero as its secretary from 1944 following the death of George Morris, had been increasingly active in south Wales plugging the gaps. But clearly, as with all political parties, the constituency parties in Wales had allowed their organization to wind down in the wartime years: Brecon and Radnor, though buoyed up by a by-election victory on the eve of the war in August 1939, was but one party that spoke of local decay.[14] Much depended on the trade unions, especially since in areas like mining seats individual membership was traditionally low. In 1942 there were accounts of falling membership in several south Wales constituencies, including Swansea, Neath and Newport.[15] In fact, in south Wales from Llanelli to Ebbw Vale the SWMF had kept the local political machinery in being. Elsewhere, the National Union of Railwaymen had been active in places ranging from Carmarthen to Anglesey. In

Cardiff South, where the Labour candidate, Lieutenant James Callaghan, was on naval service in the Far East, his own union, the Inland Revenue Staff Federation, partly through such Welsh figures as Dai Kneath, worked with the agent Bill Headon to keep the local party apparatus in working order.[16] In the end, Labour fought every one of the thirty-six Welsh constituencies save for Montgomeryshire and the University of Wales. It was as well equipped as the local Tories and Liberals but it was a mood not machinery that dictated the result.

Of course, the outcome in July 1945 was a massive electoral transformation, a seismic change. It was the last old-fashioned party-political campaign before the television era changed the nature of politics for ever. Candidates spoke at street corners or at factory gates; there were noisy and boisterous public meetings – dozens in Cardiff alone, culminating in a mass rally at the Cory Hall on 4 July, the eve of polling day. There was heckling and face-to-face contact of the most direct kind between candidate and electors. In Cardiff South, Labour hecklers pursued the Tory member, Sir Arthur Evans, and his Penarth mistress with renderings of 'Hello! Hello! Who's your lady friend?'[17] Churchill was heckled with reminders of Tonypandy thirty-five years earlier.

The results were dramatic. Labour made seven gains: the three Cardiff seats, Newport, Swansea West, Llandaff and Barry, and Caernarfon. It ended up with twenty-five seats in Wales. In Britain as a whole it won 48 per cent of the vote. In Wales it was 58 per cent. There were majorities of over 20,000 in Caerphilly, Neath, Ogmore, Pontypridd, Aberdare, Abertillery, Bedwellty and Ebbw Vale: in Abertillery local Labour Party workers called for a recount to see if the Tory really had lost his deposit.[18] In Llanelli, James Griffiths won by over 34,000, the largest majority in Britain. There were some interesting new MPs. Llandaff and Barry was won by a prominent Labour lawyer, Sir Lynn Ungoed-Thomas, the son of a Nonconformist minister. In Newport, Peter Freeman, a vegetarian, theosophist, former tobacco manufacturer and tennis champion, defeated a Conservative who had held the seat for only two months. Cardiff produced three talented new members: Professor Hilary Marquand for Cardiff East, professor of industrial relations in the local university college, who went straight into government; George Thomas, a leftish school teacher in Cardiff West, who was to become in due time Speaker of the House; and in

Cardiff South, young James Callaghan comfortably straddled a constituency that extended from the villadom of Penarth to Butetown and Tiger Bay. In time he was to rise to the highest office of all.

Labour's strength in the industrial valleys was wholly predictable. But elsewhere, in the more rural areas, there was also Labour progress. Somewhat surprisingly, Moelwyn Hughes lost Carmarthenshire to the Liberal, R. Hopkin Morris, a KC and former regional director of the BBC, who benefited from the absence of a Tory candidate. But the Liberals found themselves under threat in Pembroke where Gwilym Lloyd George defeated Wilfred Fienburgh by only 168 votes, while in Merioneth Huw Morris Jones failed by a mere 112. Labour's vote rose substantially too in Anglesey where Cledwyn Hughes, an Aberystwyth-trained solicitor, was the candidate, while in Caernarfon, Goronwy Roberts, a Bangor-trained lecturer, easily defeated the sitting Liberal to show that Welsh national sentiment was alive and well in the modern Labour Party. A victory of a different kind came in Rhondda East where the veteran one-time syndicalist, W. H. Mainwaring, very narrowly defeated the Communists' general secretary, Harry Pollitt, by just 972 votes. In fact, it was to prove the Communists' last effective stand in this old left-wing stronghold, indeed their last significant political effort ever in Wales.

The 1945 triumph was as much sociological as political. Of the twenty-five all-male Labour MPs, all save two (Callaghan and Freeman) were Welsh; nineteen were of working-class background, if one includes the miner's son, George Thomas, a school teacher; James Callaghan, a union official; and the National Union of Teachers' spokesman, W. G. Cove, a former miner at the coalface. Twelve of the MPs were from the mining industry, nearly all former workers underground. In general they were senior figures, usually former councillors as well, whose presence in Parliament reflected their stature in the local community. Dai Grenfell (born 1881), W. H. Mainwaring (born 1884), S. O. Davies (born 1886), Jim Griffiths (born 1890), Ness Edwards (born 1897) and Aneurin Bevan (born 1897) had been socialist activists during the First World War. In a by-election in 1946, they were to be joined by John Evans, another miner, entering Parliament for Ogmore at the advanced age of seventy-one. Mainwaring (as a tutor), Edwards, Griffiths and Bevan had been at the famous left-wing Central

Labour College, part of its new post-war socialist élite; Davies had led miners' protests against conscription during the First World War and had been prominent in the Minority Movement afterwards; Mainwaring had been a leading author of the famous syndicalist pamphlet *The Miners' Next Step* published by the Unofficial Reform Committee at Tonypandy in 1912. They symbolized revenge, the conquest of power by a victimized generation. Truly, in Wales they were the masters now.

The Labour hegemony after 1945 did not begin well. The SWRCL had to record sadly that its victory celebration that autumn had to be cancelled because no national speaker could be persuaded to come down.[19] There were frequent complaints at the difficulty in getting Cabinet ministers to visit Wales to listen to local complaints. Cripps in October 1945 was only just able to squeeze in an early-morning visit to the SWRCL during a trip to see local businessmen as President of the Board of Trade. Far from an immediate unveiling of the New Jerusalem, the first months after Labour's election victory saw a rapid rise in unemployment to over 70,000 (over 10 per cent) by January 1946. There were bitter complaints at Aneurin Bevan's initial slow progress in building new homes, at Ellen Wilkinson for not creating multilateral schools and at Cripps's delays in adapting wartime ordnance factories and bringing in new work to the valleys. Rationing, shortages and general austerity were the pervasive features of what Labour chose to call 'fair shares'. By the end of 1946, however, when the economy was now thriving to meet post-war demand in continental Europe and North America, the response was much more cheerful.

From the outset, Wales was well to the fore in the new Attlee government. In the Cabinet was Aneurin Bevan, the most charismatic socialist of his time, now about to achieve his greatest triumph in the National Health Service. Of only slightly lesser rank was James Griffiths, Minister of National Insurance in 1945 and architect of the 1946 Social Insurance Act, the most notable legislation in this area since the Lloyd George measure of 1911. Others in government were Hilary Marquand at Overseas Trade, Lord (George) Hall at the Admiralty, Ness Edwards at the Board of Trade and, from October 1947, James Callaghan, junior minister at Transport and (from 1950) the Admiralty. The Welsh Labour members were a solid phalanx and the Welsh table at lunchtime well-attended (though seldom by Bevan who, claimed Callaghan, only joined them when he was in trouble[20]). They were seldom critical of the government. Predictable exceptions were S. O. Davies, invariably on the theme of 'a socialist foreign policy' but also on Welsh Home Rule, and W. G. Cove, whose ferocious attacks on Ellen Wilkinson for her failure to promote comprehensive secondary schools alienated several Labour members.[21] Perhaps the more effective Welsh protesters were those who sat for English or Scottish constituencies, representatives of the Welsh diaspora, Rhys Davies (Westhoughton), Harold Davies (Leek) and Emrys Hughes, Keir Hardie's pacifist son-in-law, who sat for South Ayrshire near Hardie's old Cumnock home.

Elsewhere, there were powerful Welsh potentates among the union leaders at a time when the alliance and synergy between the Trades Union Congress and the Labour Party were closer than at any other moment. Among them were steelworkers' leaders like Lincoln Evans and Dai Davies; Arthur Deakin of Merthyr, the right-wing czar of the transport workers, and a range of miners' leaders. Even NUM South Wales Area president and Communist president (later NUM secretary), Arthur Horner, was remarkably loyal to the Attlee government, as were other prominent Communists such as Bill Paynter, Will Whitehead and Dai Francis. Horner was even offered a position on the NCB, which would have indeed been the poacher turning gamekeeper, but he declined, although only after careful reflection. Elsewhere, in the central recesses of Transport House, Morgan Phillips directed operations, always sensitive to his Welsh roots and friendships, but also sternly opposed to Welsh national deviations in whatever form.[22] The Welsh presence in the post-war Attlee ascendancy was active and articulate at all levels.

This was even more true in local government. In Glamorgan and Monmouthshire, along with councils like Swansea and the Rhondda, Labour's control was total, dating as it did from the mid-1920s. An overwhelming Labour ethos prevailed, intermeshed with the local worlds of the unions, the co-operative society, the world of adult education and a complex mesh of family and personal relationships. An archetypal figure at this period was the ex-railwayman Llew Heycock of Port Talbot, the dominating patriarch of Glamorgan County Council over many decades, famous for his malapropisms. He was much attacked as a tyrannical boss, but also admired for his genuine commitment to his community, including the causes of the Welsh-speaking minority and the eisteddfod. In north Wales, the dominant personality in Welsh Labour ranks was Huw T. Edwards, a fiercely patriotic and administratively gifted transport workers' leader, a pillar of local community life at many levels including local government and in 1949 the chairman of the first Council for Wales.[23] The older Liberal-chapel ascendancy worked alongside these new conquerors rather than being totally displaced; indeed it is in many ways the similarity of outlook and ethos between the old national leaders and the new that is striking about Wales after 1945. James Griffiths's brother, 'Amanwy', was a famous eisteddfodic bard; Cledwyn Hughes was a disciple of Lloyd George even while fighting his daughter in elections; in 1951 Abertillery was to be represented by a Congregationalist minister.

Labour rule after 1945 followed the imperatives of the war years and of the party manifesto in the general election. Industries were taken into public ownership; all seemed to thrive in post-war conditions. Coal after nationalization on 1 January 1947 found renewed strength and was handicapped not by shortage of demand but by shortage of workers; the resultant introduction of Italian and (in the North Wales Coalfield) Polish workers brought some local controversy. In early 1948 the south-west region of the NCB reported a record weekly production of 592,400 tons. A giant new steelworks at Margam, near Port Talbot, planned from 1947 and eventually employing nearly 20,000 men, spoke of the progress in another long-depressed industry, alongside the new merger of Richard Thomas and Baldwin, and the cold reduction works at Port Talbot, Velindre and Trostre to replace obsolescent tinplate works. The docks of Cardiff, Barry, Newport and Swansea were also galvanized with new life after 1945. Central government used its powers to establish large new works like the nylon plant at Pontypool, the rubber factory at Brynmawr and a range of government advance factories including in long-depressed rural areas like Holyhead and Blaenau Ffestiniog. Trading estates at Bridgend, Hirwaun and Fforestfach, in addition to that at Treforest, hugely increased employment opportunities, including particularly for women. By the time of Labour's fall from power in October 1951 unemployment in Wales was less than 3 per cent. The *South Wales Industrial Review* spoke of a second industrial revolution in the valleys.[24] It was due in large measure to the market opportunities temporarily opened up as defeated powers like Germany or Japan strove to rebuild, alongside the assistance of Marshall Aid from America. But Labour claimed the credit for full employment, as well as the welfare state and 'fair shares' and the great majority of Welsh people seemed disposed to agree.

These developments did not differ in kind from those elsewhere in Britain after 1945. Their impact on the Welsh labour movement and on Welsh society and national consciousness was more complicated. Broad loyalty to the Attlee government, local pride in the achievements of ministers like Bevan and Griffiths, were matched by a constant dialogue of query, complaint and protest. In particular, the total failure of Attlee, Morrison and other ministers to show any recognition of the particular needs of Wales and the distinctive outlook of its Labour Party led to much difficulty. The new creation of the Welsh Regional Council of Labour (WRCL), merging the old SWRCL with the constituencies of north and mid Wales in May 1947, was a launchpad to further complaint. Indeed, the retention of the somewhat insulting word 'regional' was a frequent grievance: Morgan Phillips had flatly refused to accept the title 'Welsh Council of Labour'.[25]

The broader protests of post-war politics did not strike any particular resonance in Wales. Hardly any of the Welsh members joined in the 'Keep Left' protests against Bevin's cold-war policy in 1946. Their supporters were largely English and urban; the Welsh and other union-based old Labour elements remained doggedly loyal. Ernest Bevin blamed 'the Welsh' with their alleged pacifist inclinations when the parliamentary party rebelled against a two-year period of national service in 1947.[26] But even though the leader, somewhat improbably, was the centrist figure of James Callaghan, member for Cardiff South, the large majority of Welsh MPs did not join him. S. O. Davies and W. G. Cove were amongst those who signed the pre-electoral telegram of support to the left-wing Italian socialist Nenni in April 1948, but again it would be difficult to claim that the Welsh were particularly to the fore in left-wing dissent.

However, they had their own local and national grievances. In 1946, the Welsh Labour MPs *en bloc*, backed by the WRCL and leading union figures like Huw T. Edwards, complained vehemently to Attlee that post-war planning was being carried out with a total neglect of the special needs of Wales. A Cabinet paper, accepted without demur in January 1946, had rejected not merely a

Secretary of State on grounds of broad economic planning but even a permanent advisory council. In language that subsequently seems prophetic, the government urged: 'It is difficult to devise a plan by which such a Council would not become either a dead letter or a dilatory nuisance.' Among the arguments against a Welsh Office was 'Wales could not carry a cadre of officials of the highest calibre and the services of high English officials would no longer be available'.[27]

But, despite these patronizing observations from Whitehall, wartime demands for a Welsh Secretary of State and further governmental devolution had certainly not gone away. After some frustrating communications, a parliamentary deputation led by Grenfell and Mainwaring met Attlee, Cripps and George Isaacs, Minister of Labour, on 25 July 1946 to complain about the rise of unemployment totals in Wales to 9 per cent. It was a somewhat bad-tempered session: the Welsh members complained of bad faith and Attlee criticized them for vagueness of detail.[28] Six days later, Attlee wrote to Grenfell detailing the government's responsiveness to Wales: the annual Welsh debate, the annual white paper, extended regional organization of government departments. But 'the appointment of a special Minister would not be in the special interests of Wales'.[29] Not surprisingly, the MPs were far from satisfied. On 14 August, Grenfell and Mainwaring on their behalf protested at the inadequacies of the government's response. This time their complaints had a more obviously nationalist ring. 'The reply of the Government seems to repudiate entirely the claims of Wales as a nation. It will not satisfy the supporters of the Government nor the majority of people in any party in Wales.' They called for a dedicated minister to look after Welsh matters.[30] Attlee's reply on 5 September was amiable in tone but offered nothing. He outlined the virtues of 'formal and regular meetings' of the various Welsh regional offices of government departments. But the government believed 'that it would be a mistake to think that Wales could achieve economic well-being altogether apart from considerations of policy for Britain as a whole; nor do I accept the view that the appointment of a Secretary of State would solve the economic problem.'[31]

The matter of Welsh nationality may have been a fringe issue for Attlee and his ministers but it continued to rumble in a way that anticipates the debates over devolution fifty years later. The Scots had made considerable strides during the wartime years, benefiting from the presence of Tom Johnston as Secretary of State under Churchill. They had gained a Scottish Council of State and a Scottish Council of Industry, along with local developments such as a North of Scotland Hydro-Electric Board. Johnston had been able to terrify Churchill and colleagues with threats of a Scottish Nationalist upsurge if the government did not make these concessions: the return of Dr McIntyre as the first Scottish Nationalist MP in a by-election at Motherwell had given his claims somewhat slender credence. 'We had got Scottish wishes and opinions respected and listened to', wrote Johnston in his memoirs, 'as they had not been respected or listened to since the Act of Union.'[32] By contrast, Wales had got nothing at all. The wartime Welsh Advisory Council had called for a Welsh Planning Authority in 1944 to deal with the post-war special needs of Wales as a region or nation, but that had been ignored.[33]

James Griffiths had been the leading figure on the Welsh Advisory Council. While Aneurin Bevan was sternly centralist and totally hostile to any form of Welsh separatism at this stage, Griffiths from within the government did his best to promote Welsh devolution. In December 1946 he circulated a Cabinet paper (CP 462) which called for the bill to nationalize electricity supplies to constitute the whole of Wales and Monmouthshire as a single Area Board. 'The proposals to divide Wales in the Electricity Bill will be criticized both on grounds of National sentiment and on the grounds that they provide an arbitrary division of areas which, for other administrative purposes, are treated as a single unit.' He pointed out that central and north Wales, including parts of Cardiganshire, would be linked with Merseyside under MANWEB and would cut across the proposals on local authority boundaries made by a recent commission chaired by R. Moelwyn Hughes KC, the erstwhile Welsh Labour MP.[34] But the government dismissed Griffiths's ideas out of hand. In August 1946 Kingsley Martin's *New Statesman and Nation* noted that, in 1945, Welsh Labour had made five main promises: a Secretary of State; a separate Welsh Broadcasting Corporation; an end to the forced transfer of labour to England; a north–south Welsh trunk road; and a central body to plan and develop the Welsh economy. 'All five have now been turned down in Westminster.'[35]

However, the WRCL and a variety of Welsh MPs, from Goronwy Roberts and Robert Richards in the north to George Thomas in

Cardiff, continued to press for more attention to Wales in the government's programme. In the autumn of 1948, a government committee, the Home Services Committee, which included both Bevan and Griffiths, debated the possibilities of a Secretary of State, or at least an advisory council of some kind. Bevan opposed even the latter but in consultation with the Machinery of Government Committee, the Cabinet came up with the idea of an advisory council for Wales. Griffiths wanted this chaired by a minister of Cabinet rank but Morrison vetoed this as likely to create a 'buffer minister' who would impede efficient government.[36] In a Cabinet paper of his own (CP 228) in October 1948 Morrison spoke of 'the difficulties that would arise between the chairman and other Cabinet ministers'. It would 'strengthen the demand for a Secretary of State for Wales', which Morrison evidently regarded as a crushing argument against the idea.[37] The council's chairman in the end was the influential north Wales trade union leader, Huw T. Edwards, and Morrison himself addressed the council's inaugural meeting on 17 May 1949. It considered a range of important economic and later cultural issues but quite soon disillusion, even boredom, set in. It enjoyed no executive power and was little more than a talking shop. The council's phantom-like existence petered out in 1966.

The demand in Labour ranks for distinct recognition for Wales continued despite the heavy-handed undemocratic centralism of Morrison and Attlee. In particular rising figures in north Wales like Goronwy Roberts, the member for Caernarfon, and Cledwyn Hughes, member for Anglesey in 1951, along with others like T. W. Jones, member for Merioneth in 1951 and Elwyn Jones, member for Conway in 1950–1, all called for greater recognition, at least a Secretary of State, even a Welsh elected assembly. In August 1950 Goronwy Roberts received short shrift from Morgan Phillips and Transport House. He cited two recent decisions imposed on a hostile Welsh opinion: the Forestry Commission taking 20,000 acres in west Wales for afforestation in defiance of the local population and the seizure of land for military use in Trawsfynydd in northern Merioneth. 'There is a growing feeling in Wales that the Movement is hostile to all suggestions of devolution.' Welsh Labour, he claimed, was 'dispirited and frustrated'. He talked of the difficulty in finding suitable candidates in Anglesey (where Cledwyn Hughes was reluctant to stand again), West Denbighshire, Montgomeryshire, West Flint, Merioneth and Cardiganshire. 'The movement for devolution will gather force. Is Labour to be placed in a position of such hostility to such a natural and indeed traditionally socialist idea' or would it continue to be treated 'as a kind of box room where the rubbish of the United Kingdom may be dumped'? He demanded that Wales be treated as a unit for all government purposes, that the advisory council be treated as a working party for specific Welsh problems and that either a minister or a national council be set up 'which may focus the whole of Welsh thought and take its views into orderly consideration'.[38] Roberts was brushed aside yet again by Transport House.

A further pointer to the potential tension between centralist socialism and forms of nationalism arose that summer when Lady Megan Lloyd George launched an all-party Parliament for Wales campaign at the traditional setting for such events, namely the spa of Llandrindod Wells.[39] The movement had been stimulated by the cultural pressure group Undeb Cymru Fydd; its secretary, the writer and broadcaster, T. I. Ellis, was the son of Tom Ellis, the visionary nationalist-prophet of Cymru Fydd in the 1890s, while the presence of W. R. P. George, the nephew of David Lloyd George, was another sign of distinguished ancestry and continuity. The movement eventually attracted the support of no less than five Labour MPs – Goronwy Roberts, Cledwyn Hughes, T. W. Jones, S. O. Davies, the Merthyr Marxist, and also Tudor Watkins from Radnor and Brecon – while several defeated candidates in north and mid Wales had also favoured the idea of a Welsh Parliament. The support for the dissident five was not widespread but their presence remained an embarrassment for the Labour Party machine, both Morgan Phillips in London and Cliff Prothero of the Welsh Council of Labour. It reminded contemporaries of an old and abiding argument that remained incomplete even in the glory years of the Attlee government.

Some months before the Parliament for Wales campaign was launched, Wales and the United Kingdom had their opportunity to give their verdict on five years of Labour government. It was clear that, after years of rationing and austerity, the Attlee government's popularity had slipped a good deal, especially in middle-class constituencies in southern and eastern England. However, in the general election of 1950 Wales remained quite as solid as before for what it regarded as peculiarly its own administration. Disputes over Welsh national recognition paled by comparison with the boons of full employment, economic growth, welfare and the National Health Service. While Labour nationally saw its majority fall from over 150 to just six, in Wales its popularity was greater than ever. Churchill was heckled at Ninian Park, Cardiff, over his role at Tonypandy in 1910.[40] Morale was high in the party: individual membership had risen sharply. Nor was Labour's energy by any means exhausted. Particular attention had been paid by the WRCL to the Welsh-speaking areas of north and mid Wales. Labour had never struck deep roots here as it had in the industrial south but there had nevertheless been a Labour MP for Anglesey as early as 1918 and for Caernarfon, with its slate quarrymen, in 1922–4. Conversely, rural Welsh Liberalism had been in decline since the fall of the Lloyd George coalition in 1922, while Plaid Cymru was as yet a minor force. This campaigning in rural areas was to bear fruit in the 1950 election campaign. There was a high poll in Wales, 85 per cent, the highest in Britain. Labour's share of the Welsh votes was 58 per cent, the same as in the high noon of 1945.

The outcome confirmed that Labour's advance in Wales continued, whatever the result in Britain as a whole. Labour now held twenty-seven of the thirty-six Welsh seats, as against five rural Liberal seats and four Conservatives. With the redistribution of Welsh constituencies, it is difficult to be certain about gains and losses. In some the absence of a Liberal gave the Conservatives a slight advantage but not enough to count. One clear Labour gain in a new area was in Pembrokeshire where Desmond Donnelly, a young left-wing journalist of Irish extraction, gained a very narrow victory over Gwilym Lloyd George.[41] Carmarthen remained Liberal by a majority of 0.4 per cent. Conversely Labour lost one of the Cardiff seats, Cardiff North. In north Wales, there was a narrow Labour victory at Conway and strong votes again in Anglesey and Merioneth as in 1945. At least nineteen of the twenty-seven Labour MPs were of broadly working-class background, twelve having originally been working miners. One novelty in the macho world of Welsh Labour politics was that there were now for the first time women Labour MPs, Eirene White in East Flint, daughter of the redoubtable Thomas Jones, Lloyd George's former secretary, and Dorothy Rees in Barry, a school teacher.[42] There were younger women organizers such as Peggy England Jones in Swansea and Megan Roach, but a labour movement so close to the unions and the world of hard manual labour was unlikely to give women socialists much encouragement: in any case the total number of women elected in Britain generally was only twenty-one, fourteen being Labour, a decline from 1945. Clearly though, in a sharply polarized political culture, the Labour dominance of Wales was amply confirmed. Welsh Labour remained loyal, solid and satisfied with Labour's years in power. In the government, Bevan remained at Health (Attlee refusing to promote him, perhaps on doctrinaire grounds) before moving to the Ministry of Labour in January 1951 at the height of the Korean War. Griffiths entered the Cabinet as Colonial Secretary while Ness Edwards became Postmaster General. On the whole, however, the performance of the Welsh MPs did not encourage the party leaders to consider them for promotion.

The final year-and-a-half of Labour government, with an overall majority of just six, was a very difficult time. From June 1950 it was caught up by the war in Korea, the arguments over the rearmament programme, the Cabinet disputes over health service charges that saw Bevan and Wilson resign, an alarming balance of payments crisis and finally possible wars in Persia and/or Egypt in its final weeks in office. On balance, the Welsh remained loyal and gave little encouragement to movements of protest. S. O. Davies voiced public opposition to lending support to for South Korea; he received widespread backing for his views but relatively little within Wales.[43] James Griffiths was but one minister worried about the scale of rearmament and the consequent charges on the health service, but there was no likelihood of resignation or overt protest here. By far the most serious challenge was that from Aneurin Bevan in April 1951. His resignation led to the prolonged civil war between the so-called Bevanites (who may or may not have included Bevan himself) and the Gaitskellite right. Wales, however, gave remarkably little support to the Bevanite persuasion. None of the original fifteen who formed the core of the later Bevanite group in May 1951 represented a Welsh seat, although they included two of Welsh ancestry, Harold Davies and Will Griffiths, both of whom represented English seats. The Welsh were in the main centre-right in these disputes but in any case trade unionists such as miners and others were hostile to acts of private rebellion, however worthy the cause. Thus while Bevan found backing from party activists in Ebbw Vale, his support in the main came from middle-class socialists operating in London, many of them journalists such as Foot,

Crossman and Driberg. Amongst the Welsh MPs, Desmond Donnelly and George Thomas made occasional statements of support but not consistently so. Donnelly in due time was to move sharply towards the far right of the party, indeed moving out of it altogether. He ended up as an erratic Tory before committing suicide. Aneurin Bevan may have been a Welshman, proud of his ancestry, but to the Welsh labour movement it was the cause not the man that counted.

When the Attlee government went to the country again in October 1951, at a particularly unfavourable time, it was widely anticipated that it would be defeated. So events turned out, although the eventual margin was a narrow one and Labour, with 49 per cent of the vote, polled 230,000 more votes than the Conservatives. Its percentage of the poll was unequalled in British history until John Major's victory in 1992. Wales, despite the Bevanite rebellion and other problems, was even more solid than in 1950. Indeed, its share of the vote at 60 per cent was higher than in 1945. The Welsh turnout at 84 per cent was again the highest in Britain. Despite a flood of Tory money and propaganda in the press for the Tory cause (the Cardiff-based *Western Mail*, resolutely Tory throughout, made scant effort to give Labour a fair hearing), the Welsh voters held to their old faith. The tally of Labour seats remained at twenty-seven out of thirty-six. Two marginal seats were lost, Elwyn Jones in Conway and Dorothy Rees in Barry. To balance this, Cledwyn Hughes finally triumphed in his third battle with Lady Megan Lloyd George in Anglesey, with a 595-vote majority, and began a long and distinguished tenure of the seat. In nearby Merioneth, T. W. Jones, an elderly ex-miner from Rhosllanerchrugog, Wrexham, defeated Emrys Roberts, the Liberal member since 1945. The Liberals retained Carmarthen, Cardigan and Montgomeryshire with some help from an electoral pact with the Tories.[44] But it made them look opportunist, while Clement Davies, their 66-year-old leader, was a failing force moving to the right. Labour had even stronger credentials to speak as the voice of progressive forces in Wales: only one Communist stood, Idris Cox in the Rhondda, and he lost his deposit. Some rising figures in Labour's ranks came from Wales, notably James Callaghan who had made a strong impression as a competent Admiralty minister. Whereas in Britain as a whole, therefore, the fall of Attlee's government marked a clear shift in national debate, from the ethos of 'fair shares' to that of 'setting the people free', in Wales there was little change. In defeat as in victory, the Labour ascendancy confirmed a turning-point at which Welsh politics resolutely refused to turn.

The years 1939–51 cast their shadow over the Labour Party and Welsh politics for much of the rest of the century. They symbolized people's power, solidarity, a collective response, central planning, a welfare democracy and social citizenship, an ethos diffused through local councils, the trade unions and the public services, to renew the nation after the suffering of the inter-war years. The main fabric of Labour's economic achievement, and the instruments of corporate government that ran it, largely survived until the 1980s. It was a period of reform, yet also of social and cultural conservatism. Labour's victory was for the old values. It was based on the communal solidarity of the pit and the choir and the co-op and the Workers' Educational Association, transmitted from the industrial valleys throughout significant areas of the Welsh-speaking north and west as well. Its most characteristic figures were working-class ministers like James Griffiths, trade unionists like Huw T. Edwards, local government bosses like Heycock, relatively senior figures whose outlook was shaped by past experience. It gave socialist values and historic images a new infusion of life. No raging now against the dying of the light. Post-war Wales handed on to future generations the potent legend of Labour in power. The anniversary of the birth of Nye Bevan in 1997, attended by Gordon Brown amongst others, gave an opportunity to replay the nostalgic tunes of Old Labour. What this pivotal period did not do was relate those achievements and that legend to the concept of a living Welsh nation. That was to remain unfinished business, to beguile or torment comrades yet unborn.

Notes

[1] K. O. Morgan, *Modern Wales: Politics, Places and People* (Cardiff, 1995), 108–9; Iorwerth Peate, *Rhwng Dau Fyd* (Denbigh, 1976), 122–9.

[2] J. Morris, 'Morale under air attack: Swansea 1939–1941', *WHR*, XI/3 (1983).

[3] S. Brooke, *Labour's War* (Oxford, 1992).

[4] See K. Jefferys (ed.), *Labour and the Wartime Coalition: From the Diary of James Chuter Ede* (London, 1987), 178–80.

[5] South Wales Regional Council of Labour minutes, 14 April 1942 (NLW).

[6] Ibid., 4 Oct. 1941.

[7] H. Francis and D. Smith, *The Fed: A History of the South Wales Miners in the Twentieth Century* (Cardiff, 1980), 403 ff.

[8] S. Bloomfield, 'The apprentice boys strikes of the Second World War', *Llafur*, III/2 (1981).

[9] A. Bevan, *Why Not Trust the Tories?* (London, 1944), 25.

[10] James Griffiths Papers (NLW), C1/2.

[11] D. Jay, *Change and Fortune* (London, 1980), 116 ff. He adds, 'I was not entirely prepared, however, for the torrent of Welsh oratory awaiting me in the Valleys'. The memory lingered on, sixty years later.

[12] E. Pride, 'The economic province of Wales', *Trans. Hon. Soc. Cymmrodorion* (1969), 111 ff.

[13] Francis and Smith, *The Fed*, 418.

[14] Brecon and Radnor constituency Labour Party papers, 1939–45 (NLW).

[15] SWRCL, 10 May 1943.

[16] K. O. Morgan, *Callaghan: A Life* (Oxford, 1997), 53–4.

[17] Ibid., 54.

[18] C. Prothero, *Recount* (Ormskirk, 1982), 57.

[19] SWRCL, 17 Sept. 1945.

[20] Personal information.

[21] B. Vernon, *Ellen Wilkinson* (London, 1982), 219–21.

[22] K. O. Morgan, 'Morgan Phillips', in idem, *Labour People: Leaders and Lieutenants, Hardie to Kinnock* (Oxford, 1992), 231–8.

[23] See the Edwards papers (NLW).

[24] *South Wales Industrial Review*, II/3 (Jan. 1950), 12–15.

[25] Welsh Regional Council of Labour (WRCL) minutes, 5 May 1947; Prothero, *Recount*, 53–4.

[26] L. V. Scott, *Conscription and the Attlee Government* (Oxford, 1993), 152.

[27] 'The administration of Wales and Monmouthshire', CP (46), 21, 23 Jan. 1946 (Public Record Office (PRO), CAB 129/6).

[28] Record of meeting, 25 July 1946 (PRO, PREM 8/272).

[29] Attlee to D. R. Grenfell, 31 July 1946 (Labour Party archives, GS 9/2); also PRO, PREM 8/1569.

[30] Grenfell and Mainwaring to Attlee, 14 Aug. 1946 (ibid.).

[31] Attlee to Grenfell, 5 Sept. 1946 (ibid.).

[32] C. Harvie, *Scotland and Nationalism: Scottish Society and Politics, 1707–1977* (2nd edn., London, 1994), 29–33.

[33] Griffiths Papers, C1/6.

[34] Note on 'Area Boards covering Wales under the Electricity Bill', 17 Dec. 1946, CP (46) 462 (PRO, CAB 129/15).

[35] *New Statesman and Nation* (24 Aug. 1946).

[36] 'The administration of Wales and Monmouthshire', CP (48) 228 (PRO, CAB 129/30); Cabinet minutes, 15 Oct., 18 Nov. 1948 (CAB 128/13); Morrison to Griffiths, 13 Oct. 1948 (Griffiths Papers, C2/9); meeting of Morrison with Welsh Regional Council of Labour and Welsh Parliamentary Group, 29 Oct. 1948 (ibid., C2/15).

[37] Griffiths Papers, C2/31.

[38] G. Roberts to G. Williams, 8 Aug. 1950 (Labour Party archives, GS 9/2).

[39] See J. G. Jones, 'The Parliament for Wales campaign', *WHR*, XVI/2 (1992), 207 ff.

[40] *WM*, 9 Feb. 1950.

[41] Desmond Donnelly Papers, B1–3 (NLW).

[42] See P. Stead, 'The town that had come of age: Barry 1918–1939', in D. Moore (ed.), *Barry: The Centenary Book* (Barry, 1984), 455–6, for a sympathetic portrait of Dorothy Rees.

[43] See S. O. Davies Papers, A16 (South Wales Coalfield Archive).

[44] *WM*, 2 Oct. 1951.

1. William Abraham (Mabon) unveiling a new fountain in Tonypandy, 1911.
(Photo: University of Wales, Swansea)

2. Members of the Cardiff Independent Labour Party Women's Group
campaigning in a municipal election *c*. 1905. (Photo: University of Wales,
Swansea)

3. Labour supporters on the platform at Cardiff station during an election campaign in the 1920s. (Photo: University of Wales, Swansea)

4. Keir Hardie addressing a meeting on Dowlais Top, *c.* 1900. (Photo: University of Wales, Swansea)

5. James Griffiths – a typical response to Labour conference speeches in the 1950s. (Photo: National Museum of Labour History)

6. Aneurin Bevan speaking at the South Wales Miners' Gala

7. Irene White and Dorothy Rees, the first Welsh Labour women MPs, were elected to parliament in 1950. (Photo: National Museum of Labour History)

8. Neil Kinnock – regularly pilloried by the press for his 'Welshness' (Photo: National Museum of Labour History)

9. Rhodri Morgan, Jessica Morden (General Secretary, Wales Labour Party) and Paul Murphy celebrate Labour's hundredth birthday. (Photo: Ethos Photography)

III
LABOUR WALES

8

The Structure of Power in Labour Wales, 1951–1964

ANDREW WALLING

Relatively little has been written on the Labour Party in Wales during the thirteen years of opposition between 1951 and 1964. J. Graham Jones has written detailed accounts of individual elections in specific constituencies, as well as on the Parliament for Wales campaign in the 1950s and Kenneth O. Morgan and others have written in general terms about the period. The gaps in the literature are substantial and surprising given the wealth of material available in the archives of central and often colourful figures. This chapter highlights the importance of these sources for dispelling myths about Labour's development and politics in Wales and suggests some themes which might be more fully developed by others in the future. Throughout this period, Labour looked to extend its political dominance. Not content with dominating its traditional heartlands in the industrial south, Labour was trying to become the party of all Wales. This chapter examines how it operated in the constituencies and through its Welsh office. It is argued that the Labour Party was able to promote itself as a radical party, a party of ideas, forward-looking, experienced and relevant to all Wales. Labour stood for modernization, with attractive policy proposals, the promise of services, planning and investment. It offered an all-embracing package of proposals which would cover social, political and economic life in Wales. Throughout the 1950s and 1960s, the Labour Party attempted to extend its power base into north and rural Wales, a process made all the more difficult by the shallow base of support and the lack of a Labour tradition. It pursued a radical line, setting out to increase its profile and appeal by promoting its ideas on economic planning. The party sought to modernize old industries, attract new ones and improve local amenities.

Two images of the Labour Party in post-war Wales predominate. The first is of powerful and oligarchical domination, a 'one-party state'. The second is the image of Aneurin Bevan and the idea of Welsh militancy. The nature of Labour's power and the potential for individuals to dominate areas of Labour strength has been investigated by Ian McAllister. McAllister argues that the domination of a small caucus-based party led to 'decisions on policy and strategy [being] made by small groups, and [that] during elections little attempt is made to construct a competitive electoral machine'.[1] By contrast, this chapter will examine how an oligarchy, clique or even a powerful individual could become dominant in an area. It will also show that the strength of the local powerbrokers and the electorate's habitual faith in them did not necessarily mean that these individuals lost touch with their constituents. Indeed, through their dealings with key local issues and by getting things done, such individuals earned trust and respect in their localities. Finally, it is suggested that the well-publicized, divisive and often bitter left/right national splits, barely scratched the surface of local politics. Instead, local issues such as paving, lighting, parks, buses and houses remained at the centre of local politics and in fact did not fall into left/right categories. The more politically divisive arguments only really occurred sporadically and especially during selection or reselection processes when groups or individuals were attempting to ensure that their candidate succeeded.

In this respect, the chapter echoes Chris Williams's work on the Rhondda. Williams argues that Labour's local power did not deteriorate into machine politics; that Labour remained a 'popular' party. He shows that 'party leaders [were not] manipulating an electorate whose political sense had been dulled by habitual tradition' and contends that this loyal support 'was a product of a class-conscious society that elevated its own representatives in a process of community redefinition that rested upon deep collective and personal loyalties and upon a rich associational culture'.[2]

Williams's views about the Rhondda clearly apply in other parts of Wales. By pursuing local issues and topics of local importance, the electorate unstintingly returned the same few individuals to power, confident that they would look after their locality's best interests. This chapter extends Williams's views by suggesting that, despite Labour's domination throughout industrial south Wales and despite the power of party officials which this created, it did not lose touch with rank-and-file supporters; it did not become insular, nor did it neglect Welsh-speaking, rural and north Wales areas. Labour's local domination did provide a central focus for a few organizers, agents and local party workers, but there was a genuine commitment from Welsh party organizers and officials in Cardiff to developing new policies for the whole of Wales. If the party was not uniformly enthusiastic about devolution (the issue which dominates the literature to the exclusion of all else), on balance it was still a party of progress, with a perceived relevance in the north as well as the south.

The sheer magnitude of Labour's electoral domination in its urban heartlands cannot fail to impress. In 1945, Labour's victory had been even more sweeping in Wales than in Britain as a whole. The trend of Labour's massive ascendancy in Wales continued throughout the 1950s and 1960s. Particularly in urban Wales, voting Labour was a way of life, passed on from one generation to the next. Safe seats really were safe seats and thrashing Conservative opponents was the norm not an exception. Whilst the party spent long periods in decline nationally between 1951 and 1964, in Wales, quite the reverse was true, as Wales became an even-more-pronounced bastion of Labour strength. Labour made gains, returning twenty-seven MPs from thirty-six constituencies in 1951 and reaching a high-water mark of thirty-two in 1966.

Wales was also increasingly important to the British Labour Party. Its MPs were moving up the political hierarchy, rather than remaining as backbench MPs. In Aneurin Bevan and Jim Griffiths, Labour supplied two leading national figures. Moreover, Labour's growing success in Wales was a major contributory factor to its success in British elections. Labour's national appeal was not unattractive in Wales. Throughout Britain, the Labour Party was attempting to couch itself in a progressive rhetoric, presenting the face of a modernizing party. At the top of the party the intellectual advance of revisionism, led by Gaitskell and Crosland, helped Labour to shift the emphasis of its message. Crosland felt that socialism was about alleviating social want. Equality lay at the centre of his and of the Labour Party's beliefs. Of course, Bevan – the apparent embodiment of Welsh Labour – at times opposed the leadership. However, he, Jim Griffiths and many other Labour 'left-wingers' found much in the domestic programme which was valuable. The important factor remained Crosland's commitment to higher public expenditure through progressive taxation. Labour's message was one of services and investment. This national message provided great scope at the local level for creative, modern and attractive adaption to Welsh needs, as in the Welsh Labour version of the popular policy document *Signposts for the Sixties*. Thus, the new revisionist approach to nationalization, seen in the 1957 document *Industry and Society* stressed the growing desire for greater efficiency within nationalized industries, yet did not advocate denationalization. In the Welsh industrial heartlands, this message could be made highly attractive to miners and steelworkers, who recognized the need for investment and change. In rural areas, the promise of higher investment was matched by what was being said on the ground with promises of new roads and social amenities, as well as the desire to invest in and attract new industry. Thus, the issues being discussed by national figures could be seized on and used to promise practical benefits locally. Labour was the modernizing practical party talking about services, investment, planning, jobs, an infrastructure and a strong economy.

Kenneth O. Morgan has noted how 'the domination of the Labour Party and the trade-union movement over the social and political élites of the land became . . . seemingly impregnable between 1945 and 1966'.[3] What needs to be stressed is not just the way that industrial Wales became securely Labour (as it had not been in 1939). Labour also expanded into new areas. Increasing Labour dominance was at the expense of the Liberals. Throughout the 1950s and 1960s, the Labour Party was able to tap the Liberal tradition, exude a progressive, radical and modernizing air, and, as a result become increasingly credible in many areas of north and rural Wales. In the 1950 general election, the Liberals retained just five seats in Wales, all largely rural, and lost Pembrokeshire to Labour. The 1951 election saw the Liberals lose their tenuous grips on Anglesey and Merioneth. The victory of Holyhead solicitor Cledwyn Hughes over Lady Megan Lloyd George symbolized the shift from Liberal to Labour. Hughes was a Welsh-speaking radical from the professional classes whose father had been a prominent Liberal. Such important personal connections made his candidature as a Welsh radical all the more credible. He was able to present the Labour Party's programme as progressive and modern. Electrification, rural housing, comprehensive education and the modernization of agriculture meant Labour was able to paper over its lack of a firm social base to both win and then retain the seat.

In Merioneth, Labour's victory in 1951 can be seen more as a shift in rural communities. As Kenneth O. Morgan argues, 'the workers in Blaenau Ffestiniog and Trawsfynydd were sufficiently numerous to return T. W. Jones, a senior trade unionist from Wrexham/Maelor, at the expense of Emrys Roberts'.[4] In 1955, the Liberals hung on to their three remaining seats: Cardiganshire, Montgomeryshire and Carmarthen. However, in February 1957 Lady Megan Lloyd George, standing as a Labour candidate, won Carmarthen with a majority of 3,069. Finally, at the 1966 election, Cardiganshire (a Liberal seat since 1880), was gained by the Labour candidate Elystan Morgan. As Kenneth O. Morgan notes, the 'Welsh speaking barrister from UCW Aberystwyth, was precisely the kind of articulate, progressive young professional man who would have been a natural Liberal less than a generation earlier'.[5] Labour was choosing candidates in these areas who would promote its image as a Welsh party of modernization.

In addition to absorbing an element of the Liberal tradition, Labour was also not inattentive to the national issue. During this period there was greater recognition of Wales as a distinct political area. There was a weakening of Labour's 'long-standing antagonism towards the separate political recognition of Wales'.[6] However, difficulties arose over the form and extent of decentralization. Constituencies sent resolutions calling for the decentralization of administrative authority from London to Cardiff and stronger demands came from Goronwy Roberts and S. O. Davies, through their 'Parliament for Wales' campaign. They enlisted the support of Lady Megan Lloyd George, Tudor Watkins (MP for Brecon and Radnor) and John Morris (future MP for Aberavon). Another group, comprising James Griffiths and his supporters, sought a Secretary of State for Wales.

The attitude of Welsh Labour as a whole was complex. The Welsh Regional Council of Labour (WRCL), which had initially supported the objective of a Secretary of State, by 1948 sought only a greater measure of self-determination, feeling the appointment of a 'Secretary of State for Wales was no longer practicable'. It, 'therefore, prepared an alternative policy of a more comprehensive nature, based on Democratic Devolution'. The meeting called for the establishment of 'an Advisory Council composed of representatives of Welsh life, for the purpose of advising the Government and its Agents on the need for appropriate legislation to meet the requirements of Wales from time to time'.[7] Following a deputation to the government, agreement was reached when the government formed a 'Council for Wales Plan', to include representatives from local authorities (twelve), industry and agriculture (four), trade unions (four), the national eisteddfod (one), the joint education committee (one), the University of Wales (one), the Welsh Tourist Board (one) and the Prime Minister's Appointments (three). The government then satisfied the WRCL's requests. The Council for Wales and Monmouthshire played a purely advisory role. It could neither legislate nor administer. Its first reports for the Labour government in 1949 covered the issues of unemployment, marginal land and rural depopulation. However, the toothless nature of the council was exposed once the Conservatives gained power. Cliff Prothero saw the change of government as the end of the council as a viable and trusted body. Huw T. Edwards felt 'it was not until much later . . . that the Council really succeeded in justifying its existence'.[8] The composition of the council was changed to suit the incumbent government. Henry Brooke, the Conservative Home Secretary and Minister of State for Wales, replaced the representation of cultural organizations with more members appointed by the Prime Minister. The council's function, purpose and standing were tarnished.

As the council has been studied largely as a retreat from devolution, its work and policy statements have received little attention. In fact the council produced some valuable reports. Its emphasis was on achieving a platform for development by improving the infrastructure of Wales. Work on rural areas highlighted numerous problems and suggested ways of improving housing, roads, water, sewerage and amenities. The government fully accepted the conditions were as described, but 'whilst accepting the Panel's diagnosis, the Government completely rejected the Panel's prescription'. The Conservative government's poor working relationship with the council is further highlighted by Edwards, who noted 'there was not a single instance of the Council or Panel being brought into consultation by the Government about its report and contents. The first indication the Council received of Government opinion was when it published its report.'[9]

The main concerns of the Council for Wales were also the main concerns of the Welsh Labour Party. The WRCL offered ideas on improving Welsh life. It was not simply the voice of south Wales's trade unions. The Labour Party's attempts to break into Liberal or Conservative areas of rural (particularly north) Wales are clearly visible through the attention they gave to rural areas. The WRCL's comprehensive agenda attempted to improve everyday standards of life, from housing, transport, work and the economy to the more grandiose schemes: airports, the Severn Bridge, industrial estates, new road networks and new factories. Other sections of the Labour Party had even more ambitious schemes. For example, from 1945, the Parliament for Wales group, made up of north Wales Labour candidates, had established their own broadsheet, *Llais Llafur*, which 'promised not only a Secretary of State, but an economic planning authority for Wales, a radio corporation, an end to emigration and a north–south road link'.[10]

The WRCL addressed real issues and long-term problems. In rural areas, these problems included a lack of jobs, poor roads and the decline of old industries, as well as the need for water, electricity and mechanization in some areas. These deprivations were seen as inegalitarian and as a spur to depopulation. The WRCL noted:

The greater part of the majority of school-leavers who can not be absorbed by the country towns, leave Wales to find employment elsewhere, hence low unemployment figures in these areas . . . not only bodies but also intelligence is being drained away from these areas at an alarming rate.[11]

Caradog Jones, Labour's candidate in Montgomeryshire throughout the 1950s, echoed such sentiments, stating that: 'youth and particularly the more vigorous elements could not find opportunities for satisfactory employment in Rural Wales. Thus emigration . . . is breaking down Welsh Rural Society and can only be arrested by developing the natural resources of the area.'[12] The WRCL's solution was clear: a healthy economy providing a variety of employment, which 'can be achieved with the minimum expenditure by the establishment in the main of ancillary industry to deal with the primary products and natural resources of these areas'. Labour also felt that 'the establishment of the industry of the type proposed would bring a return on capital expended, and would help local authorities by providing them with additional sources of local revenues'.

The introduction of new factories had begun under the Attlee administration. Labour now set out more substantial plans. Having witnessed the introduction of trading estates in depressed industrial areas of Britain, the WRCL felt they had 'proved their worth, socially and economically'.[13] It demanded a variant of these estates for rural areas and called for similar estates in the towns. The plans aimed at long-term prosperity for Wales. Generally, they did not advocate throwing money at problems. The Severn Bridge scheme was to play a pivotal role, opening up the south and south-east of England to Wales, a link that would be a boon for trade. The WRCL investigated ways of tapping the natural resources and primary products of the countryside and believed that its practical policy measures should be implemented by the next Labour government.

Of course, these 'modernizing' plans stressed the 'industrialization' of the countryside and were hardly what many rural traditionalists wanted. However agriculture was not entirely neglected. On the contrary, the WRCL felt improvements to agriculture were fundamental to the re-creation of prosperity in rural Wales. The rapid transition in the nature of the land, from lowland to marginal and hill farms was not ignored, with plans to increase fertility and improve drainage in upland areas and the proposal of a 'ten year programme'. Existing subsidies for fertilizers were to be maintained with additional aid for transport to remote hill farms. Farmers would receive financial aid to improve their pastures, as well as capital for building, drainage and water supply. Co-operatives were encouraged to reduce the excessive costs of agricultural machinery and foodstuffs and to provide smaller farmers with the advantages of selling on a larger scale. Producer marketing boards would be introduced for eggs, poultry, pigs, cattle and sheep. It was hoped marketing boards would produce 'order and stability out of the existing chaos'.[14] It was felt the problematic drift of the young from the land could at least be slowed by providing training courses on cropping, land improvement and similar developments in secondary schools. The package was completed by a scheme to improve unclassified roads, clear recognition that efficient farming practice meant reasonably modern transport facilities in rural areas. Forestry was also recognized as an expanding element of life in rural areas and was set to continue expanding. Proposals to increase the acreage of plantations were meant to create up to 15,000 jobs.

Benefits were stressed for smaller rural businesses with the same vigour. Making use of primary products from rural areas was important. The WRCL argued this provided the raw materials which sustained other industries. It called for numerous small concerns to be established. Medium-sized abattoirs also were encouraged in selected centres, the hides and skins to be dealt with in 'fellmongering' units, and the wools and hides to be 'cured' and 'tanned' in these areas. The raw materials for a new leather industry were on the doorstep. Further plans were mooted for the creation of creameries to produce butter and cheese. As for the maturing forests, over the 'next ten years wood would become available in steady quantities in many parts of rural Wales. Steps will be taken to establish saw-mills, tanneries etc., to deal with felled timber . . . also furniture, window frames and doors could be produced'.[15] The WRCL commissioned surveys to discover whether deposits of lead had been exhausted in central and south Wales. Research was undertaken to discover if slate could be used for purposes other than the roofing of houses. Other once prosperous but now declining industries were to be given a new lease of life. The woollen textile industry had virtually disappeared by 1945 and there had been no attempts to re-establish it. The WRCL believed that, given power, modern textile machinery and good designs, the industry could become a sound economic proposition. Small and medium-sized industries based on Wales's raw materials were to be encouraged.

The WRCL also looked beyond these local industries and suggested that industries bearing no relation to the resources of rural Wales needed to be enticed into these areas. Whilst recognizing that towns were better able to attract such industries, the WRCL felt rural areas could also sustain light industries, including engineering.

The WRCL was a forward-looking body, providing an all-embracing package of economic proposals for rural regeneration but social amenities were not neglected. Some schemes were already in progress through Labour local authorities. Improvements to housing and the development of water and sanitation were to proceed systematically. The need for a progressive programme of road development was recognized, as was the need for local meeting places, which would not add to the prosperity of areas, but would provide better social amenities. Noises made about costs and funding became noticeably more muted. Some funds were to be made available, but predominantly loans with low rates of interest were proposed. Any outright grants would be for the provision of buildings and machinery, according to need and only after careful examination. In order to be successful each application would have to be judged as a viable economic and social venture. It was felt investment could be undertaken by private firms as well as co-operative organizations, with the possibility of local authorities providing loans.

Of course, these proposals were also part of a political strategy. The Labour Party aimed to break into north and rural Wales and extend its electoral domination. By the end of 1955, a tripartite committee was established. The committee included members of the Parliamentary Labour Party Welsh Group (Desmond Donnelly, T. Jones, Goronwy Roberts and Tudor Watkins), members of the WRCL (including Cliff Prothero), and members of Labour's National Executive Committee (NEC) (including David Ginsburg and Peter Shore). James Griffiths was the chairman. The twin issues of attracting new industries into the rural areas and developing old and existing industries dominated proceedings. Goronwy Roberts advocated promoting and attracting new industry, whilst Desmond Donnelly saw the provision of work in rural areas as the means to a full life in Wales. He looked to 'joint enterprises', with the state providing some (or indeed all) of the early capital. The tripartite committee found defining its objectives particularly difficult. Peter Shore felt the committee's reports on new industry and reviving older traditional industries were confusing. He argued that unemployment was not a problem in rural areas, apparently missing the point that the reason for low unemployment was the high level of rural depopulation. However, Shore felt that any revival in agriculture would be restrained by physical limits and that if depopulation was the problem then 'it raised different problems to those we have previously tackled in development areas and elsewhere'.[16] By 1955 these fine ideas had failed to go beyond the discussion phase, but an agenda had been set and discussions had reached higher levels within the party. Jim Griffiths summed up the position, redefining the objective as the 'use of socialist planning to preserve Welsh culture and traditions. This is what people of the area wanted and policy should be shaped as far as possible to meet their requirements'. Griffiths took a far broader view than the tripartite committee and, along with the members of the NEC, seemed interested in more generalized plans, thus shelving the detailed schemes. Labour's 'failure' stemmed not from a lack of ideas but from the inability to turn those ideas into implementable policies.

Nor can Labour be justly accused of seeking solutions solely of an economic form, through enforced modernization. The WRCL felt that rural difficulties could not be solved on the cheap and that winning public support was necessary. They attached equal importance to the

> psychology and tradition of the people in these areas which must always be in the fore . . . care must be taken to make people feel that any proposed development is what they want and need in the circumstances, and that is not to be imposed on them from above, or outside. This can not be emphasised too heavily or too often.[17]

The lack of progress made by the Labour Party in addressing the problems of rural areas was at least partially due to an unsympathetic Conservative government. In 1961, Cardiganshire Labour Party president D. J. Davies lambasted the Tories, telling his annual general meeting that he viewed 'with disapproval the failure of the government to declare the County a development area and reaffirm the belief that the introduction of light industries was the only method of halting rural depopulation in the county'. Aberavon's MP John Morris also laid the blame for lack of rural development at the door of the Conservatives, stating

> that in spite of the many reports which had been produced, nothing had been done. They have all been pigeon-holed and so our young people continued to drain away. No nation could afford this . . . the government should invest in essential works not luxuries. Factories not cinemas, houses not luxury flats.[18]

Clearly Labour had a series of economic ideas which it could not deliver whilst in opposition. None the less, its domination of local government meant that, despite financial constraints, it could deliver some positive policies. Party minute books show that practical local issues dominated discussion at ward meetings. Issues such as street lighting and paving, bus routes and park benches, new buildings, new homes and attracting new industry hogged agendas. These were not easily described or perceived as socialist issues but they did affect the way in which people lived and the way in which the community viewed the councillors who served them. For instance, the party in the Llwchwr district of Gower attempted to set up a home help scheme as well as aiming to combat unemployment through the attraction of a new steelworks to the area.[19] Unusually, the local party also held monthly discussion groups on broader issues, hoping that by discussing topics such as health, housing, education and election procedure, knowledgeable and well-informed activists would result. The Brynlliw ward council spent more time discussing local issues. Each monthly meeting addressed different concerns. November 1960 covered roads, house repairs and a park bench being placed in a children's play area. The ward also secured an assurance from the water board that in future warnings would be given before water was turned off. December brought dismay that lights for Bryncunling and the painting of various houses were not in the year's budget. The disappointment may have been tempered by the fact that the engineer had recommended a new sports hall and bowls' pavilion. In March 1961 the ward requested that 1,200 new houses be built. Individual concerns over house repairs were also discussed. Clearly, left/right posturing was not a feature of local politics. The only time that national-level politics really had an impact at this level was the debate over Clause IV. Brynlliw was aggrieved enough to send forward a resolution which 'deplore[d] the conduct of Hugh Gaitskell in his attempt to break down Clause IV'.[20]

Local authorities had their hands tied by the growing centralization of authority and their limited financial resources. Since the 1920s there had been calls for larger local units to be formed so that more ambitious projects could be tackled. However, those holding the reins of local power were reluctant to give up their positions of strength and local standing. For example in 1948, the Council for Wales put forward a scheme for the reorganization of local government, proposing reducing the number of north Wales local councils from sixty-seven to ten. According to Huw T. Edwards, the scheme 'commended itself to each of the public

Table 8.1: Labour's electoral strength and membership in its heartlands,
1950–1966

Constituency		1950	1951	1955	1959	1964	1966
Newport	% of vote	51.0	52.8	53.7	53.1	57.5	59.8
	membership	3294	3040	2509	2116	1000	
Neath	% of vote	72.9	76.9	76.4	71.4	73.5	79.7
	membership	832	793	790	800	1000	
Pontypridd	% of vote	68.9	72.3	71.1	68.2	71.3	74.9
	membership	1591	1276	1416	1068	1476	
Merthyr	% of vote	78.8	79.6	77.2	77.1	75.3	74.5
	membership	850	750	700	800	1000	
Rhondda East	% of vote	75.9	81.2	72.6	65.2	71.2	77.4
	membership	329	377	319	800	1000	
Rhondda West	% of vote	82.4	81.0	73.8	72.0	79.3	76.1
	membership	389	347	459	800	1000	
Abertillery	% of vote	86.5	86.9	82.7	85.0	85.9	88.1
	membership	624	706	648	800	1000	
Bedwellty	% of vote	83.4	83.3	82.4	81.1	83.5	86.2
	membership	1050	1010	790	870	1331	
Ebbw Vale	% of vote	80.7	80.7	79.3	81.0	83.3	85.1
	membership	641	620	727	810	1477	
Pontypool	% of vote	72.3	75.7	72.9	70.1	74.5	77.0
	membership	861	885	567	800	1000	

Sources: WRCL Annual Reports; F. W. S. Craig, British Parliamentary Election
Results 1950–1970 (London, 1970).
Note: All contests Labour victories.

meetings called to consider it'. He added 'what killed the scheme
without any doubt was the opposition of officers who were afraid
of losing their jobs and the aldermen and councillors who feared
that they too would lose the power and authority which they
wielded in their various areas'.[21]

Whilst Labour was reinforcing its electoral strength and expanding its policies, it declined as a party of mass participation, a
situation best seen through looking at the party's membership
figures (Table 8.1). They clearly reveal a period of contraction. For
though high levels of membership were greatly encouraged by the
national party and its Welsh organization, they never materialized.
The problems of collecting subscriptions and the nature of the

party's organization in many wards meant little was actually done. Some powerful local figures were actually opposed to the idea of mass participation, as new recruits could pose a threat to their positions. This was an opportunity missed, as particularly in Labour's industrial heartlands potential membership levels were huge. As Fielding has recently commented, 'safe seats remained Labour's great unmilked cash cows'.[22] In north Wales, an area the party was looking to break into, membership shrank. Between 1951 and 1956, Anglesey's membership fell from 987 to 718. During the same period, Caernarfon's membership fell from 2,014 to 952. In Wrexham, an area of Labour strength, membership fell from 1,500 to 774. The situation was little better in Labour's heartlands. Caerphilly's membership tumbled from 1,437 to 845; Merthyr's from an already low 850 to 700. Pontypridd lost 200 members, and the three Cardiff seats lost nearly 1,000 members between them. Furthermore, a close examination often reveals that true membership levels were even lower than the official figures, a characteristic exposed by the raising of the minimum number of members (to 800 in 1957 and to 1,000 in 1963) required for a constituency to return a delegate to conference.

Labour had created an elected local élite which was enshrined in office by the party's huge electoral strength. This was especially apparent in south Wales, where real power was often vested in the hands of a few people. MPs often clung to office, inhibiting change. In the Gower constituency, it took considerable effort to remove the long-standing MP Dai Grenfell. In May 1958, the minutes of the Llwchwr district of the Gower Labour Party signal early signs of disaffection. Following discussion 'concerning the future of our MP . . . the general feeling of the meeting was that Mr Grenfell should retire after the present government had run its course'. By the July meeting, there were definite calls for Grenfell's resignation. Though Grenfell had been a good MP, and had 'given very good service in the past', the meeting expressed the view that 'he was not now able to carry out the duties expected of an MP today'.[23] A motion calling for his resignation was carried by an overwhelming majority and forwarded to the Gower Divisional Executive Committee.

For a man who had been the incumbent MP since 1922, this must have been a bitter pill to swallow and in November 1958 a surprised Grenfell wrote to Ifor Davies (who ultimately replaced him) complaining about his treatment. Grenfell asked Davies for a clear view of his position; he also asked why Davies had not mentioned that trouble was brewing in the two days they had spent together at the recent Labour Conference. He had been summoned to a meeting at which he had not realized his candidature was to be an issue. He 'was told that the Group, with whom you [Davies] are associated had decided to vote unanimously against me if I became a candidate at another parliamentary election in the Gower constituency'.[24] Cliques could be established and could hold onto power but they could also be removed in organizational manœuvres which became common features of Welsh Labour politics. By February 1959, Davies was the nominee of the Pontarddulais joint wards and Pontybrenin and Loughor ward Labour parties. By April, he was the official Gower constituency candidate. He was returned to Westminster the same year.

There was always a danger that those who held power in local government or in the party would lose touch with opinion, or would become inert. Very few individuals made up the committees which ran councils and ultimately made the decisions concerning their areas. Labour's overall ascendancy in Welsh local government throughout this period meant that the majority of these local 'barons' or powerbrokers came from within the party's ranks. Such people were hugely powerful. The papers of Alderman W. Douglas Hughes (agent to James Griffiths and leader of Carmarthenshire Labour Party for three decades), provide us with a rich insight into how things 'got done' locally. Clearly, if a helping hand was needed, Douglas Hughes could be a major influence. Letters requesting help or offering thanks for his help are numerous.[25] Though Hughes's support was not a guarantee of success, he could certainly influence outcomes, as a newly installed headmistress exemplified by writing 'to express my sincere thanks to you for your kindness in supporting my application for the post of headmistress at the Queen Elizabeth Grammar School, Carmarthen'.[26] The power of local barons could be disturbed by scandals (Hughes survived several) or by internal political revolts. However, as Hughes's case again illustrates, local leaders did not necessarily neglect the activists and could rule by consent. Hughes kept his finger on the pulse of the local party. In 1950, he wrote to the ward secretaries, group secretaries, women's and youth sections, stressing the need to keep the political machine in good working order.

He was also seen to be keen to increase membership levels, stating that in a constituency where 32,000 people voted Labour, membership levels should number 4,000. He further stressed the need for good speakers and subjects, good knowledge of party policy and current affairs and the need for social events to attract new members. However, membership levels remained low throughout the period, and Hughes's ascendancy was scarcely challenged.

In many respects, Hughes symbolizes how the Labour Party in Wales worked. A small but dedicated group of diligent individuals, agents or councillors maintained the party in most constituencies. Power rested firmly in their hands. In Ebbw Vale, Ron Evans, agent first to Aneurin Bevan and then to Michael Foot, became a key public and political figure. National figures such as Bevan and Foot could not dedicate as much time to constituency affairs as they may have wished. Bevan in particular was always in demand. In addition to his role at Westminster, he was a regular first-choice speaker at meetings all over Britain. Numerous letters to Evans from Bevan's Parliamentary Private Secretary (PPS) reveal how little constituency correspondence reached him. Even less was dealt with personally. For example, in 1959, a letter addressed to Bevan described how a family of four constituents was crammed into one small room in a shared house. The situation was obviously desperate, for also in the house was a 'large bedroom occupied by a Mother, Father and daughter aged fifteen and a half, and a box room occupied by an eighteen year old boy'.[27] Bevan's PPS recognized the situation 'seems a bit desperate' but passed the buck to Evans, stating 'you will know about it best'. Evans was asked if he 'would mind doing the whole thing direct', because Bevan was on holiday and his PPS was also about to begin holidays. The secretary ends by stating that 'if this kind of letter can be kept away from him [Bevan] it will help'.[28]

Ron Evans was Bevan's eyes and ears in Ebbw Vale. When Bevan failed to attend constituency meetings, Evans explained away the circumstances. When a Gaitskell speech received a poor reception in Cardiff, Evans gleefully reported the news to Bevan. However, Evans seemed willing to risk sharing his power. He was increasingly frustrated by the poor quality of the party's organization and more particularly by the low membership levels. Following discussions within the Divisional Labour Party, Evans wrote to the party's national agent, A. L. Williams. He explained: 'our greatest difficulty has been to get the decisions to make a drive implemented. It seems that the very people who give lip service to a membership drive at the divisional level baulk it at local and ward level'. He called for the use of the National Association of Labour Student Organisations (NALSO) Canvass Team; 'to undertake a mass canvass to test the potential for membership', even though NALSO was normally reserved for work in the rural and marginal constituencies. He further suggested 'a constituency like ours would make a good pilot scheme for industrial constituencies, with good results showing what could be done in all constituencies if there is the will to win'.[29] Whilst not solving the perpetual problem of collecting membership dues (a source of many a membership decline), Evans's scheme seemed to offer a way of neatly side-stepping those keen to keep membership low. The reply Evans received from Williams was not even lukewarm. Whilst not dismissing the scheme, Williams stated that the use of NALSO was in fact 'paid for out of the Regional Schemes of Assistance to Marginal Constituencies . . . I am afraid it would not be possible for expenses to be met'.[30] Ebbw Vale was unwilling to pay for student labour and the idea collapsed.

If historians have barely begun to explore the role of key Labour Party figures in the industrial heartlands, even less has been written about their central role in areas where Labour was weaker. In Brecon and Radnor, far from a Labour Party heartland, the local party structure and organization was very fragile. Not unusually, the MP, Tudor Watkins, held a semblance of local party activity together. Watkins was the key Labour Party figure in the area, constantly trying to improve local links and the party's level of organization: to build up, improve or indeed in some areas create a local party structure. However, frustration and a lack of progress sum up the results of his efforts. The Labour Party in Brecon and Radnor embarked on frequent rural campaigns year on year in an attempt to attract rural workers. Results were disappointing, as they had been since the party was founded. Watkins' requests to 'strengthen our list of contacts' in May 1953 appears to have fallen on deaf ears, for in November 1954 he remained 'disturbed by the small number of village correspondents on file and stressed the importance of the occasional visit to them'.[31] Brecon and Radnor was clearly an area where decrepit organization, inactivity, infighting and apathy was common place. In 1954, a confidential report on the standard of organization in Brecon and Radnor's local Labour parties noted that Abercrave's membership had halved, with no more than 30 per cent of members active. Brecon's 1953 membership of 151 was 'purely a card membership . . . the number of active workers appear to be very few'. The poor organization was blamed on 'local personalities'. Brynmawr, a mining area, had a card membership of 140 in 1953 (ninety in 1955 and fifty-three in 1959), though 'the same old trouble between the Local Party and the Women's section still remains' and 'personalities' were described as a 'danger to the organisation and long term planning'. Bwlch had no members because it was defunct; Cefn Coed's organization appeared 'to lack any life at all' and attendance at meetings apparently peaked at five! Crossgates only met for their AGM. Colbren had just recently re-formed and in Crickhowell, though the 1953 individual card membership was 150, it was 'purely a card membership . . . [and it was] doubtful if even a quarter of these [cards] were ever issued quite apart from collections made on them'.[32] When a local party within Brecon and Radnor was doing well, one or two individuals were responsible. If, as happened in Llangynidr and Llanfrynach, they moved or became ill, the party ceased to function. In a more extreme case, though membership of the local party in Presteigne was good, nobody wanted to be seen as publicly working for the party.[33] The situation was hardly helped by the NEC's decision to no longer regard Brecon and Radnor as a marginal constituency and thus withdraw the special support and funding afforded to such seats.

This was not a unique example. In north Wales, Labour's organization (whilst not plumbing the depths to which Brecon and Radnor's had sunk) still apparently left 'much to be desired'. Only two branches of the Labour League of Youth were functioning: 'The combined total membership is less than twenty.'[34] Although the position improved, the role of the youth sections was rarely political. Indeed a report on the state of young socialists in north Wales revealed 'that in the main their activities were of a social nature'.[35]

Clearly, the Labour Party faced a substantial task breaking into north and rural Wales. In part the difficulty lay in securing suitable candidates. The WRCL was forced to rely on local activists to produce lists of potential people who could serve in local government. The only help the council could give was arranging for speakers with local government experience to address these potential candidates.[36] Yet by 1954, four of north Wales' eight constituencies (Anglesey, Merioneth, Flint East and Conway) were considered marginal. The general picture is of a decrepit organization, lacking direction and without agents or MPs to provide it. The minutes of the WRCL North Wales subcommittee in January 1954 reveal that Flint East and Conway had not even begun campaigning. This inactivity was mirrored in Caernarfon (a Labour seat), where 'the main problem remains membership'. Though Denbigh's organization was improving, progress was being stalled by the fact that 'as one area improves with attention, another falls behind'. In Flint West, the organizational difficulties were made all the more acute through a problem with the secretaryship; and whilst Wrexham, a traditionally strong Labour area was maintaining itself, activity was described as 'not exceptional'.[37] By 1957, Wrexham's women's sections were in unchecked decline. Megan Roach, representing the WRCL, stated that 'six years ago there were nine women's sections in the seat and now there were just six. Ruabon, Ley and Wrexham had just collapsed'. Indeed, the chair of Wrexham's membership subcommittee stated that 'he was absolutely disgusted with the apparent lack of interest and effort shown by so many local Labour parties'.[38]

The party's limited membership may not have been an indication of declining support in south Wales but in north Wales it reflected the party's shallow roots and made it difficult to build popular commitment. Labour could not prove its practicality by using its position on local councils. When the WRCL received reports on the north Wales local government elections of 1958, the nature of the party's position becomes clear. In fact, only Wrexham and Flint East Constituency Labour Parties (CLPs) had invited and endorsed nominations. The report concluded 'it was obvious that some of the constituencies do not interest themselves in County Council Elections, and in fact elections are not fought on political party issues'.[39] The Labour Party had its work cut out in providing itself with a platform from which it could expand. The aims of the WRCL were often thwarted by apathy at local level. Organizational issues thus dominated the discussions and plans for north Wales. The need for marginal constituencies to produce marked registers was highlighted at virtually every meeting of the WRCL's North Wales subcommittee, but with little progress, the subcommittee revisiting the same narrow organizational matters year on year.[40] Improvements were slow and hard to implement. Plans to improve the organizational situation of the north Wales CLPs included a week-long school for election agents, as well as various weekend schools for key workers. Though some were successful, others, including the week-long school, failed to get off the ground, the 'poor response from the north Wales constituencies' being blamed for the school's cancellation. Regular demands for membership campaigns to be undertaken by the north Wales constituencies met with similarly unenthusiastic responses from constituency parties. One of the more promising statements about the state of membership across north Wales was that the constituencies had 'reported some progress in their membership campaigns, though there is nothing really spectacular to report'.[41] It suggested the trade union movement would provide a rich field for the recruitment of new members. The response of the local parties was poor once again.

Organizational 'solutions' tended to predominate when party committees discussed how to expand support. However, some members of the WRCL recognized the need to go beyond this, aiming to use the Welsh language and Welsh culture to promote the Labour Party in north Wales by developing real community links. Thus Tom Jones, a member of the North Wales subcommittee, persuaded his district committee of the Transport and General Workers' Union to pay for space in *Y Cymro*, so that a Labour Party policy document could be published in a serial form in Welsh. Copies of the policy document could also be 'run off' cheaply, thus arming local workers with Labour Party material published in Welsh. Owen Edwards, another subcommittee member, secured a promise from Cliff Prothero for financial help from head office towards the cost of publishing Labour Party material in Welsh. Though the CLPs also had to find some finances for any such project, it shows some high-level backing for attempts to broaden the Labour Party's appeal in north and rural Wales. None the less, whilst there was considerable thinking on policy for rural areas, there were fewer attempts at conducting consultation or in securing the local respect and credibility which would make their policy proposals seem real. Labour remained a pragmatic party, in which presentation and election psychology were marginalized.

A declining membership was less electorally and organizationally important in south Wales, where Labour MPs often had huge majorities, and local parties sometimes received considerable financial help from a trade union sponsor. But it still meant that parties could lose contact with the people. This was especially significant (although less common) in the coastal seats, some of which were marginal. None the less, the party still aimed at promoting organization almost as an end, rather than a means to identify, reflect or create local opinion. There was little analysis of why people did not see Labour as their 'natural' representatives. Newport is a fine example of a vibrant local party which ran into organizational and electoral difficulties. Before 1939, Newport had one of the largest party memberships in Britain, including an especially strong women's section. After 1945, the party came to rely on financial help from Peter Freeman, their MP. In 1945, for example, he pledged to give £100 to the election fund and a further £400 per annum to the constituency.[42] This was perhaps just as well, because as early as 1946, the problems of collecting membership dues and putting active ward committees together were becoming all too familiar. Re-established youth sections soon disintegrated, a formerly successful Labour Party newspaper, the *Newport Citizen*, was relaunched, but the expected success failed to materialize. At the 1948 AGM, 'anxiety was felt at the financial position of the party'.[43] The paper was suspended in March 1949. There were also attempts to organize in Newport's ever-growing council estates. However, such activity proved impotent. There was no participation in the activities of tenants' associations or other 'new' community developments.[44] Though a membership drive boosted numbers slightly, the party had lost its old energy.

Genuine efforts to improve the situation continued. There was a youth officer and a League of Youth representative on Newport's executive throughout the 1950s. The women's sections had some strong and positive features: women who could not attend meetings through illness were sent 'sunshine' (a present) by one of the appointed 'sick visitors'.[45] Their impressive programme of talks, outings and socials meant that women continued to outnumber men amongst party members. Despite the fact that the women's section showed more life, imagination and vibrancy than any other section of the party, their efforts were little valued, reflecting a common enough view of women's 'social' activities. The Labour agent told the St Julian's women in 1955 that the party had to 'foster [the] ideas and ideals of socialism' so that support was automatic. Hard work, not play, was needed. The agent went on to say that 'whilst many members were eager to take part in any social activities, not everyone could or would do the various jobs of work especially the canvassing which is an absolute necessity'.[46] Making Labour a part of people's lives – including social lives – was less important than turning them into (often menial) workers for the labour movement.

The downward trend continued. The once comfortable financial position reached its nadir in the late 1960s, when the party had to request a bridging loan from Labour's HQ to 'assist your party to meet its pressing liabilities'.[47] Nor was this position unusual. Coalfield parties with huge majorities often lacked ambition. Caerphilly Labour Party's organizer reported his pleasure at the state of the party's membership in 1951. However, the party decided against employing a full-time agent on financial grounds and followed that up by deciding that a local news sheet would be impractical.[48] Across the coalfield, membership fell, the number of trade unions participating in politics seemed to be in decline and parties relied on their huge strength and affiliated membership to keep in touch with the voters' needs.

Ultimately, the Labour Party in Wales relied on a small number of dedicated individuals to carry out its work. There is clear evidence that many of the local individuals were tremendously hard-working, attending numerous time-consuming meetings. They attempted to serve their community, to improve local conditions and amenities. Their reward was generally the faith that the electorate showed in them by returning them to office time and time again. Other aims, some of a less noble nature, were occasionally identified but were hardly dominant. Throughout the period, Labour attempted to impose itself as the party of all Wales. Clearly, it had a series of economic and social ideas which culminated in a programme of radical and progressive proposals. Most local Labour parties were respected because of their commitment to the delivery of a modernized Welsh economy and an improvement of conditions in their localities. The Labour Party of the 1950s and 1960s preached a radical tone. Modernization was the key refrain.

None the less, there were a number of failings during this period which stored up trouble for the future. Despite impressive levels of support and new electoral victories throughout the 1950s and 1960s the party contracted as a mass movement. Labour's declining – in north Wales always limited – membership and community roots may have contributed to a weakening of its position and of its ability to change. A small number of people became decision-makers in their localities. Generally, apathy seemed to exist amongst party workers. Many had neither the time nor the inclination to change the way their party functioned. The very real danger for the party was that it might lose touch with its supporters: as times changed, values altered, expectations revised. In rural Wales, where Labour failed to put down strong social roots, gaining acceptance was difficult. Labour did not necessarily speak in a voice which was appreciated, or on concerns which matched the voters' preconceptions and values. Here, Labour's ability to deliver economic gains may have facilitated electoral support but conversely Labour would face increasing difficulties during the economic downturn of the 1970s. Labour had perhaps been the party of modernizing ideas in the 1950s and 1960s. In the 1970s – when it also failed to deliver economic prosperity – it could no longer make that claim.

Notes

[1] I. McAllister, 'The Labour Party in Wales: the dynamics of one-partyism', *Llafur*, III/2 (1981), 81.

[2] C. Williams, *Democratic Rhondda: Politics and Society, 1885–1951* (Cardiff, 1996), 207–8.

[3] K. O. Morgan, *Rebirth of a Nation: Wales 1880–1980* (Oxford and Cardiff, 1981), 340.

[4] Ibid., 341.

[5] Ibid., 342.

[6] K. O. Morgan, 'Wales since 1945: political society', in T. Herbert and G. E. Jones (eds.), *Post-War Wales* (Cardiff, 1995).

[7] C. Prothero, *Recount* (Ormskirk, 1982), 65.

[8] H. T. Edwards, *Hewn from the Rock* (Cardiff, 1967), 137.

[9] Ibid., 137.

[10] J. G. Jones, 'The Parliament for Wales campaign 1950–66', *WHR*, XVI/2 (1992).

[11] D. Caradog Jones MSS, NLW, file 1. 'Memorandum on rural development', Sept. 1955.

[12] Ibid., 'Discussion Papers of Tripartite Committee', file 2.

[13] Ibid., file 1.

[14] Welsh Regional Council of Labour, 'Development of Rural Areas in Wales Interim Report'. Annual Meeting 1957.

[15] Caradog Jones MSS, file 1, 'Memorandum on Welsh rural areas'.

[16] Ibid. 'Summary of discussion of meeting 15/12/55', file 2.

[17] Ibid. 'Memorandum on Welsh rural areas'.

[18] Speeches at Cardiganshire Constituency Labour Party annual general meeting, Jan. 1961. Loti Rees Hughes MSS in the Deian R. Hopkin MSS, A1991/187/136.

[19] Llwchwr Ward Committee Mins, 19 March 1958. Gower Labour Party Offices.

[20] Brynlliw Labour Ward Council Mins, 9 March 1960. Gower Labour Party Offices.

[21] Edwards, *Hewn*, 133–4.

[22] S. Fielding, 'The "Penny Farthing" machine revisited: Labour Party members and participation in the 1950s and 1960s', in C. Pierson and S. Tormey (eds.), *Politics at the Edge* (London, 2000). EPOP panel on the past, present and future of intra-party democracy (1).

[23] Llwchwr District Labour Party Mins, 21 May 1958, 16 July 1958.

[24] D. R. Grenfell to I. Davies, Gowerton, 12 Nov. 1958. West Glamorgan Record Office, D207/1/Box 9.

[25] Alderman Douglas Hughes MSS, Deian R. Hopkin MSS, A/1991/187/43.

[26] N. Evans to D. Hughes, 1 June 1953. A/1991/187/144.

[27] Mr Bull to A. Bevan, 19 July 1959, NLW, Ron Evans Papers. File 17.

[28] Bevan's PPS to R. Evans, 12 Aug. 1959, Evans MS file 17.

[29] R. Evans to A. L. Williams, 28 April 1957, Evans MS file 17.

[30] A. L. Williams to R. Evans, 2 May 1957, Evans MS file 17.

[31] Brecon and Radnor Labour Party Mins. NLW, vol. 7, 16 May 1953, 6 Nov. 1954.

[32] Report on the standard of organization in Brecon and Radnor Local Labour Parties attached to the Brecon and Radnor Mins, vol. 7, 17 July 1954.

[33] Brecon and Radnor Mins. Meeting of the North Breconshire and Radnorshire Federation of Labour Parties, vol. 7, 6 Nov. 1954.

[34] WRCL Mins, NLW. H. Morgan's report on organization, North Wales subcommittee, 24 June 1954.

[35] WRCL Mins, H. Morgan's report on Young Socialists, 9 June 1962.

[36] WRCL Executive Committee (EC) Mins, 25 June 1951.

[37] Ibid. North Wales subcommittee, 16 Jan. 1954.

[38] Wrexham Trades Council and Divisional Labour Party, EC Mins, 8, 22 Oct. 1957, TUC Archives, Warwick University.

[39] WRCL Mins, North Wales subcommittee, 15 Feb. 1958.

[40] Ibid., 16 May 1959.

[41] Ibid., 23 Aug. 1958.

[42] Newport Labour Party, Finance Committee Mins, 27/8/45 (SWCA).

[43] Ibid., Annual Meeting, 1948.

[44] Ibid., 21 April 1947.

[45] Newport Labour Party, St Julian's Women's Section. Mins, 26 Oct. 1954 and Malpas Ward Women's Section, 14 Jan. 1958.

[46] Newport Labour Party, St Julian's Women's Section. Mins, 12 Jan. 1955.

[47] Newport Labour Party, Correspondence, LP/c3.

[48] Caerphilly Labour Party and Trades Council. Annual Report 1951, TUC Archives, University of Warwick, MSS 292 9R/137.

9

'To Help Forward the Great Work of Humanity': Women in the Labour Party in Wales

NEIL EVANS and DOT JONES

In the late nineteenth century the established political parties found it expedient to create auxiliary organizations for women: the Conservative and Liberal Parties both came to rely on woman power in adapting to the political reforms of the 1880s. Women could participate in the parties only via these auxiliaries and were not admitted to membership until after 1918. Socialist parties, by contrast, prided themselves on the admission of women to full membership from the beginning. Reminiscences of early socialist crusades in England tell of comradeship across divisions of gender and often sex equality was seen as part of the better world to come. This was also true on a wider international front. The German Social Democratic Party adopted votes for women as an integral part of its programme in 1891 and women were amongst the founders of the Socialist Party of America in 1901. Socialist parties began, if not without strong elements of chauvinism within them, at least with glimpses of a better future for women amongst their ideals.[1]

In Britain, once the early optimism of the socialists faded from the mid-1890s so did their vision of gender relations. The clearest expression of this is the emergence of women's auxiliaries in both the Social Democratic Federation and the Independent Labour Party, though women were still full members. When the Labour Party crystallized out of the Labour Representation Committee in 1906 it was quickly complemented by the Women's Labour League (WLL), which grew quite rapidly with 112 branches by 1911: its most important work, aside from elections, was local pressure on welfare measures such as school meals, medical insurance and

Table 9.1. Branches of the Women's Labour League, 1906–1918

Branch	Formed
Aberdare	1917
Abergavenny	1911
Abertillery	1910; reformed 1911; 1917; closed 1917
Bargoed	lapsed 1911
Barry	1911; reformed 1917
Briton Ferry	1913; lapsed 1913
Cardiff	nd
Cwmavon	nd
Ebbw Vale	nd
Griffithstown	1911
Merthyr Tydfil	1910; 'dead' 1912
Newport	1910
Ogmore Vale	1911
Pontypool	1916
Swansea	1909
Wrexham	1913
Ystalyfera	closing 1915

Source: C. Collette, *For Labour and for Women: The Women's Labour League, 1906–18* (Manchester, 1989), appendix 2.

infant welfare. It aimed at women whose sphere was the home rather than the trade union and consequently addressed their needs as wives and mothers. Such an emphasis gave women both an important role in politics and a different one from men.[2]

Women's participation in early socialist movements in Wales was broadly but belatedly within this pattern. Socialism was a relative latecomer to Wales and women were not prominent in its pioneering days. The WLL took some time to establish itself in south Wales. By 1910 when it held its conference in Newport there were only five branches: at Barry, Cardiff, Merthyr, Newport and Swansea (Table 9.1).[3] Significantly all but one were in the coastal strip: the serious colonization of the valleys had not yet begun and the Merthyr branch was short-lived. Cardiff had a vigorous branch: Grace Scholefield, its leading member, was the most prominent in south Wales. The Newport conference stimulated more activity in the coalfield and in the years before the First World War a network of branches was established. By the spring of 1911 a

Cardiff conference attracted thirty-two delegates including some from Abertillery, Nantyffyllon and Ogmore Vale.[4] The latter was newly formed, in the context of a local strike. It was soon sending a resolution to the Ogmore and Garw Urban District Council urging a minimum wage for its workmen and proclaiming that when women were voters they would ensure sweating ended in local government.[5] When Keir Hardie opened Cardiff's new ILP rooms in 1913 he paid fulsome tribute to the role of women in the labour movement and clearly remembered the days when sex equality had been a central aspect of the socialist vision: 'they would never understand the meaning of democracy until men and women were equal and working together for the elevation of the race'.[6]

Other branches continued the WLL's usual work. Swansea joined with the local Women's Co-operative Guild (WCG) to send a deputation to Glamorgan County Council to press for school clinics and followed this up with a public meeting urging the same cause. At Cardiff relief work for those thrown out of work by the 1912 coal strike involved the giving of 5,000 meals. Similar efforts were undertaken at Griffithstown and Barry Dock. At Abertillery women played a significant part in the campaign which returned ten Labour men out of eighteen members to the local council. Women more often helped men into office than stood themselves. Outside London few had the necessary qualifications to become councillors and this limited their direct ambitions. Ironically at Griffithstown, when the WLL branch became moribund, the local trades council ran the president of the WLL for the board of guardians. It was in this particular arena that the WLL had its greatest electoral success, with two guardians in Swansea and another in Bargoed.[7] The next year there were victories at Barry Dock, Abertillery (two), Bargoed and Swansea for Labour women guardians.[8]

By 1912 organization was improving and women were being recruited into trade unions. Yet clearly the coalfield remained only tentatively explored.[9] Having some footholds in the valleys was vital for the campaign for pithead baths which the WLL now began to undertake.[10] In June 1912 there were complaints of apathy towards the issue in some of the mining villages visited by Katherine Bruce Glasier but by November the work was seen as being 'wonderful'.[11] Grace Scholefield took the issue in hand in the eastern part of the coalfield, organizing a house-to-house

campaign in the Caerphilly area and securing help from the South
Wales Miners' Federation (SWMF).[12]

The 1913 conference reported mixed success, with some new
branches established and some old ones becoming moribund.
Twenty-one delegates came to Abertillery but they represented
only five branches.[13] Agnes Brown was appointed as the WLL's first
paid organizer in 1913 and the first area she turned to was south
Wales. Her meetings were well-received and members recruited. At
Pontycymmer the hope was expressed that a branch would be
established which: 'is built up on a solid foundation which will
withstand all storms'. Few enough of these existed in south Wales.
Early in 1914 three branches in south Wales reported activities in
the *Labour Woman*. Predictably they were Cardiff, Ogmore Vale
and Swansea. All claimed considerable activity but Swansea's
report had an élan which the other two lacked: 'We are really
waking the Labour members on the council up, and we are doing
work that ought to have been done by the men years ago.'[14]

The curious feature of WLL activity is its absence from the
Labour strongholds of the Rhondda and Aberdare Valleys and
from Merthyr Tydfil. The early branch in Merthyr disappeared
after 1910. Women's participation in the labour movement in the
centre of the coalfield took different forms. Women's concerns
were recognized in the weekly *South Wales Worker*, where there
was a regular column contributed by 'Matron' which discussed
relevant political issues, especially women's suffrage. The local
labour movement responded to this with a well-attended series of
meetings addressed by Women's Social and Political Union organizer Annie Williams in 1912–13.[15] In Merthyr Sylvia Pankhurst was
a frequent contributor to Hardie's *Pioneer* and support for
women's suffrage was central to the local ILP rally in 1912.[16] Yet
there was clearly a limit to this, a position which 'Matron' articulated with her usual bluntness. She dismissed the WLL as a creation
of middle-class women wanting to do good for the working class
and looked forward to women making their own salvation from
economic servitude. But there was little to hope for from the ILP,
whose affairs:

> are conducted almost with a total disregard to the existence of women
> in the district or to matters in which women are interested. How many
> women members are there in the valley? Where are the wives, daughters

and sisters of the men who run affairs? Are the women wanted as members?[17]

Cardiff was the centre of WLL activity in south Wales but it lacked a single Labour (even Lib-Lab) councillor by 1912. The WLL helped breathe some life into the local labour movement by participating in the trade union membership drives and also in campaigns to sell the *Daily Citizen*. A League of Woman Workers was established in Cardiff which in May 1913 organized aid for the wives of striking builders' labourers. WLL activity was supported by other bodies. In 1912 Cardiff ILP women established a women's guild to organize women members and to carry on propaganda amongst women in the city. It clearly thought women had a distinctive voice which needed to be heard by organized labour: 'Our aim is to bring to bear upon the Labour movement of our country the point of view of the woman as well as the man.'[18]

This pattern of activity continued in south Wales until 1914. Branches were added in areas like Ystalyfera and Abercrave and conferences were held. In the western part of the coalfield the need for a Welsh-speaking organizer was recognized. Women's labour organization had at least become significant enough to encounter this problem.[19] Deputations to local authorities calling for clinics and similar welfare reforms were organized. The pithead baths campaign culminated in joint propaganda actions with miners' wives and the WCG in 1914 and in seeking the support of school mistresses and religious bodies. South Wales was one of the WLL's better organized areas: only in Lancashire and Durham was it more densely established.[20]

Lack of progress in north Wales, where Labour's general grip was much more precarious, is less perplexing than it is in certain parts of south Wales. In her first tour of duty Agnes Brown visited Bangor or Caernarfon for several days. However, the first signs of activity came from Wrexham after Marion Phillips addressed a packed meeting of the local ILP. Agnes Brown followed up with a visit and a branch was duly formed.[21]

War changed the position and diverted attention from many of these issues. The WLL annual conference was postponed in 1914 and districts were advised to hold their own conferences and to consider the issue of women's part in the making of peace.[22] The WLL's next conference in 1916 revealed organizational problems in south Wales, as Scotland gained a member of the Executive Committee at Wales's expense.[23] War work involved efforts to organize the growing numbers of women workers, especially tramway women in Swansea and railway women in Cardiff. Welsh delegates spoke up for smaller classes in elementary schools and for outdoor relief to OAPs without disqualification from pensions. But by 1919 there were only three WLL branches left in south Wales: at Cardiff, Swansea and Newport.[24]

The end of the war meant a new start for women's organizations, as the 1918 constitution absorbed the WLL into the Labour Party. Branches became women's sections and one seat on the National Executive Committee (NEC) was reserved for women. An annual women's conference continued to be held. Regional advisory committees were created through which women's views could be formulated. Their influence was felt mainly over reconstruction policy and particularly in the design of council houses. Woman organizers were appointed to garner the new women's vote. Elizabeth Andrews, who took up her duties in 1919, initially translated leaflets into Welsh for north and mid Wales: *Why Women Should Join the Labour Party, To the Woman in the Home* and *Home Rule All Round*. The first new women's section was established at Ton Pentre in 1918 on her own territory. She had been born in Hirwaun in 1882 but lived variously in Mardy, Dowlais and Ystrad Rhondda, and had pursued a successful career in dressmaking. In 1910 she married Thomas Andrews, one of the Rhondda's ILP pioneers. In 1919 she reinvigorated the pithead baths campaign and gave it prominence in her evidence before the Sankey Commission. The issue was placed firmly on the SWMF's agenda by the early 1920s and the union and the Labour Party could now fight the issue in the wider world.[25]

From 1919 until her retirement in 1948 Elizabeth Andrews was the central figure in this story. She was indefatigable in her efforts and built up a formidable organization. Yet while she was inspirational, vigorous and forceful, she was also warmly regarded. When she died the East Glamorgan Women's Advisory Council over which she had long exercised a profound influence referred to her as 'our beloved Elizabeth'. Perhaps the best way to frame her achievement is through statistics. According to official party statistics in 1933 there were 11,207 male members and 9,160 women: that is, women formed 45 per cent of individual party membership in Wales. Although women constituted only 40 per cent of Welsh membership in the year she retired, absolute numbers had increased by around a quarter in that time, with 12,814 women members in 1947 (14,157 in 1946). These figures were close to the British ratio of male:female membership. The peak of 46 per cent was reached in 1955 and the share remained at around 42 per cent when the figures ceased to be published in 1970. Within this, several constituencies had a large female membership: in 1933 all three Cardiff seats, Merthyr, Ogmore, Abertillery, Bedwellty and Newport had more female than male members. The weak points were the rural areas where male membership was much higher than female, and industrial areas in north Wales like Wrexham and Flint and some industrial seats in south Wales like Neath and Pontypool.

The general tendency was for women's organization to be most noticeable in seats which were either Labour but with relatively small majorities or held by political opponents but potentially winnable. Organization spread quickly through industrial south Wales soon after Elizabeth Andrews's appointment and by 1927 there were advisory committees and sections in the north-east and the north-west as well as in Cardiganshire. These rural areas would always prove the hardest for her to organize. Andrews ascribed this to the strength of Nonconformity, to the lack of experience of women in industrial struggles in the area, their shyness at speaking in public and to the substantial Liberal influence produced by having two Liberal Prime Ministers who were associated with north Wales: Gladstone and Lloyd George. If this latter point has substance, it was mainly with regard to north-west Wales where organization was always precarious. In general, the north-east had a much steadier Labour women's presence. Andrews also admitted a difficulty with the north Wales dialect but claimed to have overcome it by keeping strictly to biblical Welsh which was understood in both north and south. Perhaps this robbed her of the homeliness of style which is so much a feature of her English-language public addresses. If the evidence of the use of Welsh in written propaganda is any indication, there was little enough effort to use the language.[26]

By 1920 there is evidence of work outside the coalfield in Pembrokeshire and by 1921 advisory councils had been established for East Glamorgan, Monmouthshire, West Wales and Pembrokeshire. In industrial south Wales such organization was increasingly strong. By 1929 there were ninety-five sections in the East Glamorgan area, while its conference in 1926 had attracted 350 delegates and visitors. When Philip Massey visited Nant-y-glo and Blaina in the late 1930s he found three women's sections to complement the area's three ward parties and stressed the considerable support which the wives of trade unionists gave to the Labour Party. In such areas women's organization had produced deep roots.[27] By the mid-1920s sections were beginning to appear in industrial north-east Wales. North-west Wales was slower to get off the ground but by December 1925 there was an advisory council in Caernarfonshire and Anglesey and two years later the first women's conference in Merioneth.[28] In Cardiganshire real organization seems to have come only after 1945 while most of north Wales had to be reorganized in the aftermath of the war.[29] By 1948 there were two advisory councils covering north Wales and some centres like Porthmadog and Blaenau Ffestiniog appear to have been well-organized.[30]

Women's organization was clearly part of electoral machinery. Organizer's reports in *Labour Woman* detail work done by women in elections. Elizabeth Andrews spent five weeks in Caerphilly in 1921 organizing the women's canvassing and street meetings and took a similar approach in Gower the next year where there was a large turnout of women for the tasks.[31] Children were also enrolled to help as politics became a communal activity. Women who had demonstrated against the policies of Sir Alfred Mond in 1922 were particularly proud of their part in defeating him at Swansea West in the December 1923 election. 'Mond must Go!' they had proclaimed and they gave him the necessary push by their electioneering work.[32] Particular efforts were made by women in the Llanelli by-election of 1936. At an eve of poll meeting at the Market Hall a record 2,000 women turned out to hear Margaret Bondfield.[33] By the late 1930s it was common to praise women's efforts in canvassing at election time. Indeed it seems that much of this was left to women's sections, Clement Attlee observing in 1938 that the progress of the party depended to a large extent on the work done by women.[34] Candidates' wives were also enrolled for this work from early on, though the mandatory picture of the (male) candidate with his happy family around him seems only to have become the norm after 1945.[35] In Tredegar in 1935 it was decided to have one day of women's meetings with only women speakers, apart from Aneurin Bevan by virtue of his position as candidate. It was claimed this resulted in some of the best women's meetings ever in the area.[36]

Women in the party also aimed at generating support in a wider sense. The women's sections drew general attention to the party. The organization of 'women's days' was especially significant. Started in 1923 they quickly became 'women's weeks' and 'women's months'. Such work combined recreation with spreading the word. Charabanc trips ending at the seaside or some beauty spot gave opportunities to distribute leaflets or to hold meetings. In the summer of 1928 women from the Llanelli and Carmarthenshire Advisory Council distributed leaflets on the sands at Tenby. The next year Brecon and Radnorshire women went to Talgarth and Builth Wells, holding village meetings along the way. The rural idyll of Radnorshire had already been disturbed by women who had held the first Labour meeting in Rhayader in 1921.[37] There was a good deal of feeling that the advanced industrial areas owed a duty to show a political lead to the more politically backward rural areas. Foundations were being laid for Labour's post-war victories in rural contituencies.

But women's months were not confined to rural outreach work. There was also a concern to demonstrate the vitality, size and commitment of the socialist movement through the public spectacle. Such performances were best put on in urban arenas where streets and open spaces provided a suitable stage. In the inter-war years this parading of structured crowds was of considerable impact: democratic movements understood this as much as did fascists. At Port Talbot in 1928 the colourful demonstration was a mile and a half long, with striking floats and various national costumes on display; Wrexham and Caernarfonshire had scaled-down versions.[38] Similar demonstrations were reported in 1930 at Swansea where there was a carnival, fête and gala and 2,000 people present to listen to speeches, music and dance. Tableaux included 'Internationalism', 'Emancipation of the Child, 1830–1930', 'Co-operative Productions' and 'Riches and Poverty in Child Life'. Not all such events were roaring successes. There was some disappointment at the size of the turnout at the Cardiff event of the same year, while Merioneth's meeting at Barmouth can hardly have expected huge crowds.[39] But often there was enough life and energy to mark society with Labour's presence.

Such activity was founded on the strength of section life. How vital was the intellectual and political activity produced in them? At least one observer of the south Wales scene was not impressed with what he saw:

> I have some knowledge, and my wife has considerable experience, of Women's Organisations, . . . the Railway Women's Guilds, the Co-operative Women's Guilds, and the Women's section of the Labour Party . . . I have been appalled at the restricted outlook usual in these organisations. The working man has had opportunities in his Trade Union, his Co-operative Society, and in public life generally, which hitherto has not been available to his women folk . . . [40]

Elizabeth Andrews understood this and saw much educational potential in party work for women. Frequently she referred to the sections as 'the working woman's university' and press accounts of meetings do not suggest intellectual and political torpor.[41] Occasionally we catch a glimpse of what the section meant to the individual member. The unnamed woman from the Barry Dock Section whose views were published in 1931 felt that the sections were an experience of serious social concern and contrasted them with the entertainment provided by Liberal and Tory women's auxiliaries which attracted people through the possibility of a social encounter with the rich and titled. Labour, by contrast, offered serious work to women, a fact underlined by its women MPs and organizers. In the end it was her adherence to her class which was decisive and her desire to be an active, not a passive member of society: 'I want to feel that I am part of this great evolutionary movement, inviting progress, not retarding it.' Similarly, Margaret Davis of Pontnewynydd stressed the sections' role as an outlet for thinking women, as a means of appreciating (through visiting speakers) the value of sound trade unionism and 'doing constructive work in building up the new social system'.[42]

Women could participate in the party in a variety of ways. Some might simply make the tea and demonstrate other domestic skills. All listened to lectures and political speeches and took part in the programmes of political education. Some went on to attend summer schools and speakers' training sessions where more intensive political education was on offer. Those elected to advisory councils entered a world which was much more conventionally political than was that of the sections. This was even more true as the heights of the party structure were scaled. Yet the strongest impression of the women's movement is its effective combination of politics and pleasure, its sense that politics was integral to life rather than something apart from it. Women often expressed the desire to have a pleasant or good meeting and sent their love to ill and absent comrades. Something of what it all meant comes from a sad entry closing the minute book of the Flintshire and Denbighshire Advisory Council in 1971: 'This brings the last minutes of our Flint & Denbigh Advisory Council to a close, and I am not ashamed to say that I am wiping my tears away, thinking of happy years spent together with these delegates.'[43]

The women's sections of the labour movement helped humanize its public face. Particularly in south Wales this presence was essentially masculine and dominated by trade unions. The Labour Party, of course, stood for humanity as much as for the interests of a class. But it was frequently women who manifested this wider human concern: loyal to class in disputes like that of 1926, they concentrated on relieving suffering in the home and beyond that in stressing the welfare of mothers and children. Internationally they espoused the cause of peace. Labour had to speak to the nation as well as to class in order to win elections and women helped to give it that voice. They rounded out the appeal of what might otherwise have been more narrowly based and in providing a persona for the party which was not exclusively male and bureaucratic they helped win it mass support, as on May Day 1933 in the Rhondda where: 'In addition to the usual mass meetings for miners, special functions for the women and children were organized – Crowning the May Queen, Maypole Dancing, Children's Sports, Welsh Teas etc. They all proved a huge success.' Elizabeth Andrews stressed this: 'Our Socialist propaganda had to have a sense of reality. We were not only a political party, but a great Movement concerned about human personalities and their well-being.'[44]

How much of a feminist agenda was there in Labour women's politics in Wales? Perhaps more than might have been expected. Women were after all a large part of the electorate after 1918 and from 1928 around half of it. Some appeal to their specific interests was inevitable. From 1918 onwards Labour had confidently announced that it was the 'woman's party'. This arose from its championing of issues which would improve the economic lot of women. It was the major carrier of the 'new feminism' of the 1920s and reflected a shift away from issues of legal equality which had come to the fore during the campaign for the vote. But Labour attitudes were not confined to this and included a belief that more jobs in public life should be held by women. This was frequently a demand made at women's meetings in Wales and Elizabeth Andrews articulated what seemed to be a wider conviction in the party: that while family would be the prime concern for most women, the old belief that this should be their sole concern had to be challenged.[45] In arguing this she was in line with popular attitudes and it is argued by some analysts of working-class culture that such roles did give many women a sense of worth and dignity. Connecting with these concerns, and addressing them through suggesting means to improve women's lot, was part of the party's appeal.[46] It was often implied that women could mainly play these political roles if they were unmarried or childless.

It was possible only rarely for women to have prominent roles in politics. Rose Davies carved her path out in local government, a sphere more compatible with the care of her five children than was Parliament. She became the first woman to sit on Glamorgan County Council and in due course its first woman chairman. She concerned herself primarily with issues which would be seen as 'women's causes': welfare, education and the care of the mentally ill.[47] She was supported by Dorothy Rees, almost twenty years her junior, who made her most significant mark as a county councillor. Leonora Davies was the first Labour woman on Pontardawe Council as well as being the first local woman magistrate. Much of her work was voluntary, concerning prisoners and juvenile delinquents.[48] Yet women remained a rare presence in the council chamber. A Labour local election manifesto in south Wales gave a list of the occupations of its councillors and added proudly: 'There is one Labour Woman Councillor.'[49] Women were seen as an interest to be represented rather than a sex which needed equality and, as late as the 1930s, some councils in the valleys were electing their first woman to office.[50]

Other activists were career women, unable to combine their vocation with marriage and a family. Miss Alice Williams, the head-mistress of Wern Girls' School, Ystalyfera, took her feminist values into her occupation by fostering the careers of 2,017 pupils, 119 of whom became teachers and fifty-five of those were still teaching

Table 9.2. Number of women candidates in general elections

General election	Labour[a]	Conservative	Liberal[b]	Plaid Cymru	Other[c]	Total
1918	1	-	-	-	-	1
1922	1	2	-	-	-	3
1923	-	-	1	-	-	1
1924	-	1	-	-	-	1
1929	-	1	2 (1)	-	-	3 (1)
1931	1	1	1 (1)	-	-	3 (1)
1935	-	2	1 (1)	-	-	3 (1)
1945	1	-	1 (1)	1	-	3 (1)
1950	2 (2)	-	1 (1)	-	1	4 (3)
1951	3 (1)	-	1	-	-	4 (1)
1955	2 (1)	1	-	1	1	5 (1)
1959	3 (2)	1	-	-	1	5 (2)
1964	2 (2)	2	-	1	1	6 (2)
1966	2 (2)	-	1	-	1	4 (2)
1970	1	2	1	-	-	4
1974 Feb.	-	-	3	2	-	5
1974 Oct.	-	1	4	1	-	6
1979	-	1	2	1	3	7
1983	2	1	3	6	1	13
1987	3 (1)	-	5	9	2	19 (1)
1992	4 (1)	2	8	7	4	25 (1)
1997	5 (4)	4	10	7	11	39 (4)

[a]Figures in brackets are the numbers elected. Only two Labour women candidates have won seats at by-elections: Megan Lloyd George (Carmarthen, 1957), 47.3%; Ann Clwyd (Cynon Valley, 1984), 58.8%.
[b]Includes Independent Liberal, Social and Liberal Democrats, Social Democrats.
[c]Includes Communist, Green Party, Ecology Party, Natural Law Party, Referendum Party, Pro-Life.
Source: B. Jones, Etholiadau Seneddol Yng Nghymru/Parliamentary Elections in Wales 1900–75 (Talybont, 1977); F. W. S. Craig (ed.), British Parliamentary Election Results 1974–1983 (Chichester, 1984) and Britain Votes, IV. British Parliamentary Election Results 1983–87 (Aldershot, 1989); C. Rallings and M. Thrasher (eds.), Britain Votes, V. British Parliamentary Election Results 1988–92 (Aldershot, 1993) and Britain Votes, VI. British Parliamentary Election Results 1997 (Aldershot, 1998).

when she retired in 1934. Her many activities included work for the ILP, Trades and Labour Council and Co-op. While her occupation would have precluded work in local government, she campaigned for infant and child welfare and for peace. She was referred to as 'a foster mother to many of the people of Ystalyfera'.[51]

As for Labour's female parliamentary candidates in Wales, two had fought the University seat in the elections of 1918 and 1922 but

Table 9.3. Labour women candidates in general elections and the percentage of votes (*indicates success)

1918	H. M. Mackenzie (University of Wales), 19.2%
1922	Dr Olive Wheeler (University of Wales), 24.6%
1931	Frances Edwards (Flint), 28.6%
1945	Eirene Ll. Jones (Flint), 37.4%
1950	Dorothy M. Rees (Barry), 44.5%*; Eirene White (Flint East), 48.5%*
1951	Dorothy M. Rees (Barry), 48.3%; Eirene White (Flint East), 53.8%*; Josephine Richardson (Monmouth), 44.4%
1955	Eirene White (Flint East), 52.6%*; Josephine Richardson (Monmouth), 42.8%
1959	Loti Rees Hughes (Cardigan), 28.2%; Megan Lloyd George (Carmarthen), 47.9%*; Eirene White (Flint East), 50.1%*
1964	Megan Lloyd George (Carmarthen), 45.4%*; Eirene White (Flint East), 54.2%*
1966	Megan Lloyd George (Carmarthen), 46.2%*; Eirene White (Flint East), 51.3%*
1970	Ann Clwyd (Denbigh), 26.3%
1983	Betty H. Williams (Caernarfon), 19.4%; Jane E. Hutt (Cardiff N), 20.0%
1987	Betty H. Williams (Conwy), 22.3%; Ann Clwyd (Cynon Valley), 68.9%*, Katrina Gass (Monmouth), 27.7%
1992	Sharon Mainwaring (Caernarfon), 15.5%; Julie Morgan (Cardiff N), 38.9%; Betty H. Williams (Conwy), 25.8%; Ann Clwyd (Cynon Valley), 69.1%*
1997	Julie Morgan (Cardiff N), 50.4%*; Betty H. Williams (Conwy), 35.0%*; Ann Clwyd (Cynon Valley), 69.7%*; Angharad Davies (Montgomery), 19.1%; Jackie Lawrence (Preseli Pembs.), 48.3%*

Source: As Table 9.2.

it was 1931 before a Labour woman stood for an ordinary constituency (Tables 9.2 and 9.3). Frances Edwards was a teacher working in Lancashire when she fought Flint in 1931: the worst election of the century in which to be a Labour candidate.[52] Perhaps she laid the ground for Eirene Lloyd Jones to contest it in 1945 when circumstances were much more propitious. Huw T. Edwards, the Transport and General Workers' Union leader in the area, later confessed to having some doubts about whether the electorate was ready for a woman candidate, but her distinguished Oxford career, her background in journalism and her famously political father (Thomas Jones, former deputy secretary of the Cabinet) won him over. This was not enough for the electorate and she lost, despite a good performance at the polls. Boundary changes delivered the prize to her (as Mrs Eirene White) at the next election, when Flint was divided and she stood in the more industrial East Flint, which included the Shotton steelworks. Her campaign managers clearly still thought her sex was a problem. One of her election leaflets constructs an imaginary dialogue between two voters: the one who raises doubts about having a woman as MP is answered by another who stresses her Oxford education, journalistic experience and work for the film industry. She would serve the constituency for another twenty years, hold ministerial office under the Labour governments of 1964–70 and be chairman of the Labour Party in 1969 before moving on to the House of Lords as a base for a further extended period of public service.[53]

Eirene White had to share the distinction of becoming the first female Welsh Labour MP. Barry had been held by Labour's Ungoed-Thomas since 1945 but boundary changes made it a more difficult proposition and, in 1948, he announced that he was not going to contest the seat at the next general election, pleading that it was too diverse and scattered to be managed by a candidate who did not have a home in the constituency. Dorothy Rees, who had experience as a local councillor and who had been a Glamorgan county councillor since 1934, was nominated for the vacancy. She had been a school teacher in her earlier days, like so many prominent Labour women but had married a Barry sea pilot which gave her a connection with the dominant activities of the port. She won the seat narrowly at the election of 1950, the beneficiary of a three-way split in the vote, becoming one of only three new women Labour MPs. In 1951, however, the Liberals did not bring forward a candidate and their vote went by two to one to her new Conservative opponent, Raymond Gower, who ran a campaign of relentless activity, stressing the 'housewives' issues' which did much to dent Labour's cause in the post-war period. Here they displaced a female MP. Dorothy Rees never again tried to win the seat and Gower remained inviolable to a string of Labour contenders because of his effective, highly personal nursing of the constituency.[54] Eirene White's position as the solitary Welsh Labour woman MP would remain until Megan Lloyd George won Carmarthen for Labour in a by-election. Like Eirene White she benefited from having a famous father and perhaps from the political ambiguity of having crossed the floor in a constituency which had not wholeheartedly endorsed the Labour cause.

In post-war Britain Labour's synthesis of socialist and feminist issues came apart. Labour failed to adapt quickly enough to a world where more married women worked and failed to capitalize on new political issues like consumerism which were giving the Conservatives an increasing appeal to women. Then, magically, Labour won a majority of women's votes in 1966, having taken no effective action to secure them: but followed it with significant steps to retain them. This meant coming to terms with the new feminist issues like equal pay and equal rights. Women's issues which had been dormant in the 1950s became prominent in the party again, to some extent promoted by a career politician who rejected the feminist tag – Barbara Castle.[55]

In Wales, by the 1950s problems were apparent at the grassroots of Labour women's organization. After Elizabeth Andrews retired in 1948 she was briefly succeeded in her post by Ismay Hill, who left shortly after her marriage. Megan Roach became another long-serving organizer of women in Wales at the beginning of the 1950s. Clearly it was a different world by then. The era of Elizabeth Andrews had ended with plentiful celebrations of silver jubilees of women's sections and advisory councils. Nostalgia for this 'golden past' became a feature of party activity, as did votes of sympathy in illness and for death. Megan Roach started her work by complaining about the state of women's organization and stressing the need to rebuild it. More problems were apparent in north Wales than south but the underlying issues seem to have been the same. In East Denbighshire by the mid-1950s most sections were not functioning.[56] Roach laboured hard to resurrect the bodies but they usually sunk back into torpor or worse once she left for her work in south Wales or in elections.[57] There was some local discontent that she did not spend enough time in north Wales, though clearly the job pulled her in many directions at the same time. By 1961 there were only ten sections in East Denbighshire compared with twenty-two in 1945.[58] Elsewhere in north and mid Wales there had only really been pockets of women's organization, with places like Blaenau Ffestiniog and Porthmadog standing out. Holyhead had the sole women's section on the whole of Anglesey and other largely rural constituencies had similar positions. Roach expressed her frustration with the task of organizing here more in geographical terms than through comments on political tradition and culture, which Elizabeth Andrews had stressed. She was fond of saying that these seats were more like continents than constituencies and blamed the lack of focus of scattered rural communities for the difficulties she encountered.

Shortly after the huge victory at the polls in 1966 the same position was discussed with regard to the whole of Wales.[59] Some of it reflected general social changes. Television was blamed for the lack of support at meetings. In an era when the party had to be careful not to canvass during *Coronation Street*, this carries some force. Certainly the vigorous street culture of working-class communities, of which women's organization had been a key part, was coming under pressure from more privatized lifestyles. Many sections seemed to have settled back into the easy option of having speakers rather than adopting the arduous task of undertaking political education. Perhaps they became too much like the WI for their own good. As early as 1951 there had only been forty-seven sections in East Glamorgan, compared with ninety-five in 1929. In 1955 not one section in East Glamorgan organized a women's week.[60] Yet Wales seemed to be doing better than other areas of Britain and was one of the last redoubts of women's organization in the party. In 1961 there were still 161 sections in Wales and in 1966 it had the second highest total of sections in the country.[61] Flickers of new interest were shown with attempts to start sections on new housing estates which lacked social facilities – like Penrhys in the Rhondda – and some younger women were drawn in as attempts were made to address newer issues. Advisory councils were dissolved in 1970 in favour of more broadly based women's committees, and an era in the party's history had come to an end.[62]

By 1980 many in the party felt that the existing structure of women's organizations had fulfilled their purpose. They believed that women's organization perpetuated sexual divisions and that women's rights had now been achieved to such an extent that there was no need for separate organization. The Conwy party felt that a revised approach was necessary:

> The women's organisation should be abolished, and women Party members encouraged to take their rightful place within the main Party structure. The issues which have hitherto been defined as 'of interest to women' should still be promoted, but by the establishment of a sub-committee which would deal with them specifically.

The position of women in the party was summed up in the report which was prepared on the basis of these replies: 'There is traditionally a strong women's organisation in Wales with 110 women's sections and 25 Labour Women's Councils. One Assistant Organiser is the Secretary of the North and South Wales regional committees and has overall responsibility for the Women's Organisation.'[63]

Obituaries for women's organizations proved to be a little premature. In the 1980s women's organization revived in the party in unexpected ways, though not with the coverage and élan of earlier times. The Conservative government returned in 1979 proved hostile to women's issues and the feminist movement which had erupted in the 1970s outside the party structure began to seek a sympathetic party location. As Labour's electoral crisis made it responsive to new approaches, it proved to be the beneficiary of this move. Many women reinvigorated the peace issue. Welsh women created the peace camp at Greenham Common and many others in the Labour Party supported them through revived women's sections and conferences.[64] To some extent, industrial struggles amplified the trend. During the miners' strike of 1984–5 and the Blaenau Ffestiniog quarrymen's strike of 1985–6 there was much talk and some reality of a changed position for women in the most socially conservative areas of Labour support. Women's support groups were part of the conflict and the role that women played on picket lines and in addressing public meetings led many to claim that gender relations had altered irrevocably in Wales.

Labour women's conferences became features of the Welsh political scene in the 1980s, reflecting a growth of women's sections in response to hostile decisions against women by the Thatcher government. The conference held in Swansea in 1983 attracted 150 delegates and 100 visitors. Women's committees were formed for north and south Wales and schools to encourage the political education of these newly active women were held. One reflection of this activity was the selection of women as parliamentary candidates, though neither Betty Williams in Caernarfon nor Jane Hutt in Cardiff North West was selected for a seat which would be winnable in 1983.[65]

Women pursued the new issues that concerned them particularly, such as cuts in contraceptive services, cervical smears and abortion. They were also concerned about discrimination, including that practised by some workingmen's clubs where Labour meetings were often held. But concerns were expressed about the whole range of domestic policy and extended through to international issues like the Falklands War and Greenham Common. Complaints about the obstacles in the way of women participating in policy-making in the party began to surface, including the right of the women's conference to elect its own representatives to the NEC and the party conference.[66]

By 1984 Welsh Labour women were fully supporting the moves to achieve equality which were by then having an influence in Britain: 'Conference recognizes that to achieve socialism we must first enable women and men to work together as equals . . . Feminism and Socialism are complementary ideals, and the Labour Party should change its structure to demonstrate this.'[67] By then the Parliamentary Labour Party included one woman from a Welsh constituency in its ranks, after Ann Clwyd won the 1984 Cynon Valley by-election. There is no evidence that she used women's issues to win the seat. Her press releases stressed many diverse issues and particularly the bitter strike that was then just beginning. She had a good deal of support from the local miners' lodges. But her real victory was in the selection conference. It was not news for a Labour candidate to win in Cynon Valley, but that a woman was selected was lightning striking the ground.

Clearly the impetus for changes within the party came from south Wales women. At the 1985 Labour women's conference the over-whelming proportion of delegates were from south Wales with twenty-four from Gwent, twenty-seven from Mid Glamorgan, thirty-two from South Glamorgan and forty-five from West Glamorgan out of a total of 142 delegates. Clwyd, Gwynedd and Dyfed could muster only fourteen between them (and Powys none).[68] In the 1987 election only three Labour women fought seats and only Ann Clwyd won. Katrina Gass in Monmouth and Betty Williams (Conwy) had little prospect of success with the tide still running strongly in the Conservatives' direction.[69] Some were beginning to feel frustration at the lack of success in promoting women's issues within the party at large. Gill Jenkins reflected sadly on her two years on the National Women's Committee: 'on the whole, I've been disillusioned and disappointed. Despite the enthusiasm of the women on the NLWC, I soon realized that even at National level, women still have very little influence on Party Policy.'[70]

Table 9.4. *Labour women candidates in European elections*

European election	Labour[a]	Conservative	Liberal	Plaid Cymru	Other	Total
1979	1 (1)	2 (1)	1	–	–	4 (2)
1984	–	2 (1)	1	–	1	4 (1)
1989	–	1	–	1	1	3
1994	2 (2)	2	2	1	3	10 (2)

[a]Candidates (all successful): 1979, Ann Clwyd (Mid and West Wales), 41.5%; 1994, Glenys Kinnock (South Wales East), 74.0%, Eluned Morgan (Wales Mid and West), 40.5%.
Source: F. W. S. Craig and T. T. Mackie (eds.), *Europe Votes I, European Parliamentary Elections, Results 1979* (Chichester, 1980) and *II, 1984* (Chichester, 1985); T. T. Mackie, *III, 1989* (Aldershot, 1990); Denis Balsom (ed.), *The Wales Yearbook 1995* (Cardiff, 1995).

Some breakthroughs had been made and the women's committee has continued to meet regularly, as has a women's conference. Many other things stayed the same. There was still a need to discuss ways to increase the number of women in public life, despite having the results of the 1997 election to celebrate. The Labour landslide of 1997 saw four Labour women returned for Welsh seats, the highest total ever. Ann Clwyd was joined by Julie Morgan for Cardiff North, Jackie Lawrence for the new seat of Preseli and Betty Williams, who finally reaped the fruits of a decade and a half of effort in Conwy.[71] The ground had been prepared by the new European seats which women had more success in contesting. Ann Clwyd had served her apprenticeship there, while in 1994 Glenys Kinnock and Eluned Morgan had been returned to the European Parliament (Table 9.4).[72]

Yet this breakthrough was the product of particular circumstances as much as of any fundamental change in the ethos of Labour in Wales. The women who won seats did so because unique opportunities arrived in the 1990s. The party's modernizers became particularly responsive to increasing women's representation under the leadership of John Smith. During this time an effective form of positive discrimination was adopted. All-woman shortlists were made mandatory for half the winnable and safe seats. The pressure for this came from the Socialist International, and the experience of Scandinavia where such policies have rapidly altered the gender balance of parliaments. All three of the new Labour women were adopted on all-woman shortlists before a legal decision held these to be a breach of the Sex Discrimination Act in

1996. The women MPs were in many ways rather different from their male counterparts: all were close to (or above) fifty; all had substantial experience in local government, a background which is becoming rarer amongst MPs in general. All three had raised their families before gaining a parliamentary seat.[73]

Nor was it a great result in the context of Britain as a whole. Four women in Parliament represents exactly an eighth of the Labour MPs elected in Wales. After the 1997 election women constitute a quarter of Labour MPs in Britain. Welsh women with political aspirations were the victims of an unhappy conjuncture: Labour's revival began in Wales in 1987 but the policy of positive discrimination was adopted only after 1992, with the consequence that there were few new victories in 1997.[74] The situation in Wales is hardly a major breakthrough in historical terms either when set against the three women elected for Welsh constituencies in 1950. Only two of these were Labour women, but the 1997 transformation is only a breach with the immediate past: it is hardly unprecedented. Nor have women made any substantial breakthrough in local government. Marion Drake is still among a very small band of women to have become Lord Mayor of Cardiff and she achieved the office only after bringing up a family.[75]

More disturbing is the realization that maintaining this advance is fraught with difficulty. The seats gained in 1997 will become vulnerable. The procedures which ensured that women were the Labour candidates chosen for these seats have been struck down by the courts. Further advances for women in Welsh politics will depend on having non-sexist selection procedures, something we may justly be sceptical about achieving. One test was the outcome of the first elections to the Welsh Assembly to be held in May 1999. Here a great problem emerged because a dual commitment to a cheap assembly (which meant that it had a mere sixty seats) and some attachment to gender balance produced a series of embarassing conflicts. Had the assembly had eighty or more seats the issue of gender balance could have been addressed by ensuring that a man and a woman were selected as Labour candidates for each of the forty constituencies. As it was it was resolved by 'twinning'. Adjacent constituencies drew up their shortlists together, with one being required to select a man and the other a woman. The four Labour women MPs led a successful campaign to have this adopted as party policy. But it raised considerable opposition on the grounds that the bigger of the two parties selected not simply its own candidate but that of its weaker neighbour. Overtly, at least, it was contested as an issue of local democracy, though anyone with a historical sense must feel that male chauvinism can wear many disguises. Plenty of party democracy was trampled upon by modernizers in London without arousing the intense opposition that twinning encountered.[76]

Whatever the conflicts over twinning, there can be no doubt that it achieved its object of raising women's representation in the Welsh Assembly. After the 1999 elections, Labour's successful delegation of fifteen women and thirteen men was the major component in giving the new body a 40 per cent women's representation, the most even gender balance of any elected body outside Scandinavia. The Liberal Democrat representation of three men and three women also contributed to this result, but Plaid Cymru's eleven men and six women and the Conservative Party's nine men pulled in the opposite direction.

So what has been the experience of women in the Labour Party in Wales? From the standpoint of a commitment to equal representation, the record is lamentable.[77] The party has been dominated by men who have formed the vast majority of those elected to office. Women have stood as Labour parliamentary candidates in general elections in Wales on thirty-three occasions and over one-third of these have been since 1983. Only seven women have ever been Labour MPs and four of these are currently in Parliament. Labour's total of candidates is better than the record of the Conservatives who number only twenty-two and 'others', who combined muster twenty-six. By contrast the Liberals have forty-five and Plaid Cymru thirty-seven. Nor is absence at Westminster compensated for by dominance in the council chamber. A radical feminist would duly convict the party at the bar of discriminatory attitudes.

Yet in many ways this would be an unsafe conviction. Political parties exist in a world which has been dominated by discriminatory attitudes and no other political party can boast a better performance.[78] For much of the period under review Labour was the pre-eminent party for nominating women to the highest public office in Wales. The Liberal Party and Plaid Cymru only nose past Labour in 1992 and 1997. Indeed women nominated for Labour Party seats, unlike those in other parties, have a relatively high likelihood of becoming MPs. Few have fought entirely hopeless seats. The worst result by a Labour woman in Wales was Sharon Mainwaring's 15.5 per cent of the poll in Caernarfon in 1992. Only three others have got less than 20 per cent of the vote. Yet Wales does not compare very favourably with Britain as a whole in the return of women to Parliament. Up to 1992 166 women had become MPs in Britain and only four of these were from Wales. Given an average British distribution, there would have been twice as many. The figures for candidates are slightly better. Only 1,721 women stood as parliamentary candidates in Britain between 1918 and 1992; Wales, with eighty-four, is in line with its share of the population.[79]

A similar conclusion emerges if we take a more general and more impressionistic gaze at women's place in Welsh politics in the twentieth century. Labour has been the party which has best expressed the political aspirations of women in Wales. Its large membership in inter-war and post-war Wales was almost 50 per cent female and they quite frequently expressed positions on women's rights as well as adopting a clear stance on welfare issues. Labour women were very much more prominent than women in Plaid Cymru in the period, though its membership may have been just as female in composition. Plaid's women's section seems to have been concerned with social events and fundraising and not to have raised any kinds of distinctively women's issues. In the inter-war period only four women were prominent in the party.[80] Labour was different: it was a serious electoral machine while Plaid Cymru was until 1945 largely a Welsh-language pressure group.[81] Only since the mid-1970s has Plaid adopted feminist issues and, although it fielded seven women candidates in 1992 and eight in 1997, none were in anything close to a winnable seat. Nor did it make any special provision for selecting women candidates for the assembly elections. Of the Conservatives there is little to be said. Only in the European Parliament do they have a lead over the other parties in running women candidates.

For the whole century women played an important part in the work of the Labour Party in Wales. Women helped to make Labour the kind of party it was and shaped important parts of its political agenda. When it has succeeded in speaking for humanity and not simply for a class it has often done so because of the promptings of its women members. Women have had the subsidiary but important role in the party that Rose Davies articulated perfectly when she declared in 1930 that it was their part to 'help forward the great work of humanity'. Women's active participation and separate organization faded in the 1950s but has been revived under the influence of feminist movements and the party's need to win the votes of women. Labour was the 'party of Wales' in the twentieth century: furthermore it justified its early claim to be 'the party for women' in the sense that it has provided most of the political outlets for them and garnered most of their votes. From the standpoint of anyone with a commitment to the equality of women its record is appalling: worse is the fact that this is the best that women have achieved in Welsh party politics.

Notes

The chapter heading is a phrase used by Rose Davies, National Library of Wales (NLW), Labour Party Collection (LPC), Mins, East Glamorgan Women's (Labour) Advisory Council, Meeting at Pontypridd, 8 March 1930.

[1] J. Rendall (ed.), *Equal or Different: Women's Politics, 1800–1914* (Oxford, 1987); R. Evans, 'German social democracy and women's suffrage, 1891–1918', *Journal of Contemporary History*, XV (1980); M.-J. Buhle, 'Women and the Socialist Party, 1901–1914', in E. H. Altbach (ed.), *From Feminism to Liberation* (Cambridge, MA, 1971).

[2] C. Rowan, 'Women and the Labour Party, 1906–1920', *Feminist Studies*, XII (1982); C. Collette, *For Labour and for Women: The Women's Labour League, 1906–1918* (Manchester, 1989).

[3] *WM*, 8 Feb. 1910.

[4] *LL*, 21 April 1911.

[5] *LL*, 19 May, 6, 13 Oct. 1911; 5 Jan. 1912.

[6] *LL*, 19 Jan. 1912; *SWDN*, 1 Dec. 1913.

[7] *LL*, 2 Feb., Mar.–May *passim*, 19 Sept., 28 Nov. 1912; 27 Mar., 17, 31 Apr. 1913.

[8] *Labour Woman* (May 1913).

[9] *LL*, 18, 25 July, 8 Aug. 1912.

[10] N. Evans and D. Jones, ' "A blessing for the miner's wife": the campaign for pithead baths in the South Wales Coalfield, 1908–1950', *Llafur*, VI/3 (1994).

[11] *LL*, 13 June, 21 Nov., 5 Dec. 1912.

[12] *LL*, 30 Jan., 7 Aug. 1913.

[13] *LL*, 19 Dec. 1912; 27 March, 1 May 1913.

[14] *LW* (Feb. 1914).

[15] K. Cook and N. Evans, ' "The petty antics of the bell-ringing boisterous band": the Women's Suffrage Movement in Wales, 1890–1918', in A. V. John (ed.), *Our Mothers' Land: Chapters in Welsh Women's History, 1830–1939* (Cardiff, 1991).

[16] *Pioneer*, 11, 25 May 1912.

[17] *Rhondda Socialist*, 21 Dec. 1912.

[18] M. J. Daunton, *Coal Metropolis: Cardiff, 1870–1914* (Leicester, 1977); N. Evans, 'Cardiff's Labour tradition', *Llafur*, IV/2 (1985); *LL*, 24 May 1912, 31 April 1913.

[19] N. Evans and K. Sullivan, ' "Yn llawn o dân Cymreig" (Full of Welsh fire): the language of politics in Wales, 1880–1914', in G. H. Jenkins (ed.), *The Welsh Language and its Social Domains, 1801–1911* (Cardiff, 2000); *LL*, 23 July 1914.

[20] Collette, *For Labour*, 60.

[21] *LL*, 27 May, 31 July, 4 Sept. 1913.

[22] *LL*, 3 Dec. 1914.

[23] *LL*, 3 Dec. 1916.

[24] Women's Labour League, Report 1914, 1915 and Proceedings of 10th Annual Conference, 1916, 14–15, 48, 51–2; E. Andrews, *A Woman's Work is Never Done* (Ystrad Rhondda, 1948), ch. 4; *LW* (May 1919).

[25] Andrews, *Women's Work*, chs. 1–2; *LW* (June, Sept. 1919; Jan. 1920).

[26] Andrews, *Woman's Work*, ch. 6.

[27] LPC, Mins of the East Glamorgan Women's Advisory Council, 16 Feb. 1929; *LW* (March 1926); P. Massey, *Portrait of a Mining Town* (London, 1937), 40–1.

[28] *LW* (Aug., Oct. 1920; May–June 1921; May, Dec. 1925; Nov. 1927).

[29] *LW* (Jan., Mar.–Apr., July–Aug. 1945).

[30] *LW* (Jan., Dec. 1948, Nov. 1958).

[31] *LW* (Aug.–Sept. 1921, Aug. 1922, Jan. 1924).

[32] *LW* (Oct. 1922, Jan., Nov. 1924, Dec. 1931).

[33] *LW* (May 1936).

[34] *LW* (May 1937, Jan. 1938).

[35] *LW* (Jan. 1929, Sept. 1939); NLW, XJN 1171–1180, Labour Party Election Literature, 1912–79.

[36] *LW* (Jan. 1936, May 1937).

[37] *LW* (Nov. 1921, Aug. 1928, March 1929).

[38] *LW* (May, July 1928).

[39] *LW* (July–Aug. 1930).

[40] NLW, Thomas Jones Papers, Class H. vol. 14, item 26, Joint Committee for the Promotion of Educational Facilities in the South Wales and Monmouthshire Coalfields [April 1930], 8.

[41] *LW* (June 1933); *Aberdare Leader* (*AL*), 8 May, 25 Sept. 1926, 4 July 1936; *SWV*, 11 May 1929.

[42] *LW* (Nov. 1931, Oct. 1932).

[43] LPC, 124 Mins of Flintshire and Denbighshire Labour Women's Advisory Council, 18 March 1971.

[44] *LW* (June 1933).

[45] J. Lewis, 'Beyond suffrage: English feminism in the 1920s', *Maryland Historian*, VI (1975); Andrews, *Women's Work*, ch. 11.

[46] J. Bourke, 'Housewifery in England, 1860–1914', *Past and Present*, CXLIII (1994); R. Crooks, 'Tidy women: women in the Rhondda between the wars', *Oral History*, X (1982).

[47] Glamorgan Record Office, D/DX ik, Rose Davies Papers.

[48] *SWV*, 9 June 1934.

[49] *Where Labour Rules: Monmouthshire County Council. A Record of Labour Administration* (1928), 2.

[50] *AL*, 29 Sept. 1934.

[51] *SWV*, 22 Dec. 1934, 5 Jan. 1935.

[52] *Liverpool Daily Post*, 28 Oct. 1931.

[53] NLW, Ex 730 Press Cuttings on East Flints Election, Oct. 1951; XJN 1171–1180; J. G. Edwards, 'Flintshire since 1801', *Flintshire Historical Society Publications*, XV (1954–5), 81–2.

[54] *Barry Herald*, April 1948–Nov. 1951.

[55] A. Black and S. Brooke, 'The Labour Party, women and the problem of gender, 1951–1966', *Journal of British Studies*, XXXVI (1997); O. McDonald, 'Women in the Labour Party today', in L. Middleton (ed.), *Women in the Labour Movement: The British Experience* (London, 1977).

[56] LPC, East Denbighshire Women's Labour Advisory Committee, 6 Nov. 1954; 1 Jan. 1955.

[57] Ibid., 5 March 1959.

[58] Ibid., 24 Jan., 4 March 1957, 20 April 1961.

[59] Ibid., 16 March 1967.

[60] LPC, East Glamorgan Women's Advisory Committee Minutes, 16 Feb. 1929, 17 Jan. 1951, 29 Oct. 1955.

[61] Ibid., 14 Oct. 1961, 14 May 1966.

[62] Ibid., 14 April 1966, 14 Oct. 1967.

[63] LPC, 212. Replies to Questionnaire sent out Nov. 1979 on the Organisation and Structure of Labour Party Wales.

[64] S. Perrigo, 'Women and change in the Labour Party, 1979–1995', *Parliamentary Affairs*, XXXXIV (1996); J. Liddington, *The Long Road to Greenham: Feminism and Anti-Militarism in Britain since 1820* (London, 1989), 222–9.

[65] LPC, 239. 3rd Annual Labour Women Wales Conference, 13 Nov. 1982.

[66] LPC, 240. 4th Annual Conference, Nov. 1983.

[67] LPC, 241. 5th Annual Conference of Labour Women in Wales, Cardiff, 10 Nov. 1984.

[68] LPC, 242.

[69] LPC, 243. 7th Annual Conference, Swansea, 1987.

[70] Ibid., 8.

[71] D. Balsom (ed.), *The Wales Yearbook, 1998* (Cardiff, 1997), 58–9, 74–5, 76–7, 104–5.

[72] *Labour Party Wales Annual Conference Report*, 1998, 7; see Table 9.1.

[73] HTV Wales, 'Now We Are Four', Dec. 1998.

[74] K. Milne 'Labour's quota women are on a mission to modernise', and J. Taylor, 'How to make the gender revolution real', *New Statesman/Society*, 16 May 1997.

[75] *WM*, 3 June 1998.

[76] BBC Wales, 'Week in Week Out', 12 May 1998; *WM*, 18 May 1998; *South Wales Echo*, 25 May 1998; K. Brennan, 'Twinning for a better balance', *Welsh Democracy Review*, III (1998).

[77] P. Graves, *Labour Women: Women in British Working Class Politics, 1918–1939* (Cambridge, 1994).

[78] P. Thane, 'Women of the British Labour Party and Feminism, 1906–1945', in H. L. Smith (ed.), *British Feminism in the Twentieth Century* (Cheltenham, 1990) and Thane, 'Visions of gender in the making of the British welfare state: the case of Women in the British Labour Party and social policy, 1906–1945', in G. Bock and Thane (eds.), *Maternity and Gender Policies: Women and the Rise of European Welfare States, 1880s–1950s* (London, 1991).

[79] A. Lockwood, 'After Astor', *New Statesman/Society*, 5 Feb. 1993.

[80] C. A. Davies, 'Women, nationalism and feminism', in J. Aaron *et al.* (eds.), *Our Sisters' Land: The Changing Identities of Women in Wales* (Cardiff, 1994).

[81] D. H. Davies, *A Call to Nationhood: The Welsh Nationalist Party, 1925–1945* (Cardiff, 1983).

10

Labour and the Nation

R. MERFYN JONES and IOAN RHYS JONES

On 18 September 1997 the Welsh people voted by the narrowest of majorities to establish a National Assembly for Wales. This positive outcome was the direct result of the Labour victory in the general election of 1 May in the same year. The Labour Party, so often denounced as a 'centralist' and 'British' party, had delivered a degree of democratic autonomy to Wales for the first time in the nation's history. In terms of the Welsh 'national question' this was, undoubtedly, the most significant step ever taken towards giving Wales a concrete political reality. It was achieved, moreover, despite the indifference of much of the Welsh electorate and the active hostility of a large minority, as was demonstrated in the referendum result.[1] Labour was not responding to massive public pressure in taking this momentous step.

Why, therefore, did the Labour Party commit itself to this policy, given that there appeared to be relatively little electoral advantage which could be expected or delivered as a result? There were, of course, as we shall see, a number of considerations which arose directly out of the political calculations of the 1990s which affected the final decisions, but to understand more fully Labour's attitude to the 'national question' and devolution we must survey the history of the whole century. In that perspective the achievement of 1997 can be seen as not only the consequence of immediate political imperatives and options but also the culmination of a debate which had always been closer to Labour's heart in Wales than political allies or opponents were willing to concede.

In this chapter we shall intercept that debate at various points, not in any attempt to establish a devolutionary pedigree for Labour and to proclaim the existence of a long march through the committee rooms and conference halls but rather to examine the nature of the arguments deployed by supporters and opponents of devolution at various times. There has been a tendency to portray this debate as one between more or less 'pro-Welsh' and 'anti-Welsh' elements within the Labour Party in Wales. While this chapter will suggest that such an analysis is inadequate and misleading, it will seek to demonstrate that the debate within Labour's ranks was a complex affair in which political priorities and programmes intersected with electoral calculation, cultural considerations and political analysis and commitment. Different elements within the party prioritized different reasons for supporting or opposing devolution at various periods; during some years one consideration would predominate, but for most of the century different factors can be seen at play, varying in relevance and intensity as the situation changed. At heart the Labour debate was fundamentally pragmatic and political but these arguments also invoked references to deeper cultural and national allegiances and to the inner cultural divisions which characterized Welsh life.

The original impulse toward devolution was part of the heavy ideological baggage inherited from Liberalism, but it also represented a political terrain which some attempted to capture from the Liberals. The electoral alliance which became the Labour Party at the beginning of the century happily accepted the old Liberal and radical demand of Home Rule All Round and Keir Hardie was often to refer to the need for Home Rule. The political charge which this demand had held in Wales in the 1880s and 1890s had, however, been largely extinguished by what appeared to be the new agenda of the twentieth century and, following the collapse of the Cymru Fydd project in 1896, the demand for Home Rule was not a major policy initiative in any political party.

The 'national question', however, did not disappear and it gave rise to a significant political debate within the Labour movement in 1910–12. In 1910 in a parliamentary question Keir Hardie asked whether the government intended to create a Secretary of State for Wales and a separate administration for the country.[2] In the columns of the *Labour Leader* and elsewhere David Thomas, the most active Labour activist in north Wales and at that time based in the Nantlle Valley in Caernarfonshire, proposed a 'Socialism in Welsh Dress'.[3] At the Carmarthen National Eisteddfod in 1911 Thomas held a meeting in an attempt to create a Welsh structure for the Independent Labour Party (ILP). He was later vehemently to deny that his intention had been to construct a separate Welsh party, but there is no doubt that this was how his appeal was interpreted by many.[4] In response to Thomas's letter to the *Labour Leader* in July 1911 a correspondent from south Wales the following month supported the aim of 'our comrade David Thomas to establish a National Labour Party for Wales'.[5] Thomas has been described as the one 'who came closest during these years to achieving the required synthesis between Socialism and the Welsh spirit'.[6] There is no denying Thomas's commitment to Welsh devolution, a cause he continued to espouse in the 1940s and 1950s, but some caution is required in interpreting his actions at this time.[7] This was not an unthinking acceptance of a Liberal cause. Thomas was nothing if not totally committed to the building of a successful labour movement and his initiative had running through it a thread of political calculation which made eminent strategic sense. In 1911 Wales was still dominated by the Liberal Party and socialists were regularly accused by Liberals and their allies in the Nonconformist denominations of being somehow 'foreign' to Welsh culture and history.[8] In these circumstances it made good political sense to attempt to appropriate elements of this Welsh history and culture to the socialist movement. This is what Thomas and his allies clearly attempted to do by arguing, with some justice, that figures such as Jack Glan y Gors, the Chartists and Welsh radical figures such as Michael D. Jones, not to mention Robert Owen, belonged as much to a socialist pantheon of heroes as to a Liberal, Nonconformist tradition. Edgar L. Chappell, at that time secretary of the West Wales ILP Federation, seemed to go further by arguing that, in accepting 'honours and posts of emolument', the Welsh Liberal MPs, including Lloyd George, had betrayed the national tradition which the Labour Party in Wales could now claim as its own.[9] Both Thomas and Chappell were quite clear that the purpose of this strategy was not only to uphold Welsh national aspirations but also to prise the Welsh electorate away from what they considered to be a defunct and corrupt Liberalism. If this was nationalism it was a nationalism laced with a high dose of political calculation; if it was

Liberalism it was a Liberalism aimed at the heart of the Liberal Party.

The same approach can be found in the use which Thomas and others made of the Welsh language. In a country where almost half the population still spoke Welsh, and in which 8.5 per cent spoke only Welsh, it made good political sense to provide literature in the language. *Llais Llafur* in the Swansea Valley, the *Merthyr Pioneer*'s Welsh pages (edited by the Revd James Nicholas of Glais) and *Y Dinesydd Cymreig* in Gwynedd all aimed to get a socialist message across in a palatable form and in Welsh. A number of Fabian pamphlets were also translated into Welsh.[10] David Thomas himself made a large contribution in this regard and in 1910 published the first and only full-length Welsh-language defence of socialism ever to be published, *Y Werin a'i Theyrnas*. It is an impressive volume but in the context of this discussion what is, perhaps, most noteworthy about it, is that it did not address specifically Welsh strategies. On the contrary the volume was a Welsh-language version of propaganda available and current in English. Thomas was preaching socialism and he was doing it in Welsh because that was the language of his target audience. As early as 1911, therefore, we can discern not only a consciousness of Wales as a nation but also a strong pragmatic and electorally strategic political element in Labour's attempt to construct a 'Socialism in Welsh Dress', a pragmatic thread which, it will be argued here, can be discerned running through the century-long debate on the Welsh Question.[11]

The influence of Liberalism can also be discerned in the immediate post-war period, when the question of Welsh Home Rule re-emerged at least in part because of the efforts of recruits from the Liberal Party such as E. T. John, Liberal MP for East Denbighshire until 1918 who fought elections in 1922 and 1923 as a Labour candidate. John was a passionate pan-Celticist and in 1918 he advocated the setting up of a Welsh Labour Nationalist Party.[12] This agitation attracted some considerable attention in Wales, particularly in the pages of the *Welsh Outlook*, and a Government of Wales Bill was introduced by the Liberal MP for Wrexham, Sir Robert J. Thomas, in 1922. There were well-publicized conferences at Llandrindod Wells and elsewhere in support of the demand for Home Rule. Historians have been sceptical as to the significance of this activity and have rightly emphasized that this was a transitional period during which the whole ground of Welsh politics underwent a shift from the old Liberal agenda to a new Labour agenda. Home Rule was unmistakably part of the old Liberal agenda, albeit now espoused by some Labour supporters. This analysis is surely right in placing the emphasis on the fundamental changes taking place and yet during that period of transition there were signs that the Home Rule demand was actively considered by a number of Labour activists. George Barker, for example, a member of the South Wales Miners' Federation Executive and future Labour MP for Abertillery, argued in 1918: 'Why not go for the real essential thing, a Parliament for Wales . . . Devolution is bound to come, and the sooner the better', and he went on to marry Labour's economic demands with a national perspective claiming that if Welsh nationalists would agree to 'see the miners own and control the mines and the steel and tinplate workers the mills . . . then Welsh workers will welcome a Welsh National Party'.[13] The original Liberal demand, therefore, could in Labour hands be informed with socialist content and purpose. In 1918 the South Wales Labour Federation passed a motion in favour of Home Rule and organized a conference in support of the idea in Cardiff.

In April 1918 the *Welsh Outlook* had initiated a debate on Labour and devolution and received strong support for Home Rule from a number of trade unionists, including R. T. Jones, the General Secretary of the North Wales Quarrymen's Union. Ramsay MacDonald also pledged his support for the idea. A number of respondents, however, although sympathetic, were more sceptical and circumspect and their arguments and doubts were to be repeated often during the coming century. The Revd Herbert Morgan, Labour candidate for Neath, expressed his doubts as to whether Labour was really interested in the national project; Sam Fisher of the Cardiff Coaltrimmers' Union, although supportive, warned that non-Welsh-speakers 'should not be tabooed and left out' and D. R. Grenfell, then a miners' agent, opposed Labour becoming 'engrossed in a movement that may divert its energies and create new antagonisms from within'.[14]

The resurgence in Home Rule agitation in the immediate post-war period, therefore, can be seen to have attracted the attention and allegiance of some within the labour movement, even though the provenance of the demand lay in the Liberal past. Like the Home Rule movement of the late nineteenth and early twentieth centuries, this agitation emerged in a period of relative economic success for the Welsh economy and it shared much of the rhetoric of earlier decades. The Depression, which afflicted Wales from the early 1920s, brought a different vocabulary and new, urgent, priorities.

The Depression not only undermined business and communities but also conditioned social and political attitudes and it inevitably lay at the heart of Labour's policy-making for many decades. As James Griffiths recalled in 1969, 'Wales has still to recover from the wounds of the thirties . . . Notwithstanding all that has since been attempted and achieved, the fears persist, the doubts remain and the wounds are unhealed.'[15]

From the 1920s onwards the cardinal aspect of any Labour political programme had to be its ability to offer solutions to the terrible blight which had descended onto the party's heartlands in industrial south Wales. The Labour Party's official economic policies dissolved with the collapse of the Labour government in 1931 and there were no easy solutions. It took a decade of tortuous debate and discussion before Labour arrived at an alternative economic policy. In Wales there appeared to be a number of broad options or, perhaps more accurately, of emphases, but given the ravages wreaked on south Wales it was abundantly apparent to most Labour politicians and their supporters that Wales could only be resuscitated by the intervention of central government: the resources for internal solutions were not available. This view was universally and rationally held within the Labour Party; as representatives of a wrecked area, what could Labour MPs do but draw attention to their constituents' plight and press for central support? In that sense they were all 'centralists' and the demand for the nationalization of the coal industry was a crucial tenet of a shared faith.

In fact, Wales received precious little assistance until the late 1930s but the forced dependence of the region was apparent to all; as one Conservative remarked, 'South Wales would be in complete collapse but for the fact that the rest of the country has helped, to a certain extent, to carry the distressed areas on their backs.'[16] This response of looking to a government transfer of resources and investment from the richer areas of Britain to derelict Wales was, and continued to be, the common strategy of most Welsh politicians. The discussion concerning Welsh devolution at that time has to be located primarily within this context. Cultural issues also came into play but they were not the primary considerations.

Much of the debate surrounding devolution in the mid decades of the century, long after the Depression had passed, reflected this central dilemma of regional economic dependency and the related emphases placed on economic and regional development, nationalization and planning. Within these broad parameters, however, there were available a number of sharply differentiated options and emphases and one of those was what can be termed a 'regionalist' response which, in dramatically changed circumstances, revisited the devolutionary project.

As has been seen, the Home Rule demand did not disappear after the war and the ILP in the 1920s continued to display an interest in the issue. In 1930 Peter Freeman, Labour MP for Brecon and Radnor, who demanded the establishment of a Secretary of State, received the enthusiastic support of at least the north Wales constituencies but not, it seems, that of Ramsay MacDonald.[17] But by the 1930s elements of a more pronounced regionalist project can be discerned in the politics of a number of Labour politicians, prominent amongst whom was D. R. Grenfell MP. Grenfell, who had been opposed to Home Rule in 1918, was elected as Labour MP for Gower in a 1922 by-election and was to become one of the longest-serving MPs and a formidable advocate of some measure of devolution. In Grenfell's rhetoric in the 1930s we can hear a rage at the dependent posture which Wales had been forced to adopt and an insistence that Wales had the capacity to overcome her problems, albeit within a structure of state support and planning. In 1936 Grenfell argued in the House of Commons that:

> The people in this part of Britain are no less competent than those in any other part. We intensely dislike having to come here in the character of supplicants asking for favours. We have proved our capacity in the world of industry. We have built up those industries . . . We live in a community which is governed by as near a democracy as this country or the world can show. . . . In this area where all the powers of disintegration and demoralisation are at work, we are not demoralised. We are still alive . . . We are fighting to maintain our position, and are meeting with a large measure of success. If we receive the encouragement and help of this House we can pull our people through this period even now.[18]

Here can be heard the genesis of what might be defined as a 'regionalist' strategy for (south) Wales: an emphasis on the internal human resources within Wales and the need for effective representation at the centre. By the Second World War this response had hardened into a policy: the demand for a Secretary of State for Wales and a Welsh Office based on the arrangements already existing in Scotland.

There was some Labour support for a Liberal motion demanding a Secretary of State in 1937 and in 1938 Morgan Jones, the Labour MP for Caerphilly, led a deputation from the Welsh Parliamentary Party to meet with the Prime Minister on the issue. Neville Chamberlain was not impressed but this marked the beginning of a long campaign which was finally to bear fruit when James Griffiths became the first Secretary of State for Wales in 1964. The war years witnessed an intensification of the pressure and the South Wales Regional Council of Labour (SWRCL) supported the call for a Secretary of State in 1942 and 1943.[19] In response to this pressure the government approved a Welsh day in Parliament in 1943 and the first debate took place in 1944. James Griffiths, MP for Llanelli, argued passionately and with eloquence 'not for complete self-government, but for a measure of administrative devolution'. The elements of the Welsh devolutionary case were woven together carefully in his speech but it was clear what the primary consideration was. He spoke with fervour about Welsh culture but he also insisted on the primacy of the economic question: 'culture', he declaimed, 'does not live in a vacuum . . . I have lived as closely as anyone to the tragedy of Wales in the inter-war period. Our people are determined not to go through that again.'[20]

The SWRCL reiterated its call for a Secretary of State in 1944 and 1945. When the NEC refused to adopt two resolutions (one from the SWRCL, the other from Flintshire) calling for a Secretary of State at the 1944 annual conference, it greatly disappointed Flintshire trade unionist Huw T. Edwards, who, as a fraternal delegate from the North Wales Federation of Labour Parties at the SWRCL's conference in 1945, gave prominence to a theme that was to become a familiar one:

> The Welsh Nationalist's Party is growing more rapidly than any other political party in Wales. I feel that it is growing because the other political parties have ignored problems that are essentially Welsh. Unless there is a re-awakening, unless there is a re-dedication of this

Movement to problems that are essentially Welsh, then I am afraid that instead of going forward we are going to go backward.[21]

The call for administrative devolution in Wales was to remain, as was the emphasis on the perceived threat from, what was in fact, a very marginal political party for some time yet.

Labour policy on Wales was not settled by the time of the 1945 general election and, in its aftermath, battle was joined between the proponents of a Secretary of State and those opposed to this decentralization of power such as Ernest Bevin and Herbert Morrison. The Welsh Parliamentary Party and Welsh Labour MPs attempted strenuously to pressure Clement Attlee and his government in this direction but no advance was made at Cabinet. During the debate on the government's white paper on Wales in October 1946 the divisions within the Labour Party again became apparent. The chairman of the Welsh Parliamentary Party, D. R. Grenfell, and the secretary, W. H. Mainwaring, both veteran mining MPs, volubly expressed the demand for change, as did other mining MPs such as George Daggar of Abertillery. As in 1944 the shadow of the Depression continued to hang over the debate, for Daggar explained, 'as Welsh members we are not going to tolerate the return of those inter-war years'.[22] For many in the Parliamentary Party securing a Secretary of State for Wales was a guarantee against such a repetition (and a post-war slump was widely expected by the labour movement at this time), although, with James Griffiths silenced by his position in government, it took the sympathetic Conservative MP for Flint, Nigel Birch, succinctly to explain, 'I do not believe that Wales would have gone through what she has gone through if she had had a Minister in this House to speak for her.'[23]

But for others, particularly those in government, any suggestion of devolution was seen as threatening to leave Wales in a state of permanent poverty. Sir Stafford Cripps, President of the Board of Trade, introduced the White Paper and dismissed the idea of a Welsh economic plan by arguing that none of the economic developments then taking place 'was local in character in the sense of being either financed or originated from Wales'.[24] As for a Secretary of State, he argued that such a development would isolate Wales and, moreover, given the small population of Wales, 'it would be quite impossible to maintain the standard of administration'.[25] D. J. Williams of Neath explained, 'What Wales needs

– and I want to stress this – is not separation from Britain but closer integration with the British economy. In the past Wales has not had a fair share of British prosperity.'[26]

It is clear that the Cabinet had already rejected the notion of a Secretary of State by this time, because it was not convinced by the case put forward by Welsh MPs that this would be an useful constitutional device in achieving the economic reconstruction of Wales. To the contrary, as Bevan, Cripps and Herbert Morrison argued, a Welsh minister was seen as a potential hindrance rather than as a facilitator in such a process. This was a genuine dispute about the efficacy of government in which those in Cabinet such as Bevan and George Hall, not to speak of Morrison and Attlee himself, but not James Griffiths, emphasized the practical value of existing instruments of government in implementing policy, while many MPs and Labour's north and south Wales councils sought more direct intervention in policy-making through a Welsh minister. This point was made by Goronwy Roberts, newly elected MP for Caernarfonshire. He was not, he explained, opposed to central planning, 'and I should like my hon. Friend the Minister of Health to pay particular attention to this', planning had to be centred in London but in order for it to 'penetrate the perimeter', he argued, a Welsh minister was required.[27]

Much of the debate concerning a Secretary of State for Wales in the immediate post-war period therefore, and naturally, pivoted on the issue of the state's role in economic reconstruction and the most effective way to prevent Wales ever again being visited by economic disaster. This argument was essentially concerned with a regionalist perspective in which Wales was viewed as a vulnerable region which, many in the Labour Party in Wales argued, required a direct voice in government.

The dispute did not evaporate quickly and a number of compromises were aired within the government during 1946 and 1947, including the notion of a Welsh minister of non-Cabinet rank proposed by Ness Edwards. The creation of the Welsh Regional Council of Labour (WRCL) in 1947, which brought together the previously existing north and south Wales organizations into one all-Wales body, was a significant pointer to the increased profile of the Welsh dimension within Welsh Labour politics. Despite what the journal *Wales* called in 1947, 'the great public interest and controversy over the Government's attitude towards Welsh devolution, policies and cultural problems', in the end all that emerged from the whole debate was the Council for Wales and Monmouthshire, a non-elected body with minimal powers and no ministerial chair.[28] There was support for a council for Wales at the local level and the Swansea Labour Party Annual Report for 1948 declared: 'It is felt that this arrangement (a Council for Wales) would be far more satisfactory than the appointment of a Secretary of State.'[29] The Council for Wales was established, under the chairmanship of Huw T. Edwards, in 1949. This has subsequently been viewed as a total rout of the pro-devolution forces but the Council did at least acknowledge the existence of Wales, including Monmouthshire, as an administrative, economic and cultural unit.

During the 1950s the Council, and its chairman, were to play a crucial role in effectively retaining the issue of devolution on the political agenda. As the memory of the Depression faded and as Wales started to benefit from the increased affluence of the period, as well as from strong regional development policies and central economic planning, the Council shifted the emphasis away from the narrowly economic to the even narrower but in many respects more effective terrain of the efficacy of the machinery of government in Wales. The conclusions of the Council for Wales and Monmouthshire's Third Memorandum on Government Administration in Wales (1957) criticized the existing arrangements which involved a large number of uncoordinated government departments with Welsh offices and units.[30] In order to achieve co-ordination and efficiency in the implementation of government policy in Wales, they argued, a Secretary of State and a Welsh Office would be necessary. These recommendations were based entirely on a consideration of the efficacy of the operation of government departments in Wales. This was not a new issue but by the late 1950s this now became the major argument of pro-devolutionists. Posing the issue in this way had also the benefit of divesting the debate of some of its more emotional and rhetorical aspects. Devolution was now being proposed as a bureaucratic rationalization rather than as a nationalistic gesture. There followed a tense dialogue between the Conservative government and the Council during 1957 and 1958 and, when it became clear that the government was not going to act, the chair of the Council, Huw T. Edwards, a prominent figure in the labour movement, dramatically resigned.

These events helped to fashion a new focus for the debate by offering both a limited and relatively uncontroversial aim and also by ensuring that devolution was seen as an anti-Tory policy. This pragmatic approach was hugely successful within the Labour Party. Even a deeply sceptical figure such as James Callaghan, who had been opposed to a Secretary of State, now swung into support for the most pragmatic of reasons – as he saw it, the Scots were getting a lot more out of central government, including the Forth Bridge, than was Wales and Cardiff, by now desperate for the Severn Bridge.[31]

A further consideration by the 1950s was the influence of a small group of Labour MPs who could be categorized as 'nationalistic' and who saw the establishment of a Secretary of State as only the first step towards the establishment of a Welsh Parliament. The general elections of 1945, 1950 and 1951 had brought a new element into the House of Commons – Welsh Labour MPs representing rural or semi-rural seats. These new representatives included Tudor Watkins (Brecon and Radnor) and Goronwy Roberts (Caernarfon), both elected in 1945, and Cledwyn Hughes (Anglesey) elected in 1951 and T. W. Jones (Merioneth) who, when elected in the same year, stated, 'I trust the Welsh Nationalists in Meirioneth will find in me a true friend of the ideals for which they stand.'[32] They all came to play a prominent role in the campaign for devolution. Goronwy Roberts had been a member of the Gwerin group at the University College of North Wales in the 1930s, a group which had attempted to marry socialism with a belief in Welsh self-government.[33] In the Commons in 1946 he attempted to explain his position in a rational and explicit fashion, arguing that a Secretary of State was only an interim measure and that what was required was a 'democratic revolution' including the establishment of national assemblies in Wales, Scotland and England. Only thus, he argued, could 'perverted nationalisms' be avoided.[34]

The Parliament for Wales campaign (1950–6) pressed these sympathetic MPs to support the campaign, but the response of the Labour Party, and especially of the Welsh organizer Cliff Prothero, was hostile and, despite an element of cross-party support, the campaign was viewed as a nationalist plot.[35] Moreover, as the 1950s progressed under a Conservative government, and as the fears of a returning depression subsided, so the urgency which had marked the

debates of the 1940s receded. It was in this unpromising context that
S. O. Davies, MP for Merthyr Tydfil since 1934, introduced his
Parliament for Wales Bill in 1955, with the support of the Parliament
for Wales campaign.[36] S. O.'s private member's bill was drafted by
Dewi Watkin Powell, a lawyer with nationalist allegiances.[37] The
issue succeeded in dividing the Labour Party and in isolating the
small group of active devolutionists from the mass of south Wales
Labour MPs. The bill had little chance of success and as the
campaign involved co-operation with the nationalists it was anath-
ematized by many Labour activists. As a political organization the
Labour Party was uncompromising in its opposition to those it saw
as electoral challengers; its party organizers had fought remorselessly
against the much smaller Communist Party since the 1920s and its
attitude to Plaid Cymru was not dissimilar. The debate, moreover,
opened Labour divisions in an election year, an offence which the
party machinery would find hard to forgive. Cliff Prothero, the
party's organizer in Wales, now had the perfect weapon with which
to beat the devolutionists. S.O.'s tactics, therefore, although successful in campaigning terms, were counter-productive in the internal
struggles of the Labour Party and there were efforts to discipline the
campaign's supporters. The debate forced the advocates of devolution such as James Griffiths and D. R. Grenfell fiercely to oppose the
proposal and W. H. Mainwaring, who in 1946 had been such a
forceful supporter of devolution, now denounced the whole enterprise. If the Labour Party was to move towards devolution it was
clear that this had to be a measure of administrative devolution in the
first place. Any more ambitious scheme awoke all the fears of
separatism and cultural isolationism from which the political
instincts of those whose politics was based on anti-fascism and the
solidarity of the labour movement recoiled.[38] Whatever its longer
term impact, the Parliament for Wales campaign can, therefore, be
viewed as counter-productive in the short term, but it is also
important to emphasize that it did open up a debate within the
Labour Party and that its chief parliamentary advocate was a left-
wing miners' MP. His active supporters in Parliament were from
north-west Wales but it is clear that there was more general, although
minority, support within the labour movement, including a minority
voice within the South Wales Area of the National Union of Mineworkers. It might even be the case that this debate made it easier for
less ambitious demands to be justified.

Cledwyn Hughes and the other pro-devolutionists understood the dangers of backing S. O.'s bill but felt that they had little option in the circumstances.[39] It was not long before they switched to striving for more attainable ends. The existence within the Labour Party of a group of politicians dedicated to a strong devolutionary stance should not, however, be underestimated. These were the people who George Thomas was later to accuse of having 'nationalist aspirations', an accusation which at least one of those accused has subsequently been ready to concede had some basis.[40] One of the most active pro-devolution advocates within the Welsh Labour Party during the latter half of the twentieth century was Gwilym Prys Davies who graduated from membership of Plaid Cymru to the Welsh Republicans before he joined the Labour Party in Pontypridd.[41] He believed that only the Labour Party could deliver real benefits for Wales, although he also realized that this would take twenty or twenty-five years. He was later to be an adviser to John Morris at the Welsh Office and a Labour peer. Ironically this politician, whose commitment to a national strategy within the Labour Party was never in question, was also the Labour candidate defeated by Gwynfor Evans in Carmarthen in 1966.

If the presence of these elements within the Labour Party should not be overlooked nor should they be overestimated, and progress, when it came, was rarely on nationalistic grounds. Indeed, it was the narrow issue of the efficiency of governmental machinery in Wales, highlighted by the Council for Wales and Monmouthshire, which proved to be the most effective lever. Following the Conservative government's 1951 creation (without a government department) of a Minister of Welsh Affairs, the Labour Party went into the 1955 election with a policy of improving the status of the Minister. By the general election of 1959, however, the party had a more ambitious policy: the demand for a Secretary of State and a Welsh Office, lost in the 1940s, now became party policy.

Resolutions had been passed at the WRCL conference stating clearly the call for a Secretary of State or minister with a seat at Cabinet in 1954, 1957 and 1958.[42] That this became party policy was largely the result of the efforts of James Griffiths. He persisted with the demand for a Secretary of State and it was his influence on Gaitskell which was crucial in getting the manifesto pledge through the NEC, although Gaitskell also appeared to be impressed by the support of Welsh Labour MPs. As Lord Cledwyn recalled:

I remember very well a special meeting of the Parliamentary Labour Party to discuss this and Hugh Gaitskell and James Griffiths came to listen to the debate . . . and we had two meetings and in the end Gaitskell said 'well I think a very good case has been made'. And it was clear that Jim Griffiths was in favour and that he had, I would imagine, have had a long conversation with Gaitskell and had influenced him in favour. . . . When we were leaving the meeting Bevan was close to me and he said, 'You've got what you wanted, now you've got to make the best of it.' Jim Griffiths also emphasized the importance of Gaitskell's support.[43]

This was the culmination of a long debate and was to prove to be a decision of the utmost significance to Wales. The debate was not reopened following the defeat of Labour in 1959, although the Conservative government, under strong pressure from Ness Edwards and others, did establish the Welsh Grand Committee in the House of Commons in 1960 to scrutinize measures pertinent to Wales. The policy was confirmed in the booklet 'Signposts to the New Wales', to all intents and purposes Labour's 1964 Welsh manifesto, which also called for a review of the position of the Council for Wales and pledged a Welsh Planning Board.[44] In November 1964, following his election victory, Harold Wilson addressed the House on the new arrangements in Wales: 'the interests of Wales are now represented in the Cabinet by my right hon. Friend the Secretary of State. My right hon. Friend will have a Welsh Office in Cardiff . . . and a small Ministerial Office in London.'[45] In the following debate the range of opinions within the Welsh party became apparent as Ness Edwards declared his apprehension, raising the quite serious point that it would be unclear which minister was to be approached on various measures, the Welsh Office or the departmental minister in Whitehall? T. W. Jones had no such apprehensions and thanked the Prime Minister, in Welsh, 'On behalf of the people of Wales'. The measure of devolution so long campaigned for was at last achieved but the debate on further devolution was only just beginning.

The late 1960s was a tempestuous time in Wales as elsewhere and the 'national question' dominated much of the political agenda, especially following Gwynfor Evans's victory in the Carmarthen by-election in June 1966 and the success of the Scottish National Party. The rise of nationalism and, in particular, the strength of the Plaid Cymru challenge to Labour's heartland in Caerphilly and in

Rhondda West was totally unexpected and caught the Labour Party off-balance. The Labour Party was seriously concerned about the threat and J. Emrys Jones, secretary of the WRCL, wrote to the secretary of Newport Labour Party, Aubrey Hames, that the Caerphilly by-election was 'crucial to the fortunes of the Labour Party in Wales', continuing: 'following upon the results of the Carmarthen and the Rhondda By-elections the Welsh Nationalists naturally have to consolidate their position and to be able to claim that they are the party of the future in Wales.'[46]

For decades the national question had been debated within the Labour Party and what remained of the Liberal Party with the nationalists contributing from a very weak political base which, however eloquent, was largely irrelevant to policy implementation. Following 1966 all that changed and the national ground which David Thomas and others had sought to seize from the Liberals early in the century was now claimed by a nationalist party which was dismissive of the Welsh credentials of the Labour Party. The debate intensified and soured. Although a resolution to make the Council for Wales a 'democratically elected and a more effective organ of administration' at the 1964 WRCL conference was remitted to the Executive Committee, the 1965 conference called on the Secretary of State to look at the possibility of an elected council for Wales within the context of local government reorganization. In 1966 Conference passed a resolution in favour of an elected body and when Cledwyn Hughes became Secretary of State in that year he attempted, unsuccessfully, to create an elected assembly as part of a package to reform local government.[47] As if to confirm his defeat at Cabinet George Thomas, virulently opposed to nationalism and to further devolution, succeeded him as Secretary of State. In the circumstances of heightened tensions including direct action by language activists and a bombing campaign, and with growing support for the Scottish National Party in Scotland, the Wilson government established the Royal Commission on the Constitution and in its evidence to the commission the Labour Party declared their commitment to further devolution.[48] The unexpected victory of Labour in 1974 brought the Kilbrandon Report onto the political agenda and devolution was to dog the government until its downfall in 1979.

The Labour Party was now committed to devolution and in J. Emrys Jones they had a Welsh organizer who was himself an enthusiastic and effective supporter of the cause. There was growing support also in some trade unions and the establishment of the Wales Trades Union Congress in 1973 had been a significant development. However, the prolonged and convoluted process of the devolution measure through Parliament witnessed the energetic opposition of a group of Labour MPs including Neil Kinnock and Leo Abse. The referendum campaign which led to the 'St David's Day massacre' of 1979 was vicious and bitter. The 'No' campaign adopted a raft of objections but prominent amongst them was an adamantine opposition to nationalism and to nationalists, even those secret ones who were suspected of existing even within the Labour Party. Leo Abse MP, when speaking upon Wales's contribution on a British level, colourfully argued this case:

> Is the Welsh contribution to shrivel? Is the Welsh political genius to have no future expression except in a miserable parish pump Assembly at Cardiff? When high certitudes collapse, and faith becomes overclouded with doubt, the resulting alienation in society can lead, as we know from the example of Nazi Germany, to regressive choices being made; the choices of xenophobia and nineteenth century nationalism are being offered to us on March 1st but Wales, whose spirit refused to be cribbed and cabinned will surely reject such demanding options.[49]

But this too was an argument based upon Welshness. As *Facts to Beat Fantasies*, a publication which sought to answer 'the claims of the yesmen and guess men', and which carried the stamp of Neil Kinnock's thoughts, illustrated,

> We *are* a nation, proud of our nationality. But there is little or no desire for the costs, responsibilities of nationhood as the puny voting support for the Nationalists shows. We do not need an Assembly to prove our nationality or our pride. That is a matter of hearts and minds, not bricks, committees and bureaucrats.

To the claims of being 'anti-Welsh' they retorted,

> The truth is the opposite. It is fundamentally *because* we are Welsh, directly *because* we represent Welsh interests, and strictly *because* we wish to maximise the opportunities of economic, social and political

support for our country that we strive to defeat the Assembly proposals on March 1st.[50]

In the circumstances of the 1970s it was inevitable also that the Welsh language would emerge as a deeply divisive issue. It had rarely been a political issue before, although in 1946 Bevan had expressed his concerns eloquently, claiming 'There is too great a tendency to identify Welsh culture with Welsh speaking'. He sought to express what he saw as the 'unease' and 'disquiet' of the English-speaking majority at this 'psychosis'. A Secretary of State, he suspected, would have to be Welsh-speaking and so, in due course, would civil servants. 'Our nationalist friends are making an enclave', he declared, 'and the vast majority of Welshmen would be denied participation in the government of their own country.' The majority, including the people of Monmouthshire, would be 'tyrannised over by a few Welsh speaking people in Cardiganshire'.[51] In the heightened tensions of a referendum campaign these fears re-emerged and helped ensure the scuppering of the devolution measure by the people of Wales: 'Bitterness or resentment from a long dead history must be left to cranks . . . belief in a narrow, linguistically isolated semi-nation will divide the Welsh people and stifle the possibility of the expansion of the use of the Welsh language.'[52] The people of Wales were quick to rally to the 'No' camp and 1979 was not to see the flowering of nationhood. On a 58.8 per cent turnout, not a single county voted 'Yes' and Wales voted against the Wales Act by 956,330 to 243,048. That the Welsh electorate voted by four to one against the measure suggests that Neil Kinnock and his allies had a surer grasp of the mood of the voters than had the official Labour Party.

Kinnock and his allies did not explicitly oppose this measure on linguistic and cultural grounds; like Bevan in the 1940s and 1950s they also offered a rational left-wing, socialist opposition to devolution, which was to do with the nature of political power and its use. Aneurin Bevan had famously expressed this in 1944 when he appeared to dismiss the Welsh Question by confessing that he did not know the difference between 'a Welsh sheep, a Westmorland sheep and a Scottish sheep'.[53] In this contribution in 1944 Bevan was quite clear; in his view the economic salvation of Wales relied on the centralized planning of the economy and as power resided in London that required the seizure and the extension of power at the centre. This was not a matter of being pro- or anti-Welsh; rather it was a socialist analysis which he had enunciated for two decades. The attempt to control the capitalist monster through planning and nationalization was at the core of Bevan's politics and he could see no way of solving either the coal problem or the agricultural problem in Wales without reference to a strategy that would tackle the problems of these industries throughout the UK. Kinnock's position in 1979, and that of a number of other left-wingers, was based on similar reasoning. What differentiated Bevan from Griffiths and his allies was not primarily the question of Wales but the much wider issue of socialist strategy. And this was not a simple debate between left and right; the Communist Party had since its first All-Wales Congress in 1945 called for a range of 'Welsh national rights', including equal status for the Welsh language and a Welsh Parliament.[54]

The 1979 referendum was followed shortly afterwards by Margaret Thatcher's general election victory, a victory which was to remove Labour from office for a generation. In the face of the Thatcherite onslaught which caused massive unemployment in Wales and in reaction to the referendum defeat, devolution seemed a lost cause. By the mid-1980s, however, it reappeared but this time in a less emotional and more pragmatic fashion than in 1979. Devolution was now increasingly viewed as a possible barrier against Thatcherism and, moreover, as a potential Labour power-base. Ron Davies, MP for Caerphilly, who had opposed devolution in 1979, now argued that 'We voted Labour (in Wales), we got Thatcherism'.[55] Devolution, once again, seemed to make eminent political sense and became party policy; in the election manifesto in 1992 it was pledged 'Within the lifetime of a full parliament we will establish a directly elected Welsh Assembly'.[56] In addition, during the 1990s the debate, as in the 1950s, came to focus more and more on the machinery of government in Wales and, in particular, on its undemocratic character as quasi-autonomous governmental organizations (quangos), often manned by Tory placemen, increasingly assumed responsibility for governing much of Welsh life. These were the arguments which were continuously repeated by the 'Yes' campaign in 1997: the emphasis was on democracy and efficiency, not national identity. However, Ron Davies, the prime advocate of devolution in 1997 within the Labour government, manœuvred importantly to safeguard the support of nationalists. Although Ron Davies highlighted questions of democracy throughout the referendum campaign, in many ways he also came to symbolize the ever-present, practical, patriotic side to Labour in Wales, learning the Welsh language and emphasizing the distinctiveness of Wales not only culturally but also politically and socially. Indeed, at the British Labour Party Conference in 1994, Ron Davies stressed national distinctiveness as a very important part of the call for legislative devolution:

> Like the Scots we are a nation. We have our own country. We have our own language, our own history, traditions, ethics, values and pride . . . We now in Wales demand the right to decide through our own democratic institutions the procedures and the structures and the priorities of our own civic life.[57]

Analysis of the referendum vote suggests that in the end many people did vote, either way, out of a sense of wider national allegiance and identity.

Throughout the century, therefore, the Labour Party has been concerned with devolution and has attempted to construct the political debate around pragmatic political objectives in an attempt to remove the apparent divisiveness which the issue engendered. Finally, in 1997, this strategy succeeded. But the Labour concern with devolution was not simply based on a wish to see more efficient and democratic systems of government. There is no avoiding either the deep emotional charge of this issue, a patriotism and a concern for Welsh culture which is repeated in generation after generation. By no means everyone subscribed to such a view and there were many socialists, as we have seen, who rejected devolution on the grounds of political strategy. Bevan is an intriguing figure in this regard.[58] He rejected the case for devolution until 1959 but at the same time he argued that, 'There is a place for Welsh culture – I subscribe to it as warmly and as sincerely as my hon. Friends – there is a place for Welsh independence, there is a place for Welsh national self-consciousness and pride.' In an article in *Tribune*, reprinted in *Wales* in 1947, he even went further:

> In so far as Wales is different to England, it is the difference, and not the similarity, which requires special recognition and a special constitutional medium of expression. Wales is different . . . in that she

has a language of her own, and an art and a culture, and an educational system and an excitement for things of the mind and spirit, which are wholly different from England and English ways.[59]

Nor is such an approach absent from Neil Kinnock, the first Welsh leader of the Labour Party and a man who was electorally destroyed by a hostile press in part because of his Welshness. In a party-political broadcast in 1992, over pictures of male voice choirs and the valleys, he claimed that 'I've always felt Welsh . . . particularly in the sense of the kind of community from which I came that gave you a confidence and an identity and I think it's important to have roots.'[60] Even those who opposed devolution, therefore, expressed a certain kind of patriotism and to oppose nationalism was not necessarily to subscribe to a hostile attitude towards Wales. But it is, above all, in the rhetoric of Jim Griffiths that we can hear this patriotic element. Griffiths, who had served as president of the South Wales Miners' Federation until his election to Parliament in 1936, always insisted on the unity of Wales and refused to see Wales only as a south Wales industrial region. This belief was demonstrated when he argued for a Welsh Regional Council of Labour in 1942:

> It is my privilege, partly because I speak what is unquestionably the finest language in the world – to pay fairly frequent visits to North Wales. There is one thing this Movement must take note of in Wales, and it is that in these days, particularly among intelligent Welsh men and women, there is a growing consciousness of nationhood. I want the Labour Movement to become the voice of young Wales. If we are to do that it is essential that there should be much closer association between the Labour Movement of North Wales and South Wales.[61]

In government from 1945 he put the rhetoric to the test by arguing strongly for all-Wales structures during post-war reconstruction.

During the twentieth century, therefore, Labour and the national question have been inseparable. A movement as diverse as Labour and representing by the 1950s such diverse parts of the country could not be expected to be united on such an issue, as it did, inevitably, raise difficult issues of nationalism, language and culture. As a result the party operated most effectively on the issue when its programme was pragmatic and politically strategic, but that should not be allowed to disguise the very real commitment to Wales and the varieties of Welsh culture which drove the process on.

Notes

[1] Yes: 559,419; No: 552,698. *WM*, 20 Sept. 1997.

[2] 'Mab Gwalia', *Wales – the Next Step: Devolution, Secretary of State, Parliament for Wales and All That* (Cardiff, 1959), 6.

[3] *LL*, 12 Sept. 1912.

[4] D. Thomas, *Diolch am Gael Byw* (Liverpool, 1968), 40.

[5] *LL*, 4 Aug. 1911.

[6] R. Pope, *Building Jerusalem: Nonconformity, Labour and the Social Question in Wales, 1906–1939* (Cardiff, 1998), 24.

[7] D. Thomas, *Llafur a Senedd i Gymru* (Bangor, 1954).

[8] W. F. Phillips, *Y Ddraig Goch ynte'r Faner Goch? Ac Erthyglau Eraill* (Cardiff, 1913).

[9] *LL*, 2 Sept. 1910.

[10] C. Parry, *The Radical Tradition in Welsh Politics: A Study of Liberal and Labour Politics in Gwynedd, 1900–1920* (Hull, 1970), nn. 23, 26, 27.

[11] D. Hopkin, 'Y *Werin a'i Theyrnas*: ymateb sosialiaeth i genedlaetholdeb, 1880–1920', in G. H. Jenkins (ed.), *Cof Cenedl: Ysgrifau ar Hanes Cymru*, VI.

[12] J. G. Jones, 'E. T. John, devolution and democracy, 1917–24', *WHR*, XIV/3 (1989).

[13] *Welsh Outlook* (March 1918).

[14] *Welsh Outlook* (April 1918).

[15] J. Griffiths, *Pages from Memory* (London, 1969), 170.

[16] Sir H. Croft, *Hansard Parliamentary Debates*, 15 July 1936, 2095.

[17] NLW, Thomas Jones Papers, H21.

[18] D. R. Grenfell, *Hansard*, 15 July 1936, 2089, 2090.

[19] South Wales Regional Council of Labour, *Report of the Annual Conference 1942, 1943*.

[20] Griffiths, *Hansard*, 28 Oct. 1946, 297–407.

[21] SWRCL, *Report of the Annual Conference 1945*.

[22] *Hansard*, 28 Oct. 1946, 247–407; G. Daggar, at 371.

[23] Ibid., 370.

[24] Ibid., 311.

[25] Ibid., 314.

[26] Ibid., 303.

[27] Ibid., 380.

[28] *Wales* (Spring 1947), 141.

[29] *Swansea LP Annual Report for 1948*, Swansea LP MS, West Glamorgan RO.

[30] HMSO, The Council for Wales and Monmouthshire, *Third Memorandum* (1957).

[31] RMJ interview with Lord Callaghan, 25 Sept. 1998.

[32] Denbighshire RO, J. Idwal Jones Papers, DD/DD/698/2.

[33] RMJ interview with John Roberts Williams, 19 April 1996.

[34] *Hansard*, 28 Oct. 1946, 278–81.

[35] C. Prothero, *Recount* (Ormskirk, 1991), 68.

[36] R. Griffiths, *S. O. Davies: A Socialist Faith* (Llandysul, 1983), 161–94.

[37] RMJ interview with Dewi Watkin Powell, 24 Aug. 1995.

[38] J. G. Jones, 'The Parliament for Wales campaign 1950–1956', *WHR*, XVI/2 (1992).

[39] RMJ interview with Lord Cledwyn of Penrhos, 12 April 1995.

[40] G. Thomas, *Mr Speaker* (London, 1985). Those accused were Cledwyn Hughes, Elystan Morgan, John Morris and Tom Ellis.

[41] G. P. Davies, *Llafur y Blynyddoedd* (Denbigh, 1991).

[42] Welsh Regional Council of Labour, *Report of the Annual Conference 1957, 1958*.

[43] RMJ interview with Lord Cledwyn, 12 April 1995; J. Griffiths, *James Griffiths and his Times* (Ferndale, n.d.), 43.

[44] *Signposts to the New Wales* (Labour Party, 1963).

[45] *Hansard*, DCCII 17 Nov. 1964, 623–4.

[46] J. E. Jones to A. Hames, Newport Labour Party MS C9 (South Wales Coalfield Archive).

[47] WRCL, *Report of the Annual Conference 1964, 1965, 1966*.

[48] HMSO, Commission on the Constitution, *Written Evidence 5 Wales* (1972).

[49] L. Abse, speech at 'Highbury Club', 2 Feb. 1979. NLW, Leo Abse Papers, D/g/36.

[50] Labour No Assembly Campaign Wales, *Facts to Beat Fantasies* (Feb. 1979), 6 and 1.

[51] *Hansard*, 28 Oct. 1946, 401.

[52] Labour No Asssembly Campaign Wales, 10.

[53] *Hansard*, 17 Oct. 1944, 2312.

[54] *Communist Policy for the People of Wales: Report of the First All-Wales Congress of the Communist Party*, 1945.

[55] *WM*, 18 July 1988.

[56] Labour Party Wales, *It's Time to Get Wales Moving Again, Labour's Election Manifesto April 1992*.

[57] J. Osmond, *Welsh Europeans* (Bridgend, 1995), 79–80.

[58] D. Smith, 'The ashes onto the wind: Bevan and Wales', in G. Goodman (ed.), *The State of the Nation: The Political Legacy of Aneurin Bevan* (London, 1997).

[59] *Hansard* (1944), 2312. 'The claim of Wales: a statement', *Wales* (Spring 1947), 151–3.

[60] N. Kinnock, Party Political Broadcast, 1992.

[61] J. Griffiths, WRCL, *Report of the Annual Conference 1942*, NLW Film 688, Labour Party Wales Papers.

11

Facing the New Challenge: Labour and Politics, 1970–2000

DUNCAN TANNER

The conditions which helped mould the Labour Party in Wales during its infancy almost disappeared during the last three decades of the century. After a period of partial decline, the old staple industries experienced pronounced crisis. Mines and steel mills closed, leaving whole areas bereft of alternative employment. The occupational groups which once supported the Labour Party in vast numbers all but vanished. Rapid economic change was matched by challenges to old ideas and social structures, by the appearance of new injustices and inequalities, as well as new expectations. Labour needed to reassert the relevance of its values and policies whilst facing more serious political competition from a cultural and political nationalism on the one hand and (for part of the period) a populistic conservatism on the other. It faced a serious test of its dominant position in Welsh politics.

This chapter identifies the nature and significance of these challenges and charts elements of Labour's response. It does not and cannot offer a comprehensive analysis. If many phases in the Welsh Labour Party's history are underexplored, the period since 1970 is almost virgin terrain. Although the Labour Party and its members generally allow very open access even to quite recent material, few historians have exploited this vast and revealing resource.[1] There are no studies of Welsh Labour politics since 1945, no surveys of the party at the grass roots, no extensive oral history projects as there are for England.[2] Although there are excellent compendia of statistics and studies of recent elections, there is no historically based study of Welsh electoral change to rival those of

Scotland. Indeed, there has been little recognition of the extent to which Labour's fortunes waxed and waned after 1970. Accounts of recent events, based on non-archival sources or the participant's own experiences, are difficult to evaluate.[3]

Given the gaps in the literature and the difficulties of seeing the most recent events in context and through the primary sources, this chapter offers an interim interpretation, based on necessarily selective archival research and statistical analysis and focusing in the main on the period for which primary sources are available. It draws out some themes highlighted throughout this collection and discernible electoral and other trends, to analyse the fortunes of Labour in a period of substantial change. It has been argued in particular that for much of the century Welsh Labour politics contained (in both senses) a radical socialism and passionate varieties of nationalism, advocating practical policies in a manner which was frequently consistent with the values and desires of people in the differing parts of Wales. It is suggested here that during the 1970s this traditional Labour synthesis fell apart. Labour suffered so much because it was in office during a period of economic decline, because of a leftward drift (which for some of those involved developed into a carefully thought-out, radical, decentralized but ultimately unpopular socialism) and because reinvigorated opponents were credible rivals. Finally, the chapter evaluates the nature and extent of Labour's revival in the 1980s and 1990s, and its difficulties following the 1997 general election. It then details the challenge which the party faces if it is to maintain its dominant position within Welsh politics.

The economic transformation of Wales over the last century has presented Labour with a series of problems. In 1900 Wales lacked an economic infrastructure, a cohesive internal economy and any real means of exerting economic control – but at least much of the economy was buoyant. However, problems were looming. Most industrial activities were labour-intensive, manual and male dominated. By 1920 nearly 60 per cent of the male workforce was employed in mining, engineering, transport and building, with domestic service as the main employment for women. During the Depression of the 1930s these were all sectors where unemployment was high or wages low. Post-war recovery masked many underlying economic problems, but neither cured them nor hid the fact that Welsh voters had lower incomes and fewer opportunities than those in England. Levels of unemployment were higher than the United Kingdom average across the 1950s and 1960s, reaching 4 per cent in 1967. Although Labour spent more than 30 per cent more on public services in Wales than in England and took action to relocate industry and government offices in Wales, few new and highly paid forms of employment moved in to compensate for the decline in manufacturing and mining.[4] To match the economic position, social indicators – diet and health, for example – were worse and educational advancement less common. Labour developed into the party which sought to overcome the problems of the past, to offer Wales the opportunities evident elsewhere through the provision of state aid and the delivery of jobs and services.

This presented political problems in the 1970s. The economic weaknesses increasingly evident in the 1960s became transparently obvious after Labour returned to power in 1974. Unemployment reached 10 per cent by 1980, and peaked at 14 per cent in 1986. The traditional staples of the Welsh economy collapsed. In the steel industry, 50,000 jobs were lost between 1971 and the mid-1980s. Mining, one of the major industries at the turn of the century, fell into decline and then virtually disappeared after the 1984–5 miners' strike.[5] The decline in agriculture, caused by low prices and falling EEC subsidies, meant rural areas were hit hard. Cheap foreign holidays, changing lifestyles and a changing local population meant that Welsh tourist areas also faced severe difficulties.

The economic crisis hit many Labour voters directly. The closure of large steelworks such as Shotton and Ebbw Vale seriously threatened confidence in Labour, even when British Steel succeeded in bringing in new jobs.[6] The closure of pits in south Wales had an even greater impact. In addition to being an economic catastrophe, mining areas had become symbols of Labour's strength and values. Alongside this, other public-sector occupations – the occupations most likely to vote Labour – declined in number. Whilst across Britain as a whole Labour's social base was contracting, in Wales the change was probably especially pronounced.[7] The occupational base changed in other politically significant respects. New private-sector manufacturing initiatives – often high-technology enterprises – moved in during the 1970s and 1980s, transforming the economy of the south Wales coast and of Deeside. By the late 1990s, overseas-owned companies accounted for 30 per cent of manufacturing employment. This process provided more employment opportunities for women, especially part-time workers (by 1986, 46 per cent of women were employed part-time). The number of jobs in the service sector also increased. This was different work with a different culture. Although the economic consequences of these changes have received much expert attention, the political and psychological impact has yet to be properly studied.[8]

By the 1980s Labour could no longer focus its appeal on male manual workers employed in the public sector. Changing social structures and trends reinforced the challenge which economic change presented to the party's traditional approach. In the past Labour had encased its appeal in the language of religion and passed it through the prism of trade unionism. Neither chapel nor union exerted as much influence by the 1970s and both went into greater decline thereafter. Labour had also appealed to notions of family life in which women held the family unit together and were the core of every community. In Welsh-speaking areas it had presented itself as the party of the common people and their ways and values. Social statistics certainly indicate that key institutions and structures changed dramatically across the last thirty years of the century. For example, the nuclear family became less common, with divorce increasing and around 40 per cent of children born outside marriage. A way of life was challenged, both in the south and in the north (where in-migration, unemployment and rural depopulation combined to threaten both economic prosperity and existing social patterns). Labour's language, rhetoric, values and policies had not seemed inappropriate to the needs of many areas and groups of people in the 1950s and early 1960s. Now the party needed to change to match and interpret the changing realities of peoples' lives.[9]

None the less, Labour could not simply abandon its old ways. Many of its supporters, rooted in a world Labour had created and regularly dependent on it for their livelihood, wanted the party to resist change and preserve the benefits and gains of the post-war period. Thus Labour needed to inject new life into declining areas, whilst preserving their culture and values. At the same time, there were many – including plenty in the declining areas themselves – who wanted the benefits of an affluent and privatized society, much removed from the collective and communal world of many working-class communities, even though good public services remained popular across the United Kingdom. People purchased their own homes, sought advancement through the education system and valued a more individualized lifestyle.

Adapting to this new world was not necessarily a problem. Challenges had been faced in the past. Labour had not achieved its primacy through an automatic class attachment to the party. The habit of voting Labour had to be created in the 1920s and 1930s. In the 1950s and 1960s Labour renewed its appeal and adapted it to different communities, gaining new seats in rural and Welsh-speaking areas as a result, although it was not always as 'modern' and 'progressive' as its propaganda suggested. Its success was made easier by comparatively full employment, by Labour local authorities having the money to provide services and Labour governments promising to deliver jobs and other improvements. When circumstances altered, Labour faced greater difficulties. As the economic position declined from the 1960s onwards, so many of Labour's old prescriptions (such as Keynesian economics and nationalization) were either discredited or ruled out by the opposition of international investors.

The challenges outlined above were especially serious because the party faced two resurgent rivals. Plaid Cymru's connection with the linguistic and cultural renaissance in Wales during the 1960s is well known. The conservatism of some of its supporters rooted in that movement should not be understated. Initially at least Plaid was not a serious threat, both because of its outlook and because many on the left of Plaid Cymru wished to pressurize Labour into acting on Welsh nationalist issues, rather than rival it as a party.[10] In the 1950s there was some movement between the two organizations. Plaid recruited Labour activists who felt the party was no longer defending ordinary communities in the Welsh-speaking heartlands. Huw T. Edwards, the north Wales trade union organizer and Labour baron, left the party when it failed to oppose the flooding of the Tryweryn Valley in 1956. Plaid's inability to reconcile linguistic nationalism with radical policies led him to return shortly after. Such doubts were not uncommon. Others sympathized with nationalist views but remained with Labour. Gwilym Prys Davies, for example, a deeply patriotic Labour activist who in his youth had flirted with the Welsh republican movement, felt Plaid was 'too negative, that they weren't alive enough to the needs of the person travelling on the bus in Pontypridd'.[11] A dialogue between Labour and nationalists was possible because of the long and understudied support for Welsh national claims within the Labour Party. In the 1920s a number of Labour intellectuals tried to root the party in a Welsh/nationalist tradition and argued for Home Rule. Cross-party discourse between Labour advocates of greater national independence and others continued even after the formation of the nationalist party. The Mudiad Gwerin movement of the 1930s embraced intellectual nationalists and Labour supporters such as Goronwy Roberts. Nor did Labour's shift to the left in the 1950s and 1960s make a socialist/nationalist concord impossible, since new generations of socialists and nationalists shared a radical and socialist vision. The intellectual nationalist journals *Aneurin* in the early 1960s and *Radical Wales* in the 1980s sought to crystallize this affinity. The charismatic historian Gwyn Alf Williams produced a radical, democratic and decentralized socialism with both a nationalist and an internationalist flavour. It inspired a series of Labour and nationalist activists, set the tone for the journal *Radical Wales* and was part of a more generalized intellectual challenge to 'traditional' Labour ideas.[12]

Plaid Cymru became a more serious electoral rival to the Labour Party during the 1966–70 Wilson government. In 1966 Gwynfor Evans of Plaid Cymru defeated Labour's Gwilym Prys Davies in the Carmarthen by-election, largely because Labour policies on agriculture, regional development and education were successfully represented as a threat to the continued viability of small Welsh communities. In 1967 and 1968 Plaid nearly captured two Labour strongholds, Rhondda West and Caerphilly, with swings of 30 and nearly 40 per cent respectively.

Labour won all three of these seats at the 1970 election (despite Plaid Cymru's exceptionally strong performance across much of south Wales). Plaid's subsequent electoral successes in 1974 were in the more thoroughly Welsh-speaking areas of north Wales. None the less, this did not indicate a diminishing threat to the Labour Party; on the contrary, Labour seats in north Wales were increasingly vulnerable. In north-west Wales Plaid Cymru had already converted a portion of the professional classes, establishing itself in local government and in education, well before the 1974 elections. Sympathy for 'Y Blaid' was becoming a badge of 'Welshness'. The pressures to conform and embrace this association amongst the Welsh-speaking middle classes gradually became as powerful as the pressures to conform in Labour-dominated south Wales. With economic decline suggesting that Labour was no longer the party of economic modernization, Labour's position was doubly undermined, its support in the working-class areas progressively eroded. Caernarfon and Merioneth, both Labour-held seats since 1945 and 1951 respectively, fell to Plaid Cymru and gradually became secure political strongholds.

The threat to Labour was also maintained in the south. As economic circumstances worsened in the 1970s, nationalists attacked Labour for failing to invest in infrastructural development and for giving cash incentives to the private sector. *Radical Wales* was set up in 1983 in order to stimulate socialist ideas within Plaid Cymru itself, to encourage debate between nationalists and Labour and to win support for the nationalist cause 'in the industrial, mainly English-speaking parts of the country'.[13] Bread-and-butter issues were not ignored. The lassitude of Labour councils and MPs was attacked. There were successes in local government too, including the capture of Merthyr council in 1976 and later of Taff Ely, where Plaid stood for 'clean streets, rubbish collected regularly on the right night of the week, council houses that are in good repair . . . play-grounds . . . and an adequate supply of sports pitches'.[14]

In the 1970s Labour also faced competition from a resurgent Conservative Party. A substantial Tory vote in rural, middle-class and in some strongly working-class areas was augmented by affluent English voters retiring to parts of north Wales in particular. As Labour struggled to manage its internal divisions over devolution, Tories proclaimed themselves the party of the union. They offered ordinary voters a chance to buy their council houses and enjoy lower taxes. In 1983 they also stood for toughness and resolve, as exemplified by their defence of Britain's standing in the Falkland Islands. Even the Liberal Party presented a stronger challenge. It gained from the formation of the SDP, which – if never strong in Wales – still converted three Labour MPs and a number of Labour activists to its cause. In several north Wales seats the Alliance combined community politics with elements of Labour's moderate past, making it much more difficult for Labour to recapture lost ground.[15]

The impact of this growing competition and of growing voter dissatisfaction with the Labour Party, is presented in Tables 11.1 and 11.2. Table 11.1 shows that, in the early 1970s, Labour's traditional domination of local government in Wales was

Table 11.1. Political composition of district councils, Wales, 1973–1976 (%)

	Labour	Independent	Liberal	Conservative	Plaid Cymru	Others	% Councils Labour-controlled
1973	43.2	39.9	2.8	8.8	2.6	1.9	54.0
1976	29.3	38.9	2.6	14.2	8.0	7.2	29.7

Source: D. Balsom and M. Burch, A Political and Electoral Handbook for Wales (Farnborough, 1980), 66–7.

Table 11.2. General election results, Wales, 1966–1997

	Labour		Conservative		Liberal[a]		Plaid Cymru		Others		Seats
	seats	% vote	seats	% vote	seats	% vote	seats	% vote	seats	% vote	
1966	32	60.7	3	27.0	1	6.3	0	4.3	0	0.9	36
1970	27	51.6	7	27.7	1	6.8	0	11.5	1	2.4	36
1974 Feb.	24	46.8	8	25.9	2	16.0	2	10.7	0	0.6	36
1974 Oct.	23	49.5	8	23.9	2	15.5	3	10.8	0	0.2	36
1979	22	47.0	11	32.2	1	10.6	2	8.1	0	2.2	36
1983	20	37.5	14	31.0	2	23.2	2	7.8	0	0.4	38
1987	24	45.1	8	29.5	3	17.9	3	7.3	0	0.2	38
1992	27	49.5	6	28.6	1	12.4	4	8.8	0	0.7	38
1997	34	54.7	0	19.6	2	12.4	4	9.9	0	3.4[b]	40

Source: The Wales Yearbook 1999 (Cardiff, 1999); F. W. S. Craig, British Electoral Facts, 1832–1987 (London, 1989).
[a]Alliance 1983–7; Liberal Democrats 1992–7.
[b]Includes the Referendum Party (2.4%).

dramatically overturned. By 1973 Labour was the majority party on less than half the larger local authorities in Wales. In part this reflected its weakness in rural areas. However, the same cannot be said for the 1976 local government elections, after which Labour lost control of all but twelve of the thirty-seven councils. Fewer than a third of all wards returned Labour councillors. Cardiff and Newport fell to the Tories, Merthyr and the Rhymney Valley to Plaid Cymru.

Labour also saw its primacy challenged in parliamentary contests (Table 11.2). The 1974 general elections witnessed some recovery over the 1973 local council results, but Labour's vote remained below that obtained in 1970. More dramatic was the collapse in parliamentary representation, as enhanced support for Plaid Cymru and the Liberals turned solid Labour seats into marginals and in some cases led to Labour defeats. Nor was the slide easily reversed. Only some of the support lost at the 1976 local elections returned to Labour in the 1979 general election. The party nearly fell back to the position it held in the 1930s. However, the real débâcle came in 1983. Labour support fell below 40 per cent. The Tories – just 6 per cent behind – captured fourteen Welsh seats. Only the nature of the electoral system prevented an even more dramatic collapse in Labour's parliamentary representation.

From 1983 onwards Labour regained support, as Table 11.2 also indicates. The impact of Conservative policies in Wales, notably growing unemployment, helped create massive pro-Labour majorities in some seats.[16] Although Labour polled better in 1987 the party still amassed fewer votes than in 1974 and failed to regain sufficient support in the more affluent areas. In 1992 there were further improvements. However, Plaid Cymru also polled more effectively, mopping up Alliance support and hence making it more difficult for Labour to recapture seats from the nationalists. Plaid's own representation increased from two to four as its ability to rival Labour in Welsh-speaking Wales continued to grow.

Although a substantial revival took place across the 1980s and early 1990s it was not until the advent of New Labour that Labour captured several traditionally Tory seats. In the 1997 general election Labour polled 55 per cent of the vote. Tory representation was wiped out; the Liberals were squeezed. Of Labour's opponents, only Plaid Cymru polled well. Similarly, in the 1997 local government elections, Labour candidates were elected in 57 per cent of contests and the party gained control of all but five of the twenty-three county councils and county boroughs (Table 11.3).

None the less, New Labour had not developed a new message which was unquestioningly popular with the Welsh electorate. The challenges presented by social and economic change had not been fully addressed. The 1997 results were in part a consequence of Tory failure, not Labour success. In the 1999 local government elections (Table 11.4), Labour support plummeted. The number of Labour victories declined in relation to 1997 (from 57 to 45 per cent). The party fared little better than in 1973. The main

Table 11.3. *Political composition of county boroughs and county councils before the 1999 elections (numbers of councillors by party affiliation)*

	Labour	Indep.	Lib. Dem.	Cons.	Plaid Cymru	Total
Blaenau Gwent	33	6	1	1	1	42
Bridgend	40	3	2	2	1	48
Caerphilly	54	3	1	0	10	68
Cardiff	55	0	9	2	1	67
Carmarthenshire	40	32	1	0	8	81
Ceredigion	1	24	10	0	9	44
Conwy	18	10	17	10	5	60
Denbighshire	19	19	3	0	7	48
Flintshire	46	15	7	3	1	72
Gwynedd	10	22	4	0	47	83
Isle of Anglesey	5	29	0	0	6	40
Merthyr Tydfil	29	4	0	0	0	33
Monmouthshire	26	4	1	11	0	42
Neath Port Talbot	50	10	2	0	2	64
Newport	46	0	0	1	0	47
Pembrokeshire	12	40	4	0	4	60
Powys	8	61	10	3	1	83
Rhondda Cynon Taff	56	5	0	0	14	75
Swansea	56	10	7	2	0	75
Torfaen	41	1	1	1	0	44
Vale of Glamorgan	35	0	0	7	5	47
Wrexham	36	10	0	6	0	52
Totals	766	318	82	49	124	1139
Percentages	**57.2**	**23.7**	**6.1**	**3.6**	**9.2**	

Source: Balsom, *Wales Yearbook*.

beneficiary was Plaid Cymru, with 16 per cent of all councillors returned. The first National Assembly results suggested even greater problems for Labour. As Table 11.5 shows, Labour support fell below 40 per cent, with Plaid Cymru polling nearly 30 per cent. In Tory seats which Labour had captured in the 1997 general election, the party was pushed out. At the same time, a series of talismanic Labour seats fell to Plaid Cymru, including Islwyn and centres of historic Labour triumphs such as the Rhondda and Llanelli. Finally, the European election results (Table 11.6) confirmed Labour's misery, with Plaid Cymru coming within 2 per

Table 11.4. Political composition of county boroughs and county councils following the 1999 elections (numbers of councillors by party affiliation)

	Labour	Indep.[a]	Lib. Dem.	Cons.	Plaid Cymru	Total
Blaenau Gwent	34	7	1	0	0	42
Bridgend	41	5	5	1	2	54
Caerphilly	29	3	3	0	38	73
Cardiff	50	1	18	5	1	75
Carmarthenshire	28	31	1	0	14	74
Ceredigion	1	22	7	0	14	44
Conwy	20	13	14	5	7	59
Denbighshire	13	23	1	2	8	47
Flintshire	42	20	7	1	0	70
Gwynedd	12	21	6	0	44	83
Isle of Anglesey	4	26	0	1	9	40
Merthyr Tydfil	16	13	0	0	4	33
Monmouthshire	18	4	1	19	0	42
Neath Port Talbot	40	12	2	0	10	64
Newport	40	2	0	5	0	47
Pembrokeshire	13	39	3	3	2	60
Powys	7	58	6	1	0	72
Rhondda Cynon Taff	26	5	2	0	42	75
Swansea	47	9	10	4	2	72
Torfaen	39	3	1	1	0	44
Vale of Glamorgan	19	0	0	22	6	47
Wrexham	26	15	7	4	0	52
Totals	565	332	95	74	203	1269
Percentages	**44.52**	**26.17**	**7.49**	**5.83**	**16.0**	

Source: Western Mail, 8 May 1999.

[a]Includes Ratepayers, Independent Labour, etc.

cent of Labour. In many 'safe' Labour seats in the south Wales valleys, Plaid pushed Labour very close or defeated its candidates.

The true meaning of the election results was disputed by politicians. Labour did not accept it had paid the price for 'arrogance, sloth, incompetence and frequent corruption across huge swathes of Wales', nor that this was an epoch-making 'political earthquake', as Plaid Cymru claimed.[17] Whilst recognizing that there were problems to be addressed, Labour stressed the impact of mid-term protest, made effective through the low turnouts of just

Table 11.5. National Assembly election results, 1999

	Votes cast	% vote
Labour	384,671	38.47
Plaid Cymru	290,570	29.06
Conservatives	162,133	16.21
Liberal Democrats	137,657	13.77
Others	24,879	2.49

Source: Western Mail, 8 May 1999.

Table 11.6. European election results, 1999

	Votes cast	% vote	Seats
Labour	199,690	31.9	2
Plaid Cymru	185,235	29.6	2
Conservatives	142,631	22.8	1
Liberal Democrats	51,283	8.2	
Others	47,586	7.6	
Turnout		28.33	

Source: BBC News and Independent, 15 June 1999.

46 and 28 per cent in the Assembly and European elections and a similarly low figure in the local government elections. Protest voting and a series of other factors inflated support for Labour's opponents. The proportional system introduced for the National Assembly elections probably influenced the way some people voted (as well as the distribution of seats). Having elections which focused on the various parties' policies for Wales and for Europe, rather than on their suitability as a party of government for the United Kingdom, helped Plaid Cymru and the Tories respectively. Labour had faced similar difficulties in the 1970s and subsequently effected a recovery, as the preceding analysis has demonstrated. Indeed, the strength of the Labour Party – and the patchy challenge from its rivals – should not be understated. Plaid Cymru made little headway in some Labour areas, for reasons which have still to be explained. The Tories' recovery was strongest when Europe – and Europe alone – was the issue. Habit, tradition, the pattern of past events, the party's ability to restate its relevance and the

limitations of its rivals' appeal, all suggest that Labour is likely to remain a powerful force. None the less, the party's collapse was not simply a consequence of some recent and unresolved local difficulties, nor of the fiasco surrounding Alun Michael's selection as the party's leader in Wales. Labour cannot safely assume it will regain all its lost support. Across this period, Plaid Cymru gained support incrementally, seldom losing all its hold where once it made a breakthrough. The following section attempts to explain the erosion of Labour's primacy and the nature of the challenge which the party now faces if it is to rebuild its former domination.

By the late 1930s Labour had established a successful approach which it reinforced in the 1950s and 1960s. Provision of local services and support for Welsh industries, articulated in a language that local people understood as their own, helped make Labour voting an unconscious habit, especially but not uniquely amongst working-class electors. The changing composition of the population explains some of Labour's problems since the 1960s but not the depth of the party's decline in the 1970s and 1980s nor the scale of its recovery in the 1990s. Moreover, whilst many in Wales have probably developed a stronger national identity as a result of cultural and institutional developments since the 1960s, this too cannot explain the erosion of Labour's support. Plaid's success has been paralleled by limited popular enthusiasm for devolution, causing the party to drop separatism from its immediate programme. Rather, Labour's problems developed when the basis of its historic success in Wales was eroded in the 1970s, and when it failed to replace this with a new alternative in the 1990s. Political as much as social changes have to be explored.

When Plaid Cymru began to gain support in the 1960s Labour was shocked. Ted Rowlands, on the verge of becoming MP for Merthyr in the mid-1960s, records that Labour activists were 'rocked to the back of our heels by the nationalist challenge'.[18] The party's reaction was swift. Before the Caerphilly by-election in 1968 the Welsh Labour Party's chief organizer wrote to local party secretaries seeking their organizational assistance, noting that the election was 'crucial to the fortunes of the Labour party in Wales'. He continued, 'Following upon the results of the Carmarthen and Rhondda by-elections the Welsh Nationalists naturally have to consolidate their position to be able to claim that they are the Party of the future in Wales . . . We must contradict this'.[19] Rowlands argues that Labour was taught a lesson – not to take the electorate for granted. As a result the party looked to a new generation 'to carry the banner forward in a rather different manner' and a series of younger Labour candidates were adopted in 1970 and 1974. This is an important and perceptive point. Huge efforts were made by Labour Party officials and by individual Labour MPs in the 1960s and 1970s to revitalize the party. This was necessary to ensure electoral success but it was also the natural desire of an idealistic, committed and confident younger generation, anxious to mould the party in its own image.

The need to revitalize Labour politics in the constituencies had long been apparent. For organizational purposes, Labour divided Britain into geographical subsections. In the mid-1960s Wales had more MPs than any other organizational area but more than 60 per cent of its constituency associations affiliated on the minimum number of members (1,000) and less than a quarter had a full-time agent (one of the lowest figures in Britain). This pattern of organizational decline was not unnatural in areas where Labour was seemingly invincible, but it stripped the party of its ability to identify popular opinion and fight its rivals.[20]

The initial spur to greater activism was not the challenge of nationalism but the challenge of Conservatism. The Swansea Labour Party, for example, had been 'repeatedly pressed' to increase its membership in the late 1950s and early 1960s, but only reacted after the party lost the Swansea West constituency to the Tories in 1959. The new Labour candidate selected in the wake of this defeat, Alan Williams, seems to have promoted a more active approach, including propaganda campaigns, a membership drive, jazz concerts and participation in the National Executive Committee (NEC)'s attempt to address apathy, the 'Festival of Labour', held in 1962.[21] The Newport MP, Roy Hughes, held surgeries and visited the Labour clubs and halls which had in the past been a substantial political asset to the party. The Newport party also developed an extensive programme of political education, designed to teach leading activists about the party's municipal policy. This was accompanied by a leaflet campaign, with voters receiving letters addressing the concerns of their specific street. Again the spur was apathy and its assumed electoral consequences.[22] In the 1970s, a new influx of candidatess did much the same. After his selection at Bedwellty Neil Kinnock made a conscious effort to 'liven up the constituency' with speakers and rallies, later arguing that Labour's failure to maintain contact with the people, not the failure to devolve power, was the real crisis of Welsh democracy. For similar reasons, in 1984 Alun Michael set up a group in Cardiff 'to take action on publicity and to establish a single and effective method of enabling all local branches to publish *local* information'.[23]

Ted Rowlands's new generation of candidates were working-class grammar-school boys, often the first in their family to attend university and regularly employed as teachers, lecturers or workers in the public sector. They were more 'metropolitan' in outlook than their predecessors, a reflection of their generational interest in American and European culture and their time spent at university or in cities such as Cardiff and Liverpool. Abse and Rowlands, and later Kinnock, Flynn and Michael, all had Cardiff connections. Kinnock at least was involved in new political causes whilst at university, causes characterized by attempts to secure active participation: the anti-apartheid protests, the Vietnam War, the Campaign for Nuclear Disarmament (CND). Such enthusiasms could inject new life into Labour politics; but the new breed of Labour candidates was not necessarily concerned with issues which Labour voters found attractive. The causes championed by Leo Abse, notably his support for homosexual law reform, hardly inspired his constituents. Nor was the enthusiasm for CND displayed by a newer generation, like Paul Flynn and Neil Kinnock, wholly shared by the voters.[24] None the less, it would be inappropriate to argue that the influx of new candidates tore Labour away from its community roots. In many cases younger candidates combined support for 'new' political issues with strong attention to local social, economic and educational concerns. They seemed to represent a means of moving Labour forward, of keeping the party in touch with younger voters and a more liberal age without deserting the past.

Considerable attention was also paid to the nature of Labour policy in the 1960s and 1970s. Although much historical attention has focused on the strong opposition of some Labour MPs to devolution, archival evidence confirms Peter Stead's observation that Welsh Labour officials such as Emrys Jones played a major part in pushing devolution forward. They developed detailed research papers for the Royal Commission on the Constitution in

1969, including a case for extending a Welsh Assembly's remit, a proposed organizational structure and details of the financial and other powers which this body should possess.[25] Opponents of devolution were well aware of the position. George Thomas, Secretary of State, expressed his concern to the general secretary of the party: 'I am deeply concerned at the course that events are taking in Transport House Cardiff, for I feel that unless we are very careful we are heading for a major row amongst ourselves as to the evidence that is to be submitted to the Royal Commission.'[26]

The Welsh submission was eventually 'watered down' by the NEC, to the disquiet of the Welsh executive.[27] When a referendum on devolution was agreed, officials put all their weight behind the campaign. Emrys Jones, the party agent, warned the Welsh Labour executive that, whilst it was possible for leading figures to abstain on the devolution vote, 'any action apart from support for Party policy or abstention would be doing harm to the Party. Party policy is decided at Conference, and not separately by Constituency Labour Parties.'[28]

A number of Welsh Labour officials, and a group of young radical candidates and activists whose political careers they assisted, saw devolution as one component of a programme of democratization. They supported popular control of economic planning machinery, of the University of Wales, and of the police force and social-security arrangements. The Welsh executive produced a lengthy twenty-seven-point memorandum on the erosion of democracy, which included comments on the powers of the House of Lords, the civil service and the machinery of government. This programme united moderates (such as Tom Ellis MP and the party's Welsh research officer, Gwynoro Jones) and more radical elements, although only the latter were enthusiastic about the final element of the programme, the expansion of industrial democracy.[29] For socialists who were 'devolutionists', the creation of a devolved assembly meant supporting public accountability and control and was a means of empowering and radicalizing the people. The chairman of the Welsh Labour Party, Emlyn Hughes, claimed the devolution proposal was

> based on far more study and understanding than any other political party has ever brought to bear on the problem of democracy in an industrial society. If our official policy had carried the day on 1st March

it is not too far-fetched to believe that it would have brought a permanent shift of political balance in Wales that would be favourable to the growth of socialism.[30]

Similarly, the Welsh Labour executive passed a bitter and prophetic resolution following the referendum vote against devolution:

> We are deeply disappointed at the result of the Referendum . . . [which] solves none of the problems of Wales or of Britain. The problems which the Assembly was designed to deal with, will still remain . . . The lack of public accountability in the regions in Britain and the democratic control of the great public sector set up by Governments of all parties will become more and more important as an issue. The Tories have their answer to it – smash the machinery, destroy the public services, and hand everything back to private enterprise. Unless Labour carries out radical and effective proposals to create real democratic control of our public services and industries, the Tory party will destroy all we have built up over generations.[31]

Nor was devolution the only policy area where a section of the party made efforts to address specifically Welsh issues. Labour's growing support for Welsh-language education in the 1970s similarly reflected a desire to devolve control of important issues to local communities. A discussion document, *The Place of the Welsh Language in Education*, supported 'urgent action' to stem the decline in the Welsh language, by ensuring that every child in Wales had the opportunity to learn Welsh or have their education conducted in Welsh. At the same time, Labour argued that the language could 'be saved only if the people wish it' and not by compulsion, adding that language should not become 'a divisive issue among the people of Wales'. Labour became committed to producing a Welsh education system extending from pre-school to university. The party increased support to the pre-school Ysgol Meithrin movement from almost nothing in 1973–4 to £60,000 in 1978–9. By 1979 it was proposing further to increase resources for all levels of Welsh-language education, including the training of Welsh-speaking teachers. It also pushed for the Home Office to 'introduce the fourth channel in Wales at the very earliest opportunity'.[32]

If such issues were enthusiastically supported by some party officials and party members, especially in north Wales, there was considerable disquiet in other sections of the party. Young and committed MPs like Neil Kinnock expressed a preference for 'modernization' and for centralized economic planning, highlighting the romantic illusions behind a linguistic nationalism which catered for a small percentage of the Welsh people and ignored the needs of the English-speaking majority. Such people fought devolution through conviction; not because they were anti-Welsh, but because they had a different vision of the country. Passions were high on both sides and soured Welsh politics for many years. If Kinnock suffered from this in some circles, a number of left-wing devolutionists shared his distaste for the xenophobic aspects of nationalism and his commitment to radical policies. Their *bête noire* was George Thomas, a robust anti-devolutionist whose enthusiasm for the investiture of the Prince of Wales symbolized the conservatism of the Labour establishment.[33]

Industrial and employment issues also caused considerable internal disquiet within Welsh Labour politics. The 1966–70 Wilson government's decision to cut public expenditure rather than devalue the pound exacerbated tensions within an already divided and highly competitive Cabinet. Expenditure was seen even by many on the 'right' as a means to address social disadvantage. Welsh rank-and-file disquiet was publicly echoed by several Welsh Labour MPs. None the less, by 1970 Labour could stress an economic record within Wales which included £60 million spent on grants to aid developments in the Valleys, use of industrial development certificates to attract new private industries (such as Firestone tyres at Wrexham and Ford at Swansea) and direct relocation of state organizations to Wales (the Royal Mint at Llantrisant, the Census Office in Newport, the Driver Vehicle and Licensing Centre in Swansea, the RAF to St Athan).

Labour's victories in the 1974 general elections gave it an opportunity to implement its ideas for Wales. Its new strategy recognized the limitations of regional policy in the past. Labour established a series of bodies to promote new economic development, notably the Welsh Development Agency, the Development Board for Rural Wales, and the Land Authority for Wales. The Welsh Trades Union Congress (TUC) contributed a plan for using development area status as a means of helping Deeside; constructive suggestions were made by constituency parties following an extensive consultation exercise in 1976–7 and 1979–80, notably in relation to the need for skills training.[34] There was a realization that the Welsh economy was overcommitted to industries which were in decline.

None the less, economic crisis brought on by international problems and a continuing balance of payments deficit threatened the viability of Labour's plans for Wales. In 1976 the Labour government made huge cuts in public expenditure. Alan Williams reported to Welsh constituency parties that 'the options for the Government were limited . . . The main areas of hope were the hope for growth in world trade and the prospect of revenue from North Sea Oil.'[35] Again, these public expenditure cuts caused considerable internal disquiet, with voluble activists attacking the government and the Welsh Parliamentary Party as 'right-wing'. The proudly egalitarian and non-deferential traditions of south Wales Labour politics hardly encouraged quiet and uncritical understanding of the party's dilemmas.

This is not to suggest that activists were critical without good cause. Even if it was now obliged to make cuts, the government had failed to anticipate problems. It had focused too much on the public sector and on the importance of attracting manufacturing jobs. However, the views advanced by Welsh critics of the government at the time were equally problematic. There was considerable resistance to inward investment by multinational companies and to the development of the tourist industry (almost instinctively seen as an inferior development, involving the exchange of 'real', masculine, manufacturing jobs and well-paid work for 'servile', non-productive and low-paid employment). Labour's policy now seems like a well-intentioned resistance to trends which were irresistible but, as in the 1930s and 1960s, it was not a policy based on a refusal to accept economic realities. Michael Foot's view merits serious consideration:

> If it hadn't been for the disruption of that government in 1979, in my opinion, we could have carried through in Ebbw Vale and in the whole of Blaenau Gwent area a proper changeover from the old industries to new industries. So it isn't just a case of people saying these Labour people . . . they don't understand how you've got to do away with the old methods and bring in the new . . . but the most important thing that we were trying to insist upon was that the pace of changeover must be one which the communities could take.[36]

In the face of mounting economic problems this was not an easy policy to put across. Both the affluent and those adversely affected by change felt aggrieved. Welsh Labour officials tried to address the problem, to ensure Labour's increasingly disgruntled supporters understood the party's actions. Efforts were made to involve more trade union officials, both as advocates for the party and in election campaigns.[37]

Campaigning techniques were also reviewed, although advocates of change faced several obstacles, notably limited funds and London's distrust of Welsh initiatives. When Gwynoro Jones tried to obtain details of research into the attitudes of young people conducted for the Labour Party by Mark Abrams, he was allowed only a verbal briefing by NEC officials. When Ted Rowlands wanted to produce material aimed at the young and at countering nationalism, the request was rejected.[38] None the less, with no Labour press in Wales to speak of and with the newspapers in both north and south largely hostile, Labour had a real communications problem. Good relations with the BBC in Bangor and party-political broadcasts focusing on Welsh issues were no substitute.[39] Labour was failing to mount an effective resistance.

This problem was increasingly significant because organizational problems evident in the 1960s became even more pronounced in the 1970s and 1980s. In several coalfield seats, where a few trade unions had always played a substantial role in party organization, atrophy had set in. When Jeffrey Thomas tried to fight off an attempt to deselect him in Abertillery he found that many of the trade unions 'which one could normally count on for support are not affiliated'.[40] Nor was the position in Labour's target seats any better. In north-west Wales Labour 'organization' rested on pockets of strength and a few key and ageing individuals in the scattered towns, combined with the candidates' own considerable efforts. Nor was Labour securely rooted in local government in these areas, as it was in the south. There was scarcely any organization in Caernarfon during the February 1974 election. Despite an unusual surge of enthusiasm thereafter, Hubert Morgan reported in 1978 that the 'organization' created during the October 1974 campaign had again collapsed, noting 'the complete lack of personnel to drive [the party] forward'. In north Wales Labour was seen, by its own admission, 'as an urban party, a South Wales Party, a Party out of tune with the needs of rural areas . . . In

Gwynedd, too, there appears to be a polarization developing – If you're Welsh you're Nationalist, and if you're English you're Conservative, and Labour is squeezed in the middle.'[41]

The failure of devolution, supported in north Wales by many on the 'right' as well as the 'left' of the party, hardly helped Labour's case, especially when coupled with the party's apparent inability to deliver the economic benefits it had always promised in the past. Nor did the position improve after 1979. Twin defeats – of the party in the 1979 election and of devolution in the referendum – resulted in a huge and devastating crisis, the nature of which is only now being recognized. The devolution débâcle traumatized many intellectuals on the left. Socialist and nationalist intellectuals sought explanations for their defeat through discussion and analysis of Welsh identity and Welsh culture, assuming that something had gone wrong, that Wales had somehow 'failed'. John Osmond, an analyst of devolution and democracy and a campaigner for changes within Wales, founded the journal *Arcade* to stimulate debate on these issues. John Davies, Gwyn Alf Williams and others carried the debate forward. Welsh intellectuals pioneered discussions of the way myth, symbol, memory, assumed identity, institutions, language and other factors could create an 'imagined' sense of nationhood. On the socialist left historians such as Hywel Francis and Dai Smith warned that a mythical past was being manufactured by nationalists anxious to construct a sense of nationhood. Gwyn Alf Williams, seeking both to explain the failure of devolution and to unite socialism and nationalism, argued that many nationalists regarded the English-speaking Welsh as inferior, identifying the Welsh-speaking establishment as a particular problem. New and cross-party campaigns for devolution eventually grew out of this debate, little of which took place at Labour's official instigation. Indeed, in the years following devolution Labour lost its hold on Welsh intellectual life, as many intellectuals withdrew from participation in party activity.

In the aftermath of the 1979 defeat, Labour also became embroiled in factional disputes over the future direction of the party. The product of this cathartic period – the 1983 election manifesto – was famously labelled 'the longest suicide note in history' by Gerald Kaufman. Labour's shift to the left was not just unpopular in England. Although Thatcher's government introduced major cuts in regional aid grants and followed policies which increased unemployment in Wales, only a few Welsh seats produced a pro-Labour swing in 1983. Election studies show that, even in industrial south Wales, likely Labour voters were deeply unhappy with Labour policy. Three-quarters of the voters from this area in 1983 thought their personal circumstances had deteriorated under the Tories but only around a quarter of these voters thought Labour's policies were more likely to improve the situation. Less than 20 per cent thought that Michael Foot was the best of the party leaders. Whilst some of this may have reflected the rather non-Thatcherite policies pursued in Wales between 1979 and 1983, Labour was still in a deep trough.[42]

Supporters of the Trotskyite *Militant* newspaper were particularly active and vocal in this period. Although Militant was not strong in Wales, it had a number of full-time Welsh officials, claimed complete control of the Welsh Labour students' organization and possessed considerable support in parts of Cardiff and Swansea.[43] Several leading Labour figures (including Kinnock, Abse and Callaghan) faced pressure from Militant supporters in their constituencies. Callaghan in particular suffered 'poisonous' meetings in Cardiff South East, where Jack Brooks, his long-standing agent, battled through 'almost a decade of infighting'. Militant and its allies tried to get certain MPs deselected, only succeeding with Jeffrey Thomas in Abertillery (he subsequently joined the Social Democratic Party (SDP)).[44]

The internal battle for organizational control occupied considerable time, but party members were also anxious to advance the positive and radical socialist policies embedded within the Bennite agenda. Various constituencies supported increased public expenditure and especially state control of finance via the nationalization of banks, building societies and insurance companies. Through this industrial investment could be controlled and legislation passed to prevent inward investors operating against the long-term interests of the community. Many rank-and-file activists supported the abolition of private medicine and opposed the sale of council houses. These were not policies which attracted support from voters in 1983 but they were part of a practical programme, not a vacuous 'leftism'.[45] Militant were the parasitic fringe, not the core of a Welsh constituency left, some of which wished to focus on 'constructive' policies.

Beneath the acrimony, division and conflicts, many struggled to create a popular and practical alternative to Thatcherism. MPs like

Michael Foot fought hard to attract new industry. He and other
Labour MPs worked with Labour-dominated groups such as the
Heads of the Valleys Standing Conference, or through Labour
local authorities, to try and obtain EEC funds.[46] Welsh Labour
officials were similarly constructive. To heal wounds and involve
the constituencies, they had circulated branches with a draft of the
party's proposed policy commitments in 1980. Branches immediately called *en masse* for a new referendum on EEC membership
(which was outside the remit and rejected by London). They also
pushed for costed and practical policies and for a specific commitment to relocate industry in Wales and develop real industrial
democracy. The Mid Glamorgan party noted that the draft
manifesto contained too much dogma, 'without there being a consistent approach to how such ideas can be given a practical application'. Cardiganshire too argued that the manifesto was 'deficient in
firm proposals for Welsh affairs'. This was hardly the style of the
London left. Individual branches called on the party to construct
policies which recognized the reality of social changes. One Cardiff
branch noted that the elderly, 'this large and increasing section of
the population', went unmentioned in the manifesto. Some
suggested more attention be paid to the disabled and housebound,
especially in the 'dead ends which are becoming more dead as
industry departs', and to community-based medical care. From
north and mid Wales there was support for greater attention to
Welsh-language education and to the problem of second homes. A
few responses pushed the need to develop tourism; others stressed
encouragement of indigenous small businesses.[47]

Following the 1979 defeat a number of Welsh MPs began to feel
that the party had to change direction. The Ebbw Vale MP and
party leader, Michael Foot, realized that retaining unpopular but
radical policies left the electorate at the mercy of Thatcherism.
Neil Kinnock too shifted his views, courting hostility with his
constituency party by not supporting Benn in the 1981 deputy
leadership election. Most Welsh Labour MPs voted for Denis
Healey, prompting deselection battles in several constituencies.[48]
Jim Callaghan, an increasingly isolated figure, had long argued
that the Labour left was peddling fantasies. Backbench MPs with
their feet firmly on the ground were also well aware of what
disunity was doing. As Ted Rowlands commented in a constituency
report, by 1983 Labour had become 'a shambles, divided,

introspective, out of touch with the feelings even of some of our most loyal supporters'.[49]

There is much still to be learnt about the causes of Labour's collapse in the 1970s and about the internal political developments which helped structure the party's political actions in the 1980s and 1990s. Until the archives are opened full analysis is impossible; none the less some broad themes stand out. It is clear that Labour's traditionally successful approach in Wales was falling apart. The party could no longer deliver jobs and services. It had failed to contain nationalism within its own ranks. Subsequent Tory policy, leading to the miners' strike of 1984–5, provided Labour with an electoral opportunity. However, like Labour local authorities whose wings were clipped by legislation and spending cuts, the parliamentary party was powerless to mount effective resistance to this or other Tory assaults on Labour communities and Labour values. Expecting power rather than seemingly permanent opposition, and committed to some ideals which seemed increasingly unpopular with voters and with their own party, several MPs seemed to lose enthusiasm for the patient reconstruction of policy and organization. Deep rifts were created in a parliamentary party which contained many strong views and individualistic temperaments.

These were also tragic years for Neil Kinnock. Elected to the leadership of the party as Labour's superman in 1983, he faced a barrage of opposition from the left within a year of taking office. His views on the miners' leader Arthur Scargill, his attacks on picketline violence during the miners' strike and his attempt to drop unpopular aspects of party policy all attracted opposition. He was attacked by Plaid Cymru for opposing devolution but castigated in the popular press for his 'Welshness'.[50] If Kinnock's contribution to rebuilding the British Labour Party is increasingly recognized, his indirect contribution to rebuilding the party in Wales has scarcely even been noted.[51] Tory policy was so destructive after 1983 that some reaction was likely. However, it was Kinnock's approach – rational, practical, strongly Welsh in tone and sentiment – which helped ensure that the Liberals and Plaid Cymru were not the major beneficiaries. Moreover, under Kinnock a new and more sympathetic approach to devolution developed. If Kinnock himself was not initially particularly keen to reopen old wounds by pushing hard for devolution, Ron Davies and other equally practical MPs and activists became converts to the merits of a devolved assembly. Given that more MPs had been elected who were at home with the Welsh language and with devolution, including Alun Michael, Jon Owen Jones and Paul Flynn, a shift in policy became more likely. The enthusiasm of first John Smith and subsequently Tony Blair for constitutional reform turned a changing climate into a concrete commitment, backed by the full weight of central office, although the process of creating a national assembly was hardly straightforward and many retained reservations about the new approach to power-sharing, national-ism and nationalists.[52]

In 1997 Labour won a decisive election victory in Wales, followed by the narrowest of majorities for devolution in the care-fully constructed referendum campaign which followed. Internal dissent, which hindered the Labour devolution campaign in 1979, was crushed. However, Labour had not reinvented itself as a new party with a new agenda. It benefited from the impact of Tory policies on Welsh households and the popularity and profession-alism of its approach at the British level. New Labour had not yet devised a practical set of policies for economic and social regenera-tion in Wales, a means of revitalizing the Welsh Labour Party, nor a means of recapturing the intellectual agenda.

This is not to say that New Labour made no changes. For whatever reason, it committed itself to devolution and worked closely with Plaid Cymru within the new National Assembly. It was far more open to women, who in some areas formed a substantial part of Labour council groups by 1997. The policy of 'twinning' ensured that half of all National Assembly candidates were women. Some such candidates evidently supported a different, more inclusive, form of politics.[53] New Labour was addressing two problems evident in previous years – failures to deliver devolution and to adopt a less masculine focus.

Perhaps the devolution debate – unresolved business for many since 1979 – dominated discussion for too long, to the exclusion of other pressing issues. As Labour's campaign manager Peter Hain recognized after the National Assembly elections, New Labour had much work still to do at constituency level. As the elections took place, a number of Labour (and other) councillors had been embroiled in well-publicized corruption cases. Deselection battles, with former Labour councillors standing as Independents, were a further problem. Some local councils, dominated by the party for many years, had failed to take account of public opinion and focus on value-for-money services. Several 'surprise' Labour defeats were attributed to the actions of such Labour councils. Some local parties also lacked the capacity to reach, enthuse and mobilize their supporters, a significant fact as Labour had to contend with a hostile press and with swathes of voters in border areas who do not even receive Welsh television.[54] Local commitment, local leadership and local ideas had declined, to be replaced by strategic leadership from London. Although Wales had developed its own vibrant debate on Welsh identity and policy and its own critique of past regional policies, the party outside Wales seemed not to have noticed. The Fabian Society finally asked in March 1999 how it should address the new constitutional structures so far as Wales was concerned (having previously focused almost exclusively on Scotland). Its first response was to hold a conference in Oxford on the 'English Question'. A recurrent theme within Welsh Labour politics – London's problems with a distinct Welsh line and the absence of a Labour policy forum in Wales – again became apparent.[55]

There was a further problem. As Glenys Kinnock perceptively noted immediately after the National Assembly elections, and as the TUC argued in its own post-election analysis, New Labour had structured its policies and its image in order to recapture middle England.[56] If this helped the party in Wales capture several traditionally Tory seats in 1997, by 1999 many traditional Labour voters in Wales may have felt alienated by both the style and content of Labour politics (which was certainly not the case when Neil Kinnock was leader). London's support for Alun Michael rather than the locally popular Rhodri Morgan as the party's Welsh leader exemplified the problem, whilst its use of trade union block votes to get him elected blurred its 'modernizing' image. The constituencies in south Wales which Labour lost were some of the most decidedly 'Welsh' seats in the country (that is, they largely contained people born in Wales). To maintain its success of 1997 New Labour had simultaneously to satisfy these traditionally Labour and very Welsh voters, while also retaining the support of more affluent Tory converts, largely in the border areas and in Cardiff. As New Labour seemingly abandoned the party's traditional emphasis on public expenditure and attracting new industry, it needed to develop support and enthusiasm for a more market-based 'third way' to replace it. The main steps taken by 1999 – notably skills development and the welfare to work programme – were long-term measures valued by experts but not by the electorate. Although the new constitutional framework promised to facilitate more strategic thinking and a more distinctly Welsh approach, allowing Labour to utilize the considerable amount of research being undertaken into the policy issues facing Wales, in 1999 the party fell between two stools, sure neither of its traditional supporters nor its new sympathizers. It offered neither a revitalized 'Old Labour' approach nor a clear and articulate 'New Labour' philosophy that was known to and supported by the party and the electorate.

The challenge which Labour faces at the end of the century is radically different from that which it faced a century ago.[57] A party rooted in the working class, in trade unions and in mining communities, now heads a government with a huge majority, dependent on support from very different voters. Labour governments did a great deal for Wales between the beginning and the end of the twentieth century, both through the creation and funding of a substantial public sector and through direct intervention and support of industry and services. They were responsible for changes in education and in the constitutional structure. Labour councils have regularly delivered high-quality administration of these services, tailored to local needs. In all these areas there have been successes and failures, good ideas badly implemented, bad ideas administered with care. A new type of Welsh electorate now has to be convinced that New Labour can serve the peoples' interests and represent their hopes and values, as Labour did in the past. At the end of the century Labour can feel pride, but no complacency. Victories made in the past will need to be remade in the future.

Notes

[1] D. M. Tanner and A. Walling, *The Labour Party in Wales: An Electronic Guide to Archival Resources* (Bangor, 2000).

[2] E. Shaw, *The Labour Party since 1945* (London, 1993); P. Seyd, *Labour's Grass Roots: The Politics of Party Membership* (Oxford, 1992); D. Weinbren, *Generating Socialism: Recollections of Life in the Labour Party* (Stroud, 1997).

[3] D. Balsom and M. Burch, *A Political and Electoral Handbook for Wales* (Farnborough, 1980); D. Balsom (ed.), *The Wales Yearbook 1999* (Cardiff, 1999); B. Jones, *Etholiadau'r Ganrif: Welsh Elections 1885–1997* (Talybont, 1999); P. Stead, 'The Labour party and the claims of Wales', in J. Osmond (ed.), *The National Question Again: Welsh Political Identity in the 1980s* (Llandysul, 1985); and L. Andrews, *Wales says Yes: The Inside Story of the Yes for Wales Referendum Campaign* (Bridgend, 1999).

[4] A. H. Birch, *Political Integration and Disintegration in the British Isles* (London, 1977), 43–4.

[5] Welsh Office, *Welsh Economic Trends* (Cardiff, 1974–94), I–XV.

[6] S. Venn, 'The management of change in the British Steel Corporation 1967–1989: an analysis of the management perspective', Univ. of Wales M.Phil. thesis, 1999, 381–6.

[7] A. Heath, R. Jowell and J. Curtice, *How Britain Votes* (London, 1985), 17–39; and A. Heath, R. Jowell and J. Curtice with B. Taylor, *Labour's Last Chance? The 1992 Election and Beyond* (Aldershot, 1994), 281–8.

[8] S. Brand, J. Bryan, S. Hill, M. Munday, A. Roberts, 'An economic strategy for Wales', *WER* X (1997/8), 21.

[9] Welsh Office, *Welsh Inter-Censal Survey 1986* (Cardiff, 1987); and Welsh Office, *Digest of Welsh Local Area Statistics* (Cardiff, 1997–9).

[10] A. Edwards, 'Labour and the challenge of nationalism: political argument and political strategies in Welsh-speaking Wales', University of Wales (Bangor) MA thesis, 1998.

[11] Interview with Gwilym Prys Davies (all interviews courtesy of R. Merfyn Jones, Cymru 2000 project).

[12] Edwards, 'Challenge of nationalism', ch. 3.

[13] *RW*, I (Winter 1983).

[14] *RW*, XXX (Summer 1991).

[15] For views on politics in north-west Wales during this period I am grateful for conversations with Edmund Halliday, Deian Hopkin, Cyril Parry and Emlyn Sherrington.

[16] D. Butler and D. Kavanagh, *The British General Election of 1983* (London, 1984), 341.

[17] *WM*, 8 May 1999.

[18] Interview with Ted Rowlands.

[19] J. Emrys Jones to Constituency Labour Parties (CLPs), 13 June 1968, Newport Labour Party (NLP) MS C9 (South Wales Coalfield Archive).

[20] S. Fielding, 'The "Penny Farthing" machine revisited: Labour Party members and participation in the 1950s and 1960s', in C. Pierson and S. Tormey (eds.), *Politics at the Edge* (London, 2000).

[21] Swansea Labour Association, *Annual Report* (1963) (West Glamorgan RO).

[22] A. Hames to R. Hughes, 19, 25 Jan. 1968 NLP MS C7, circulars and papers from J. Newham, Jan., Feb. 1968, NLP MS C9 and C10.

[23] R. Harris, *The Making of Neil Kinnock* (London, 1984), 55, 100; Alun Michael circular, 17 April 1984, Labour Party Wales (LPW) MS 80 (NLW).

[24] Interviews with Leo Abse, Paul Flynn, Ted Rowlands; P. Flynn, *Baglu 'Mlaen* (Caernarfon, 1998), 70–3 (I am grateful to Andrew Edwards for this reference).

[25] Stead, 'Claims', 155–6. The Welsh study groups sent 22 pages of detailed proposals to the Labour Party in Oct. 1969 (Labour Party archives, Museum of Labour History, Manchester, National Agent's Department (LPNAD) box file on Wales).

[26] G. Thomas to H. Nicholas, 19 June 1969, LPNAD.

[27] J. Emrys Jones, report to National Agent, 22 Dec. 1969, LPNAD.

[28] LPW Executive Committee (EC) mins, 16 Oct. 1978.

[29] LPW EC memo., 13 Oct. 1978.

[30] Address at Llandudno, 18 May 1979, LPNAD.

[31] LPW EC mins, 5 Mar. 1979.

[32] LPW discussion document by J. Emrys Jones, 'The place of the Welsh Language in education', 27 Feb. 1978, LPNAD; LPW EC mins, 6 May 1974.

[33] G. Thomas, *Mr Speaker: The Memoirs of the Viscount Tonypandy* (London, 1985), 96, 118–19; Flynn, *Baglu 'Mlaen*, 41. I am grateful to Emlyn Sherrington, Labour candidate for Caernarfon in October 1974, for his comments on this section of the chapter.

[34] Dennis Gregory, 'The Deeside economy: results and prospects', June 1976, LPW MS 136.

[35] Consultation meeting at Llandrindod Wells, 27 Nov. 1976, LPW MS 136.

[36] Interview with Michael Foot.

[37] Organizer's reports, 31 Aug. and 3 Sept. 1974, LPNAD.

[38] G. Jones to P. Clark, 27 Aug. 1969, J. Gwyn Morgan to G. Thomas, 14 Aug. 1969, LPNAD.

[39] Hubert Morgan, organizer's memo, 17 Jan. 1974, LPNAD.

[40] J. Thomas to F. Taylor, 1 June 1981, Jeffrey Thomas MS file 6, NLW.

[41] Organizer's report, 17 Nov. 1978, speech at Llandudno, 18 May 1979, LPNAD. For Caernarfon, author's conversations with Cyril Parry and Emlyn Sherrington and interview with Eleri Carrog.

[42] R. Johnston, *A Nation Dividing? The Electoral Map of Great Britain 1979–1987* (London, 1988), 236–8.

[43] Minutes of Militant Tendency meetings, 22 Nov. 1982 (Preston), and 'extracts from a conversation with the current Militant Treasurer in Gwent', 23 Jan. 1982, LPNAD.

[44] K. O. Morgan, *Callaghan: A Life* (Oxford, 1997), 712–13, 725–6; J. Thomas to R. Hayward, 12 Oct. 1981, Jeffrey Thomas MS file 6.

[45] 'Constituency reports on draft manifesto 1980', LPW MS 144.

[46] Gwent County Planning Office, Industrial development subcommittee, 3 Dec. 1984 and 25 Aug. 1987 and letters to Nicholas Edwards and Lord Young, 30 Nov. 1984, 14 Oct. 1987, National Museum of Labour History, Michael Foot MS CO3, CO9.

[47] 'Constituency reports', LPW MS 144, incl. G. Parry to H. Morgan, 3 Feb. 1981.

[48] Andrews, *Wales Says Yes*, 35–6.

[49] Merthyr Tydfil and Rhymney CLP, *Annual Report* (1983–4), in Ted Rowlands MS 3/17 (NLW).

[50] J. Thomas, 'Taffy was a Welshman, Taffy was a thief: anti-Welshness, the press and Neil Kinnock', *Llafur*, VII/2 (1997).

[51] M. J. Smith, 'Neil Kinnock and the modernisation of the Labour Party', *Contemporary Record*, VIII (1994), 555–66 and the subsequent piece by Steve Fielding, pp. 589–99.

[52] K. Morgan, 'Labour's devolution policy', in D. Balsom and J. B. Jones (eds.), *The Road to the National Assembly for Wales* (Cardiff, 2000). See also R. W. Jones and B. Lewis, 'The Welsh Labour Party and Welsh civil society: aspects of the constitutional debate in Wales', PSA conference paper, University of Keele 1998.

[53] By 1997 at least 30% of Labour councillors in Torfaen, Cardiff, Monmouthshire and Wrexham were women (calculated from Balsom, *Wales Yearbook 1999*). See also interview with Cherry Short, Labour's National assembly candidate for Monmouth, *Independent*, 10 April 1999.

[54] For attacks on the efficiency and honesty of Labour councils in Blaenau Gwent, Cardiff, Vale of Glamorgan and Maesteg, *Independent*, 3 May 1999, *WM*, 7, 8 May 1999. In Islwyn, which also fell to Plaid, a hitherto strong local party had suffered a fall in membership spanning several years (Islwyn CLP, *Annual Meeting* (1997)).

[55] M. Jacobs (Fabian General Secretary) circular to Fabian society members, 18 March 1999, in author's possession. See also J. Osmond, 'Welsh politics in the new millennium', reported in *WM*, 30 July 1999.

[56] *Independent*, 8 May 1999.

[57] Reviews of issues facing Labour at the turn of the century include J. Osmond, 'Addressing the Welsh policy vacuum', *Welsh Economic Review*, X/2 (1997/8), 40–8, and R. Macdonald and H. Thomas (eds.), *Nationality and Planning in Scotland and Wales* (Cardiff, 1997). For elections, B. Taylor and K. Thomson (eds.), *Scotland and Wales: Nations Again?* (Cardiff, 1999) and M. Balsom *et al.*, 'The red and the green: patterns of partisan choice in Wales', *British Journal of Political Science*, XIII (1994), 299–325.

Appendix I

Labour Party Electoral Statistics, 1900–1999

Table I.1. *Parliamentary elections, 1900–1997*

Year	Seats won	Seats contested	Unopposed returns	Total seats	% share of vote
1900	2[a]	3	0	34	10
1906	5[b]	6	2	34	13
1910 (J)	5[c]	6	0	34	16
1910 (D)	5[d]	8	1	34	19
1918	10	28	5	36	34
1922	18	29	1	36	41
1923	20	28	2	36	42
1924	16	34	7	36	41
1929	25	34	0	36	44
1931	16[e]	30	4	36	47
1935	18	34	10	36	46
1945	25	34	1	36	58
1950	27	36	0	36	58
1951	27	36	0	36	60
1955	27	36	0	36	58
1959	27	36	0	36	57
1964	28	36	0	36	58
1966	32	36	0	36	61
1970	27	36	0	36	52
1974 (F)	24	36	0	36	47
1974 (O)	23	36	0	36	50
1979	22	36	0	36	47
1983	20	38	0	38	38
1987	24	38	0	38	45
1992	27	38	0	38	50
1997	34	40	0	40	55

[a] W. Abraham was returned as a 'Lib-Lab' for the Rhondda constituency. Keir Hardie was returned in second place for the dual-member seat of Merthyr Boroughs.

[b] W. Abraham (Rhondda), W. Brace (South Glamorgan), T. Richards (West Monmouth) and J. Williams (Gower) were all returned as 'Lib-Labs'. Keir Hardie was returned in second place in Merthyr Boroughs.

[c] Keir Hardie was returned in second place in Merthyr Boroughs.

[d] Keir Hardie was returned in second place in Merthyr Boroughs.

[e] R. C. Wallhead stood as the ILP candidate in Merthyr Tydfil, but was not opposed by a Labour candidate.

Table I.2. European elections, 1979–1999

Year	Seats won	Total seats	% share of vote
1979	3	4	42
1984	3	4	45
1989	4	4	49
1994	5	5	56
1999[a]	2	5	32

[a]This election was the first European election to be conducted under a system of proportional representation.

Table I.3. Election for the Welsh Assembly, 1999

	Seats won	Total seats	% share of vote
Constituency vote	27	40	38
Regional vote[a]	1	20	37

[a]Electors had two votes in this election. The first was cast for a candidate standing in the constituency, the second for a list of candidates standing in one of five regions. The election of candidates from the regional lists was conducted under a system of proportional representation designed to counteract any imbalance generated by the operation of the traditional first-past-the-post system in the constituencies. Hence, as Labour had won 68% of the constituencies (on only 38% of the vote), its share of the regional list seats was minimal, despite attracting 37% of the vote in this ballot. Labour's share of the seats in the Assembly, at 28/60, was still higher (47%) than its share of either vote.

Appendix II
Labour MPs and Other Public Representatives, 1900–1999

1900–1918

Glamorgan
William Abraham (Rhondda), 1885–1918; (Rhondda West), 1918–20
William Brace (South Glamorgan), 1906–18; (Abertillery), 1918–20
Keir Hardie (Merthyr Boroughs), 1900–15
John Williams (Gower), 1906–22

Monmouthshire
Thomas Richards (West Monmouth), 1904–18; (Ebbw Vale), 1918–20

1918–1945

Anglesey
Sir Owen Thomas, 1918–22; (Independent Labour, 1922–3)

Brecon and Radnor
Peter Freeman, 1929–31; (Newport), 1945–56
W. F. Jackson, 1938–45

Caernarvonshire
R. T. Jones (Caernarvonshire), 1922–3

Carmarthenshire
James Griffiths (Llanelli), 1936–70
Daniel Hopkin (Carmarthen), 1929–31, 1935–41
R. M. Hughes (Carmarthen), 1941–5
Dr J. H. Williams (Llanelli), 1922–36

Denbighshire
Robert Richards (Wrexham), 1922–4, 1929–31, 1935–55

Glamorgan
William Abraham (Rhondda West), 1918–20
E. N. Bennet (Cardiff Central), 1929–31
W. G. Cove (Aberavon), 1929–59
D. L. Davies (Pontypridd), 1931–8
S. O. Davies (Merthyr Tydfil), 1934–70; (Independent Labour, 1970–2)
J. E. Edmunds (Cardiff East), 1929–31
Ness Edwards (Caerphilly), 1939–68
D. R. Grenfell (Gower), 1922–59
George Hall (Aberdare), 1922–46
Vernon Hartshorn (Ogmore), 1918–31
Arthur Henderson Jr. (Cardiff South), 1923–4, 1929–31
William Jenkins (Neath), 1922–45
William John (Rhondda West), 1920–50
Morgan Jones (Caerphilly), 1921–39
T. I. Mardy Jones (Pontypridd), 1922–31
C. Ellis Lloyd (Llandaff and Barry), 1929–31
J. Ramsay MacDonald (Aberavon), 1922–9
W. H. Mainwaring (Rhondda East), 1933–59
David Watts Morgan (Rhondda East), 1918–33
D. L. Mort (Swansea East), 1940–63
Alfred Onions (Caerphilly), 1918–21
Arthur Pearson (Pontypridd), 1938–70
H. W. Samuel (Swansea West), 1923–4, 1929–31
R. C. Wallhead (Merthyr Tydfil), 1922–34
David Williams (Swansea East), 1922–40
D. J. Williams (Neath), 1945–64
E. J. Williams (Ogmore), 1931–46
John Williams (Gower), 1918–22

Monmouthshire
George Barker (Abertillery), 1920–9
Aneurin Bevan (Ebbw Vale), 1929–60
William Brace (Abertillery), 1918–20
George Daggar (Abertillery), 1929–50
Evan Davies (Ebbw Vale), 1920–9
Charles Edwards (Bedwellty), 1918–50
Thomas Griffiths (Pontypool), 1918–35
Arthur Jenkins (Pontypool), 1935–46
Thomas Richards (Ebbw Vale), 1918–20
James Walker (Newport), 1929–31

University of Wales
George M. Ll. Davies, 1923–4

1945–present

Anglesey
Cledwyn Hughes, 1951–79

Brecon and Radnor
Caerwyn Roderick, 1970–9
Tudor Watkins, 1945–70

Caernarvonshire
Ednyfed Hudson Davies (Conway), 1966–70; (Caerphilly), 1979–83
W. E. E. Jones (Conway), 1950–51
Goronwy Roberts (Caernarvonshire), 1945–Feb. 1974
Betty Williams (Conwy), 1997–

Cardiganshire
D. Elystan Morgan, 1966–Feb.1974

Carmarthenshire
Denzil Davies (Llanelli), 1970–
James Griffiths (Llanelli), 1945–70
Megan Lloyd George (Carmarthen), 1957–66; (previously Liberal MP)
Gwynoro Jones (Carmarthen), 1970–Oct. 1974
Roger Thomas (Carmarthen), 1979–87
Dr Alan Williams (Carmarthen), 1987–97 (Carmarthen East and Dinefwr),
    1997–

Denbighshire
Tom Ellis (Wrexham), 1970–83
J. Idwal Jones (Wrexham), 1955–70
Martyn Jones (Clwyd South West), 1987–97; (Clwyd South), 1997–
John Marek (Wrexham), 1983–
Robert Richards (Wrexham), 1945–55
Chris Ruane (Vale of Clwyd), 1997–
Gareth Thomas (Clwyd West), 1997–

Flint
David Hanson (Delyn), 1992–
Barry Jones (Flint East), 1970–83; (Alyn and Deeside), 1983–
Eirene White (Flint East), 1950–70

Glamorgan

Donald Anderson (Swansea East), Oct. 1974–

James Callaghan (Cardiff South), 1945–50; (Cardiff South-East), 1950–83; (Cardiff South and Penarth), 1983–7

Martin Caton (Gower), 1997–

Ann Clwyd (Cynon Valley), 1984–

Donald Coleman (Neath), 1964–91

W. G. Cove (Aberavon), 1945–59

Ednyfed Hudson Davies (Caerphilly), 1979–83

G. Elfed Davies (Rhondda East), 1959–Feb. 1974

Ifor Davies (Gower), 1959–82

Ron Davies (Caerphilly), 1983–

S. O. Davies (Merthyr Tydfil), 1945–70; (Independent Labour, 1970–2)

Ness Edwards (Caerphilly), 1945–68

Fred Evans (Caerphilly), 1968–79

Ioan Evans (Aberdare), Feb. 1974–83; (Cynon Valley), 1983–4

J. Evans (Ogmore), 1946–50

D. R. Grenfell (Gower), 1945–59

Win Griffiths (Bridgend), 1987–

Peter Hain (Neath), 1991–

George Hall (Aberdare), 1945–6

Kim Howells (Pontypridd), 1989–

Brynmor John (Pontypridd), 1970–89

William John (Rhondda West), 1945–50

Alec Jones (Rhondda West), 1967–Feb. 1974; (Rhondda), Feb. 1974–83

Jon Owen Jones (Cardiff Central), 1992–

Neil McBride (Swansea East), 1963–Oct. 1974

W. H. Mainwaring (Rhondda East), 1945–59

Professor Hilary Marquand (Cardiff East), 1945–50

Alun Michael (Cardiff South and Penarth), 1987–

Julie Morgan (Cardiff North), 1997–

Rhodri Morgan (Cardiff West), 1987–

John Morris (Aberavon), 1959–

Percy Morris (Swansea West), 1945–59

D. L. Mort (Swansea East), 1945–63

Walter Padley (Ogmore), 1950–79

Arthur Pearson (Pontypridd), 1945–70

Ray Powell (Ogmore), 1979–

Arthur Probert (Aberdare), 1954–Feb. 1974

Mrs D. M. Rees (Barry), 1950–1

Allan Rogers (Rhondda), 1983–

Ted Rowlands (Cardiff North), 1966–70; (Merthyr Tydfil), 1972–

John Smith (Vale of Glamorgan), 1989–92, 1997–

D. Emlyn Thomas (Aberdare), 1946–54
George Thomas (Cardiff Central), 1945–50; (Cardiff West), 1950–79
Iorwerth Thomas (Rhondda West), 1950–67
A. L. Ungoed-Thomas (Llandaff and Barry), 1945–50
Gareth Wardell (Gower), 1982–97
Alan Williams (Swansea West), 1964–
D. J. Williams (Neath), 1945–64
E. J. Williams (Ogmore), 1945–6

Merioneth
William Edwards, 1966–Feb. 1974
T. W. Jones, 1951–66

Monmouthshire
Leo Abse (Pontypool), 1958–83; (Torfaen), 1983–7
Donald Anderson (Monmouth), 1966–70; (Swansea East), Oct. 1974–
Aneurin Bevan (Ebbw Vale), 1945–60
George Daggar (Abertillery), 1945–50
Sir Charles Edwards (Bedwellty), 1945–50
Huw Edwards (Monmouth), 1991–2, 1997–
Harold Finch (Bedwellty), 1950–70
Paul Flynn (Newport West), 1987–
Michael Foot (Ebbw Vale), 1960–83; (Blaenau Gwent), 1983–92
Peter Freeman (Newport), 1945–56
Alan Howarth (Newport East), 1997–
Roy Hughes (Newport), 1966–83; (Newport East), 1983–97
Arthur Jenkins (Pontypool), 1945–6
Neil Kinnock (Bedwellty), 1970–83; (Islwyn), 1983–95
Paul Murphy (Torfaen), 1987–
Llew Smith (Blaenau Gwent), 1992–
Sir Frank Soskice (Newport), 1956–66
Jeffrey Thomas (Abertillery), 1970–
Don Touhig (Islwyn), 1995–
D. Granville West (Pontypool), 1946–58
A. Clifford Williams (Abertillery), 1965–70
Revd Llewelyn Williams (Abertillery), 1950–65

Pembrokeshire
Nick Ainger (Pembroke), 1992–7; (Carmarthen West and South Pembs.), 1997–
Desmond Donnelly (Pembroke), 1950–70
Jackie Lawrence (Preseli Pembrokeshire), 1997–

Labour Members of the European Parliament

Ann Clwyd (Mid and West Wales), 1979–84
Wayne David (South Wales), 1989–94; (South Wales Central), 1994–9
Win Griffiths (South Wales), 1979–89
Glenys Kinnock (South Wales East), 1994–9; (Wales), 1999–
Eluned Morgan (Mid and West Wales), 1994–9; (Wales), 1999–
David Morris (Mid and West Wales), 1984–94; (South Wales West), 1994–9
Allan Rogers (South East Wales), 1979–84
Llew Smith (South East Wales), 1984–94
Joe Wilson (North Wales), 1989–99

Labour Members of the National Assembly for Wales, elected in 1999

Lorraine Barrett (Cardiff South and Penarth)
Rosemary Butler (Newport West)
Christine Chapman (Cynon Valley)
Jane Davidson (Pontypridd)
Andrew Davies (Swansea West)
Ron Davies (Caerphilly)
Richard Edwards (Preseli Pembrokeshire)
Sue Essex (Cardiff North)
Val Feld (Swansea East)
Brian Gibbons (Aberavon)
Janice Gregory (Ogmore)
John Griffiths (Newport East)
Christine Gwyther (Carmarthen West and Pembrokeshire South)
Alison Halford (Delyn)
Edwina Hart (Gower)
Jane Hutt (Vale of Glamorgan)
Ann Jones (Vale of Clwyd)
Carwyn Jones (Bridgend)
Peter Law (Blaenau Gwent)
Huw Lewis (Merthyr Tydfil and Rhymney)
John Marek (Wrexham)
Alun Michael (South Wales West)
Tom Middlehurst (Alyn and Deeside)
Rhodri Morgan (Cardiff West)
Lynne Neagle (Torfaen)
Alan Pugh (Clwyd West)
Karen Sinclair (Clwyd South)
Gwenda Thomas (Neath)

Appendix III
Labour Party Membership Statistics, 1928–1955

Throughout its history the Labour Party has had 'affiliated members' (largely those who pay the political levy) and 'individual members' (those who join the party separately, in order to play an active part in branch affairs). Both groups were represented on the party's local executive committees. The importance of these groups – and of regional union organizers and local election agents – is discussed in the text.

Figures for the number of individual members in constituency parties were recorded centrally from 1928 and reported in the party's annual report. From 1933 figures for the number of male and female members were given separately. However, the figures have to be treated with considerable care. First, it is often argued that some very strong parties had powerful links to the community through the trade unions. A low individual membership did not necessarily indicate a party which was unable to identify and involve the local community (although links through the trade union were generally links to the male community, given the employment patterns within Wales for much of the century). Second, the figures themselves are regularly inaccurate. From 1929, all parties had to affiliate a minimum of 240 members, whether they had that many members or not. After 1956 the minimum affiliation figure rose to 800, despite the fact that a very large number of parties across the United Kingdom (and at least half the constituency parties in Wales) had a declining membership which was already below the minimum affiliation level. After this date figures were no longer given for constituency membership and the national figures became progressively inaccurate.[1] Third, even during this period, some parties misreported their membership figures. Many lacked the bureaucratic machinery necessary to record and track party members. Branch secretaries did not always supply the necessary figures, let alone record with accuracy the number of new or lapsed members, especially in scattered seats containing many small local parties. In times of financial hardship, some parties affiliated only a proportion of their members in order to avoid paying a larger affiliation fee to head office. Changes between one year and the next thus have to treated carefully.

At the same time, the figures are far from being useless as a historical source. A high membership could be an index of vitality, to be more fully explored through other sources. Equally, falling membership figures may indicate a party's declining ability to reach its constituency and keep in touch with its community, especially given Labour's inability to use an often hostile mass media to communicate its message. Membership figures are also particularly useful as a means of identifying high and changing levels of active support for Labour amongst women. These figures were compiled by Dot Jones from the Welsh Labour Party's annual reports. There are no figures for 1939–44.

Note

[1] See P. Seyd and P. Whiteley, *Labour's Grass Roots: The Politics of the Party Membership* (Oxford, 1992), 13–19.

Table III.1. Constituency party membership, 1928–1932

	1928	1929	1930	1931	1932
Anglesey	–	180	423	270	240
Brecon and Radnor	160	240	1000	485	860
Caernarfon	600	600	720	640	240
Caernarfon Boroughs	327	168	329	240	266
Cardiganshire	163	159	240	240	360
Carmarthen	–	–	240	240	240
Llanelli	180	180	240	320	480
Denbigh	180	150	240	240	240
Wrexham	360	360	670	828	925
Flint	360	360	670	828	925
Aberavon	180	360	620	519	1277
Llandaff and Barry	–	360	1198	1244	2238
Caerphilly	180	199	769	1008	2552
Gower	180	180	449	600	536
Neath	180	180	269	240	291
Ogmore	517	180	530	464	452
Pontypridd	180	180	315	286	404
Aberdare	240	60	240	240	240
Cardiff Central	514	624	376	400	450
Cardiff East	421	550	442	487	642
Cardiff South	489	522	260	339	498
Merthyr Tydfil	210	252	282	240	300
Rhondda East	467	360	240	240	270
Rhondda West		360	240	240	270
Swansea East	60	180	627	647	779
Swansea West					
Merioneth	252	250	910	331	928
Abertillery	–	180	240	240	240
Bedwellty	250	250	280	500	240
Ebbw Vale	180	180	240	240	240
Monmouth	300	300	550	553	959
Pontypool	395	315	751	281	771
Newport	1440	1605	2206	1793	3356
Montgomery	180	158	240	348	240
Pembroke	–	180	447	408	277
Total membership	9145	10362	17845	16074	23151

Table III.2. Constituency party membership, 1933–1938

	1933		1934		1935		1936		1937		1938	
	men	women	men	women	men	women	men	women	men	women	men	women
Anglesey	120	120	120	120	180	60	200	40	205	35	200	40
Brecon and Radnor	404	218	315	155	961	403	650	300	436	207	490	123
Caernarfon	120	120	225	115	487	120	202	79	312	100	903	210
Caernarfon Boroughs	147	93	137	103	255	90	210	150	180	60	281	64
Cardiganshire	325	65	200	70	–	14	200	40	320	60	485	55
Carmarthen	186	140	621	148	850	150	904	253	450	160	321	89
Llanelli	241	138	400	200	500	100	400	200	522	178	500	400
Denbigh	120	120	120	120	120	120	140	100	202	88	160	80
Wrexham	554	169	441	211	568	187	664	246	557	244	455	172
Flint	334	147	356	124	405	172	203	171	220	100	402	160
Aberavon	453	249	584	184	792	417	740	344	1381	492	1021	386
Llandaff and Barry	1258	1008	1056	1028	941	961	968	1040	821	923	674	818
Caerphilly	966	959	936	711	1142	984	1320	865	1000	700	600	400
Gower	291	231	258	262	342	192	397	230	462	244	372	248
Neath	225	57	463	159	415	266	491	596	834	594	371	395
Ogmore	210	283	438	436	323	443	390	400	725	455	416	294
Pontypridd	240	160	380	199	440	310	431	280	731	631	586	415
Aberdare	185	106	370	190	249	202	285	208	224	190	211	218
Cardiff Central	154	228	180	265	239	486	249	357	238	303	193	295
Cardiff East	174	261	155	243	128	330	134	435	103	305	108	298
Cardiff South	137	273	178	286	346	566	311	477	293	462	261	475
Merthyr Tydfil	90	150	124	240	204	270	205	207	356	314	250	200
Rhondda East	–	–	–	–	–	–	–	–	–	–	–	–
Rhondda West	441	–	–	–	–	–	–	–	245	385	324	170
Swansea East	410	282	1208	887	1273	880	1132	937	883	848	748	674
Swansea West	–	–	–	–	–	–	–	–	–	–	–	–
Merioneth	384	222	528	115	634	239	318	96	426	238	189	51
Abertillery	93	153	268	240	126	189	261	617	150	235	161	195
Bedwellty	152	186	255	266	514	303	337	306	336	298	282	291
Ebbw Vale	120	120	538	76	266	103	400	200	345	212	345	189
Monmouth	565	371	543	443	457	235	221	143	269	215	154	86
Pontypool	711	454	573	355	1953	537	838	629	992	538	458	349
Newport	855	1941	855	1975	1057	2319	978	2182	802	1964	753	1979
Montgomery	180	60	120	120	180	60	180	60	180	60	180	60
Pembroke	182	76	253	89	230	70	201	54	180	60	180	60
Wales	11027	9160	13198	10135	16577	11778	14560	12242	15380	11997	13034	9939
Total membership	20187		23333		28355		26802		27377		22973	
Women as % total	45.4		43.4		41.5		45.7		43.8		43.3	

Table III.3. Constituency party membership, 1945–1947

	1945		1946		1947	
	men	*women*	*men*	*women*	*men*	*women*
Anglesey	435	209	420	150	353	99
Brecon and Radnor	744	289	969	630	720	394
Caernarfon	1351	600	2337	781	909	154
Caernarfon Boroughs	275	223	348	242	500	200
Cardiganshire	460	120	613	128	420	90
Carmarthen	476	119	649	121	662	138
Llanelli	800	400	1270	335	1136	503
Denbigh	341	152	218	109	257	96
Wrexham	522	185	763	334	958	316
Flint	1539	445	1074	370	966	384
Aberavon	796	669	726	670	624	724
Llandaff and Barry	872	803	1060	985	944	978
Caerphilly	850	500	871	578	670	373
Gower	875	425	1048	597	873	471
Neath	610	288	738	349	660	317
Ogmore	615	345	744	451	520	346
Pontypridd	667	469	856	698	927	661
Aberdare	247	186	239	196	248	204
Cardiff Central	240	324	230	430	292	354
Cardiff East	209	267	250	350	240	337
Cardiff South	250	460	420	480	350	650
Merthyr Tydfil	350	250	400	200	450	220
Rhondda East Rhondda West	427	295	452	377	361	347
Swansea East Swansea West	485	492	675	575	685	593
Merioneth	959	241	804	268	318	290
Abertillery	600	550	426	272	300	390
Bedwellty	609	348	801	603	701	507
Ebbw Vale	347	225	614	403	437	212
Monmouth	564	460	696	598	442	462
Pontypool	406	303	319	349	422	382
Newport	368	1033	489	1185	506	1185
Montgomery	299	66	616	239	645	253
Pembroke	788	304	827	1041	756	184
Wales	19376	12045	22962	14157	19252	12814
Total membership	31421		37119		32066	
Female as % total	38.3		38.1		40.0	

Table III.4. Constituency party membership, 1949–1955

	1949		1950		1951		1952		1953		1955	
	men	women	men	women	men	women	men	women	men	women	men	women
Anglesey	392	191	685	302	287	224	583	385	447	310	358	360
Brecon and Radnor	726	486	796	562	713	546	971	682	967	739	586	528
Caernarfonshire	2008	369	2018	682	1600	906	1882	1204	1153	865	1321	823
Caernarfon	1253	251	1581	433	1214	624	1100	782	416	418	563	389
Conway	755	118	437	249	386	282	782	422	737	447	758	434
Cardiganshire	289	137	478	204	228	108	220	96	222	40	279	93
Carmarthenshire	1667	495	1605	678	1764	704	1986	896	1579	880	1482	598
Carmarthen	777	142	700	200	864	186	1075	271	786	168	537	64
Llanelli	890	353	905	478	900	518	911	625	793	712	945	534
Denbighshire	1233	471	1470	330	1340	400	1759	784	1319	660	848	368
Denbigh	110	110	200	100	140	100	359	184	319	160	327	115
Wrexham	1123	361	1270	230	1200	300	1400	600	1000	500	521	253
Flint	2700	1360	2540	1511	1738	1278	2225	1942	1572	1441	1207	992
East Flint	1500	710	1425	881	1061	807	1435	1327	1039	985	857	654
West Flint	1200	650	1115	630	677	471	790	615	533	456	350	338
Glamorgan	8903	7576	9325	8111	7942	7280	9145	8227	9167	8233	7801	7472
Aberavon	601	843	606	860	579	663	598	892	602	872	580	786
Barry	564	547	795	845	704	821	946	979	1087	1158	834	893
Caerphilly	1100	600	905	532	722	513	883	629	775	550	526	319
Gower	1009	631	751	309	705	335	750	300	761	389	728	371
Neath	516	205	497	325	543	250	477	382	505	388	453	337
Ogmore	898	494	936	625	839	613	933	772	798	743	721	653
Pontypridd	837	566	955	636	761	515	724	597	923	253	784	632
Aberdare	237	205	274	205	301	226	304	203	348	215	296	222
Cardiff North	524	609	550	601	410	462	673	450	305	525	443	473
Cardiff South East	500	800	606	820	414	765	678	873	662	953	489	646
Cardiff West	532	708	707	809	463	719	561	704	650	768	420	680
Merthyr Tydfil	400	300	500	350	450	300	460	261	506	282	400	300
Rhondda East	157	162	159	170	167	180	187	185	168	176	148	171
Rhondda West	176	193	184	205	170	207	183	240	238	236	199	260
Swansea East	435	434	452	429	360	411	449	457	396	447		
Swansea West	417	279	448	390	354	300	339	303	443	278	780	729
Merioneth	895	301	993	378	566	412	995	508	999	600	979	490
Monmouthshire	3416	3749	3727	4181	4273	4551	4231	5198	4007	4614	3762	4544
Abertillery	287	426	216	408	331	375	290	360	245	337	308	340
Bedwellty	551	380	567	483	519	491	488	640	489	530	369	421
Ebbw Vale	450	258	378	263	351	269	392	351	507	260	363	364
Monmouth	787	516	864	574	1486	1077	1664	1496	1579	1341	1665	1400
Pontypool	471	339	495	366	536	349	483	410	363	349	276	291
Newport	870	1830	1207	2087	1050	1990	914	1941	824	1797	781	1728
Montgomery	845	293	752	291	514	184	661	257	582	369	600	289
Pembroke	849	315	1373	629	1498	778	1893	1092	1346	824	1172	760
WALES	23923	15743	25762	17859	22463	17371	26551	21271	23360	19575	20395	17317
Total membership	39666		43621		39834		27822		42935		37712	
Female as % total		39.7		40.9		43.6		44.5		45.6		45.9

NB No membership figures were given for 1954. Figures in normal type are county totals, in italics for constituency parties (where different)

Select Further Reading

Andrews, Leighton, *Wales Says Yes: The Inside Story of the Yes for Wales Referendum Campaign* (Bridgend, Seren, 1999).

Cleaver, David, 'Labour and Liberals in the Gower constituency, 1885–1910', *Welsh History Review*, XII/3 (1985), 388–410.

David, Wayne, 'The Labour Party and the "exclusion" of the Communists: the case of the Ogmore Divisional Labour Party in the 1920s', *Llafur*, III/4 (1983), 5–15.

Evans, Eric Wyn, *Mabon (William Abraham 1842–1922): A Study in Trade Union Leadership* (Cardiff, University of Wales Press, 1959).

Evans, Neil, 'Cardiff's Labour tradition', *Llafur*, IV/2 (1985), 77–90.

Fagge, Roger, *Power, Culture and Conflict in the Coalfields: West Virginia and South Wales, 1900–22* (Manchester, Manchester University Press, 1996).

Foot, Michael, *Aneurin Bevan* (London, Granada, 1975).

Fox, Kenneth O., 'Labour and Merthyr's Khaki Election of 1900', *Welsh History Review*, II/4 (1965), 351–66.

Francis, Hywel, *Miners Against Fascism: Wales and the Spanish Civil War* (London, Lawrence & Wishart, 1984).

Francis, Hywel and David Smith, *The Fed: A History of the South Wales Miners in the Twentieth Century* (Cardiff, University of Wales Press, 1998).

Gilbert, David, *Class, Community and Collective Action: Social Change in Two British Coalfields, 1850–1926* (Oxford, Oxford University Press, 1992).

Gregory, Roy, *The Miners and British Politics, 1906–1914* (Oxford, Oxford University Press, 1968).

Griffiths, James, *Pages from Memory* (London, J. M. Dent & Sons, 1969).

Griffiths, Robert, *S. O. Davies: A Socialist Faith* (Llandysul, Gomer, 1983).

Hopkin, Deian, 'The rise of Labour: Llanelli, 1890–1922', in Geraint H. Jenkins and J. Beverley Smith (eds.), *Politics and Society in Wales, 1840–1922* (Cardiff, University of Wales Press, 1988), 161–82.

Hopkin, Deian, 'Y *Werin a'i Theyrnas*: ymateb sosialaeth i genedlaetholdeb 1880–1920', in G. H. Jenkins (ed.) *Cof Cenedl: Ysgrifau ar Hanes Cymru*, VI (Llandysul, 1991), 163–92.

Hopkin, Deian, 'The rise of Labour in Wales, 1890–1914', *Llafur*, VI/3 (1994), 120–41.

Howard, Chris, 'Reactionary radicalism: the Mid-Glamorgan bye-election, March 1910', in Stewart Williams (ed.), *Glamorgan Historian*, IX (1973), 29–41.

Howard, Chris, ' "Expectations born to death": the local Labour Party expansion in the 1920s', in Jay M. Winter (ed.), *The Working Class in Modern British History: Essays in Honour of Henry Pelling* (Cambridge, Cambridge University Press, 1983), 65–81.

Howard, Chris, ' "The focus of the mute hopes of a whole class": Ramsay MacDonald and Aberavon, 1922–29', *Llafur*, VII/1 (1996), 68–77.

Howell, David, *British Workers and the Independent Labour Party, 1888–1906* (Manchester, Manchester University Press, 1983).

Howell, David, 'Labour organisation among agricultural workers in Wales, 1872–1921', *Welsh History Review*, XVI/1 (1992), 63–92.

John, Angela V., *Our Mothers' Land: Chapters in Welsh Women's History, 1830–1939* (Cardiff, University of Wales Press, 1991).

Jones, Ieuan Gwynedd, 'Franchise reform and Glamorgan politics, 1869–1921', in Prys Morgan (ed.), *Glamorgan County History*, VI, *Glamorgan Society 1780–1980* (Cardiff, Glamorgan County History, 1988), 43–70.

Jones, J. Barry, 'Dénouement: Glamorgan County Council 1960–1974', in Prys Morgan (ed.), *Glamorgan County History*, VI, *Glamorgan Society 1780–1980* (Cardiff, Glamorgan County History, 1988), 419–29.

Jones, J. Graham, 'Wales and the "New Socialism", 1926–29', *Welsh History Review*, XI/2 (1982), 173–99.

Jones, J. Graham, 'Welsh politics between the wars: the personnel of Labour', *Transactions of the Honourable Society of Cymmrodorion* (1983), 164–83.

Jones, J. Graham, 'Glamorgan politics, 1918–85', in Prys Morgan (ed.), *Glamorgan County History*, VI, *Glamorgan Society 1780–1980* (Cardiff, Glamorgan County History, 1988), 71–87.

Jones, J. Graham, 'The Parliament for Wales campaign', *Welsh History Review*, XVI/2 (1992), 207–36.

Jones, R. Merfyn, *The North Wales Quarrymen, 1874–1922* (Cardiff, University of Wales Press, 1981).

Jones, R. Merfyn, 'Beyond identity? The reconstruction of the Welsh', *Journal of British Studies*, XXXI (1992), 330–57.

Lewis, Richard, *Leaders and Teachers: Adult Education and the Challenge of Labour in South Wales, 1906–1940* (Cardiff, University of Wales Press, 1993).

Lewis, Richard, 'The Welsh radical tradition and the ideal of a democratic popular culture', in Eugenio F. Biagini (ed.), *Citizenship and Community: Liberals, Radicals and Collective Identities in the British Isles, 1865–1931* (Cambridge, Cambridge University Press, 1996), 325–40.

Lieven, Michael, *Senghennydd: The Universal Pit Village, 1890–1930* (Llandysul, Gomer, 1994).

McAllister, Ian, 'The Labour Party in Wales: the dynamics of one-partyism', *Llafur*, III/2 (1981), 79–89.

McAllister, Laura, 'The Welsh devolution referendum: definitely, maybe?', *Parliamentary Affairs*, L/2 (1998), 149–65.

May, Eddie, 'Charles Stanton and the limits to "patriotic" labour', *Welsh History Review*, XVIII/3 (1996), 145–66.

Morgan, Kenneth O., *Keir Hardie: Radical and Socialist* (London, Weidenfeld & Nicolson, 1975).

Morgan, Kenneth O., *Wales in British Politics, 1868–1922* (Cardiff, University of Wales Press, 1980 edn.).

Morgan, Kenneth O., *Rebirth of a Nation: Wales, 1880–1980* (Oxford, Oxford University Press, 1981).

Morgan, Kenneth O., *Modern Wales: Politics, Places and People* (Cardiff, University of Wales Press, 1995).

Morgan, Kenneth O., *Callaghan: A Life* (Oxford, Oxford University Press, 1997).

Mòr O'Brien, Anthony, 'The Merthyr Boroughs election, November 1915', *Welsh History Review*, XII/4 (1985), 538–66.

Morris, Dylan, 'Sosialaeth i'r Cymry – trafodaeth yr ILP', *Llafur*, IV/2 (1985), 51–63.

Parry, Cyril, *The Radical Tradition in Welsh Politics: A Study of Liberal and Labour Politics in Gwynedd, 1900–1920* (Hull, Hull University Press, 1970).

Parry, Cyril, 'Gwynedd Politics, 1900–1920: the rise of a Labour Party', *Welsh History Review*, VI/3 (1973), 313–28.

Parry, Jon, 'Trade unionists and early Socialism in south Wales, 1890–1908', *Llafur*, VI/3 (1986), 43–54.

Parry, Jon, 'Labour leaders and local politics, 1888–1902: the example of Aberdare', *Welsh History Review*, XIV/3 (1989), 399–416.

Pope, Robert, *Building Jerusalem: Nonconformity, Labour and the Social Question in Wales, 1906–1939* (Cardiff, University of Wales Press, 1998).

Prothero, Cliff, *Recount* (Ormskirk, Hesketh, 1982).

Pretty, David A., *The Rural Revolt that Failed: Farm Workers' Trade Unions in Wales, 1889–1950* (Cardiff, University of Wales Press, 1989).

Smith, Dai, *Aneurin Bevan and the World of South Wales* (Cardiff, University of Wales Press, 1993).

Smith, Dai, 'The ashes onto the wind: Bevan and Wales', in Geoffrey Goodman (ed.), *The State of the Nation: The Political Legacy of Aneurin Bevan* (London, Victor Gollancz, 1997), 68–87.

Smith, J. Beverley (ed.), *James Griffiths and his Times* (Ferndale, W. T. Maddock, 1977).

Stead, Peter, 'Vernon Hartshorn: miners' agent and cabinet minister', in Stewart Williams (ed.), *Glamorgan Historian*, VI (1970), 83–94.

Stead, Peter, 'Working class leadership in south Wales, 1900–1920', *Welsh History Review*, VI/3 (1973), 329–53.

Stead, Peter, 'The language of Edwardian politics', in David Smith (ed.), *A People and a Proletariat: Essays in the History of Wales, 1780–1980* (London, Pluto Press, 1980), 148–65.

Stead, Peter, 'Establishing a heartland: the Labour Party in Wales', in Kenneth D. Brown (ed.), *The First Labour Party* (Beckenham, Croom Helm, 1985), 64–88.

Stead, Peter, 'The Labour Party and the claims of Wales', in John Osmond (ed.), *The National Question Again: Welsh Political Identity in the 1980s* (Llandysul, Gomer, 1985), 99–123.

Tanner, Duncan, *Political Change and the Labour Party, 1900–18* (Cambridge, Cambridge University Press, 1990).

Tanner, Duncan, 'The Labour Party and electoral politics in the coalfields', in Alan Campbell, Nina Fishman and David Howell (eds.), *Miners, Unions and Politics, 1910–47* (Aldershot, Scolar, 1996), 59–92.

Taylor, Bridget and Katarina Thomson (eds.), *Scotland and Wales: Nations Again?* (Cardiff, University of Wales Press, 1999).

Williams, Chris, ' "An able administrator of capitalism"? The Labour Party in the Rhondda, 1917–21', *Llafur*, IV/4 (1987), 20–33.

Williams, Chris, *Democratic Rhondda: Politics and Society, 1885–1951* (Cardiff, University of Wales Press, 1996).

Williams, Chris, 'Democracy and nationalism in Wales: the Lib-Lab enigma', in Robert Stradling, Scott Newton and David Bates (eds.), *Conflict and Coexistence: Nationalism and Democracy in Modern Europe: Essays in Honour of Harry Hearder* (Cardiff, University of Wales Press, 1997), 107–31.

Williams, Chris, *Capitalism, Community and Conflict: The South Wales Coalfield, 1898–1947* (Cardiff, University of Wales Press, 1998).

Williams, John, *Was Wales Industrialised? Essays in Modern Welsh History* (Llandysul, Gomer, 1995).

Williams, Siân Rhiannon, 'The Bedwellty Board of Guardians and the Default Act of 1927', *Llafur*, II/4 (1979), 65–77.

Index